Introduction to Islamic Economics

The Wiley Finance series contains books written specifically for finance and investment professionals as well as sophisticated individual investors and their financial advisors. Book topics range from portfolio management to e-commerce, risk management, financial engineering, valuation and financial instrument analysis, as well as much more. For a list of available titles, visit our Web site at www.WileyFinance.com.

Founded in 1807, John Wiley & Sons is the oldest independent publishing company in the United States. With offices in North America, Europe, Australia, and Asia, Wiley is globally committed to developing and marketing print and electronic products and services for our customers' professional and personal knowledge and understanding.

Introduction to Islamic Economics

Theory and Application

HOSSEIN ASKARI
ZAMIR IQBAL
ABBAS MIRAKHOR

WILEY

We dedicate this book to all those
who feel the pain of injustice and poverty

Contents

Acknowledgments

We are indebted to Omar Fayoumi for assisting with Chapter 5 and to Hamid Shafiezadeh for his work on Chapter 6. The suggestions of the Wiley editorial staff have been invaluable. As always, we are grateful for the support of our families.

About the Authors

Hossein Askari is the Iran Professor of International Business and International Affairs at the George Washington University. Before coming to GW, he was a professor of Business and Middle Studies at the University of Texas at Austin and assistant professor of Economics at Tufts University. He has also served on the executive board of the International Monetary Fund and as consultant to a number of governments, institutions, and multinational corporations. He received all his university education at the Massachusetts Institute of Technology, where he earned a BS in civil engineering and a PhD in economics.

*   *   *

Zamir Iqbal is a lead specialist at Finance and Markets (F&M) Global Practice of the World Bank. He heads the World Bank Global Center for Islamic Finance Development in Istanbul. He has more than 20 years of experience in risk management, capital markets, and asset management at the World Bank Treasury. Islamic finance is his research focus, and he has coauthored several books on Islamic finance topics such as banking risk, financial stability, and risk sharing. His most recent coedited book, *Economic Development and Islamic Finance*, was published by the World Bank in 2013. He earned his PhD in international finance from the George Washington University and serves on the professional faculty at the Carey Business School of Johns Hopkins University.

*   *   *

Abbas Mirakhor is currently the first holder of the chair of Islamic Finance at the International Center for Education in Islamic Finance (INCEIF). He served as the dean of the executive board of the International Monetary Fund from 1997 to 2008 and as the executive director representing Afghanistan, Algeria, Ghana, Iran, Morocco, Pakistan, and Tunisia from 1990 to 2008. He has authored numerous publications and research papers on Islamic finance; among them are *Introduction to Islamic Finance* (Wiley 2011), *Risk Sharing in Islamic Finance* (Wiley 2011), and *The Stability of Islamic Finance* (Wiley 2010).

CHAPTER 1

Economic Systems

Learning objectives:

1. *The differences between economic systems and the role that government plays.*
2. *How the ideal Islamic system differs from the Western market capitalist system.*
3. *The role of markets and how they differ in Islam and in the market capitalist system.*
4. *What institutions are and why they matter for economic prosperity.*
5. *Governments have an important role no matter the system.*

Over the years, a number of different economic ideologies and systems have been proposed and promoted. As with most other things in life, economic doctrines and systems have a limited shelf life and evolve with time. While in 2014 the mixed capitalist market system of the Western world, especially that in the United States, may appear preeminent, it received a number of shocks at its very foundation. The financial crisis of 2007–2008 with its extensive fallout and the rapid rise of China as an economic power have raised new and fundamental questions about the long-term direction and viability of the laissez-faire mixed capitalist system practiced in the United States and other Western nations.

After World War I, economists generally realized that neoclassical economics was not well equipped to address the reasons underlying unemployment, business cycles, and their mitigation and amelioration. During the Great Depression, John Maynard Keynes's *General Theory of Employment, Interest, and Money* provided some answers.[1] As a result,

---

[1] Published in London by Macmillan in 1936.

Irving Fisher and Alfred Marshall's neoclassical theories were resurrected and reborn into the Keynesian framework. After World War II, a number of economists, including Hicks, Samuelson, Tobin, Solow, and Modigliani, further developed the Keynesian approach in what came to be known as neo-Keynesian macroeconomics. Although the Keynesian theory of demand management with its further refinement became the most widely accepted macroeconomic framework after World War II, the Chicago school of economics later criticized it, largely on libertarian grounds and on the grounds that it could not explain a number of observed economic developments in the 1970s and 1980s. These economists argued against discretionary macroeconomic policies in favor of the market's "invisible hand" (Adam Smith's famous words that, ironically, were mentioned only once in his famous work, *The Wealth of Nations*) and passive fiscal and monetary policies. Milton Friedman argued against the effectiveness of fiscal policy and instead pointed to passive (by a rule as opposed to discretionary) monetary policy. This approach was further supported and advocated in the early 1970s by Robert Lucas and his followers in their rational expectations framework to macroeconomics. While downplaying the promise of macroeconomic policies to fine-tune the economy, they generally advocated supply-side policies and programs to enhance economic prosperity. Today, in 2014, with the devastating fallout of the financial crisis of 2007–2008 still with us, economists are even more divided about the effectiveness of Keynesian macroeconomic policies and the broader role of government intervention in economic management.

WHAT IS AN ECONOMIC SYSTEM?

Any economic system is essentially a network of relationships (among households, businesses, and government), organizations, and the framework for producing, distributing, and consuming the goods and services produced in an economy while protecting the rights of future generations to the earth and the environment that all must share. An economic system includes how the output of the economy is produced and divided among members of society, how incentives and decision making are formulated, the extent of government intervention and its provision of goods and services, the role of markets and their regulation and supervision, and, in the legal system of property rights, ownership of factors of production and contracts and their enforcement. Although there are a number of ways to classify the range of economic systems, one classification could divide them into these five traditional economies, market economies, mixed market economies, mixed socialist economies, and command (planned) economies. In 2014, the most prominent economic system is the mixed market economic system, which is still evolving, followed by the mixed socialist economic system, the communist (command) system, and the recent rebirth of the Islamic economic system.

The most critical characteristic that distinguishes economic systems is the *relative* importance of markets and governments in determining what goods and services are produced, how they are produced, and who gets the output. A secondary distinguishing attribute has increasingly become the role of morality and justice in the economic system.

Traditional Economic Systems

Today, traditional economic systems are those that prevail largely in the tribal regions of a number of developing countries. They are predominantly agricultural with little or no labor specialization. Government services, where governments exist, are severely limited. These economies invariably rely on tradition, customs, and religion to decide what and how goods are produced and distributed, what occupations are chosen, and what form of governance is followed. Paper money is rarely used. Commodities, animals, and land provide a store of wealth, and barter is quite common.

Pure Market (Capitalist) Economic System

The father of modern capitalist market system was Adam Smith, the author of two books that have shaped the capitalist market economic systems around the world. His most widely cited text is *The Wealth of Nations* (more precisely, *An Inquiry into the Nature and Causes of the Wealth of Nations*), published in 1776. It was preceded by what we consider his masterpiece, the much less quoted *The Theory of Moral Sentiments*, published in 1759. For many mainstream economists, the year 1776 marks the birth of modern economics. In *The Wealth of Nations*, Smith took the bold stance that markets, left alone, were self-regulating and required no government rules, intervention, and regulation, and that government intervention would, in practice, do more harm than good. At the foundation of a market economy is the belief that the best outcome for all involved—namely the maximum output of goods that people want at the lowest price—results from individual sellers and buyers, acting individually and independently through the language of price (as the signaling device). Consumers vote what they want with their purchases; producers respond by producing what is demanded by consumers. If demand goes up, prices increase to balance supply and demand, and the higher price is a signal to producers to increase output. Producers, in pursuit of profits, produce the goods demanded most efficiently depending on the relative price of factors of production (land, labor, and capital) by increasing their inputs into the production process. People acquire goods and services on the basis of their voting power (ownership of factors of production and accumulated wealth).

For Smith, markets worked best if largely left alone. He saw markets as being self-regulating and having the special feature that they afforded the needed incentive to market participants. Profit incentives drive producers to produce the goods and services demanded in the most efficient way. Consumers are given a wide range of choice by registering their demand (what they buy) through the markets and can increase their income through education and savings. Smith coined the now-famous term "invisible hand" that would lead consumers and producers to pursue their self-interest *and*, unknowingly, in the process support the economic interests of all. Smith went even further and also argued that well-intentioned government rules and regulations were not needed and might in fact be detrimental to the growth of economic prosperity. He thus advocated a laissez-faire economic philosophy. This was the foundation of the capitalist economic system that fueled the Industrial Revolution in England and later in the rest of Europe and the United States.

Smith saw markets at the center of the economic system. Markets are not limited to those for final goods and services. Markets for factors of production, labor, and capital work in the same way as those for goods and are just as crucial for a smooth functioning economic system. Without factors of production, goods and services cannot be produced. In fact, one can imagine a market for almost everything in life.

Although Smith preached laissez-faire market economics, he was also a man of God. Smith believed in the deity and that "the Author of Nature" had prescribed the rules of human behavior in all things, including for economic behavior. It was left to humans to operationalize these rules and develop laws to provide the required institutional scaffolding for the ideal and efficient economy, an economy in which the government plays a minimal role but where rules (institutions) and especially the rule of law (and rule enforcement) guide the economy along its ideal path. Smith saw effective institutions as the scaffolding of the economic system. He was anything but the cold-hearted promoter of market economics that has become his mantra in most justifications of laissez-faire market economics. The Smith of *Moral Sentiments* envisaged the market system functioning if market participants complied with rules, including the rules of human behavior that had been prescribed by the Author of Nature. In *Moral Sentiments*, he advocated the importance of morality; he believed that for market participants, the love of self would result in sympathy for others as they entered market (more on this in the following paragraph). Without morality and government rule/legal intervention, the pure market system could lead to a veritable jungle—possibly maximum output but with the rise of harmful monopolies and price gauging; extreme income inequalities (poverty alongside great wealth); inhumane working conditions; discrimination by race, religion, age, and sex; unsafe foods and medicines; harmful spillovers or externalities (such as environmental degradation that is not cleaned up by those responsible); information that is not shared (asymmetric) with all market participants; and broken social systems. In others words, there could indeed be market failure in a number of areas with adverse social consequences. Adam Smith, the champion of free enterprise and limited government intervention, still acknowledged as fact that businessmen left to themselves could not be trusted and that they might take advantage of consumers through collusion or natural monopolies.

Because our description of the "real" Adam Smith may not be familiar to most, it may be helpful to give an extensive quote from his other book— *The Theory of Moral Sentiment*. Smith expresses his remarkable insight regarding rules of conduct, which he believed were:

> *the ultimate foundations of what is just and unjust in human conduct. . . . Those general rules of conduct, when they have been fixed in our mind by habitual reflection, are of great use in correcting the misrepresentations of self-love concerning what is fit and proper to be done in our particular situation. The regard to those general rules of conduct is what is properly called a sense of duty, a principle of the greatest consequence in human life, and the only principle by which the bulk of mankind are capable of directing their actions. . . . Without this sacred regard to general rules, there is no man whose conduct can be much depended upon. It is this which constitutes the most essential difference between a man of principle and honor and a worthless fellow. . . . Upon the tolerable observance of these duties depends the very existence of human society, which would crumble into nothing if mankind were not generally impressed with a reverence for those important rules of conduct. This reverence is still further enhanced by an opinion which is first impressed by nature, and afterward confirmed by reasoning and philosophy, that those important rules of morality are the commands and Laws of the Deity, who will finally reward the obedient, and punish the transgressors of their duty. . . . The happiness of mankind as well as of all other rational creatures seems to have been the original purpose intended by the Author of Nature when he brought them into existence. No other end seems worthy of that supreme wisdom and benignity which we necessarily ascribe to him; and this opinion, which we are led to by the abstract*

consideration of his infinite perfections, is still more confirmed by the examination of the works of nature, which seem all intended to promote happiness, and to guard against misery. But, by acting according to the dictates of our moral faculties, we necessarily pursue the most effectual means for promoting the happiness of mankind, and may therefore be said, in some sense to co-operate with the Deity, and to advance, as far as is in our power, the plan of providence. By acting otherwise, on the contrary, we seem to obstruct, in some measure, the scheme, which the Author of Nature has established for the happiness and perfection of the world, and to declare ourselves, if I may say so, in some measure the enemies of God. Hence we are naturally encouraged to hope for his extra-ordinary favor and reward in the one case, and to dread his vengeance and punishment in the other. . . . When the general rules which determine the merit and demerit of actions comes thus to be regarded as the Laws *of an all-powerful being, who watches over our conduct, and who, in a life to come, will reward the observance and punish the breach of them—they necessarily acquire a new sacredness from this consideration. That our regard to the will of the Deity ought to be the supreme rule of our conduct can be doubted of by nobody who believes his existence. The very thought of disobedience appears to involve in it the most shocking impropriety. How vain, how absurd would it be for man, either to oppose or to neglect the commands that were laid upon him by infinite wisdom and infinite power. How unnatural, how impiously ungrateful not to reverence the precepts that were prescribed to him by the infinite goodness of his creator, even though no punish-ment was to follow their violation! The sense of propriety, too, is here well supported by the strongest motives of self-interest. The idea that, however, we may escape the observation of man, or be placed above the reach of human punishment, yet we are always acting under the eye and exposed to the punishment of God, the great avenger of injustice, is a motive capable of restraining the most headstrong passions, with those at least who, by constant reflection, have rendered it familiar to them.*[2]

As we shall see through this volume, Smith's deist views, the sacred rules of nature, the required legislation, and the well-functioning market system *converge* with what we visualize as an "ideal Islamic system." Viewed in this light, Smith's thoughts then become systematic and complete in the sense

---

[2]Smith (2006, pp. 186–198).

that the *Moral Sentiments* covers the first part, his *Lectures on Jurisprudence* covers the second part, and *The Wealth of Nations*, the third part. This view holds the promise of opening a line of communication between Islamic economics and conventional economics to illuminate how the original visions of Islam and Smith converge. Our position in this regard is of course diametrically opposed to the position held by most that the two disciplines have nothing in common and that the only way to define Islamic economics is to jettison conventional economics: throw the baby out with the bathwater.

Because of market failures and social considerations, truly pure market economies do not exist today. Instead, market or capitalist economies are mixed systems, with the word "mixed" referring to government participation and intervention. Crucially, the questions have become: How much government intervention is acceptable? In what areas?

Mixed Market (Capitalist) Economic System

A number of the shortcomings of a pure market economic system have been noted. We also should add that markets need a "referee" to make sure that important market rules are respected and negative fallouts are contained and limited. Markets are the medium for effective economic performance; they are not an ideology to be placed on a pedestal and untouched, as some would have it.

Private property rights and secure contracts are essential features of a market economy. Property rights give individuals the right to own property and to use that property as they wish. Property rights, in turn, are of no value unless they are secure and legally enforced. Similarly, most economic transactions that are outside the simple retail sphere rely on contracts that must be secure and enforced. In other words, business development needs security and confidence. Without government intervention as the referee, business conditions could become problematic. Moreover, in the absence of business regulations, supervision, and enforcement, businesses could collude and fix prices to the detriment of consumers and society at large. Even without price fixing, monopolies could develop to the detriment of society. At the same time, there are a number of areas where there are natural monopolies, such as defense and some areas of infrastructure. Again, we see a role for government. Most important, even if markets are self-regulating and operate smoothly without government intervention, (namely, how market output is divided among members of society) they may yield results that are socially abhorrent—a few wealthy individuals alongside mass poverty. And most practically, governments needing revenues have to collect taxes to provide even the minimum level of public and social services.

Mixed Socialist Economic System

In large part because of significant income inequality, poverty, human dissatisfaction, and increasing social concerns, some mixed market economies adopted a socialist mantle as an offshoot of Marxism. In Western Europe, socialist parties emerged as strong political contenders to nurture key nationalized industries and expand the available welfare programs. Some countries adopted limited industrial plans. Key sectors, such as banking, telecommunications, railroads, energy, healthcare, and education, were nationalized. The provision of social benefits was expanded to include free education and healthcare, extended unemployment benefits, early retirement for those in hardship industries, minimum retirement benefits, and reduced working hours. These programs increased the role and economic contributions of the state while reducing the role of markets. In the 1980s, the United Kingdom reversed a number of earlier socialist decisions, denationalized some industries, and reduced a number of social programs. This reversal of socialist policies and programs spread to a number of other countries in Western Europe. It was adopted by the International Monetary Fund as the recommended policy prescription and was even forced on some countries during the financial crisis of 2007–2008, in part because of significant public debt and the belief that societies could no longer afford what became considered to be social programs that were too generous.

Command (Planned) Economic System

A command or planned economic system is the polar opposite of a market-based economy. In a command economy, a central public authority makes decisions on the specific goods to be produced, decisions that would be made by individual producers and consumers in a market system. Moreover, in a command economic system, there are no private property rights. Property and resources are collectively owned by groups or by the state. The state or planning organization determines the output of each final good and service sector and those of intermediate goods and services. It decides on wages to be paid and on all remuneration of incomes. From these wage and income figures, consumption and savings are determined. In order to have useful consumption (demand) figures, the planning directives literally go down to the kind and even sizes of shoes to be produced. The output of shoes is so specified (what to be produced), and the inputs have to be dictated (how the goods are produced and the required materials), and so on down the line. In a planned economy, the authorities use an input-output model to derive the needed inputs of different sectors. The planners determine prices and thus the incomes (who can buy the economy's output).

Thus the planning entity determines all that the markets do "invisibly" in a market system.

In practice, no planner can predict individual demands for goods as well as the invisible hand of the market as consumers register their votes (by what they demand) and prices send the signal to producers. Similarly, planners cannot tell producers the best (most efficient) way to combine the inputs they need to produce the planned output. Instead, producers who have the profit incentive and who know the technologies and the relative cost of inputs are best placed to produce the highest-quality output at the lowest cost. Moreover, there is little incentive to innovate and work hard in a system where there are no private property rights and no ownership. It is easy to see why it would be difficult to develop a thriving economy in such a system. Economic waste, chaos, and stagnation are the likely outcome.

Planned economies had their heyday after World War II in the Soviet Union and China but lost their cachet as the Soviet economy faltered. With the collapse of the Soviet Union, the mixed market economic system began to rule almost supreme. Russia turned to a market-supported system through shock therapy, and China started to gradually move toward a market-based system. We say "almost supreme" because income and wealth inequalities became glaring in a number of market economies. Economists began to question the relative importance of economic output for individual well-being as material success was no longer seen as synonymous with human happiness and welfare. Since the financial crises of the 1980s, excessive national debt and, more recently, the most serious economic downturn and stagnation since the Great Depression have renewed doubts about the ability of markets and governments to deliver economic prosperity and well-being.

CURRENT STATE OF THE GLOBAL ECONOMIC SYSTEM

Due to market failure and other reasons, there is no "pure" market economy in the world of 2014. There is a role for governments in any economic system, and hardly anyone denies an important role for the government. The questions relate to the areas and extent of government intervention. Generally speaking, the wealthy argue for very limited government intervention and low taxes to maximize their earnings and wealth, while the poor want extensive intervention to address unequal opportunities (education and healthcare), wealth disparities, and social safety nets.

But even though they recognize these safeguards and address them, mixed market economies in practice all over the globe have come under considerable criticism. In 2014, there are five major criticisms of the mixed market economic system:

1. Wide and growing income and wealth disparities
2. Recurring and highly disruptive financial crises accompanied by rising unemployment and severe economic hardships, especially for the poorer segments of society
3. Neglect of the human and societal well-being dimension of economic development
4. Irrational assumption of rational self-interest
5. Continuing environmental degradation

Growing Income and Wealth Disparities

In the United States, for example, income and wealth inequalities have deteriorated significantly over time.[3] In 1982, those in the top 1% of the U.S. income distribution received 12.8% of the total national income; this percentage rose to 21.3 by 2006 and fell back to 17.2 in the aftermath of the financial crash of 2007–2008. Another popular indicator of growing income disparity is a comparison of average chief executive officer pay relative to the pay of an average factory worker; this ratio rose from 42 times in 1960 to a high of 531 in 2000 and fell back to 344 in 2007. An often-used comparator of income distribution across countries is the Gini coefficient (with zero representing perfect equality and 100 representing total inequality, or in other words, one person earning the entire national income); the most recent numbers for some countries are:

United States: 45.0

Iran: 44.5

Japan: 38.1

Egypt: 34.4

United Kingdom: 34.0

Switzerland: 33.7

France: 32.7

Norway: 25.0

Sweden: 23.0

---

[3] For the U.S. data cited here, see G. William Anderson, "Who Rules America?" (http://www2.ucsc.edu/whorulesamerica/power/wealth.html). For Organisation for Economic Co-operation and Development (OECD) data, see "Growing Unequal? Income Distribution and Poverty in OECD Countries" (http://www2.ucsc.edu/whorulesamerica/power/wealth.html).

The rankings among 133 countries (with 1 representing the most equal income distribution among countries, namely Sweden):

South Africa: 133
United States: 93
Iran: 90
Sweden: 1

A standard method of addressing income inequality in a capitalist system is through progressive taxation. But this is not always the case in countries that profess progressive taxation. As the following article excerpt notes:

> *The lowest 20% of earners (who average about $12,400 per year), paid 16.0% of their income to taxes in 2009; and the next 20% (about $25,000/year), paid 20.5% in taxes. So if we only examine these first two steps, the tax system looks like it is going to be progressive.*
>
> *And it keeps looking progressive as we move further up the ladder: the middle 20% (about $33,400/year) give 25.3% of their income to various forms of taxation, and the next 20% (about $66,000/year) pay 28.5%. So taxes are progressive for the bottom 80%. But if we break the top 20% down into smaller chunks, we find that progressivity starts to slow down, then it stops, and then it slips backwards for the top 1%.*
>
> *Specifically, the next 10% (about $100,000/year) pay 30.2% of their income as taxes; the next 5% ($141,000/year) dole out 31.2% of their earnings for taxes; and the next 4% ($245,000/year) pay 31.6% to taxes. You'll note that the progressivity is slowing down. As for the top 1%—those who take in $1.3 million per year on average—they pay 30.8% of their income to taxes, which is a little less than what the 9% just below them pay, and only a tiny bit more than what the segment between the 80th and 90th percentile pays.*

While income figures represent one measure of inequality, a more comprehensive measure is wealth; these figures are even more discouraging. In 2000, the percentages of the national wealth held by the top 10% of the adult population in a number of Western countries were:

Switzerland: 71.3
United States: 69.8
France: 61.0

Sweden: 58.6

Norway: 50.5

Germany: 44.4

Finland: 42.3

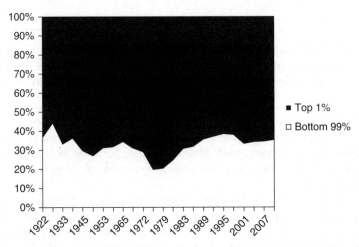

FIGURE 1.1   Share of Wealth Held by the Bottom 99% and Top 1% in the United States, 1922–2010

The numbers for the United States, where figures are readily available, are even more alarming when we look at the top 1%. (See Table 1.1 and Figure 1.1.) Generally speaking, in 1976, the top 1% held about 20% of the total national wealth. This figure nearly doubled to 40% in 1995 and in 2010 stood at over 35%. The corresponding dollar figures (wealth and income) for the various percentiles are shown in Table 1.2.

Instability of Economic and Financial Systems

A second major criticism of the mixed market system is the recurring financial crises and the heavy economic toll that follows, especially on the less fortunate members of society. While the Great Depression and the financial crisis of 2007–2008 are the two most prominent standouts, they are not alone.[4] The conventional financial system is based on fractional reserve banking and debt, whereby banks create money though loans and investors

---

[4]Kindleberger (2011).

TABLE 1.1 Share of Wealth Held by the Bottom 99% and Top 1% in the United States, 1922–2010

	Bottom 99%	Top 1%
1922	63.3%	36.7%
1929	55.8%	44.2%
1933	66.7%	33.3%
1939	63.6%	36.4%
1945	70.2%	29.8%
1949	72.9%	27.1%
1953	68.8%	31.2%
1962	68.2%	31.8%
1965	65.6%	34.4%
1969	68.9%	31.1%
1972	70.9%	29.1%
1976	80.1%	19.9%
1979	79.5%	20.5%
1981	75.2%	24.8%
1983	69.1%	30.9%
1986	68.1%	31.9%
1989	64.3%	35.7%
1992	62.8%	37.2%
1995	61.5%	38.5%
1998	61.9%	38.1%
2001	66.6%	33.4%
2004	65.7%	34.3%
2007	65.4%	34.6%
2010	64.6%	35.4%

TABLE 1.2 Income, Net Worth, and Financial Worth in the United States by Percentile, in 2010 dollars

Wealth or Income Class	Mean Household Income	Mean Household Net Worth	Mean Household Financial (Non-Home) Wealth
Top 1%	$1,318,200	$16,439,400	$15,171,600
Top 20%	$226,200	$2,061,600	$1,719,800
60th–80th percentile	$72,000	$216,900	$100,700
40th–60th percentile	$41,700	$61,000	$12,200
Bottom 40%	$17,300	−$10,600	−$14,800

and consumers borrow to finance investment and consumption. The assumption of excessive debt, or leveraging, exposes the financial system to bad decisions and debt that cannot be repaid, setting off a chain reaction of defaults among financial institutions and causing panic and requiring government bailouts that become a burden for average taxpayers. Moreover, serious financial crises, most notably the Great Depression and the financial crisis of 2007–2008, lead to panics, loss of business and consumer confidence, deleveraging, severe and prolonged recessions or depressions, long-lasting periods of high unemployment, and, ultimately and most ominously, unbearable pressure on families and on the fabric of society and social cohesion.

Neglect of Human Welfare Dimension of Economic Development

A third criticism of mixed market economies is the focus on gross domestic product (GDP) and not on the happiness, well-being, and welfare of individuals and society at large. In the West, under the mixed market system, the focus of economic policy is largely GDP and GDP per capita, not on the condition of all humans. Human beings are *not the end* result of all economic activity but are taken in part *as inputs* to economic production, and the economic goal has become how much goods and services are produced. Thus, other goals, especially human well-being, freedom to pursue individual goals, and social cohesion, have fallen by the wayside. These shortcomings became increasingly recognized in the West during the late 1970s and 1980s through the works of Mahbub ul-Haq and Amartya Sen.

Mahbub ul-Haq argued that all development and growth models following World War II considered humans, whether as labor or human capital, to be an input into the production process and therefore a means for development. What was missing, he asserted, was the consideration of the human as the end of the development process. He developed the idea of "basic needs," which laid the foundation for his later work on "human development," culminating in the publication of the *Human Development Report* in 1990. As he says in his book, *Reflections on Human Development*, "After many decades of development, we are rediscovering the obvious—that people are both the means and the end of economic development."[5] In his foreword to ul-Haq's book, Paul Streeten defines human development as "widening the range of people's choices. Human development is a concern not only for poor countries and poor people, but everywhere. In the high-income countries, indicators of shortfalls in human development should be looked for in

---

[5]Ul-Haq (1995, p. 3).

homelessness, drug addiction, crime, unemployment, urban squalor, environmental degradation, personal insecurity and social disintegration." Aside from the recommendation that economic development should focus on humans as ends as well as means, Mahbub ul-Haq concentrated on enhancing human productivity as a means of development, arguing that the labor force is productive when it is well nourished, skilled, and well educated.

The Human Development Index (HDI) was an attempt to devise a technical means to provide an indication of a society's level of human development and to measure its progress through time. In its initial formulation, the HDI included three variables:

1. Per capita GDP, calculated at the real purchasing power exchange rate
2. Literacy rates
3. Life expectancy at birth

This was the first major attempt to focus attention away from the growth of GDP as the measure of the development and progress of countries. By introducing literacy and life expectancy, the HDI broadened the information base of the meaning of development. Any increase in HDI could be interpreted as an improvement in the society since progress on education and health benefits the society as a whole. To a degree, the inclusion of health and education in the original HDI corrected the distributional ambiguity contained in per capita GDP as the only indicator of economic progress since it can conceal large income inequalities. The HDI also made it possible to produce a ranking of countries that would give some indication of drawbacks to affluence by showing "the troubles of overdevelopment—or, better, maldevelopment—as well as those of underdevelopment. Diseases of affluence can kill, just as the diseases of poverty can. Income statistics, by contrast, do not reveal the destructive aspects of wealth," as reported by the 1990 Human Development Report (HDR). It is thus possible for a country to rank low in terms of per capita GDP but high in terms of HDI.[6]

Amartya Sen's concept of "development as freedom" was an effort to further modify, expand, and enhance the meaning of development. Sen expanded the theoretical and empirical dimension of human development from its definition as "both the process of widening people's choices and the level of their achieved well-being" to its culmination as "freedom." The 1990 HDR had identified well-being as including, among others things: access to income; health, education, and long life; political freedom; guaranteed human rights; concern for the environment; and concern for participation. Under the influence of Sen and his colleagues, this view was revised to suggest

---

[6]Ul-Haq (1995, pp. 46–66).

that the goal of development is "to secure the freedom, well-being and dignity of all."[7]

Sen notes that in an age of "unprecedented opulence," there is also "remarkable deprivation, destitution and oppression." In both rich and poor countries, there are, in one form or another, problems of "persistence of poverty and unfulfilled elementary needs, occurrence of famines and widespread hunger, violation of elementary political freedoms as well as of basic liberties, extensive neglect of the interests and agency of women, and worsening threats to our environment and to the sustainability of our economic and social lives. Overcoming these problems is a central part of the exercise of development."[8]

Sen argues that it is the individual agency (the capacity for human beings to make choices and to impose those choices on the world) and social arrangements that, deeply complementing each other, determine the extent to which problems and deprivations can be addressed successfully. Freedoms of various kinds are essential to the exercise of human agency. Social arrangements, in turn, determine the extent of human freedom and agency; individual freedom has to become a social commitment so that human agency can become effective in solving problems. Sen conceives of the expansion of freedom "both as the primary end and as the principal means of development. Development consists of the removal of various types of 'unfreedoms' that leave people with little choice and little opportunity of exercising their reasoned agency. The removal of substantial unfreedoms, it is argued here, is constitutive of development." Freedom is multidimensional and "instrumental effectiveness by freedoms of particular kinds to promote freedoms of other kinds" serves to promote freedom as the "preeminent objective of development." These instrumental freedoms include political freedoms, economic facilities, social opportunities, transparency guarantees, and protective security.[9]

Although the human dimension became recognized, little has changed in economic management and policy in the West. In these mixed market economies, all eyes are glued to quarterly and annual GDP growth with a smattering and infrequent reference to poverty and income inequality here and there. While there are many valid criticisms of modern-day capitalist mixed economies, they still generally are perceived to be the most efficient in delivering economic output and growth, and international institutions such as the World Bank and the International Monetary Fund continue to recommend most of the capitalist prescriptions. But economic efficiency

---

[7] Sen (1999, p. xv).

[8] Ibid., p. xii.

[9] Ibid., pp. xii–xiii.

does not necessarily embrace economic justice, human well-being, and social harmony.

Irrational Assumption of Rational Self-Interest

In recent years, more and more economists have raised serious questions regarding the basic postulates of the classical-neoclassical economic paradigm. Aside from those who have focused their criticism on the separation of economics from ethics, such as Amartya Sen, others have focused on the postulate of rational self-interest of the paradigm without rejecting its other features. One example is the position of two prominent economists, George Akerlof and Robert Shiller. In their book *Animal Spirits*, they revive the concept of "animal spirits" proposed by Keynes, saying that Keynes "appreciated that most economic activity results from rational economic motivation—but also that much economic activity is governed by animal spirits." While accepting that "people rationally pursue their economic interests," they, along with Keynes, argue that exclusive adherence to this view ignores "the extent to which people are also guided by non-economic motivations. And it fails to take into account the extent to which they are irrational or misguided. It ignores the animal spirits."[10]

The concept of animal spirits refers to a restless and inconsistent element in the economy. It refers to our peculiar relationship with ambiguity or uncertainty. Sometimes we are paralyzed by it. Yet at other times it refreshes and energizes us, overcoming our failures and indecisions. According to Akerlof and Shiller, the animal spirits have "five different aspects," each of which "affect[s] economic decisions: confidence, fairness, corruption and antisocial behavior, money illusion, and stories." Confidence derives from the basic trust that people have in one another, the market, and the state "and the feedback mechanisms between 'confidence' and the economy that amplify disturbances." Fairness concerns "the setting of wages and prices." This theory acknowledges corruption and other social behaviors as playing a role in the economy and affecting it. The theory also revives another Keynesian concept, "money illusion," which refers to the fact that people are often fooled by nominal values of economic variables, such as wages, prices, income, and wealth. They are "confused by inflation or deflation" and do not "reason through its effects." Finally, by the stories aspect of animal spirits, Akerlof and Shiller mean the sense of identity people hold of themselves, their economy, and society. "Our sense of reality, of who we are and what we are doing, is intertwined with the story of our lives and of the lives of others. The aggregate of such stories is a national or

---

[10] Akerlof and Shiller (2009, p. ix).

international story, which itself plays an important role in the economy." Of the five aspects, Akerlof and Shiller consider confidence and money illusion as the cornerstones of their theory. They believe their theory, with its central concept of animal spirits, describes how the economy works. "It accounts for how it works when people really are *human*, that is, possessed of all-too-human animal spirits. And it explains why ignorance of how the economy really works has led to the current state of the world economy, with the breakdown of credit markets and the threat of collapse of the real economy in train."[11]

This digression on the view of Akerlof and Shiller demonstrates how little the classical-neoclassical economic paradigm has advanced its view of humankind, perhaps the most important cornerstone element of any social science theory. It has lasted from the eighteenth to the twenty-first century, from considering man as a purely self-interested egoist of the classical economics to the "rational" self-interested egoist of the neoclassical economics of the twentieth century and finally to the "animal spirits"–motivated, "rational" self-interested egoist of the twenty-first-century neoclassical-Keynesian hybrid conception of Akerlof-Shiller.

Negative Impact on Environment

A fourth major area of concern has been the continuing degradation of the environment and the inability of the global economic system to reverse years of environmental neglect. Generally speaking, the neglect of the environment is classified as a negative economic externality; it is the fallout of economic activities, such as electricity production, or of the manufacturing of goods, such as steel. Producers of electricity, whether using coal, oil, or natural gas, produce as by-products pollutants that damage the environment. In other words, buyers of electricity do not pay for the full cost of its production. Similarly, drivers do not pay the full price for gasoline; they pay for gas but not for the resulting pollution caused by their driving. All modern economies fail to address the environmental damage that their economies, and their citizens more generally, cause. One reason is that a major part of the environmental damage is passed on to future generations who have no vote in what goes on today. Environmental damage is not only local. Countries argue that meaningful policies to reverse global environmental damage, such as global warming, require international agreement, something that is elusive because most countries are not willing to sacrifice their economic output if they can put it off, especially if all countries (no matter

---

[11] Akerlof and Shiller (2009, pp. xi, 4–5).

what their past contribution to environmental degradation) do not make a similar sacrifice.

ISLAMIC ECONOMICS PARADIGM

Islam is a rules-based system with a prescribed method for humans and society to achieve material and nonmaterial progress and development grounded in rule compliance and effective institutions. The foundations of the Islamic economic system were laid down centuries ago in the Quran and practiced by the Prophet Muhammad in Medina during his brief time on this plane of existence. These rules laid down by the Almighty (swt) are at the foundation of the Islamic system and provide the required effective institutions. The institutional scaffolding of the Islamic economic system is thus formed by the rules of behavior defined by the Quran. As a result, the content and blueprint of Islamic economics is derived by: (1) extracting the rules that define an ideal Islamic economy and their economic implications from the Quran and the *Sunnah* (the teachings and the practice of the Prophet Muhammad [sawa]); (2) studying these institutions in the contemporary economy and determining the degree and extent of deviation between institutional scaffolding and that of the ideal Islamic economy; and (3) prescribing policy recommendations to bridge the gap between the two.

The Islamic economic system is a market-based system, where markets are seen as the best and most efficient mechanism for resource allocation (production and consumption). But efficiency of the market system must not be confused with markets as an ideology, whereby unfettered markets are seen as philosophy or the basis of the economic system, something to be revered, untouched, and placed on a pedestal. To be efficient, markets must have rules (such as information disclosure) to protect market participants (workers, producers, investors, and consumers) and must be supervised with strict rule enforcement. Private property that is legally acquired is held sacred in Islam, and property rights are fully protected. However, according to Islam, Allah (swt) is the Creator of all things on this earth and His creation has been given to humans of all generations in trust. Thus land and other natural resources must be developed in ways that benefit all humans of all generations equitably. It is imperative that the rights of the disabled and those of future generations are fully honored.

A major feature of the Almighty's rules, conveyed in the Quran and practiced by the Prophet (sawa), is *justice*. Thus the Islamic institutional scaffolding and the ideal Islamic economy exude justice. As a result, the promotion of social and human development on this plane of existence is founded on rules that promote justice. The Prophet (sawa) understood the essential objective of the message to encourage and insert justice in human societies as emphasized in the Quran. The Prophet (sawa) taught the responsibility of the individual, the collectivity, and the state. He particularly emphasized the equality of individuals before the law and that all rules that are incumbent on individuals and the collectivity must be more strictly observed by those in positions of authority, as illustrated by his famous saying: "Authority may survive disbelief but not injustice." Insistence on justice became the hallmark of the institutional scaffolding of governance, a structure with full transparency and accountability. Rule compliance that embraces the pursuit of social justice is a requirement of each and every Muslim during every day of his or her life on this earth. Justice is essential in all endeavors, as the pursuit of justice leads to spiritual fulfillment and brings humans closer to their Creator. Rule compliance and justice cannot be compromised. In Islam, social and human development is multidimensional and goes well beyond the highest level of GDP and GDP per capita. Human spiritual pursuits on this earth cannot be compromised for material ends.

In Islam, conventionally measured GDP per capita and GDP growth are not society's only economic goals. There are overriding spiritual, moral, and human dimensions to all economic endeavors. Humans need bread to live but do not live by bread alone. The goal of progress and development is the overall well-being of humans and society. While this has been the goal in Islam, it began to be recognized through the work of Mahbub ul-Haq, Amartya Sen, and numerous other economists in conventional economics only in the late 1970s. Moreover, in Islam, institutions have been seen as an essential element and the foundation of achieving human and economic development. This idea became popular in conventional economics only about 30 or so years ago; it had been almost forgotten from the writings of Adam Smith with the emergence of neoclassical economics. Institutions are the formal and informal laws and rules that shape political and economic structures of society to reduce risk and increase trust. Risk reduction and trust enhancement in turn support economic progress and prosperity.[12]

SHORT HISTORY OF ECONOMIC THOUGHT IN ISLAM

The last section provided a general description of Islamic teachings on economics, but we cannot sidestep a number of inescapable questions. Namely, given our claim that Islamic teachings on the economic system are based on the morality and ethics of centuries ago, why have the contributions of Islamic

---

[12]For a detailed discussion of these points, see Mirakhor (2010).

economics not entered into mainstream economics? Why is it that apparently none of the concepts of conventional economics is based on Islamic economics? And why is it that Islamic economics is not more developed as a social science so that it could be at least taught in Muslim countries as a stand-alone economic system? While space limitations preclude a full discussion, brief references may begin to address the issues.

Mirakhor made one of the early attempts to point to the neglect of Muslim contributions to modern economics.[13] It is disheartening that after discussing Greco-Roman economics, Joseph Schumpeter in his magnum opus, *History of Economic Analysis*, states: "So far as our subject is concerned we may safely leap over 500 years to the epoch of St. Thomas Aquinas (1225–1274) whose Summa Theologica is in the history of thought what the south-western spire of the Cathedral of Chartres is in the history of architecture."[14]

This statement is the reason he titles this section of Chapter 2 of his book "The Great Gap." The implications of this statement, as well as the rest of the material in this section of Schumpeter's book, is that for 500 years nothing was said, written, or practiced that had any relevance to economics. In this respect, Schumpeter was merely reflecting an attitude in the coverage of the history of economic thought existing since the late 1800s. The fact that his book became the locus classicus of all works on the history of economic thought only means that this idea would continue from that time on. It is a demonstrable fact that almost all books about the history of economic thought to present-day text-books echo Schumpeter's sentiments about economic thought prior to the Scholastics (the philosophers who were responsible for the economic thinking in the medieval period, which lasted from 500 to 1500).

Whatever may have been Schumpeter's reason for not recognizing and acknowledging the influence of Muslim scholars, the results were unfortunate for the history of economic thought. The fact that his book became such a celebrated reference in the discipline helped perpetuate what we may call a blind spot in the field that has continued to the present. Even if scholars wish to ignore the research in the history of philosophy, theology, ethics, and science, the mere fact that anyone who consults original writings of medieval scholars can see references to names such as Alfarabius (Al-Farābī), Avicenna, Averroes, and Algazal (Al-Ghazālī) should raise questions regarding their roles in the development of economic thought.

A number of early Muslim contributions included discussion of ideas on taxation, market regulation, usury, permissible economic behavior, wages, prices, division of labor, money as medium of exchange and as unit of account,

[13]Mirakhor (2003).
[14]Schumpeter (1954, pp. 73–74).

admonition against debasement of money, coinage, price fluctuations, and, finally, ethical prescriptions regarding observance of the mean. These works have shown that during the first two and a half centuries of Islam, ideas were developed regarding fiscal policy, monetary policy and institutions, credit and credit instruments, price determination and price policy, market and market regulation, commodity exchange, usury, government budgets, use of taxation as a tool to encourage production and discourage accumulation of wealth, public treasury, deficit financing, methods of balancing governmental budgets, supply and demand, checking and savings accounts, rudiments of banking institutions and procedures on formation of partnerships and commenda contracts, and monopoly.

By the ninth century, many of these ideas had appeared in writing in the form of Islamic legal (*fiqh*) manuals. Udovitch's studies on commercial techniques, credit, and credit instruments existing in the world of Islam by the ninth century was based on analysis of these types of manuals as well as mercantile manuals of early periods of Islam. Based on his studies, Udovitch suggests: "The earliest Muslim legal sources now justify the assertion that already in the late eighth century, and possibly earlier, credit arrangements of various types constituted an important feature of both trade and industry" in the Islamic world.[15] Similarly, the works of Abul-Fadl Ad-Dimashqi, a ninth-century scholar, show advanced ideas regarding value theory, cost and price determination.

As discussed in Chapra, historical records reveal a number of important early contributions by Muslim scholars to the development of Western economic thought and the Enlightenment movement in Europe. Unfortunately, with the passage of time, these contributions were either forgotten or attributed to others. Chapra similarly identifies a number of important Muslim contributions from secondary sources centuries before they were identified and incorporated in conventional economics, including:

> *interdisciplinary approach; property rights; division of labor and specialization; the importance of saving and investment for development; the role that both demand and supply play in the determination of prices and the factors that influence demand and supply; role of money, exchange, and market mechanism; characteristics of money, counterfeiting, currency debasement, and Gresham's law; the development of che[cks], letters of credit and banking; labor supply and population; the role of the state, justice, peace, and stability in development; and principles of taxation.[16]*

[15]Udovitch (1970).
[16]Chapra (2010, p. 10).

Chapra discusses some of these contributions in more detail and goes on to describe how these and other contributions of Muslim scholars were ignored:

> *to remove the concept of the "Great Gap" of "over 500 years" that exists in the history of conventional economic thought as a result of the false assumption by Joseph Schumpeter in his book,* History of Economic Analysis *(1954), that the intervening period between the Greeks and the Scholastics was sterile and unproductive. This concept has become well embedded in the conventional economics literature as may be seen from the reference to this even by the Nobel Laureate, Douglas North, in his December 1993 Nobel lecture (1994, p. 365). . . . Even the Scholastics themselves had been greatly influenced by the contributions made by Muslim scholars. The names of Ibn Sina (Avicenna, d. 1037), Ibn Rushd (Averroes, d. 1198) and Maimonides (d. 1204) (a Jewish philosopher, scientist, and physician who flourished in Muslim Spain), appear on almost every page of the thirteenth century summa (treatises written by scholastic philosophers) (Pifer, 1978, p. 356).[17]*

And Chapra goes on to explain the reason for the decline of Muslim economic progress:

> *The trigger mechanism for this decline was, according to Ibn Khaldun, the failure of political authority to provide good governance. Political illegitimacy, which started after the end of khilafah in 661 gradually led to increased corruption and the use of state resources for private benefit at the neglect of education and other [n]ation-building functions of the state. This gradually triggered the decline of all other sectors of the society and economy.[18]*

Even a cursory reading of the writings of the last century by Muslim scholars, social critics, and pamphleteers—beginning perhaps with Jamaluddin Asadabadi (better known as Afghani) and his students, such as Muhammad 'Abduh, Hassan al Banna, Sayed Qutb, Allamah Dr. Muhammad Iqbal, Sayyid Abul A'la Mawdudi, Shaheed M.B. Sadr, and Fazlur Rahman to social critics such as Malik Ben Nabi and Ali Shari'ati, and to contemporary scholars reveals a conviction that Islam has solutions to people's contemporary problems.

---

[17]Chapra (2010, pp. 11–21).
[18]Ibid., p. 11.

BOX 1.1 SHORT HISTORY OF ISLAMIC ECONOMIC THOUGHT

Siddiqi (2010) divides the history of economic thought of Muslims into three periods. The first period lasted from after the *hijra* (the migration of the Prophet (sawa) and his followers from Mecca to Medina) until AH 450 (AD 1058). In this period, *fuqaha* (jurists) and philosophers emerged. Some eminent scholars of this period are Abu Yusuf, Muhammad bin Al-Hassan, Abu Ubayd, and Junayd Baghdadi.

The *fiqh* concentrated on the requirements of *Shariah*, and economic issues were discussed in this context. *Fuqaha* separate the *maslaha* (utility) and *mafsada* (disutility) in economic activities. Jurists treated economics as a normative endeavor. The contributions of Sufis to economic thought can be summarized as an important attempt to give a low weight to material pursuits in favor of altruism and unselfish service to others. The philosophers' thoughts were global and rational. Their approach was toward an ideal society. In this sense, they concentrated on macro issues while jurists focused on micro issues.

The second phase lasted from AH 450 to 850 (AD 1058 to 1446). This period witnessed a flourishing of Islamic economic thought. Abu Hamid Al-Ghazali, Taqiuddin Ibn Taymiyah, and Ibn Khaldun were the eminent scholars of this period. Ali-Ghazali believed that individuals should satisfy only their basic needs, not more or less. Ibn Taymiyah concentrated on the need for society to establish a moral foundation for economic pursuits according to *Shariah*. He asserted that a ruler must preserve justice in transactions and introduced the institution of *hisab* (account) and the concept of fair price in transactions. Ibn Khaldun explained the reasons for the fall and rise of civilizations. He also discussed the importance of the division of labor and the role of trade in growth. He believed in the minimal role of the state in economic activities.

The third period lasted five centuries, AH 850 to 1350 (AD 1446 to 1932). This period is characterized by stagnation in intellectual and individual thinking. Among the scholars of this time, Shah Waliullah explained the rationality of *Shariah* rules for conducting individual and social dealings. He believed taxation to be a necessary policy for governments to provide enough funds for public needs, such as maintaining roads. However, he was strongly opposed to heavy taxes. He also believed that extravagance, luxury, and opulent living invariably led to the downfall of civilizations.

Source: Mohammad Nejatullah Siddiqi, "History of Islamic Economic Thought," in *Handbook of Islamic Economics*, edited by Habib Ahmed and Muhammad Sirajul Hoque, vol. 1: 95–110. (Jeddah, Saudi Arabia: Islamic Research and Training Institute, 2010).

The second important conviction articulated in these writings is a deep belief that Islam has prescribed rules of behavior for individuals and societies to comply with that assures felicity on this earth and in the hereafter. The third conviction expressed, in one form or another, is that the malaise of Muslim societies stems from general noncompliance with the rules of behavior prescribed by the Lawgiver.

Systematic focus on economic issues, however, began in earnest in the 1950s with Sayed Qutb's book, *Social Justice in Islam*.[19] The challenge of the two dominant systems—capitalism and socialism—and their attraction for Muslim youth during the 1950s, 1960s, and 1970s made the task of articulating an Islamic response ever more urgent. The first to respond to the challenge, positioning Islam's view on economic matters between capitalism and socialism, was Sayyid Abul A'La Mawdudi.[20] His writings and those of his students, especially Professor (Senator) Khurshid Ahmad, became a major source of thought and the standard bearer of ideas for Islamic economics.

The 1960s represent a watershed in the progress to articulating a vision of the Islamic economic system firmly grounded on the Quran and the *Sunnah*. The publication in 1968 of Shaheed M. B. al Sadr's book, *Iqtisaduna (Our Economics)*, initiated a new approach in articulating Islam's vision of an economy that serves society's needs.[21] Monzer Kahf

---

[19]The book was first published in or about 1945 in Egypt but did not become available in the rest of the Muslim world until the 1950s. It was translated into English much later by John B. Hardie as *Social Justice in Islam* (Lahore: Islamic Book Services, n.d.).

[20]For a recent rendition of Maulana Mawdudi's ideas on Islam and economics, see Ahmad (2011). This book competently culls and integrates Mawdudi's ideas from various pamphlets, speeches, sermons, and writings.

[21]See also an enlightening essay by perhaps the most brilliant student of Al Sadr, Ammar Abu Raheef, in Al–Hassani and Mirakhor (2003).

suggests that *Iqtisaduna* became a shining beacon that began a new era in Islamic studies and marked the birth of Islamic economics.[22] The central focus of the book is identifying the architecture of the Islamic economic system and then examining and understanding the behavior of its constituent elements. These are then the tasks of the discipline of Islamic economics. It is noteworthy that *Iqtisaduna* was written after al Sadr had already published *Falsafatuna* (*Our Philosophy*), a book that established the ethico-philosophical framework in which *Iqtisaduna* was later envisioned.[23]

SUMMARY

An economic system covers the type of relationships among households, businesses, and government and the framework for producing, distributing, and consuming the goods and services produced in an economy. A critical dimension of the economic structure is the extent of government intervention, the role of markets and their regulation and supervision, the legal system of property rights, ownership of factors of production, and contracts and their enforcement. The basic issues to be addressed are what goods and services are produced and how and for whom they are produced. Although there are a number of ways to classify the range of economic systems, one classification could be traditional economies, market economies, mixed market economies, mixed socialist economies, and command (planned) economies.

Adam Smith is widely considered to be the father of the modern capitalist market system. The Great Depression and the imploding global economy shook up the economics profession. In response, Keynes put

---

[22] Monzer Kahf, "Definition and Methodology of Islamic Economics Based on the Views of Imam al Sadr," paper presented in the International Conference on Imam Sadr's Economic Thoughts, Qum, Islamic Republic of Iran, May 2006.

[23] This book was published first in 1960 and *Iqtisaduna* in 1961. There is a parallel with Adam Smith who wrote his ethico-philosophical work, *The Theory of Moral Sentiments*, long before his more famous book, *The Wealth of Nations*. Until very recently the economics profession made no serious attempt to connect the two. The result of this disconnect has been the development of a "science" of economics divorced from the ethical foundations so strongly articulated and advocated in *The Theory of Moral Sentiments* by Smith, the father of the market economic system. Similarly, a study of *Falsafatuna* would provide a more complete understanding of *Iqtisaduna*. See also the essay by Ragheef in *Iqtisad*.

forward his book titled *General Theory of Employment, Interest, and Money* to provide some answers. A number of economists further developed the Keynesian approach in what came to be known as neo-Keynesian macroeconomics. Although the Keynesian theory of demand management has become the most widely accepted macroeconomic framework, the Chicago school of economics later criticized it, largely on libertarian grounds and because it could not explain a number of observed economic developments in the 1970s and 1980s. These economists argued against discretionary macroeconomic policies in favor of the market's invisible hand and passive fiscal and monetary policies. In 2014, economists are even more divided about the effectiveness of Keynesian macroeconomic policies and the broader role of government intervention in economic management. There is no "pure" market economy in the world of 2014. There is a role for governments in any economic system to limit economic cycles and financial crises, to enhance growth, to develop a social safety net, and to safeguard the interests of future generations, interests that include preservation of the environment and provision of the social and legal infrastructure for efficient operation of a market system.

The Islamic economic system is a market-based system, where markets are seen as the best and most efficient mechanism for resource allocation. But valuing markets for their efficiency is not the same as upholding markets as an ideology and a philosophy. The foundations of the Islamic economic system were laid down in the Quran and practiced by the Prophet Muhammad (sawa) in Medina. These rules that were established by the Almighty are the basis for the Islamic system and provide the effective institutions for the ideal Islamic system.

KEY TERMS

Economic systems	Market economies
Demand management	Mixed market economies
Markets	Mixed socialist economies
Institutions	Command economies
Traditional economies	

QUESTIONS

1. What is an economic system, and what are its component parts?
2. What is the function of an economic system?

3. What is the role of government in different economic systems?
4. What would happen to economies if governments did not exist?
5. What are the key features of the Islamic economic system?
6. Would you rather have the Islamic or the market capitalist system in your country? Explain your answer.
7. How does the role of markets vary in different economic systems?

CHAPTER 2

Foundation of the Islamic Economic Paradigm

Learning objectives:

1. *How Islam differs from other religions.*
2. *The difference between individual and societal goals in Islam.*
3. *The importance of rules (i.e., institutions) and rule compliance in Islam.*
4. *Why justice is so important in Islam.*
5. *The role of* Shariah *in Islamic economics and finance.*
6. *The meaning of* maqasid-al-Shariah *(objectives of* Shariah*).*
7. *The foundational elements of Islamic teachings.*
8. *The importance of agent-trustee in Islam and in preserving the rights of all generations.*

Four fundamental concepts support the rules-based religion that is Islam. First is *walayahh*, the unconditional, dynamic, active, ever-present love of the Supreme Creator for His creation, which is manifested through the act of creation and the provision of sustenance for all humans. This involves providing sufficient resources to sustain life and divine rules to sustain and flourish on this earth. Humans reciprocate His love by extending their love to other humans and to the rest of creation. Second is the concept of *karamah*, human dignity. The Quran considers humans to be the crowning achievement of His creation for whose personal and collective development everything else has been created. Indeed, humans are the purpose of creation. The third concept is the *meethaq*, the covenant in which all humans were called before their Supreme Creator and asked to testify that they recognize in Him the One and Only Creator and Sustainer of the entire creation and all other implications flowing from this testimony.[1]

The concept of *meethaq*, in turn, unfolds into three basic principles:

1. *Tawheed*, the One-and-Onlyness of the Creator, which unfolds into the one-and-onlyness of the created and its unity, including above all the unity of humankind
2. *Nubbowah*, the continuous chain of humans (prophets) appointed by the Creator to remind, warn, cleanse, teach, and induce humans to bring about and uphold justice within the created order through their position of agency-trustee assigned and empowered by the Supreme Creator
3. *Maád*, the return of creation to its origin and the accountability of humanity (individually and collectively) for acts of commission and omission—success and failure in achieving, establishing, and upholding justice toward their selves, toward others of their kind, and toward the rest of creation

The fourth concept is that of *khilafa*, agent-trustee relationship. *Khilafah* is the empowerment of humans by their Creator as agent-trustee to extend His love and compassion to one another, materially through the resources provided to them by the Creator and nonmaterially through the manifestation of unconditional love for their own kind as well as for the rest of creation.

A number of verses of the Quran affirm and confirm the unity of humankind. These verses, plus those recounting the provision of physical-material as well as nonphysical faculties and facilities created for all humans that empower them economically and spiritually, form the cornerstone of the legislative framework of rules (institutions) for the socio-economic-political behavior of humans. Resources are created for all humans of all generations, who compose one humanity. Their diversity does not and should not mean their disunity. By the primordial covenant, not only do all humans recognize their own unity, they also have full cognition of their responsibility to maintain the unity and integrity of the rest of creation through their service to humanity and to the rest of creation.

---

[1]They were collectively asked to testify to the Oneness and Uniqueness of the Creator as the *One* and the *Only* Cherisher Lord (*Rabb*) of all creation and everything else that this declaration implies, including the necessity of complying with rules of behavior, which their Lord Creator has ordained and prescribed for a life of felicity on earth. All members of this cycle of humanity, that is, all the progeny of Adam, testified so (Quran 7:172).

Unity operates at two levels, societal and individual. On the social plane, unity expresses itself in the integration of human society. Islam refuses to accept as the ultimate unit of body politic anything less than the totality of Islamic community, or the *ummah*. It is a responsibility of this collectivity to ensure that all obstacles are removed from the individual's path to Allah (swt). Whether the individual will choose this path for this ultimate happiness is then his or her own personal choice. There is only one Muslim people, no matter how scattered and far removed its members may be. Only the complete *ummah* comprises that circle which is Islam, and no segment of the Muslim community has a right to be the *ummah* any more than a segment of a circle could claim circularity. On the personal level, unity is manifested in one's actions. It is the appropriation to one's self as well as the proclamation in implementation and living a life that has integrity. The concept of Islamic community cannot be overemphasized.

META-FRAMEWORK AND ARCHETYPE OF ECONOMIC RULES

The fountainhead of all Islamic paradigms is the Quran. It provides the framework within which all relevant envisioned conceptions of reality find their source. This eternal source specifies rules of behavior (institutions) applicable to all societies at all times. These rules are immutable temporally and spatially. The meta-framework specifies the immutable, abstract rules. The archetype model articulates the operational form of these rules and demonstrates how these rules are operationalized in a human community. The abstract became operational in the hands of the one human being who was the one and only direct recipient of the source of the meta-framework, the Quran. Through the words and actions of this perfect human, the meta-framework given by the Creator in the Quran was interpreted, articulated, and applied to the immediate human community of his time. The meta-framework specifies general universal laws, rules of behavior. The archetype model provides universal-specific rules of behavior and the institutional structure needed for organizing a human society based on the immutable rules of the meta-framework.

No one understood the Quran better than the Messenger (sawa), appointed to deliver it to humankind. During his blessed life on this plane of existence, he was both the spiritual and temporal authority for his followers. In his capacity as the spiritual authority, he expounded, interpreted, and explained the content of the Quran. In his capacity as the temporal authority, he operationalized the rules (institutions) specified in the Quran in the town of Medina. The economic system, which he established in Medina, is the archetype of Islamic economic systems. This archetype contains a core institutional structure that is immutable because it is firmly established based on the Messenger's (sawa) authoritative operationalization of the rules prescribed by the Creator in the Quran.

A typical example is the institution of inheritance. The specific procedure on how the inheritance is to be distributed is described in the Quran. There are also institutions that the Messenger (sawa) established which, while not explicitly stated in the Quran, are based on his understanding of the Quran as its highest interpretive authority. An example of this type of institution is the rules of market behavior. These two types of rules are immutable: Any conception of how an Islamic economy works will have to take these two elements of the archetype model as given. A third type of institutions at the periphery of the archetype model are temporally and spatially specific to the time and the place in which the archetype model was implemented. For example, the Messenger (sawa) instituted rules of noninterference with market forces and the need for unhindered flow of information in the market. This rule is of and itself an immutable rule of the archetype model, but forces that would interfere with market functioning may vary and are time and place dependent. For instance, before Islam, one acceptable method of interfering with market forces in Arabia was that middlemen would meet caravans bringing supplies some distance outside of the cities and purchase the supplies for resale in the cities. The Messenger (sawa) prohibited this procedure. Clearly, the principle of noninterference with the market forces is unchanged, but this particular procedure is no longer relevant. The economic hermeneutics of this rule and its application to a particular time, place, and market is part and parcel of what an Islamic economic paradigm would seek to address.

The meta-framework envisions an ideal society as one composed of believers committed to rule compliance. The individual members are aware of their "oneness" and conscious of the fact that their own self-interest is served by seeing "others as themselves." Such a society is one of the "Golden Mean" that avoids extremes and is so rule compliant that it serves as a benchmark for and a witness to humanity (Quran 2:143). This is a society that actively encourages cooperation in socially beneficial activities and prohibits cooperation in harmful ones (Quran 3:104, 110, 114; 9:71). Moreover, in this society, consultation, both at the level of individual as well as the collectivity, is institutionalized in accordance with the rule prescribed by Allah (swt) (Quran 3:159; 42:38; 2:233). Similarly, all other rules of behavior prescribed in the Quran are institutionalized with sufficiently strong incentive structure to enforce rule compliance. The objective is the establishment of social justice in society.

IMPLICATIONS OF THE AGENT-TRUSTEE RELATIONSHIP

Faculties such as *áql* (intelligence of the heart), human dignity, *walayahh* and *fitrah* (the primordial nature of humankind), gifted to humankind by their Creator, were to be employed in cognition, remembrance, and fidelity to the primordial covenant (*mithaq*). The crucial importance of fidelity to this covenant drives the necessity of remaining faithful to all covenants, contracts, and promises, as long as they are permissible, which often is emphasized in the Quran (e.g., 5:1). The commitment to remain faithful to the terms and conditions of the primordial covenant (to bear witness to Divine Existence and His Unity), equipped with the gifts of their Creator (the resources of the earth), humans were then assigned the role of trustee-agent (*khalifah*, or viceroy) of the Divine on earth (Quran 2:30). This mission consisted of, *inter alia*, developing the earth (Quran 11:61); establishing social justice through the exercise of love toward their kind and the rest of creation, as a reflection of the love of the Creator; and removing the obstacles from the path of others of their kind toward Allah (swt) (i.e., their passage from the darkness of personality traits unworthy of the human state toward the light of nearness to their Creator). Once again, it is the compliance with the rules of behavior prescribed by the Creator that makes treading the path feasible.

This agent-trustee position is a divine trust that is bestowed on humans. It is by virtue of this trust and the responsibilities associated with it that humans have been invested with domination over what has been created for them. Many verses in the Quran affirm this subjugation of resources to humans. The entire human population has the collective responsibility to ensure that every human being has the opportunity to tap his or her dormant potentialities and possibilities and convert them to actualities. This collective view of humans evokes the matter of unity of humankind, which in turn reflects the recognition of Allah's (swt) Oneness and Unity, that is, *Tawheed*. The link between responsible living in this world and accountability in the next provides a means for an infinite planning horizon for human beings.

The agent-trustee office bestowed on humans requires the activation of the nonmaterial gifts from the Creator that empower humans to perform their responsibility of agent-trustee. To this end, a self-cleansing and purification process is required. Believing in Islam is not a sterile, static, superficial, and passive verbal-physical expression and pretension to Islam-icity. A process instituted by the Creator serves to energize the ascending movement and progress of the self toward its perfection.

SIGNIFICANCE OF RULE COMPLIANCE

A verse in the Quran contains the necessary and sufficient condition for the existence of an ideal society and economy: "If the members of the collectivity were to be rule-compliant and ever-conscious surely We should have opened for them blessings from the sky and from the earth. But they rejected [the Divine messages] therefore we seized them on account of their [noncompliant] deeds" (Quran 7:96). The necessary condition for an ideal economy is being rule compliant. The sufficient condition of *taqwa* (i.e., the inner torch of consciousness of the ever-presence of the Creator) requires that there be no occasional lapse in rule compliance whatsoever. That is the ideal society and the economy is one in which humans, individually and collectively, are fully rule compliant. In such a society, the members and their collectivity comply with rules specified for all in the society and other rules relating to behavior in particular circumstances, such as those relating to economic behavior. The first include, *inter alia*, the rules of enjoining the good and forbidding evil behavior; of consultation, cooperation, and avoiding harm to others; and of establishing social justice. Of these, by far, the first is the most crucial. It is an imperative without which compliance with all other rules, general and specific, will be weak or avoided altogether without impunity. It is a foundational rule that empowers all other decreed rules of behavior compliance that allow humans to tread the absolutely desirable path of closeness to Allah (swt) commanding us and others to rule compliance that derives directly from cognizance and acknowledgment of the love bond (*walayahh*) between the Creator and humankind as well as its derivative love bond among humans.

When we say that Islam is a rules-based system, we mean that the rules are prescribed by the Lawgiver, who monitors compliance, and there are rewards for compliance and sanctions for noncompliance. Accordingly, the prescriptions ordained by the Lawgiver and explained and implemented by His Messenger are rules. The most crucial and central to Islam's concept of development is the progress humans make in developing the self. Without this, balanced and appropriate progress in the other two dimensions of development is not possible; any forward movement in them without self-development leads to harmful distortions. Compliance with the rules prescribed by the Lawgiver prevents distortions. The rules constitute a network that regulates all dimensions of the human experience, individually and collectively, on this plane of existence.

The rules in Islam go beyond those considered important by economists for economic growth—property rights protection, the enforcement of contracts, and good governance. In Islam, these are the rules of seeking knowledge through education; avoiding waste, harm, or injury; pursuing hard work; and not engaging in fraud, cheating, or abuse of property. The internalization of the rules of conduct governing market participation and compliance with them ensures that the market will be an efficient mechanism to create a balance within an economy. Because fairness and justice are ensured by rule compliance, the price that emerges will be a fair price. Rules regarding the fair treatment of others ensure that those who participate in the act of production receive just payment for their efforts. Thus, market-based distribution guided by the price mechanism would also be fair. Rules governing income redistribution ensure that the rights of others to access resources are preserved before income becomes disposable. All economic transactions are governed by rules requiring strict faithfulness to the terms and conditions of contracts and promises. Hence, the probability of asymmetric information and moral hazard, and their negative consequences, is minimized. Rules governing consumption ensure that there is no opulent or wasteful consumption. Since consumers internalize these rules before entering the market, the rules also shape consumer preferences and thus demand, moderating excessive wants. Rules governing the use of disposable income and wealth (i.e., income and wealth after they have been cleansed of the rights of others) ensure that wealth is not hoarded and that it is made available in the form of investment and expenditures in the way of Allah (swt). Prohibition of interest ensures the direct participation of wealth holders in sharing risk associated with investment.

The internalization of rules of behavior by individuals and their institutionalization, along with the incentive structure and enforcement mechanism, reduces uncertainty and ambiguity in decision-action choices confronting the individual and the society. The problems associated with coordination are resolved through compliance with the rule of cooperation. Moreover, a binding rule from the archetype model resolves the negative aspects of the collective action problem. Not only cooperation is ordained as a rule-based feature of society's institutional structure; the rule of negation of harmful externalities and reciprocation of one harmful act by another (i.e., the rule of not harming third parties by one's action and the right not to be harmed by anyone's action without reciprocation) mitigates the risk of the emergence of collective action problems.[2]

IMPACT OF SCARCITY

The agent-trustee duty of humans is central in the Islamic economic vision for a number of intertwined reasons. Conventional economics

---

[2]Kamali (2006), and Mirakhor and Hamid (2009).

doctrines focused on scarcity and unlimited human wants as the central reason for the study of economics. Economic growth is presumed to create wealth and thus relax the scarcity constraints. While scarcity is a serious constraint in a world of unlimited wants, it is not so in Islamic vision. The Creator has provided humankind with sufficient resources at the global level to satisfy all human needs if humans follow His rules. The creation of the earth was not a random event. Allah (swt) created the earth by incorporating human needs and creating conditions (as a test) that require humans to share.

In Islam, scarcity takes on three different aspects. First, the Quran repeatedly asserts that from a macro-global standpoint, Allah (swt) has created all things in "exact measures" (Quran 49:52), indicating that the Lord Cherisher, sustainer of all creation, provides sufficient sustenance for all in His creation including humankind. The Quran, however, recognizes two other dimensions of scarcity. It acknowledges a micro-actual scarcity stemming from misdistribution of resources and from greed and gluttony. Hence, one encounters in the Quran the overwhelming emphasis on social justice and rules against waste, accumulation of wealth, and extravagance. The third concept refers to the real scarcity arising from the fact of finite conditions of man on this plane of existence. The physical conditions of man impose a finite constraint. "Man is finite, mortal and aging, limited in time and space."[3] Becoming aware of these constraints as well as of the potentialities of the human state, human consciousness, once awakened, not only allows humans to grasp potentialities but also permits the human realization of them and the ability to transcend the limits of their physical existence to imagine what is and what could be. Humans, thus, realize that their physical existential constraints impose limits on how much of their potentialities they can actualize; they must then "choose between the alternatives grasped by transcending consciousness."[4] The third notion of scarcity dealt with in the Quran is this "existential scarcity" arising from the finite conditions of humans on this physical plane of existence. The Quran's constant reminder of limitations of time on this earth and the rapidity of its passage is symbolized by the question humans are asked on their transition to the next level of existence. They are asked, "How long did you spend on the earth?" and their answer is "A day or part of the day!" (Quran 18:19). Similarly the Quran clearly and repeatedly reminds humans about the natural aging process that erodes their physical and mental abilities (Quran 68:36; 70:16). The existential scarcity caused by the finite conditions of existence of humans on the earth "leads to an allocation

---

[3]Weisskopf (1971, pp. 22–23).
[4]Ibid.

problem of scarce means to alternative ends . . . the resources which are ultimately scarce are life, time and energy because of human finitude, aging and mortality."[5]

Thus there can be scarcity because some humans are selfish, hoard, and do not share with others who are less fortunate, because some humans have excessive wants, or because some humans are lazy and do not work hard enough. Thus scarcity can be a factor only at the local level because some people are taking more than their fair share of resources. While self-interest is fully recognized in Islam, it must be subservient to social interest. Human wants and preferences cannot be accepted as a given but must be shaped to reflect Allah's (swt) intentions for humankind. Conventional economics assumes that humans have unlimited wants and takes this as a given; Islam abhors greed and selfishness and sees them as traits that must be changed. Conventional economics assumes unlimited wants and emphasizes economic growth and material output for human happiness; Islam emphasizes the spiritual. Humans who live in regions with high per capita incomes are not any happier than those in poorer regions, because those living in rich areas invariably focus on their relative material position and, more generally, wealth does not by itself bring happiness. The sharing of material output with the less fortunate is of spiritual importance and brings about inner joy to those who share and should not be seen as charity. It instead supports the unity of humanity and protects the rights of those who for reasons beyond their own control are deprived. Allah's (swt) bounty to humankind has other important dimensions. Allah (swt) is the Ultimate Owner of His Own Creation that is intended for all humankind of all generations. These gifts, such as all depletable resources, water, land, and the environment, generally must be managed in trust so that the rights of all humans of this and future generations are preserved.

In sum, scarcity is only a constraint at a micro-individual level; at this level, it is a test both for the person who is constrained and for the person who is not constrained. For the constrained, it is a test of the strength of belief that has been experientially revealed to the person and is a light shining on the strength and weakness of the self. For those economically better off, it is a test of their recognition of the real source of their wealth— Allah (swt)—and the strength of their rule compliance in helping remove (self-sacrifice) economic constraints, namely, barriers from the path to perfection of those in need of help, a major purpose of life on this earth. Moreover, Islam asserts unambiguously that poverty is neither caused by scarcity or paucity of natural resources nor by a lack of proper synchronization between the modes of production and distribution. Rather, it is a

---

[5]Weisskopf (1971, pp. 22–23).

result of waste, opulence, extravagance, and nonpayment of what rightfully belongs to less able segments of the society. This position is illustrated by the prophetic saying: "Nothing makes a poor man starve except that with which a rich person avails a luxury." This is why waste, abuse of wealth, extravagance, and excessive consumption are condemned as unjust, particularly when they occur in conjunction with poverty that they could help to alleviate. In the morality of property, Islam unequivocally considers all individuals entitled to a certain standard of life; it is this entitlement that entails the satisfaction of their claim as a matter of equity and justice.

RATIONALITY AND FREEDOM OF CHOICE

In recognition and acknowledgment of their dignity, the Supreme Creator has endowed humans with freedom of choice. This gift is so important that the prophets and messengers and all of the revelations sent to humanity can be understood as attempts by Allah (swt) to persuade humans to choose—through the activation of their faculties of spirit, consciousness, and intelligence (áql)—to freely recognize and acknowledge the Love of the One and Only and to then return that Love through active love (love service) to the Creation of Allah (swt). This supreme gift of the Creator affords humans the choice of rejecting the reality and existence of their own Creator. In many verses of the Quran, Allah (swt) declares that had He wished He could have created all humans fully aware, conscious, and active believers. But humans are given the gift of free choice to recognize, acknowledge, and accept the love of Allah (swt) in gratitude for His gifts and to reciprocate His Love through their own love extended to the rest of creation through service to the creatures (humans and other living inhabitants of the earth) of Allah (swt), or to reject it all. In emphasizing this freedom of choice, the Quran unambiguously states that there is to be no compulsion in belief and religion. Even the Prophet (sawa) was instructed that He was appointed to remind and to warn but not to compel humans. This freedom of choice clearly extends to economic decisions and is again a test in which humans must encounter and overcome the temptations that they face.

Consciousness and awareness of their Creator and the prescribed rules render humans rational decision makers. Rational, meaning reasoned, action in a human who is aware follows reasoning by a faculty with which the Creator endows every human. This is intelligence (áql), which initiates a process of cognition by the heart. Áql is defined as the instrument by which the All-Merciful Creator is adored and through which final felicity (al-Jannah, or Paradise) is achieved. Áql is distinguished from intellect, which is a process of cognition by the mind. The ultimate operating rule of áql is for its possessor to cognate the truth that the criterion for reason-based action is achieving the satisfaction of Allah (swt).

This faculty is dormant in *bashar* (humankind). It is activated when man embarks on the path of becoming human (*insan*). Reading the Revelation to humans, cleansing them, and teaching them how to internalize the Revelation by the messengers activates the *áql*. When intelligence is dormant, man can reason only through intellect. Without *áql*, the decision-making process takes place through reasoning via the intellect alone. The process is faulty because without cognition by the heart, reasoning is activated and governed by character traits unworthy of the human state. When humans reason through the use of *áql* while choosing among alternative decision-actions available, the one selected is the one with the best chance of achieving the satisfaction of the Creator (i.e., choosing the decision-action compliant with the rules prescribed by Allah [swt]). Choice of a decision-action in the absence of *áql* would be governed by whims (*hawa'*) and in response to stimuli to the basic of instincts of man. This discussion demonstrates that while the postulates of self-interest and rationality are crucial in decision making in both the conventional economic and Islamic paradigms, they are radically different in their substance and implications.

The autonomy provided by the freedom of choice is exercised through compliance with rules (codified in institutions) specified by the Creator that are necessary for harmonious existence. Therefore, autonomy here is the exercise of freedom of choice in light of the responsibilities incorporated in the human state. Humans are endowed with the ability to choose freely and responsibly in accordance with reflective-meditative reasoning in carrying out the duties of the office of agent-trustee. Humans can use the natural-material resources of the earth and the nonmaterial gifts of empowerment endowed by the Creator. This exercise of the freedom of choice by humans to behave on earth in accordance with the rules of behavior prescribed by their Creator implies action and dynamism on their part to act in accordance with the will of the Creator and in keeping with the unity of His creation.

This discussion provides the basis for comparing the postulates of self-interest and rationality in the classical-neoclassical and Islamic paradigms. While both postulates are crucial in decision making in both paradigms, they are radically different in their substance and moment.

INDIVIDUAL OBLIGATIONS, RIGHTS, AND SELF-INTEREST

In Islam, human freedom is envisaged as a personal surrender to the Divine Will rather than as an innate personal right. The human being is ontologically dependent on Allah (swt) and can only receive what is given to him by the

Source of his being. Human rights are a consequence of human obligations, not their antecedent. Man is charged with certain obligations toward his Creator, nature, himself, and other humans; all of these obligations are outlined by the rules prescribed by the Creator. When these obligations are fulfilled, certain rights and freedoms are gained. Limitations that are imposed by the rules on the rights and freedom of the individual are directed at removing negative possibilities from human life. The obligations, rights, and limitations defined by Islam must be observed if the individual and the system are to have an Islamic identity.

Within the Islamic framework, individuals have natural rights that are guaranteed, including the right to pursue their economic interests. Islam considers natural rights of the individual as the rights granted to him by Allah (swt). Pursuing one's economic interests, within the framework of Islam, there is first an obligation and a duty, then a right that no one can abrogate. What is significant, however, is the fact that if an individual lacks the power and ability to pursue economic interests, the obligation to do so is no longer incumbent on the person, while his or her rights are still preserved. The right to economic benefits is never negated as a result of a lack of ability to undertake the duty to pursue economic interests. The potential right remains even if a person is unable to actualize it. Conversely, if the person is able but does not perform his or her obligations, the rights are also negated.

Corresponding to the objectives of the messengers and prophets, humans are to listen to the revelation with the aim of internalizing the rules of behavior (institutions) prescribed in the message, cleanse themselves of character traits unworthy of the human state, develop the earth, establish social justice, and, finally, move from darkness into light and help others of their kind to do the same. Humans can achieve all of these simply by being fully rule compliant. Doing so, humans serve their own best self-interest. Being fully rule compliant requires humans to be fully conscious and aware of their true self-interest, which is not limited only to the life on this plane of existence but includes and incorporates, in accordance with the third fundamental principle, the life to come. This means recognition that no one knows the best self-interest of humans other than their Creator who has prescribed rules of conduct compliance that assures them of attainment of their best self-interest. In 126 verses, the Quran explains that the prescribed institutional framework ensures that compliance with the rules is "best" for humans. To emphasize that their Creator knows best, the Quran asserts that there are things that humans believe to be best for them but are in fact harmful to them and there are things humans believe to be harmful to them but are best for them. This assertion is immediately followed by the phrase "Allah knows and you do not" (Quran 2:216).

In a number of verses after prescribing a rule of behavior, the Quran immediately states that compliance with the rule "is best for you if you only knew" (see, e.g., 2:184, 271, 280; 4:25; 8:19; 9:3, 41). Continuous consciousness and awareness of the need to be rule compliant progressively actualizes the potential in humans to come to know why behaving according to a prescribed rule serves their best self-interest because their Creator provides them with "a light with which to traverse on earth" (6:122).

To summarize, in Islam, and contrary to popular opinion, self-interest is not negated. Islam, in fact, considers it a primary factor in its incentive-motivation system—a necessity in any organized society if individuals are to maximize utility by following the behavioral rules prescribed by the system. Provided that self-interest is defined to cover spiritual and temporal (i.e., eternal and temporary) interests, there is not one rule that does not carry with it its own justification for individual self-interest. Individuals are invited to follow the rules for their own benefit, material and spiritual, in this world and for their ultimate salvation and felicity in the next. This is made clear by the Quran, which generally couples injunctions with the assertion that compliance with them by individuals is for their own benefit. Often the Quran enumerates the incentives and the rewards for compliance and the retribution for noncompliance, both here and in the hereafter. It is in the context of the pursuit of self-interest that individual obligations and rights, as well as the limits and accountabilities to these rights, are specified by the rules in Islam.

CENTRAL NOTION OF JUSTICE

Justice is at the left, the right, and the center of Islamic economic teachings. Indeed, in Islam, there can be little progress unless the focus is on justice and the rights of all humans are acknowledged and preserved. But this does not translate into a socialist economic system. The economic justice that is envisaged in Islam is not equal incomes and wealth. The focus of economic justice is not solely placed on the outcome. Again, if Allah (swt) had wanted this, He would have so designed His creation. Instead, the focus of justice is on the available means and opportunities to all humankind.

Thus, the central framework and operation of these rules is justice. The Prophet (sawa) understood the essential objective of His selection, appointment, and message to be to encourage and insert justice in human societies, as emphasized in the Quran. The Prophet (sawa) taught the responsibility of the individual, the collectivity, and the state. He particularly emphasized the equality of individuals before the law and that all rules that are incumbent on individuals and their collectivity must be more strictly observed by those in positions of authority. Hence the famous saying attributed to him: "Authority may survive disbelief but not injustice." Insistence on justice became the hallmark of the institutional scaffolding of governance, a structure with full transparency and accountability. In Islam, economic justice is centered on affording all humans an equitable chance (the means) to flourish while affording the disabled a dignified life and erasing poverty everywhere.

All humans should have the same (similar) opportunity and the freedom to achieve their economic goals (a level playing field in education, healthcare, and basic nutrition) through hard work while preserving the rights (not to be confused with charity) of the disabled. After humans have worked and received their just rewards, then they must help the less fortunate to eradicate poverty and avoid great disparities in wealth; this is a test for humans to show their love for their Creator and His creation as contrasted with a love of fleeting wealth. Individuals as well as the state should remove all roadblocks, especially oppression, from the path of human development. There is a prophetic saying that on the Day of Reckoning, the oppressor, the oppressed, and the person(s) who stood by and observed the oppression will be called upon to answer: the oppressor for oppression, the oppressed for not resisting the oppression, and the bystander for not assisting the oppressed. Any injustice perpetrated by individuals against other humans and against the rest of creation is ultimately an injustice to the self. Allah (swt) loves justice; it is a central part of His universal love. Humans must live a life that is just and must stand up to and eradicate injustice wherever they find it.

As mentioned earlier, a central aim of Islam is to establish a just and moral social order through human agency. This all-embracing desideratum of the Islamic system is the ruling principle from which human thought and behavior, the substantive and regulative rules of *Shariah*, the formation of the community, and the behavior of polity and of political authority derive their meaning and legitimacy. This emphasis on justice distinguishes the Islamic system from all other systems. It is through the scaffolding of justice that the raison d'être of the rules governing the economic behavior of the individual and economic institutions in Islam can be understood. What gives the behavior of a believer its orientation, meaning, and effectiveness is acting with the knowledge that justice evokes Allah's (swt) pleasure and injustice, His displeasure. Whereas justice in Western thought is a quality of the behavior of one individual in relation to another and actions can be perceived as unjust only in relation to the other, in Islam justice has implications and consequences for the first individual as well. That is, when one does injustice to someone else, there is always reciprocity; through injustice to others, ultimately, one also does injustice to oneself and receives its results both here and in the hereafter. The concept of justice

BOX 2.1 CONCEPT OF JUSTICE IN ISLAM

Justice in Islam is a multifaceted concept, and several terms exist for each aspect. The most common word in use that refers to the overall concept of justice is *ádl*. This word and its many synonyms imply the concepts of "right," as an equivalent of "fairness," "putting things in their right place," "equality," "equalizing," "balance," "temperance," and "moderation." These latter concepts are more precisely expressed as the principle of the Golden Mean, according to which believers are not only individually urged to act in conformity with this principle but also the community is called upon, by the Quran, to be a nation in the middle. Thus, justice in Islam is the aggregation of moral and social values that denote fairness, balance, and temperance. The implication for individual behavior is, first of all, that individuals should not transgress their bounds and, second, that one should give others, as well as oneself, what is due.

permeates Islam. It is very simple: Put everything in its rightful place and give everyone his or her due (see Box 2.1).

In practice, justice is operationally defined as acting in accordance with the law as outlined in *Shariah*, which, in turn, contains both substantive and procedural justice. Substantive justice consists of elements of justice contained in the substance of the Law, while procedural justice consists of rules of procedure assuring the attainment of justice contained in the substance of the law. The underlying principles that govern the distinction between just and unjust acts determine the ultimate purpose of the Islamic path, *Shariah*, which includes: the establishment of the "general good" of society (considered to be the intent of the Quran for human collectivity; *Shariah* is the path by which it is achieved); building the moral character of individuals; and, finally, the promotion of freedom, equality, and tolerance, which are often stated as important goals of *Shariah*. Of these, protecting the interests of society is accorded the greatest importance. Although there can be no contradiction between justice for the community as a whole and justice for the individual, interests of the individual are protected so long as such interests do not come into conflict with the general interests of the community.

We should again emphasize that the cornerstone of all ethical rules and regulations in the community is the concept of social justice. All economic rules in the Quran relate one way or another to the principle of social justice. The Quran puts great emphasis on economic justice as the foundation of social justice. Social and economic justice requires a simultaneous adjustment in all aspects of human life, as required by the axiom of unity. In adopting the axiom of unity, the Quran stresses the economic and material side of life. Whenever wealth is mentioned, adjectives such as "the good" and "the bounty of Allah" (swt) are used. Muslims are told to earn and enjoy wealth with the economic dimension of life injected with a unique moral quality to become the substantive base of the Islamic social order.

A Muslim engaged in the act of production is engaged in a form of worship. Economic justice as the cornerstone of social justice becomes indispensable to social order in Islam. In the end, the existence of absolute and relative poverty along with significant income inequality is an indisputable evidence of economic, social, and political failure. These adverse developments would be attributed to rule violation and governance failure, for which members of society are, individually and collectively, responsible, no matter how strong their pretensions to Islamicity. As noted by Chapra, ethical values must be enforced.[6] The Quran and the *Sunnah* provide the framework for moral behavior, but it is up to individuals, communities, and the state to enforce ethical values. And the effectiveness of moral behavior, in turn, increases with its widespread adherence.

SHARIAH: THE LAW

Islam legislates for humans according to their real nature and the possibilities inherent in the human state. Without overlooking the limited and the weak aspects of human nature in any way, Islam envisages man in light of his primordial nature as a theophany of Allah's (swt) attributes, with all the possibilities that this implies. It considers the human as having the possibility of being perfect but with a tendency to neglect potentialities of the human state by remaining only at a level of sense perception. It asks, therefore, that in exchange for all the blessings provided by their supreme Creator, humans seek to realize the full potential of their being and remove all the obstacles that bar the right functioning of their intelligence. To order human life into a pattern intended for it by its Creator, humans are provided with a network of injunctions and rules that represent the concrete embodiment of the Divine Will. By virtue of accepting specific codes of behavior—through the exercise of free choice—a person becomes a Muslim and then lives both his private and his social life according to

---

[6]Chapra (2010).

these rules. This network of rules—called *Shariah*, a word that is etymologically derived from a root meaning "the road"—leads humans to a harmonious life here and felicity hereafter.

The emphasis on the axiomatic principle of unity forms the basis for the fundamental belief that Islam recognizes no distinction between the spiritual and the temporal, between the sacred and the profane, or between the religious and the secular realms. Islam seeks to integrate all human needs, inclinations, and desires through the all-embracing authority of *Shariah*. Life is considered as one and indivisible. Therefore, the rules of *Shariah* hold sway over economic life no less than over social, political, and cultural life; they persuade, determine, and order the whole of life. It is through the acceptance of and compliance with the rules of *Shariah* that individuals integrate themselves not only into the community but also into a higher order of reality and the spiritual center. Violations of these rules will have a disintegrative effect on the life of the individual and on the community.

Shariah rules are derived, based on the Quran and its operationalization by the Prophet (sawa), through a rigorous process of investigation and thinking across time and geographical regions. The expansion of the rules of law and their extension to new situations, resulting from the growth and progress of the Islamic community, is accomplished with the help of consensus in the community, analogical reasoning—which derives rules by discerning an analogy between new problems and those existing in the primary sources—and independent human reasoning of those who specialize in the law. As a result, *Shariah* is invested with great flexibility in handling problems in diverse situations, customs, and societies. Therefore, it has a wide range of solutions and precedents, depending on different circumstances.

History has *not* recorded instances when Muslim jurists were unable to provide Islamic solutions to new problems. Their opinions covered all aspects of life. They laid down innovative theories, exemplary rules, and solutions. However, with the decline of Islamic rule in Muslim countries, the significance of *Shariah* in running day-to-day life also declined and development of *Shariah* remained dormant. In the last few decades, however, the reawakening among Muslims has generated enormous demand for the development of *Shariah*-based rules that address the problems of modern society (see Box 2.2).

The overall aim or objective of Islamic law—that is, the concept of *maqasid-al-Shariah*—is to promote the welfare of humankind and prevent harm by preserving the faith, lives, intellect, prosperity, wealth, and interests of future generations. The preservation of these promotes society and its interests. The achievement of society's interests (*maslahah*) is essentially the same as *maqasid*; they are one and the same.

BOX 2.2 BASICS OF *SHARIAH* (LAW)

The life of a Muslim at the individual and the societal level is governed by different sets of rules. The first set, known as *aqidah* (faith), concerns the core relationship between people and the Creator and deals with all matters pertaining to a Muslim's faith and beliefs. The second set deals with transforming and manifesting the faith and beliefs into action and daily practices and is formally known as *Shariah* (law). Finally, the third set is *akhlaq*, which cover the behavior, attitude, and work ethics according to which a Muslim lives in society. *Shariah* is further divided into two components: *ibadat* (rituals) focuses on the rites and customs through which each individual comes to an inner understanding of their relationship with Allah (swt); and *muamalat* (transactions) defines the rules governing social, political, and economic life. Indeed, a significant subset of *muamalat* defines the conduct of economic activities within the economic system, which ultimately lays down the rules for commercial, financial, and banking systems.

Ijtihad (from the root *jahd*, meaning "struggle") plays a critical role in deriving rules for resolving issues arising from time-dependent challenges. *Ijtihad* refers to the efforts of individual jurists and scholars to find solutions to problems that arise in the course of the evolution of human societies and that are not addressed specifically in the primary sources. *Ijtihad* is based on the earlier consensus of jurists (*ijma'*), analogy (*qiyas*), judicial preference (*istihsan*), public interest (*maslahah*), and customs (*urf*). Secondary sources of *Shariah* must not introduce any rules that are in conflict with the main tenets of Islam.

Over the course of history, different methods of exercising *ijtihad* have evolved depending on historical circumstances and the different schools of thought (*madhahib*) that prevailed at different times. The most commonly practiced methods are Hanafi, Maliki, Shafi'i, Hanbali, and Jafari, each of which assigns different weights in decision making to each source of law: the Quran, the *Sunnah*, *ijma'*, and *qiyas*. For example, the Jafari school does not accept analogical reasoning in its entirety as a legitimate method to derive rules of *Shariah*, favoring instead expert investigation and provision of solutions to new problems by jurists.

SUMMARY

Four fundamental concepts support the rules-based religion that is Islam: *walayahh* (the love of the Supreme Creator for His Creation that is manifested through creation and the provision of sustenance for all humans), *karamah* (human dignity), *meethaq* (the covenant calling humans before their Supreme Creator to recognize in Him the One and Only Creator), and *khilafa* (agent-trustee relationship).

Islam considers self-interest a primary factor in its incentive-motivation system; it is a necessity in any organized society if the individual is to maximize utility by following behavioral rules prescribed by the system. But in Islam, self-interest is defined to cover the spiritual and the temporal (i.e., eternal and temporary). Rules are for an individual's material and spiritual benefit in this world and for his or her ultimate salvation and felicity in the next. The incentives and the rewards for compliance and the retribution for noncompliance are sometimes detailed.

A central goal of Islam is to establish a just and moral social order through human agency (*khilafah*). Justice is operationally defined as acting in accordance with the law, which, in turn, contains both substantive and procedural justice. Humans are provided with a network of injunctions and rules that embody the divine will in terms of specific codes of behavior for both private and social life. The network of rules—called *Shariah*—etymologically derived from a root meaning "the road"—leads humans to a harmonious life on this earth and happiness in the hereafter. The overall goal of Islamic law—that is the, concept of *maqasid-al-Shariah*—is to promote the welfare of humankind and preserve their faith, lives, intellect, prosperity, wealth, and the interests of future generations, which in turn promote society and its interests. The achievement of society's interests (*maslahah*) is essentially the same as *maqasid*; they are one and the same.

KEY TERMS

Shariah	*Ummah*
Maqasid-al-Shariah	Unity of creation
Maslahah	Justice
Walayahh	Freedom of choice
Karamah	Scarcity
Meetaq	Meta-framework
Tawheed	Archetype model
Khilafa	

QUESTIONS

1. What is the concept of *ummah* in Islam?
2. What are the meta-framework and the archetype model?
3. What are the four concepts that are at the foundation of the Islamic system, and what do they mean?
4. In Islam, are individuals assumed to have freedom of choice?
5. How is individual incentive preserved in Islam?
6. What is meant by the phrase "Islam is a rules-based system"?
7. What is the importance and implication of the role of agent-trustee in Islam?
8. Why is rule compliance important in Islam?
9. How is the notion of scarcity in Islam different from that in conventional economics?
10. What do the terms "*Shariah*" and "*maqasid-al-Shariah*" mean?

CHAPTER 3

Institutional Framework and Key Institutions

Learning objectives:

1. *The nature of risk and its economic implications.*
2. *How trust mitigates uncertainty and risk.*
3. *Rules are the essence of institutions.*
4. *What rules are important in all economic systems.*
5. *Islam is a rules-based system.*
6. *Rule compliance enhances trust and builds effective institutions.*
7. *Effective institutions are the foundation of economic and social progress.*
8. *The important institutions in Islam.*
9. *The importance of work ethic in Islam.*

All societies face two interrelated problems—uncertainty and coordination. The first stems from the fact that the future is unknown. Yet every human has to make decisions and take actions that affect his or her own future as well as the future of others. Making decisions is one of the most fundamental capabilities of humans, but it is bound up with uncertainty. Facing an unknown, and generally unknowable, future, humans make decisions and choose among alternative courses of action based on their expectations of future consequences of their actions. The problem becomes more complicated when uncertainty about the future is coupled with ignorance about how other individuals, or their collectivities, behave in response to unknown states of the world.

The problem of decision making under uncertainly is compounded by two additional factors: the competence of the decision maker and the difficulty of selecting the most preferable among alternative possibilities, especially if there is a once-and-for-all decision since, once made, it destroys the possibility of making that decision again.[1] The gap between competence and difficulty enhances uncertainty leading to errors, surprises, and regrets. The level of uncertainty regarding the state of the world, as well as with respect to decision-actions of other individuals, makes collective action, which is necessary if society is to survive and flourish, a challenge. It then becomes crucial for societies to find ways and means of solving the problem of uncertainty and promoting coordination among individual decision makers.

Because of the interdependence among members of society, decisions made and actions taken by individuals directly and indirectly affect others. Only omniscient individuals with no uncertainty are able to take the most preferred action regardless of the degree of complexity of the decision environment. This is not, however, the case for humans, who must make decisions under conditions of uncertain and complex environments. Consequently, societies have to devise mechanisms that render individual behavior under uncertainty more predictable in order to attenuate uncertainty and promote coordination. By and large, societies develop rules of behavior that are more or less restrictive depending on the perception of the degree of uncertainty and the impact of individual decisions on other members of the society (see Box 3.1).

The collection of the rules of behavior prescribed for individuals and collectivities constitutes the institutional structure of society. The rules of behavior—whether enshrined in instruments such as social contracts, constitutions, and legal framework or embedded in social conventions, customs, habits, and cultural values—are sustained by enforcement mechanisms that provide proper incentives of rewarding rule compliance and punishing rule violation. The incentive structure is such that "not only are deviates from the desired behavior punished, but a person who fails to punish is in turn punished."[2] The incentive structure must be such that rules of behavior become self-enforcing; it also must be such that it renders the enforcement mechanisms in place effective by providing "appropriate

---

[1] Heiner (1983).
[2] Kandori (1992, p. 3).

BOX 3.1 SIGNIFICANCE OF RULES OF BEHAVIOR

Rules of behavior are designed to accomplish three objectives:

1. Reduce the cognitive demand on individuals in the face of uncertainty
2. Specify acceptable and unacceptable behavior
3. Make actions by individuals predictable

In totality, these three objectives reduce uncertainty in the environment by making the response of individuals to states of nature in their environment predictable. These rules of behavior are referred to as institutions. In the words of Schotter (1981, 10–11), an "institution is a regularity in social behavior [that] . . . specifies behavior in specific recurrent situations, and is either self-policed or policed by some external authority."[1] Institutions impose constraints on behavior and shape interactions among individuals in the society; they "define and limit the set of choices of individuals."[2] They are "phenomena that coordinate, regulate and stabilize human activities." They "facilitate" or "hinder human coordination"; they "can be regarded as both restrictions and opportunities, in both cases facilitating action by reducing uncertainty."[3] In situations of uncertainty, individuals form expectations about the consequences of their own decision-actions as well as those of other members of the society. One crucial characteristic of institutions (rules of behavior) is to "absorb uncertainties." Another is to reduce "the demand on the cognitive capacity of the human mind. Parallel with this, institutions also stabilize expectations and coordinate actions."[4]

---

[1] Schotter (1981, pp. 10–11).
[2] Aoki (2001, p. 3).
[3] Groenwegen, Pitelis, and Sjöstrand (1995, p. 20).
[4] Ibid., p. 35.

incentives . . . for the enforcers to perform their mission properly."[3] When and if "a mechanism that was designed with the purpose of achieving a

---

[3] Aoki (2001, p. 6).

prescribed social goal is not self-enforceable, then it needs to be supplemented . . . by enforcers (the courts, police, ombudsmen, etc.)."

The stronger the rule compliance by individuals in the society, the more self-sustaining and self-enforcing the rules become. For this outcome to be attained, the rules must be internalized by individuals as endogenous elements of their own minds, which find external expression when the rules become shared beliefs among individuals in the society. The stronger the shared beliefs, the stronger would be the coordinated collective actions and the more stable the society. As Aoki suggests, an institution (rule) "by the very fact of its existence, controls agents' individual action-choice rules by coordinating their beliefs. These beliefs channel their actions in one direction against the many other directions that are theoretically possible."[4] Following Douglass North, Aoki conceives of institutions as "rules of the game" and defines "an institution" as

> *a self-sustaining system of shared beliefs about how the game is played. Its substance is a compressed representation of the salient features of an equilibrium path, perceived by almost all agents in the domains as relevant to their own strategic choice. As such it governs the strategic interaction of agents in a self-enforcing manner and in turn is reproduced by their actual choices in a continually changing environment.*

He defines "the domain" as a set of agents—either individuals or organizations—and sets of physically feasible actions open to each agent in successive periods."[5]

Each economic system has an "institutional matrix" that "defines the opportunity set, being one that makes the highest payoffs in an economy's income distribution or one that provides the highest payoffs to productive activity."[6] North contends that in all economic systems, institutions (rules of behavior) are designed by humans to impose constraints on human interaction. These institutions "structure human interaction by providing an incentive structure to guide human behavior. But an incentive structure requires a theory of the way the mind perceives the world and its functioning so that

---

[4]Aoki (2001, p. 13).
[5]Ibid., pp. 20–21.
[6]North (2005, p. 61).

institutions provide those incentives."[7] It is here where paradigms become relevant because paradigms in economics do have conceptions of man, society, and their interrelationships. Such conceptions are themselves products of a meta-framework whose elements may or may not be explicitly specified but which nevertheless exist in the mind of the designer prior to the construction and presentation of the paradigm. Two meta-frameworks underlie economic paradigms: creator centered and man centered. The former derives its economic analysis from rules of behavior (institutions) prescribed by the creator for individuals and collectivities in human societies. Examples are economic paradigms that are based on Abrahamic traditions: Judaism, Christianity, and Islam.[8] The latter, the secular tradition, takes as given or derives rules of behavior (institutions) that are designed and approved by the society.

KEY INSTITUTIONS

The institutional framework of the ideal economy is composed of a collection of institutions—rules of conduct and their enforcement characteristics—designed by the Lawgiver, prescribed in the meta-framework, and operationalized by the archetype model to deal with allocation of resources, production and exchange of goods and services, and distribution-redistribution of resulting income and wealth. The objective of these institutions is to achieve social justice. Important among their functions is reduction in uncertainty for members of the society to allow them to overcome the obstacles to decision making caused by paucity of information. Rules specify what kind of conduct is most appropriate to achieving just results when individuals face alternative choices and must take action. They impose restrictions on what society's members can do without upsetting the social order, while all members rely on the social order in forming their own actions and their expectations of the responses of others.

Central among the rules that constitute the institutional structure of the ideal economy are rules governing property; contracts and contractual obligations; trust; markets and the code of conduct; risk sharing; wealth accumulation and utilization; wealth distribution and redistribution; work and work ethics; and competition and cooperation.

---

[7] North (2005, p. 66).
[8] For Judaism, see, for example, Tamari (1987); for Christianity, see, for example, Long (2000).

Property

While the individual's right to property affirms the natural tendency in man to possess—particularly something resulting from his own creative labor—the concomitant private property obligations, from the point of view of justice, are designed to give effect to the interdependence of members of the community, with a view to recognizing explicitly that they cannot live in isolation. The private property obligations, therefore, reject the notion that a person does no harm to members of his group if as a result of his effort he is better off and others are no worse off than they would otherwise be. These obligations write the principle of sharing into the delineation of interests in property and consider private ownership to be subject to a trust, or duty, in order to effect sharing. Hence, private initiative, choice, and reward are recognized in Islam's conception of property rights, but such recognition is not allowed to subvert the principle of sharing or to lead to violations of the rights of the community. If, as a result of the growth of society, division of labor, or increasing complexities of markets, either the obligation to share is shirked or the rights of the society and the cohesion of the community are undermined, an intervention by the legitimate authority to take corrective measures would be deemed justified.

The word "property" is defined as a bundle of rights, duties, powers, and liabilities with respect to an asset. In the Western concept, it is considered the right of an individual to use and dispose of a private property, along with the right to exclude others from the use of that property. Even in the evolution of Western economies, this is a rather new conception of property that is thought to have accompanied the emergence of the market economy. Before that, however, a grant of the property rights in land and other assets included the right to use and enjoy the asset, but it did not include the right to dispose of it or exclude others from its use. For example, the right to use the revenues from a parcel of land, a corporate charter, or a monopoly granted by the state did not carry the right of disposing of the property. It is thought that the development of the market economy necessitated a revision of this conception of property since the right not to be excluded from the use of assets owned by another individual was not marketable; it was deemed impossible to reconcile this particular right with a market economy. Hence, of the two earlier property rights principles—the right to exclude others and the right not to be excluded by others—the latter was abandoned, and the new conception of property rights was narrowed to cover only the right to exclude others. In Islam, however, this right is retained without diminishing the role of the market as a mechanism for resource allocation and impulse transmission.

There are eight key principles of Islamic property rights:

1. Acknowledge the permanent, constant, and invariant ownership of all property by Allah (swt). The Supreme Creator is the ultimate owner of all properties and assets. In order that humans become materially able to perform duties and obligations prescribed by the Lawgiver, they have been granted a conditional right of possession of property. This right is granted to the collectivity of humans.
2. Acknowledge transfer by Allah (swt) of the right of possession to all of humankind, which establishes the right of collectivity to the created resources.
3. Provide equal opportunity of access by all to the natural resources provided by the Creator, to be combined with their labor to produce goods and services.
4. Individuals appropriate the products resulting from the combination of their labor with these resources, without the collectivity losing its original rights either to the resources or to the goods and services by individuals.
5. Recognize only two ways in which individuals accrue rights to property:
   a. Through their own creative labor; and/or
   b. Through transfers—via exchange, contracts, grants, or inheritance— from others who have gained title to a property or an asset through their labor.

   Fundamentally, therefore, work is the basis of acquisition of rights to property. However, work is performed not only for the purpose of satisfaction of wants or needs but is considered a duty and obligation required of everyone. This rule forbids gaining instanta- neous property rights without working to earn them. The exception is lawful transfer. This rule also prohibits property rights gained through gambling, theft, earning interest on money lent, bribery, or generally from sources considered unlawful. Just as work is a right and obliga- tion of all humans, access to and use of natural-physical resources provided by the Creator for producing goods and services are also every human's right and obligation. All humans are ordained to apply their creative labor to these resources to produce what society needs. If an individual, for whatever reason, lacks the ability to work, it does not deprive him or her of the original right to resources granted to every human by the Creator.
6. Sanctify, through the "immutability of property rights," the duty of sharing by transferring it into the principles of property rights and obligations. Before any work is performed on natural-physical

resources, all humans have an equal right and opportunity to access these resources. When individuals apply their creative labor to resources, they gain a right to priority in the possession, use, and exchange of the resulting product without nullifying the original property rights of the Creator or the rights He granted to all humans in the final product or the proceeds from its sale.

This principle regards private property ownership rights as a trust held to affect sharing. Before any work is performed in conjunction with natural resources, all members of society have an equal right and opportunity to access these resources. When individuals apply their creative labor to resources, they gain a right of priority in the possession, use, or market exchange of the resulting product without nullifying the rights of the needy to the proceeds of the sale of the product. To ensure the property rights of all members of society, property rights over natural resources (such as mines) were placed in trust of the state, to be used for the benefit of all, or in the hands of society at large as commons (e.g., surface and underground water).[9] A clear distinction was made between the right of ownership and the right of possession, particularly in the case of land. Any individual could combine labor, capital, and available land to produce a commodity over which the person would have full property rights. The land would remain in the person's possession as long as the land was in production. However, if the land was not used for continuous production (for a designated period, such as three consecutive years), the person would lose the right of possession, and another producer would have the right to take possession of the land to use labor and capital to produce a commodity.

7. Acknowledge the duty of sharing the product or the income and wealth proceeding from its sale, which relates to property ownership rights as a trust. This rule is made operational through the ordained duties imposed on income and wealth, which must be paid to cleanse income and wealth from the rights of others. This is perhaps the reason the

---

[9]Western economists have long addressed the issue of natural resource depletion and intergenerational equity. Robert Solow (1974, p. 41) reached the conclusion that "the finite pool of resources (I have excluded full recycling) should be used up optimally according to the general rules that govern the optimal use of reproducible assets. In particular, earlier generations are entitled to draw down the pool (optimally, of course!) so long as they add (optimally, of course!) to the stock of reproducible capital." This is essentially the Islamic prescription.

Quran refers to these duties as *zakah*, from the root word meaning "cleansing and purification." These duties are likened to tree pruning, which simultaneously rids the tree of its undesirable parts and allows its further growth. Although the Quran acknowledges that in His wisdom the Lord has created humans with differences, it also emphasizes that these differences are only minor and that all humans are essentially the same. The real difference between them, the one that ultimately counts, is the degree of awareness of Allah (swt) conscious. No other difference matters.

In a society in which there is poverty amid plenty, the roots of inequality must be traced to distortions in the pattern of resource endowments, in the workings of the exchange and/or distribution mechanisms, and/or in the redistributive framework. The most fundamental among these is the pattern of resource endowment. When one is granted the mental-physical capacity by the Creator to access more of these resources, it means others less able or unable to use these resources are in fact one's partners, whose rights in the final postproduction, postmarket proceeds must be redeemed. The Quran affirms that because these are rights to be redeemed rather than charity, extreme care must be taken of the recipient's human dignity.

8. Acknowledge the limitations on the right of disposing of property—a right that is absolute in the Western concept of property rights. In Islam, individuals have an obligation not to waste, squander, or destroy property, or to use property for opulence or unlawful purposes. Once the specified property obligations are appropriately discharged, including that of sharing in the prescribed amount and manner, property rights on the remaining part of income, wealth, and assets are held sacred and inviolate, and no one can force their appropriation or expropriation.

While these rules strongly affirm humankind's natural tendency to possess—particularly products resulting from individual labor—the concomitant property obligations promote interdependence and cohesion among the members of society. Private initiative, choice, and reward are recognized as legitimate and protected but are not allowed to subvert the obligation of sharing.

Islam recognizes that the Divine Providence has endowed individuals with unique and unequal abilities and that some individuals have greater mental and/or physical capacities. Consequently, they are capable of obtaining title to a larger amount of property and assets. But this only means that the responsibilities and obligations of such individuals are greater than those of others. Once these individuals have discharged their duties of sharing, in the prescribed manner and in the prescribed amount, and provided they are not in violation of the rules of *Shariah*, their rights to their possessions are held inviolate, and no one has any right to force appropriation (or expropriation) of that person's property to anyone else. This right is held so sacred that even when rules had to be developed for emergency cases of expropriation for projects of public utility, they were called "legitimate violation" (*ikrah hukmi*). Even then, such actions could be taken only after adequate compensation was paid to the owner of the property. To violate the legitimate property rights of a person is considered to be *oppression* and *exploitation*, just as there is *discord and corruption on earth* when individuals do not discharge their private property obligations.

While these principles strongly affirm people's natural tendency to possess, the concomitant obligations give rise to the interdependence of members of society. Private initiative, choice, and reward are recognized but not allowed to subvert the obligation of sharing. The inviolability of appropriately acquired private property rights in Islam deserves emphasis. As one legal expert observed, given the divine origin of Islam:

> *Its institutions, such as individual ownership, private rights, and contractual obligations, share its sacredness. To the authority of law, as it is understood in the West, is added the great weight of religion. Infringement of the property and rights of another person is not only a trespass against the law; it is also a sin against the religion and its God. Private ownership and individual rights are gifts from God, and creative labor, inheritance, contract, and other lawful means of acquiring property or entitlement to rights are only channels of God's bounty and goodness to man. . . . All Muslim schools teach that private property and rights are inviolable in relations between individuals as well as in relations with the state. . . . It is not only by their divine origin that the Muslim institutions of private ownership and right differ from their counterpart in the Western system of law; their content and range of application are more far-reaching. . . . If absolutes can be compared, it can be safely said that the right of ownership in Muslim law is more absolute than it is in modern system of law. . . . The Muslim concept of property and right is less restricted than is the modern concept of these institutions.*[10]

---

[10]Habachy (1962).

Shariah outlines the obligations concomitant with property rights. Among the obligations is, first, the responsibility of sharing the proceeds or the use of property—and, second, the obligation not to waste, destroy, squander, or use the property for purposes not permitted by *Shariah*. To do so would be to transgress the limits set on one's rights and an encroachment on the rights of the collectivity. This position of *Shariah* is in conformity with the Islamic conception of justice and the rights and responsibilities of the individual and the community.

Contracts and Contractual Obligations

The next set of rules to be understood and internalized by individuals is those governing contracts. In any economic system, individuals not only make choices for themselves, but they also interact with other members of the society through transactions facilitated by explicit and implicit contracts entered into within the bounds specified by the institutional setting of the society. A contract is a time-bound instrument with an objective that stipulates the obligations that each party is expected to fulfill in order to achieve the objectives of the contract.

The concept of contracts in Islam is not only important in the legal aspect of exchange, as an institution necessary for the satisfaction of legitimate human needs, but it is also a concept upon which *Shariah* is based. The whole fabric of the Divine Law is contractual in its conception, content, and application. Its very foundation is the primordial covenant between Allah (swt) and humans—the *meethaq*. That covenant imposes on humans the duty of remaining faithful to the affirmation of humanity: Humans recognize the Supreme Creator as their Cherished Lord and their *wali* (protector/guardian). That recognition, in turn, is an affirmation of the duty of rule compliance, which serves the best interests of humans and is a contractual obligation linking humans to their Creator and to one another. Justice demands rule compliance as a demonstration of faithfulness to the terms of the primordial covenant.

The contractual foundation of the law in human behavior is with respect not only to the Creator but also toward other humans. Performance will be judged not only in the carrying out of contractual obligations but also in the essential attributes of intending with which a party enters into a contract. These attributes are sincerity, truthfulness, and the strength and rigor of the loyalty of the fulfillment of obligations a person is intending to take on by entering into the contractual relationship. The foundation of *Shariah* is the covenant between Allah (swt) and man, which imposes on man the duty of being faithful to his word. The Quran reiterates, "Allah (swt) will not fail in His Promise."

As Habachy suggests, Islam's strong emphasis on the strictly binding nature of contracts covers private and public law contracts as well as international treaties. Moreover, "every public office in Islam, even the *Imamate* (temporal and spiritual leadership) is regarded as a contract, an agreement (*áqd*) that defines the rights and obligations of the parties. Every contract entered into by the faithful must include a forthright intention to remain loyal to performing the obligations specified by the terms of contract."[11] The highest office of the leadership of the society, *imamate* or *khilafat*, is inaugurated by *mubayaá* (from the word *bay'ah*), which is a contract between the ruler and the community stating that the leader will be rule compliant in discharging the duties of the office. This provides a strong accountable basis for governance.[12]

Throughout the legal and intellectual history of Islam, a body of rules constituting a general theory of contracts—with explicit emphasis on specific contracts, such as sales, lease, hire, and partnerships—was formulated on the basis of *Shariah*. Contracts are considered binding, and *Shariah* protects their terms, no less securely than the institution of property. This body of rules established the principle that, in matters of civil and economic dealings, any agreement not specifically prohibited by *Shariah* is valid and binding on the parties and can be enforced by the courts, which treat the parties to a contract as complete equals.

Trust

Trust is considered the most important element of social capital in Islam and the cornerstone of the relationship of individuals with Allah (swt) and with others in society. Islam places a strong emphasis on trust and considers being trustworthy as an obligatory personality trait. The root of the word for "trust" (*amanah*) is the same as that for "belief" (*iman*). The Quran insists that a strong signal of true belief is faithfulness to contracts and promises. It makes clear that performing contractual obligations or promises is an important and mandatory characteristic of a true believer.[13]

In short, Islam has made trust and trustworthiness obligatory and has rendered them inviolable, except in the event of an explicitly permissible justification. The life of the Prophet (sawa) is a shining illustration of the implementation of the guidance of Allah (swt) in maintaining trust and remaining trustworthy. Regarded as eminently trustworthy even before

---

[11] Habachy (1962).
[12] Al-Hakimi et al. (1989).
[13] See, for example, Quran 2:58, 283; 12:52; 23:1–8; and 42:107, 125, 143, 162, 178, 193.

His divine appointment (the community conferred upon him the title of *Al-Ameen*—"Trustworthy"), the Prophet (sawa) expended a great deal of effort in modifying when possible and changing when necessary the behavior of the community in respect to trustworthiness. Numerous statements, actions, and circumstances are attributed to Him in which trust was the preeminent concern.[14]

In *Shariah*, the concepts of justice, faithfulness, reward, and punishment are linked with the fulfillment of obligations incurred under the stipulations of the contract. Justice links man to Allah (swt) and to his fellow men. It is this bond that forms the contractual foundation of *Shariah*, which judges the virtue of justice in man not only by his material performance but also by the essential attribute of the intention (*niyyah*) with which he enters into every contract. This intention consists of sincerity, truthfulness, and insistence on rigorous and loyal fulfillment of what he has consented to do (or not to do). This faithfulness to contractual obligations is so central to Islamic belief that the Prophet (sawa) defined a believer as "a person in whom the people can trust their person and possessions." He is also reported to have said that "a person without trustworthiness is a person without religion." So basic is the notion of contracts in Islam that every public office is regarded primarily as a contract and an agreement that defines the rights and obligations of the parties. The highest temporal office, that of *khalifa*, is inaugurated by *mubayaá*, which is a contract between the ruler and the community that ensures the ruler will be faithful in discharging his duties.

---

[14]For example, in a few short but significant statements (quotations from Payandeh [1984]), the Prophet declares:

> *The person who is not trustworthy has no faith, and the person who breaks his promises has no religion.*
>
> *Maintaining promises perfectly is a sign of faith.*
>
> *There are three [injunctions] that no one is allowed to violate: treating parents kindly regardless of being Muslim or non-believer; keeping a promise whether to a Muslim or to a non-believer, and returning what is entrusted for safekeeping—regardless of whether the person entrusting is a Muslim or a non-believer.*
>
> *Return what is placed in your trust for safekeeping to the person who has trusted you and do not betray even the one who has betrayed you.*
>
> *Three [behavioral traits], if found in a person, then he is a hypocrite even if he fasts, prays, performs bigger and smaller pilgrimages, and says "I am a Muslim:" when he talks, he lies; when he promises, he breaches; and, when trusted, he betrays.*

Trustworthiness and remaining faithful to promises and contracts are absolute, regardless of the costs involved or whether the other party is a friend or a foe (see Quran 9:4). There is also a network of micro-level rules that ensure transparency and the unhindered flow of information. This includes, *inter alia*, the requirement incumbent upon sellers that they must inform buyers of goods the prices, quantities, and qualities of what they are buying; a body of rules governing the consumer's option to, under various circumstances, annul a transaction; the rule of noninterference with market supplies; the rule against hoarding; and the rule against collusion among market participants.[15]

It should be noted that there is a strong interdependence between contract and trust; without trust, contracts become difficult to negotiate and conclude and costly to monitor and enforce. When and where trust is weak, complex and expensive administrative devices are needed to enforce contracts. Moreover, it is generally recognized that unambiguous contracts— ones that foresee all contingencies—do not exist, as not all contingencies can be foreseen. As McMillan suggests, trust is an important element of a well-designed market. "For a market to function well, you must be able to trust most of the people most of the time. . . . Your trust in your trading partner rests on both the formal devices of the law and the informal device of reputation."[16] When and where property rights are poorly defined and protected, the cost of gathering and analyzing information is high, and trust is weak, it is difficult to clearly specify the terms of contracts and enforce them. In these cases, transaction costs—that is, search and information costs, bargaining and decision costs, contract negotiation and enforcement costs—are high. Where and when transaction costs are high, there is less trade, fewer market participants, less long-term investment, lower productivity, and slower economic growth. As North has pointed out, when and where there is rule compliance and enforcement, there is an increase in the likelihood that property rights will be protected and contracts honored.[17] Under such conditions, individuals are more willing to specialize, invest in long-term projects, undertake complex transactions, and accumulate and share technical knowledge.

Markets: The Code of Conduct

In the realm of conventional economics, reliance on markets is an ideology to some economists; this is not so in Islam. This is because markets and competition

---

[15] Mirakhor (2007).
[16] McMillan (2002, pp. 10–11).
[17] North (2003, p. 103).

do not by themselves guarantee that social and economic justices will be served. In Islam, markets are seen as affording the best signaling mechanism to producers and consumers and thus the most efficient intermediary for resource allocation, economic production, distribution and consumption. Therefore, markets are encouraged. Even then, markets must have rules that are just and ensure their proper operation, and they must be supervised to guarantee that rules are followed and enforced. While these rules and their supervision and enforcement are seen as sufficient in the workings of the conventional market system, it is not so in Islam. In Islam, market participants, both buyers and sellers, must embrace a code of morality before they enter the market. Under such a system, the price that emerges from markets can be considered "just" in the sense that it is the result of proper functioning markets that are based on just rules that are followed and enforced and with market participants who are moral in their behavior. In the absence of morality and moral behavior by all market participants, markets can result in allocations that are socially unjust and even perverse—gross income inequities, opulence alongside poverty, excessive consumption and little savings, hoarding, and the like. Thus, markets left alone may not fulfill human material needs and are also not equipped to address human spiritual needs.

The market's institutional structure is built around five pillars:

1. Property rights
2. Free flow of information
3. Trust
4. Contract
5. The right not to be harmed by others and the obligation not to harm anyone

Together, these pillars serve to reduce uncertainty and transaction costs and to enable cooperation and collective action to proceed unhindered.

Before the advent of Islam, trade had been the most important economic activity of the Arabian Peninsula. A number of thriving markets had developed throughout the area. Upon his arrival in Medina, the Prophet organized a market that was structured and governed by rules based on the Quran. He implemented a number of policies to encourage the expansion of trade and the market. The Prophet (sawa) prohibited the imposition of taxes on individual merchants as well as on transactions. He also implemented policies to encourage trade among Muslims and non-Muslims by creating incentives for non-Muslim merchants in and outside of Medina. After the conquest of Mecca and the rest of Arabia, these and other market rules were institutionalized and generalized to all markets. These rules included, in addition to the five pillars previously mentioned:

- No restrictions on international or interregional trade (including no taxation of imports and exports).
- Free spatial movement of resources, goods, and services from one market to another.
- No barriers to market entry and exit.
- Free and transparent information regarding the price, quality, and quantity of goods, particularly in the case of spot trade.
- Specification of the exact date for the completion of trade in instances when trade was to take place over time.
- Specification of the property and other rights of all participants in every contract.
- Guaranteed contract enforcement by the state and its legal apparatus.
- The prohibition against hoarding commodities and productive resources for the purpose of pushing up their price.
- Prohibition on price controls.
- A ban on sellers or buyers harming the interests of other market participants by, for example, allowing a third party to interrupt negotiations between two parties in order to influence the negotiations to the benefit of one of the parties.
- A ban on the shortchanging of buyers by, for example, not giving full weight and measure.

Moreover, sellers and buyers were given the right of annulment of a business agreement in these seven instances:

1. Before leaving the location in which it was taking place.
2. In the case of a buyer who had not seen the commodity and after seeing it found it unacceptable.
3. If either the seller or the buyer discovered that the product had either been sold for less than or bought for higher than it was worth.
4. If the buyer discovered that the quality of the product was not as expected.
5. If side conditions were specified during the negotiations that were left unfulfilled.
6. If a delivery period was specified but the product was not delivered on time.
7. If the subject of the negotiations was pack animals, the buyer had the right to return the animals up to three days after the deal was finalized.

The moral-ethical foundation of market behavior prescribed by the Quran and implemented by the Prophet (sawa) ensured the minimization of risk and of uncertainty for market participants and increased the efficiency of exchange. Its aim was to reduce transaction costs. Moreover, rules specified in the Quran regarding faith to the terms of contracts and the knowledge of their enforcement increased certainty and reduced transaction costs. Another important rule promulgated by the Prophet (sawa) was the prohibition of interference with supply before entrance into the market. From the earliest period of operation of the Medina market, the Prophet (sawa) appointed market supervisors, whose job was to ensure rule compliance, which in turn would result in markets that were just. The Prophet (sawa) advised the participants to go beyond mere rule compliance and to treat their fellow humans with beneficence. The Prophet (sawa) strongly encouraged market participants to accept the duty of "commanding the good and forbidding evil" by engaging in self-regulation.

Rules governing market conduct relate to appropriate behavior on the part of all participants in the market. The Quran acknowledges the need for markets and affirms their existence, placing emphasis on contracts of exchange (*bay'*) and trade (*tijarah*). As a rule, it emphasizes market transactions based on mutual consent; that is, based on freedom of choice and freedom of contract, which, in turn, requires acknowledgment and affirmation of private property rights. The archetype model, discussed earlier, operationalized the concept of exchange and trade as well as the use of the market as the mechanism for this purpose. A market supervisor is appointed to ensure compliance with the rules of conduct in the marketplace, rules that are internalized by participants before their entrance into the market. Compliance with the rules of market behavior ensures prices that are fair and just. So long as market participants comply, no direct interference with the price mechanism is permitted, even though the legitimate authority is responsible for supervising market operations.

Risk Sharing

Another core principle of Islamic economics is the notion of risk sharing. This is based on the principle of liability, which states that profit is justified on the basis of taking responsibility, possibly even becoming responsible for a loss and its consequences. This legal maxim, said to be derived from a saying of the Prophet (sawa) that "profit comes with liability," implies that *Shariah* distinguishes lawful profit from all other forms of gain and that entitlement to profit arises only when there is also the liability, or risk, of loss.

The central proposition of Islamic finance is risk sharing and the prohibition of interest-based transactions in which a rent (interest) is collected as a percentage of the principal loaned without the full transfer of the property rights to the lender. One result of this type of transaction is that the risk associated with the transaction is borne by the borrower. Rather, Islam proposes a mutual exchange (*al-bay'*) in which one bundle of property rights is exchanged for another, thus allowing both parties to share the risks of the transaction—something that is sanctioned. The emphasis on risk sharing is evident from one of the most important verses in the Quran with respect to economic relations. The verse states: "They say that indeed an exchange transaction (*al-bay'*) is like an *al-riba* (interest-based) transaction. But Allah has permitted exchange transactions and forbidden interest-based transactions" (2:275). The nature of property rights inherent in these two transactions hints at one of their crucial differences. *Al-bay'* is a contract of exchange of one commodity for another where the property rights over one commodity are exchanged for those over the other. In the case of an *al-riba* transaction, a sum of money is loaned today for a larger sum in the future without the transfer of the property rights over the principal from the lender to the borrower. Not only does the lender retain rights over the sum lent, but property rights over the additional sum to be paid as interest are transferred from the borrower to the lender at the time the contract of *al-riba* is entered into. Arguably, the last verse renders exchange and trade of commodities and/or assets the foundation of economic activity in the Islamic paradigm.

From this, important implications follow: Exchange requires freedom for parties to contract. This in turn implies freedom to produce, which calls for clear and well-protected property rights to permit production to proceed. To be able to exchange freely and conveniently, the parties need markets. To operate successfully, markets need rules of behavior and enforcement mechanisms to reduce uncertainty in transactions and ensure the free flow of information. They also need trust to be established among participants; competition among sellers, on one hand, and buyers, on the other; reduced transaction costs; and mitigation of the risk to third parties in having to bear externalized costs of two-party transactions.

Wealth Accumulation and Utilization

Islam encourages the human to utilize, to the fullest extent possible, all the resources that Allah (swt) has created and entrusted to humankind for his use. The nonutilization of these resources for humankind's benefit, and for that of the society, is tantamount to ungratefulness to Allah (swt) for the provision of these resources. Wealth is considered an important means by which humans can pave the way for the attainment of their ultimate objective of establishing a rule-compliant community. Islam refers to wealth as "good," an object of delight and pleasure, and a support for the community. Conversely, involuntary poverty is considered to be undesirable and a basis of unbelief. This particular conception of wealth, however, is qualified by the means employed in its earning, possession, and disposal.

Its "earning" is qualified by emphasis on the fact that wealth is only a means for the achievement of man's ultimate objective, not an end in itself. It must be earned through "good," "productive," and "beneficial" work, as defined in *Shariah*, which also outlines the methods of lawfully earning wealth. Not only are lawful methods of earning wealth specified, but the types of economic activity that may lead to unlawfully acquired wealth that are prohibited are discussed. *Shariah* specifies nonpermissible professions, trade, and economic activity that may lead to unlawfully acquired wealth. Even within each profession, *Shariah* specifies proper and improper practices. Just as wealth, rightfully earned and purposefully disposed of, is considered a blessing, wealth acquired or accumulated unlawfully for its own sake is condemned as "corruption" and retrogression to the basest of all human negative qualities—greed.

Islam regards wealth as the lifeblood of the community, which must be constantly in circulation; therefore, its possession excludes the right of hoarding (Quran 9:34). The implication is that wealth, lawfully earned, must be invested within the community to improve its economic well-being. Investing wealth is measured not only by the monetary gain associated with it but also by the benefits that accrue to society, a point that must be borne in mind at all times by the owners of wealth.

The disposal of wealth is also subject to the rules of *Shariah*. The first and foremost among these rules is the recognition of the rights of others in this wealth resulting from the principle of invariant claim to ownership. These rules include levies whose amounts are specified and others whose amounts are left to be determined by the wealth owner. These levies fall due when wealth exceeds a specific minimum amount (*nisab*). After these obligations are met, the remainder belongs to the owner, but it must be used in accordance with the rules of *Shariah*, which forbid extravagance, opulence, waste, or general abuse of wealth. It cannot be used to harm others or to acquire political power or to corrupt the polity.

While Islam treats wealth, lawfully acquired, possessed, and disposed of, as sacred and subject to the protection of *Shariah*, it regards the wealth owner as a trustee who holds the wealth as a trust on behalf of Allah (swt) and the community. Hence, a person's inability to use wealth properly provides the basis for the forfeiture of rights to that wealth. Extravagance, waste, and general abuse of wealth are the basis on which the community can consider the wealth owner a *safih*, a person of weak understanding, one in possession of "weak intellect," and one who, along with his or her own financial and moral loss, is damaging the interests of the community.

According to the principle of *hajr*, such a person's wealth can be made the ward of the community or of its legitimate representatives, who may limit the wealth owner's right to the use of only a part of the property to meet basic needs.

Wealth Distribution and Redistribution

Believers must remain fully conscious of the human partnership throughout the process of wealth creation and of the fact that they must redeem the rights of others in the created income and wealth. Being unable to access resources to which they have the right does not negate the fact that the poor are to share in the income and wealth of the more able.

One of the most important economic institutions or practices that operationalizes the objective of achieving social justice is the distribution/redistribution rule of the Islamic economic paradigm. As mentioned earlier, a crucial mission of all messengers and prophets is the establishment of social justice. In practical terms, the Quran makes clear that this means creating a balanced society that avoids the extremes of wealth and poverty, a society in which all understand that wealth is a blessing provided by the Creator for the sole purpose of providing support for the lives of all. The Islamic view holds that it is not possible to have many rich and wealthy people who continue to focus all their efforts on accumulating wealth without simultaneously creating a mass of economically deprived and destitute people. The rich consume opulently while the poor suffer from deprivation because their rights to the wealth of the rich and powerful are not redeemed.

To avoid this, Islam prohibits the accumulation of wealth and imposes limits on consumption through its rules prohibiting waste (*itlaf*), overspending, and ostentatious and opulent spending (*israf*). It then ordains that the net surplus, after moderate spending necessary to maintain a modest living standard, must be returned to those members of the community who, for a variety of reasons, are unable to work and whose share of their Allah-given resources have been utilized by the more able. The Quran considers the more able as trustee agents in using these resources on behalf of the less able. In this view, property is not a means of exclusion but inclusion, in which the rights of those less able are redeemed in the income and wealth of the more able. The result would be a balanced economy without extremes of wealth and poverty. The operational mechanism by which the right of the less able is redeemed is the network of mandatory and voluntary payments, such as *zakat* (2.5% on wealth), *khums* (20% of income), and payments referred to as *sadaqat*. Distribution takes place after production and sale, when all factors of production are given what is due to them commensurate with their contribution to the production, exchange, and sale of goods and services.

"Redistribution" refers to the postdistribution phase when the charge due to the less able are levied. These expenditures are essentially repatriation and redemption of the rights of others in one's income and wealth. Redeeming these rights is a manifestation of belief in the oneness of the Creator and its corollary, the unity of the creation in general and of humankind in particular. It is the recognition and affirmation that Allah (swt) has created the resources for all of humankind who must have unhindered access to them. Even the abilities that make access to resources possible are due to the Creator. This means that those who are less able or unable to use these resources are partners of the more able. The expenditures intended for redeeming these rights are referred to in the Quran as *sadaqat*, which is the plural of the term *sadaqa*, a derivative of the root meaning "truthfulness and sincerity"; their payments indicate the strength of the sincerity of a person's belief (2:26,272). The Quran insists that these are rights of the poor to the income and wealth of the rich; they are not charity (2:177; 19:51; 38:30; 70:25; 917:26). Therefore, the Quran asks that extreme care be taken to acknowledge the recipients' human dignity, dignity of which the recipients themselves are fully aware and conscious to the point that they are reluctant to reveal their poverty. The Quran consequently recommends that payment to the poor be done in secret (2:271–273). Moreover, it strictly forbids that these payments be made reproachfully or accompanied by ill treatment of recipients or with annoyance displayed by the person making the payment (2:262–265).

Work and Work Ethics

The concept of work in Islam (*al-amal*) is far broader, and has different characteristics and objectives, than the concept as it is understood in the Western economic tradition. In Islam, the work ethic is defined by the Quran itself, which stresses the need for work and action by human beings. It is because of this emphasis on work that Islam is considered a religion of action. The Quran exalts work and raises it to the level of worship, considering work as an inseparable dimension of faith itself. Conversely, it considers idleness—or the squandering of time in pursuit of unproductive and nonbeneficial work—as the manifestation of lack of faith and of unbelief.

Man is called on to utilize time in pursuit of work by declaring that Allah (swt) has made the day as a means of seeking sustenance. A person who, through hard work, seeks the "bounty" of Allah (swt)—which includes all appropriate means of earning one's livelihood—is most highly praised. All able-bodied persons are exhorted to work in order to earn their living. No one who is physically and mentally able is allowed to become a liability to his family or to the state through idleness and voluntary unemployment. The work that everyone is required to perform must be "good" or "beneficial" (*a'mal salih*), but no work is considered inconsequential in relation to its rewards or punishments in this world and in the next. One will have to reap whatever rewards or retributions are due as a result of one's work.

Work, therefore, is regarded not only as a right but also as a duty and an obligation. Hence, based on its notion of individual rights and responsibilities, Islam extends to individuals the right to choose the type of work they desire. Along with this freedom come the obligation to consider the needs of society and to select the type of work permitted by *Shariah*.

Since all class distinctions are negated by Islam, no line of work permissible by *Shariah* is considered demeaning by Islam, which countenances only diversification on the basis of natural talents, skills, and technology—which are considered to be a grace or blessing (*fadl*) from Allah (swt)—and which all Muslims are urged to acquire. Based on its concepts of justice and contracts, Islam makes it an obligation for workers to perform the tasks that they have contracted to the best of their abilities. But since individuals are endowed with different abilities and talents, this productivity will differ. Justice, however, demands that the return for every individual's work must be commensurate with his or her productivity, but not that all humans receive the same remuneration.

While Islam has, in no uncertain terms, decried laziness, idleness, and socially unproductive work, it maintains that those who are physically or mentally unable to work still retain a right to what the society, individually and collectively, produces. This conclusion is based on the principle of invariant claim to ownership, which maintains that all human beings have a right to the resources provided for humankind by Allah (swt). Since Allah (swt) is also the source of the physical and mental abilities that enable some members of society to possess more than others, the right of ownership to the original resources of those less able remains valid. This follows from the fact that Allah's (swt) original right of ownership of resources, which He has created, is not negated when those resources, along with the creative labor of individuals, are transformed into products, property, and wealth.

Competition and Cooperation

In the Islamic conception of humankind's ultimate goal, economic life plays a purely instrumental role. Even in this role, economic affairs are meant only to provide the institutions and mechanisms needed for satisfying man's economic needs, as man's essence as the supreme creature of Allah (swt) is allowed to be manifested in this world. Thus, the economic system designed in accordance with the fundamental principles of Islam ensures that humans can exercise their eminent dignity, freedom, responsibilities, and rights in the conduct of economic affairs. The economic system must be so ordered as not to assign to humans a purely instrumental role in achieving the goals of the economy or the state. Islam seeks to guide humans to direct individual action and responsible participation in economic affairs in a manner that commits them to community solidarity and cooperation, resulting in a dynamic and growing economy. Thus, individuals are made accountable for the moral effects of their social actions, including those in economic affairs, so that their own inner personal-spiritual transformation and growth is bound to the progress of the community.

Hence, Islam utilizes cooperation and competition in structuring the ideal society through harmonization and reconciliation between these two opposites and also between equally primeval and useful forces at every level of social organization. From this perspective, one can argue that one of the greatest distinguishing characteristics of Islam is its forceful emphasis on the integration of human society as a necessary consequence of the unity of Allah (swt). To this end, the personality of the Prophet (sawa) is inseparable from what the Quran considers as the optimal approach necessary for the emergence of solidarity in human society. Every dimension of the personality of the Prophet (sawa), manifested in his various social roles in the community, is directed toward maximum integration and harmony in society. Moreover, every rule of behavior, including those in the economic arena, is designed to aid the process of integration. Conversely, all prohibited practices are those that, one way or another, lead to social disintegration.

The Quran and the traditions of the Prophet (sawa) make clear references to the dual nature of competition and cooperation; that is, human beings can cooperate and compete for good or evil. It is this that leads to the integration or disintegration of society. The fundamental sources, however, emphasize that competition and cooperation must be utilized in probity and piety rather than in evil and enmity. Thus the Quran declares: "Cooperate with one another unto righteousness and piety. Do not cooperate with one another unto sin and enmity" (5:2). Similarly, Muslims are urged to compete with one another in beneficial and righteous deeds. These sources do not allow suppression of competition or cooperation in favor of the other when they are used within the *Shariah* framework. Rather, all of the regulatory and supervisory authority invested in the legitimate political authority is directed toward a balanced and constructive utilization of these forces. The *Shariah* rules regarding the structure of the market and the behavior of market participants are examples of such balance. Although the rules of *Shariah* regarding economic affairs demarcate limits and boundaries of desirable competitive and cooperative behavior necessary for the provision and preservation of the solidarity of society, the individual always remains the identifiable agent through whose action (and on whose behalf) all economic activity takes place.

SUMMARY

All societies face two interrelated problems—uncertainty and coordination. Compliance with the prescribed rules of behavior not only reduces uncertainty and promotes collective action through cooperation; it also promotes growth with no, or a minimal level of, poverty.

The institutional framework of the ideal economy is composed of a collection of institutions—rules of conduct and their enforcement characteristics—designed by the Lawgiver to deal with allocation of resources, production and exchange of goods and services, and distribution-redistribution of resulting income and wealth. The objective of these institutions is social justice. Rules specify what kind of conduct is most appropriate to achieving just results when individuals face alternative choices and must take action. Rules impose restrictions on what society's members can do without upsetting the social order on whose existence all members count in deciding on their own actions and forming their expectations of others' responses and actions.

Rules governing transactions, such as trustworthiness, truthfulness, fatefulness to the terms and conditions of contracts, transparency in actions, and noninterference with the workings of the markets and the price mechanism so long as market participants are rule compliant, provide a strong economic foundation where information flows unhindered and participants engage in transactions confidently with minimal concern for uncertainty regarding the actions and reactions of other participants. Because of the high level of trust, transaction costs can arguably be assumed to be minimal. Risk and return sharing in financing productive economic activities, moderate spending, and avoidance of extravagant and opulent consumption would provide financial resources for investment. Rules regarding redistribution and prohibition of idle wealth accumulation would reinforce the availability of resources for savings and investment.

KEY TERMS

Rules governing property rights

Rules governing production

Rules governing exchange

Rules governing income distribution and redistribution

Rules governing market conduct

Rule compliance

Institutions

Justice

Risk and risk sharing

Trust

Markets

Wealth accumulation

Wealth distribution and
redistribution

QUESTIONS

1. What are the different types of risks facing individuals in any economic system?
2. How is the perception of economic justice different in Islam from that in the market capitalist system?
3. How can risk and uncertainty impact economic prosperity?
4. Why is trust among individuals and institutions important for economic prosperity?
5. What is the purpose of rules in the Islamic economic system?
6. How are rules related to institutions?
7. What are the major rules in Islam governing economic behavior?

CHAPTER 4

The Islamic Economic System

Learning objectives:

1. *Role of justice and ethics in the Islamic system.*
2. *Manifestation of justice in policies in Islam.*
3. *The differences between the Islamic and conventional financial systems.*
4. *Why interest and interest-based debt instruments are prohibited in Islam.*
5. *Role of government in the Islamic and in the conventional financial systems.*
6. *Importance of ethical behavior in Islam.*
7. *Importance of modest lifestyles and sharing of income and wealth in Islam.*
8. *Islam's requirement that individuals be ethical and unselfish.*

According to Douglass North, each economic system has an "institutional matrix" that "defines the opportunity set, being one that makes the highest payoffs in an economy's income distribution or one that provides the highest payoffs to productive activity."[1] North contends that in all economic systems, institutions (rules of behavior) are designed by humans to impose constraints on human interaction. These institutions "structure human interaction by providing an incentive structure to guide human behavior. But an incentive structure requires a theory of the way the mind perceives the world and its functioning so that institutions provide those incentives."[2]

It is here where paradigms become relevant because paradigms in economics do have conceptions of humans and society, and their interrelationships.

---

[1] North (2005, p. 61).
[2] Ibid., p. 66.

Such conceptions are themselves products of a meta-framework whose elements may or may not be explicitly specified but which, nevertheless, exist in the mind of the designer prior to the construction and presentation of a paradigm. For example, the meta-framework of neoclassical economics is in classical economics, as the name implies. Basically two meta-frameworks underlie all economic paradigms: Creator centered or human centered. The former derives its economic analysis from rules of behavior (institutions) prescribed by the Creator for individuals and societies. Examples are economic paradigms that are based on the Abrahamic traditions of Judaism, Christianity, and Islam.[3] The human-centered or secular tradition takes as given, or derives, rules of behavior (institutions) that are designed and approved by society.

As discussed in previous chapters, Islam prescribes rules of behavior (institutions) that collectively define a system. Therefore, one could state that Islamic economics as a discipline is concerned with three things:

1. The rules of behavior (institutions) prescribed by Islam, as they relate to resource allocation, production, exchange, distribution, and redistribution
2. Drawing economic implications for the ideal system created by compliance with these rules
3. Providing policy recommendations for achieving the ideal economic system envisioned by Islam

Having discussed key economic institutions in previous chapters, we now turn our attention to key features of the emergent Islamic economic system based on Islam's core institutions.

SOCIAL AND ECONOMIC JUSTICE

Justice—social and economic—is at the foundation of the Islamic economic system. The Quran uses two words for justice: *qist* and *ádl*. The first is the chief characteristic of appropriate human relations and of human relations toward the rest of creation. It is a human phenomenon; it is not a divine trait. *Ádl*, however, is a feature of the Creator's actions that manifests itself in the perfect balance of the cosmos; it characterizes His action to place everything in its rightful place. Any injustice perpetrated by the individual against other humans and against the rest of creation is ultimately an injustice to the self. Allah (swt) loves justice; it is a central part of His

---

[3]For Judaism, see, for example, Tamari (1987). For Christianity, see, for example, Long (2000). See also Paul (2005).

universal love. The response of creation to universal love must mirror the justice of Allah (swt).

A just economy is part of a just, healthy, and moral society, which is the central objective of Islam. What underpins all the rules of behavior prescribed by Islam is its conception of justice, which maintains that all behavior, irrespective of its content and context, must, in its conception and commission, be based on just standards as defined by *Shariah*. An Islamic economy is an enterprising, purposeful, prosperous, and sharing economy in which all members of society receive their just rewards. Such an economy is envisioned as one in which economic disparities that lead to social segmentation and divisiveness are conspicuously absent. Another important rule is the prohibition against taking (i.e., receiving) interest. This issue is covered in some detail later in this chapter.

The three components of economic justice in an Islamic society are:

1. Equality of liberty and opportunity for all members of society with respect to the utilization of natural resources;
2. Justice in exchange; and
3. Distributive justice.

All these components are accomplished within the framework of *Shariah*.

Equality of Opportunity

In the Islamic conception, liberty means that others do not prevent a person from combining his creative labor with resources, which are designated by *Shariah* for the use of the individual members of society. Opportunity, however, represents a favorable conjunction of circumstances that gives the individual the chance to try to compete. Success is dependent on the individual's efforts and abilities. This equality of opportunity must be secured deliberately by the collectivity. It not only denotes free and equal access to physical resources but generally also extends to technology, education, and environmental resources. Islam's position that natural resources are provided for all members of society forms the basis for this equality of access to resources and equality of opportunity to use them. Even if the opportunity to use these resources is not available to some, either naturally or due to some other circumstances, their original claims to resources remain intact and are not nullified. At some point in time, they must be remunerated for these claims by the other members who happen to have or get greater opportunity to use them.

Justice in Exchange (Economic Transactions)

The idea is that, by mixing their creative labor with resources, individuals create a claim of equity to the possession of the assets thus produced, by virtue of which they can participate in exchange. To allow exchange to take place on the basis of just standards, Islam places a great deal of emphasis on the market and its moral, just, and—based on these two factors—efficient operation. To ensure justice in exchange, *Shariah* has provided a network of ethical and moral rules of behavior that covers in minute detail the behavior of all market participants. *Shariah* requires that these norms and rules be internalized and adhered to by all participants before they enter the market. A market that operates on the basis of these rules, which are intended to remove all factors inimical to justice in exchange, yields prices for factors of production (labor, entrepreneurship, capital, and land) and products that are considered "fair" and "just." Unlike the scholastic notion of "just price," which lacks an operational definition, the Islamic concept refers to the price prevailing as a result of the interaction of economic forces operating in a market in which all rules of behavior specified by *Shariah* are observed and adhered to by all participants. It is an *ex post facto* concept, meaning that a just price has been paid and received.

The rules governing exchange in the market cover *Shariah*-compatible sources of supply and demand for factors and products before they enter the market, *Shariah*-based behavior on the part of the buyers and sellers, and a price-bargaining process free of factors prohibited by *Shariah*. Hence, the term "market imperfection" refers to the existence of any factor considered nonpermissible by *Shariah*. The rules regarding supply and demand not only govern the permissibility of products demanded and supplied but also look beyond these phenomena to their origin. Not all demands for products are considered legitimate, nor are all acts of supplying products permissible. The means by which the purchasing power that gives effect to demand is obtained and the manner in which the production of commodities for their supply takes place must have their origins based on just standards. Rules governing the behavior of participants in the market are designed to ensure a just exchange. *Shariah* prescribes the freedom of contracts and the obligation to fulfill them; the consent of the parties to a transaction; noninterference with supplies before their entry into the market; full access to the market to all buyers and sellers; honesty in transactions; the provision of full information regarding the quantity, quality, and prices of the factors and products to buyers and sellers before the start of negotiating and bargaining; and the provision of full weights and measures. Behaviors such as fraud, cheating, monopoly practices, coalitions, collusion of any kind among buyers and sellers, underselling products, dumping actions, speculative hoarding, and bidding up of prices without the intention to purchase are all forbidden. All in all, any form of behavior leading to the creation of instantaneous property rights without a commensurate equity created by work is forbidden. A market in which all these conditions are fulfilled produces fair and just prices for the factors and products. These are just and equitable not on any independent criterion of justice, but because they are the result of bargaining between or among equal, informed, free, and responsible people.

Islam's emphasis on moral and just conduct in the marketplace is remarkable in its vigor. A producer or a businessperson whose behavior complies with Islamic rules is said to be like the prophets, martyrs, and truthful friends of Allah (swt). He or she is ranked with the prophets because he or she, like the prophets, follows the path of justice; with the martyrs because they both fight with heavy odds in the path of honesty and virtue; and with the truthful because both are steadfast in their resolve. Islam asks participants to go beyond the rules of *Shariah* and extend beneficence to one another as a safeguard against injustice. Beneficence implies helping others in ways not required by justice. It is thus different from justice, which prescribes just limits to selfishness.

While justice regulates and limits selfishness, beneficence rises above it. Moreover, participants in the market are responsible not only for their own just behavior. Because of the obligation of "enjoining the good and forbidding the evil," they are also made responsible for the behavior of their fellow participants. Islam maintains that when a human sees another committing an injustice toward a third and fails to attempt to remove that injustice, he or she becomes a party to that injustice. If the person failing to help is personally a beneficiary of this injustice, then the failure is considered tantamount to supporting it. Although provisions are made for coercive and corrective action by legitimate authorities, the clear preference is for self-management of the market. Any interference in the operations of such a market—through price controls, for example—is considered unjust, a transgression and a sin.

In response to the rules of market behavior imposed by *Shariah*, Muslims early in their history structured their markets as bazaars, which looked almost the same all over the Muslim world and possessed characteristics that promoted compliance with the rules. Physically, bazaars were structured to guarantee maximum compliance with these rules. Each physical segment of the market was specialized with respect to specific products, and there was little price variation from one part of the market to the next. The institution of guilds made possible self-regulation of each profession and trade. Additionally, markets were inspected for compliance by a market supervisor (*muhtasib*) who was appointed by local judges. Unfortunately, the institution of bazaars did not evolve to meet the requirements of an expanding economy or the growing complexity of economic relations. Many of the bazaars that still exist in parts of the Muslim world lack a number of Islamic characteristics and requirements. They are underdeveloped physically and in their infrastructure—most are centuries old and have not been expanded.

Distributive Justice

The last component of Islamic economic justice, distributive justice, is the mechanism by which equal liberty and equity are reconciled without the least possible infringement. Insofar as the distribution of resources—the just and equal access to these resources, as well as equal opportunity in their use—is guaranteed, the claim to equity on the basis of reward and effort is just. The moral basis of property is the importance afforded to real goods and services, which derived directly from human efforts and achievements. There are three bases of private property in Islam:

1. Property that is derived from personal ability and effort, including material property made or obtained from natural resources by combining them with personal skills, ability, and technology; income from self-made capital; assets acquired in exchange for the product of the owner's labor;
2. Property acquired by transfers from the producer; and
3. Property acquired through inheritance from the producer.

Rules regarding distributive justice operate through the second and third of these bases.

Assuming equal liberty and opportunity, whenever work has to be performed for the production of wealth, the output of humans may vary greatly both in quality and quantity. Equity then demands that, commensurate with their productivity, humans receive different rewards. Hence, starting from the equality of liberty and opportunity of access to resources, equity may lead to inequality. Moreover, the allocation of resources arising from the operation of the market will reflect the initial distribution of wealth as well as the structure of the market. Assuming that both the operation and the structure of the market are just, there is no logical reason to assume that the market outcome will automatically and naturally lead to relatively equal wealth distribution. Consequently, the result may be (and often is) that inequalities, equitably created, will have immediate and longer-term implications. It is here that the distributive mechanisms of Islamic economic justice attempt to modify inequalities that are equitably created.

As we saw earlier, Islam recognizes claims based on equality of liberty and opportunity, which are reflected in the degree of access to resources, the degree and extent of the ability of persons to actualize their potential liberty and opportunity, and the right of prior ownership. The right that the less able have in the wealth of those who have greater ability and opportunity to produce greater wealth is redeemed through the various mandated and voluntary levies (*zakat, khums, kharaj, nafaqa, sadaqa*, etc.), the payment of which is not beneficence but a contractual obligation that must be met. Islam also encourages beneficence (*sadaqa*) over and above obligatory dues, but these levies are in the nature of returning to others what rightfully belongs to them. Shirking this obligation causes a misdistribution of wealth, which Islam considers the major source of poverty.

In Islam, the rules of inheritance modify the distribution of wealth to the next generation based on the principle that the right of the owner to wealth ceases upon death. The power of the person to bequeath wealth as he or she wishes is recognized but is basically restricted to a maximum of one-third of net assets. The Quran (4:11–12) clearly specifies the exact manner in which the shares of heirs are to be determined in inheritance. Among the same category of heirs there is neither preferential treatment nor discrimination, though a woman's share is generally one-half of a man's share because, under the rules of *Shariah*, responsibility for the maintenance of the family rests on the husband. Even if the wife has a larger income and greater wealth (from her own work or from inheritance), she is not required to share that wealth or income with her husband and is under no legal obligation to make any contribution toward her family. Considering the nature of the (extended) family ties and mutual responsibilities exhorted by Islam, its institution of inheritance breaks up the wealth of each generation and redistributes it to the next in such a way that a large number should receive a modest portion of such wealth rather than it going to a single heir or a small number of heirs.

PROHIBITION OF INTEREST (*AL-RIBA*)

Al-riba technically refers to the "premium" that must be paid by the borrower to the lender along with the principal amount as a condition of the loan or for an extension in the duration of loan. At least four characteristics define the prohibited interest rate:

1. It is positive and fixed *ex ante*.
2. It is tied to the time period and the amount of the loan.

3. Its payment is guaranteed regardless of the outcome or the purposes for which the principal was borrowed.
4. The state apparatus sanctions and enforces its collection.

It is a common misunderstanding and a myth that Islam, by prohibiting interest on loans, denies the concept of the time value of money. Islamic scholars have always recognized the time value of money but maintain that the compensation for such value has its limitations. Recognition of an indirect economic value of time does not necessarily mean acknowledging any right of equivalent material compensation for this value in all cases. According to *Shariah*, compensation for the value of time in sales contracts is acknowledged, but in the case of lending, increase (interest) is prohibited as a means of material compensation for time.

The Islamic notion of the opportunity cost of capital and the time value of money can be clearly understood by reviewing the distinction between investment and lending. Time by itself does not give a yield; it can contribute to the creation of value only when an economic activity is undertaken. A sum of money can be invested in a business venture or it can be lent for a given period of time. In case of investment, the investor will be compensated for any profit and loss earned during that time. Islam fully recognizes this return on the investment as a result of an economic activity. If money is in the form of a loan, however, it is an act of charity where surplus funds are effectively being utilized to promote economic development and social well-being.

In response to the contemporary understanding that interest on a loan is a reward for the opportunity cost of the lender, Islamic scholars maintain that interest fixed *ex ante* is certain while profits or losses are not. To demand a *certain* fixed compensation for an *uncertain* return that is actually earned is indulging in *al-riba* and is, therefore, unlawful. The element of uncertainty diminishes with time as the resultant return on the investment is realized, rather than the accruing of return simply from the passage of time. In short, Islam's stand on the time value of money is simple and clear: Money is a medium of exchange; time facilitates completion of economic activity, and the owner of capital is to be compensated for any return resulting from economic activity. Lending should be a charitable act without any expectation of certain monetary benefit at the expense of another.

The Quran clearly and strongly condemns acquisition by individuals of each other's property through wrongful means (see 2:188; 4:29, 161; 9:34). Islam recognizes two types of individual claims to property: (1) property rights that are a result of the combination of an individual's labor and natural resources; and (2) rights or claims to the property that are obtained through exchange, remittances of what Islam recognizes as the rights of those less able to utilize the resources to which they are entitled, outright grants, and inheritance. Money represents the monetized claim of its owner to the property rights created by assets that were obtained or received through (1) and/or (2). Lending money is, in effect, a transfer of these rights from the lender to the borrower. All that can be claimed in return for the loan is its equivalent and no more. Interest on money loaned represents an unjustifiable and instantaneous property rights claim. It is unjustifiable because interest is a property right claimed outside the legitimate framework of individual property rights recognized by Islam and instantaneous because as soon as the contract for lending upon interest is concluded, a right to the borrower's property is created for the lender, regardless of the outcome of the enterprise for which the money is used.

Money lent on interest is used either productively, in the sense that it creates additional wealth, or unproductively, in the sense that it does not lead to incremental wealth produced by the borrower. In the former case— that is, when the funds are used in combination with the labor of the entrepreneur to produce additional wealth—the money lent cannot have any property rights claim to the incremental wealth because the lender, when lending money, does not bargain for a proportion of the additional wealth but for a fixed return, irrespective of the outcome of the enterprise. The lender, in effect, transfers the right to his property to the borrower. In the latter case, since no additional wealth, property, or assets are created by the borrower, the money lent—even if legitimately acquired—cannot be used to claim any additional property rights since none is created.

Islamic scholars advocating the elimination of interest from the economy highlight the fact that there is no satisfactory theory of interest in the conventional economic theory. This criticism is levied especially on fixed rates of interest. Muslim writers see the theories of interest as attempts to rationalize the existence of an institution that has become deeply entrenched in modern economies and not as attempts to justify, based on modern economic analysis, why moneylenders are entitled to a reward on the money they lend. Typical justifications for interest in any economy include the arguments that interest is a reward for saving, a marginal productivity of capital, and an inevitable consequence of the difference between the value of capital goods today and their value after some time.

When it is argued that interest is a reward for saving, Muslim scholars respond that such payments can be rationalized only if savings are used for investment to create additional capital and wealth. According to the scholars, the mere act of abstention from consumption should not entitle anybody to a return. When argued that interest is justified as marginal productivity of capital, Muslim scholars respond that although the marginal productivity of capital may be one factor in the determination of the rate of interest, interest per se has no necessary relation with the productivity of capital. Interest is paid on money, not on capital, and has to be paid irrespective of capital productivity. In distinguishing between interest as a charge for the use of money and a yield from the investment of capital, Muslim scholars argue that it is an error of modern theory to treat interest as the price of, or return on, capital. Money, they argue, is not capital; it is only "potential capital," and it requires the service of the entrepreneur to transform the potentiality into actuality. The lender has nothing to do with the conversion of money into capital or with using it productively. When argued that interest arises as the time value of money, Muslim scholars respond that this only explains its inevitability, not its "rightness." Even if the basis for time preference is the difference between the value of commodities this year and the next, Muslim scholars argue, it seems more reasonable to allow next year's economic conditions to determine the extent of the reward.

It is argued that when a person lends financial resources, these funds are used to create either a debt or an asset (i.e., through investment). In the first case, Islam considers that there is no justifiable reason why the lender should receive a return simply through the act of lending per se. Nor is there a justification, either from the point of view of the smooth functioning of the economy or that of any tenable scheme of social justice, for the state to attempt to enforce an unconditional promise of interest payment regardless of the use of borrowed money. If, however, the money is used to create additional capital wealth, the question is raised as to why the lender should be entitled to only a small fraction (represented by the interest rate) of the exchange value of the utility created from the use made of the funds; the lender should be remunerated to the extent of the involvement of his financial capital in creating the incremental wealth.

RISK-SHARING ECONOMIC SYSTEM

Islam endorses risk sharing as the preferred organizational structure for all economic activities, and in fact it endorses the most comprehensive application of risk sharing that goes beyond anything put forward by modern economic theories. Islam prohibits, without any exceptions, explicit and implicit interest-based contracts of any kind and requires mandatory risk sharing with the poor, the deprived, and the handicapped based on its principles of property rights. Moreover, even after these rights are redeemed, the remaining wealth is not to be accumulated. Wealth is considered the strength of the economy and a means of support for society.

Wealth must not be withheld from circulation through accumulation. Noncirculation of wealth among the members of the society creates a sclerosis in the society's body economic, restricting the flow of resources needed for the growth of the economy. To allow a healthy circulation of wealth, the Islamic paradigm envisions a financial system based on risk and return sharing. Within the Islamic framework, the central proposition of Islamic finance is the prohibition of interest-based transactions in which a rent is collected as a percentage of an amount of the principle loaned for a specific time period without the full transfer of the property rights over the money loaned to the borrower. One result of this type of transaction is that the entire risk of the transaction is shifted to the borrower. Instead, Islam proposes a mutual exchange in which one bundle of property rights is exchanged for another, thus allowing both parties in the exchange to share the risks of the transaction.

The ideal Islamic finance system points to a full-spectrum menu of instruments serving a financial sector embedded in an Islamic economy in which the institutional scaffolding (rules of behavior as prescribed by Allah [swt] and operationalized by the Noble Messenger, including rules of market behavior prescribed by Islam) is fully operational.[4] The essential function of that spectrum would be spreading and allocating risk among market participants rather than allowing it to concentrate among the borrowing class. Islam proposes three sets of risk-sharing instruments:

1. Risk-sharing instruments in the financial sector;
2. Redistributive risk-sharing instruments through which the economically more able segments of society share the risks facing the less able segment of the population; and
3. The inheritance rules specified in the Quran through which the wealth of a person at the time of passing is distributed among present and future generations of inheritors.

As will be argued here, the second set of instruments is used to redeem the rights of the less able in the income and wealth of the more able. These are not instruments of charity, altruism, or beneficence. They are instruments of redemption of rights and repayment of obligations.

The starting point of this discussion is verse 275 of Chapter 2 of the Quran, particularly the part of the verse that declares contract of *al-bay'* (exchange) permissible and that of *al-riba* (interest) nonpermissible. Arguably, these few words can be considered as constituting the organizing principle—the fundamental theorem, as it were—of the Islamic economy.

---

[4]Chapra (2000) and Iqbal and Mirakhor (2011).

Most translations of the Quran render *al-bay'* as "commerce" or "trade." They also translate *al-tijarah* as "commerce" or "trade." Consulting major Arabic lexicons[5] reveals that there is substantive difference between *al-bay'* and *al-tijarah*. Relying on various verses of the Quran (e.g., 10–13:61; 29–30:35; 111:2; 254:2), these sources suggest that trade contracts (*al-tijarah*) are entered into in the expectation of profit (*ribh*). *Al-bay'* contracts are defined as *mubadilah al-maal bi al-maal*: exchange of property with property. In contemporary economics, it would be rendered as "exchange of property rights claim." These sources also suggest a further difference in the meaning of the terms: Those who enter into a contract of exchange expect gains but are cognizant of probability of loss (*khisarah*).

First, it is worth noting also that all Islamic contractual forms, except spot exchanges, involve time. From an economic point of view, time transactions involve a commitment to do something today in exchange for a promise of a commitment to do something in the future. All transactions involving time are subject to uncertainty, and uncertainty involves risk. Risk exists whenever more than one outcome is possible. Consider, for example, a contract in which a seller commits to deliver a product in the future against payments today. There are a number of risks involved. There is a price risk for both sides of the exchange; the price may be higher or lower in the future. In that case, the two sides are at risk, which they share once they enter into the contract agreement. If the price in the future is higher, the buyer would be better off, and the price risk has been shed to the seller. The converse is true if the price is lower. Under uncertainty, the buyer and seller have, through the contract, shared the price risk. There are other risks that the buyer takes, including the risks of nondelivery and quality. The seller also faces additional risks, including the risk that the price of raw material may be higher in the future, and transportation and delivery cost risks. Again, these risks have been shared through the contract. The same argument applies to deferred payment contracts.

Second, it may appear that spot exchange or cash sale involves no risk. But price changes postcompletion of spot exchanges are not unknown. The two sides of a spot exchange share this risk. Moreover, from the time of the classical economists, it has been known that specialization through comparative advantage provides the basis for gains from trade. But in specializing, a producer takes a risk of becoming dependent on other producers specializing in the production of what the producer needs. Again, through exchange, the two sides to a transaction share the risk of specialization. Additionally, there are pre-exchange risks of production and transportation

---

[5] See leading Arabic dictionaries such as *Lisan Al-Arab, Mufradat Alfaz Al-Quran* (2009) and Lane (2003), among others.

that are shared through the exchange. It is clear that the other contracts at the other end of the spectrum of Islamic contracts—that is, *mudharabah* (a contract between a capital provider and an investment manager with the profits and losses shared according to the contractual agreement) and *musharakah* (a partnership as in the previous case, but both partners participate in the management)—are risk-sharing transactions. Therefore, it can be inferred that by mandating *al-bay'*, Allah (swt) ordained risk sharing in all exchange activities.

Third, it appears that the contract of *al-riba* is prohibited because opportunities for risk sharing are nonexistent in such a contract. It may be argued that the creditor does take risks—the risk of default. But it is not risk taking per se that makes a transaction permissible. A gambler takes risks as well, but gambling is forbidden (*haram*). Instead, what seems to matter is the opportunity for risk sharing. *Al-riba* is a contract of risk transfer. As Keynes emphasized in his writing, if interest rates did not exist, financiers would have to share in all the risks that entrepreneurs face in producing, marketing, and selling a product.[6] But by decoupling future gains, by lending money today for more money in the future, financiers transfer all risks to entrepreneurs.

Fourth, it is clear that by declaring the contract of *al-riba* nonpermissible, the Quran intends for humans to shift their focus to risk-sharing contracts of exchange.

The emphasis on risk sharing is evident from one of the most important verses in the Quran (2:275) with respect to economic relations. "They say that indeed an exchange transaction (*al-bay'*) is like a *al-riba* [interest-based] transaction. But Allah has permitted exchange transactions and forbidden interest-based transactions." The nature of property rights inherent in these two transactions hints at one of their crucial differences. *Al-bay'* is a contract of exchange of one commodity for another where the property rights over one commodity are exchanged for those over the other. In the case of an *al-riba* transaction, a sum of money is loaned today for a larger sum in the future without the transfer of the property rights over the principal from the lender to the borrower. Not only does the lender retain property rights over the sum lent, but property rights over the additional sum to be paid as interest are transferred from the borrower to the lender at the time the contract of *al-riba* is entered into.

Arguably, the verse makes exchange and trade of commodities and/or assets the foundation of economic activity in the Islamic paradigm. From this, important implications follow: Exchange requires freedom of parties to contract. This in turn implies freedom to produce, which calls for clear

---

[6]Mirakhor and Krichene (2009).

and well-protected property rights to permit production to proceed. To freely and conveniently exchange, the parties need markets. To operate successfully, the market needs rules of behavior, along with enforcement mechanisms to reduce uncertainty in transactions and increase the free flow of information. The market also needs:

- Trust to be established among participants
- Competition among sellers, on one hand, and buyers, on the other
- Reduced transaction costs
- Risks mitigated to third parties in terms of having to bear externalized costs of two-party transactions

To reduce the incidence of informational problems that plague the conventional interest-based economic system, these additional requirements are necessary:

- Rules that ordain trust
- Faithfulness to the terms and conditions of contracts
- Rule compliance and prohibition of rule violations
- Transparency and truthfulness in transactions
- Prohibition of interference with market forces, hoarding of commodities to force increases in their price, and coalitions
- Market supervision to ensure rule compliance[7]

A further implication is that finance based on risk-return sharing means that the rate of return to finance is determined *ex post facto*, by the rate of return on real activity rather than the reverse, which is the case when interest-based debt contracts finance production. This has a further economic implication in that risk-return-sharing finance removes interest payments from the preproduction phase of an enterprise and places it in the post-production and after-sale distributional phase. In turn, this has price-quantity consequences. It should be clear that compliance with the behavioral rules prescribed by Islam reduces risk and uncertainty, both of which are facts of human existence. When risks to income materialize, they play havoc with people's livelihood. It is, therefore, welfare enhancing to reduce risks to income and lower the chances of income volatility in order to allow consumption smoothing. By focusing on trade and exchange in commodities and assets, Islam promotes risk sharing.

Arguably, it can be claimed that through its rules (institutions) governing resource allocation, property rights, production, exchange, distribution and

---

[7]Mirakhor (2007).

redistribution, financial transactions, and market behavior, the Islamic paradigm orients all economic relations toward risk-reward sharing. This can be said to be a logical consequence of insistence on the unity of human-kind since through risk sharing, Islamic finance promotes social solidarity. "Massive risk can carry with it benefits far beyond that of reducing poverty and diminishing income inequality. The reduction of risk on risk on a greater scale would provide substantial impetus to human and economic progress."[8] The most meaningful human progress is achieved when all distinctions on the basis of race, color, income and wealth, and social-political status are obliterated to the point where humanity, in convergence with the Quranic declaration (31:28), truly views itself as one and united. It can be argued that implementation of Islamic finance will promote maximum risk sharing, thus creating the potential for enhanced social solidarity.[9]

In addition to its risk-sharing characteristics, an Islamic economic system has the potential of greater stability than its conventional counter-part. The main reason for this is the fact that when production is financed entirely by risk-return sharing or equity finance, in the case of rapid changes in the price, assets and liabilities both move in the same direction simulta-neously—thus the financial structure adjusts in tandem on both sides of the ledger. A number of analytic models have investigated the adjustment process and have demonstrated the stability of Islamic finance in response to shocks as well as the growth implications of such a system in closed and open economy situations.[10] An important feature of these models was the assumption of 100% reserve banking based on the understanding of bank deposits as a safekeeping operation firewalled from the risks involved in investment operations (i.e., the so-called two-windows model).[11] This fea-ture of requiring banking depository institutions to hold 100% reserves against demand deposits removes two sources of instability associated with conventional interest-based, fractional reserve banking. Nonavailability of interest-based financial transactions and 100% reserve banking eliminate the ability of the financial system to create money out of thin air and impair its ability to leverage an asset base into much larger liabilities.[12] Moreover, when risk-return sharing replaces an interest-based debt system, a much closer relationship is forged between the financial and the real sectors of the economy. As early as the 1930s, economists discussed the negative

---

[8] Shiller (2003).
[9] Askari, Iqbal, and Mirakhor (2009), Iqbal and Mirakhor (2011), and Mirakhor (2007).
[10] Khan (1987), Khan and Mirakhor (1989), and Mirakhor and Zaidi (1988).
[11] Khan (1987).
[12] Mirakhor and Krichene (2009).

consequences of interest-based debt financing for real activities in terms of income and employment.[13] The world has witnessed repeated periodic episodes of financial crises originating in systems with interest-based debt financing at their core in the last two centuries. The frequency of these crises increased in the last decades of the twentieth century and culminated in the devastating global crisis of 2007–2008. As unfortunate as these crises have been, they have held lessons for Islamic finance, which still is in its nascent stage of development, especially since Islamic finance is now operating in an institutional framework that is basically that of the conventional debt-driven system.

In the area of finance, prohibiting debt-based contracts and endorsing exchange have four significant economic implications.

1. Before parties can enter into a contract of exchange, they must have the property rights in what they are going to exchange.
2. The parties need a place or a forum to consummate the exchange: a market.
3. The market needs rules for its efficient operation.
4. Market rules need enforcement.

Exchange facilitates specialization and allows the parties to share production, transportation, marketing, sales, and price risk. Therefore, exchange is above all a means of risk sharing. From an economic standpoint, therefore, by prohibiting interest rate–based contracts and ordaining exchange contracts, the Quran encourages risk sharing and prohibits risk transfer, risk shedding, and risk shifting. Islamic finance is basically a financial system structured on risk sharing and the prohibition of debt financing (leveraging).[14] The central proposition of Islamic finance is the prohibition of transactions that embody rent for a specific period of time as a percentage of the loaned principle without the transfer of the property rights claims, thus shifting the entire risk of the transaction to the borrower. The alternative to debt-based contracts—namely mutual exchange, where one bundle of property rights is exchanged for another—allows both parties to share production, transportation, and marketing risks. In order to fit into this framework, financial intermediation and banking in the Islamic financial system (and more generally in a risk-sharing system) have been proposed as having two tiers. The first tier is a banking system that accepts deposits for safekeeping without accruing any return and requiring 100% reserves. This protects the payment system of the economy

---

[13]Keynes (1930).
[14]Askari, Iqbal, Krichene, and Mirakhor (2011).

while concurrently limiting the credit-creating ability of the banking system. Thus it obviates the need for a deposit guarantee, as in the conventional fractional reserve system. The second tier is an investment component that functions as a classical financial intermediary, channeling savings to investment projects, and where deposits in investment banks are considered as equity investments with no guarantees for their face value at maturity and subject to the sharing of profits and losses. Depositors are investors in the pool of assets maintained by the bank on the assets side of its balance sheet.

It is important to recognize—though it may be difficult, given our mindsets—that there is nothing magical about the recent historical prominence of debt financing. Before the rise of debt financing, equity financing was preeminent, but a host of factors and developments catapulted debt financing to the forefront. Risk-sharing finance is trust intensive, and trade financing during the Middle Ages was based on risk sharing, which, in turn, was based on mutual trust. Upheavals of the late Middle Ages, in the fourteenth and fifteenth centuries, including the Black Death, strife within the church and between the church and hereditary rulers, and general economic decline, contributed to the breakdown of trust in communities and among their members. While risk-sharing techniques continued to prevail in Europe until the mid-seventeenth century, beginning in the mid-sixteenth century, the institution of interest-based debt financing also began to be used more widely and extensively. The catalyst for debt financing was primarily the breakdown of trust in Europe and elsewhere and the adoption of securitization in finance. Over time, government deposit insurance schemes, tax treatments, rules, and regulations have all heavily favored debt-based contracts over risk-sharing contracts. Thus, risk sharing is still at an early stage of development in all countries, to say nothing of its even more modest international practice. These developments have helped perpetuate a system that a number of renowned economists, such as Keynes, have deemed detrimental to growth, development, and equitable income and wealth distribution. More recently, a growing literature and proposed reforms have argued that the stability of a financial system can be assured only by limiting credit expansion and leveraging; this, in turn, requires the elimination of implicit and explicit subsidies that fuel moral hazard, such as subsidized deposit insurance schemes and guarantees that support institutions that are deemed too large to fail, and policies that afford legal protection to those who manipulate the financial system for their own personal advantage and gains.

ROLE OF THE STATE

Since Islam considers economic relations and behavior as the means of social and spiritual integration, economic attainments are not to be viewed as ends in themselves. All the rules of behavior regarding economic matters are addressed to individuals and their collectivity, which is represented by the state. The state is regarded as being indispensable for the orderly organization of social life, the achievement of legitimate objectives, the creation of material and spiritual prosperity, and the defense and propagation of faith. The state is primarily a vehicle for implementing *Shariah* and derives its legitimacy from its enforcement of *Shariah* rules. It is assumed to be empowered to use, within the limits of the law, all available means at its disposal to achieve the objectives and duties prescribed for the collectivity, including the synchronization of individual and public interests.

Foremost among the collective duties is ensuring that justice prevails in all walks of social life. Thus, the establishment of a judiciary or judicial system, with all the apparatus necessary for carrying out the verdicts of the courts, free of any charges and available to all, is regarded as an indispensable duty of the state. Another of the state's duties is to guarantee equal liberty and opportunity in access to and use of resources identified by *Shariah* for the use of individuals. This covers the provision of education, skills, and technology, available to all. When both equal liberty and equal opportunity are provided, then the production of wealth and its possession and exchange become matters of equity. All infrastructures necessary for markets to exist and operate have also traditionally been the responsibility of the state. The first market for the Muslim community was built in Medina at the direction of the Prophet (sawa) who required that trade be allowed to take place in that market freely, without any charges or fees imposed on market participants. On this basis, jurists have recognized market supervision, and its control only when necessary, as a duty of the state.

As we have seen, Islam recognizes as inviolable the right of those unable to actualize their potential to have equal liberties and opportunities in the wealth of those more able. Thus, Islam establishes a practice that is a balance between libertarian and egalitarian values, whereby when the payment of the obligatory levies mandated under *Shariah* rules is shirked, the state has a responsibility to correct the resulting misdistribution.

The eradication of poverty is undoubtedly one of the most important of all duties made incumbent upon the state, second only to the preservation and propagation of faith, whose very existence is considered to be threatened by poverty. Islam regards poverty primarily as a failure on the part of the more able and wealthy members of society to perform their prescribed duties. Hence, the commitment to distributive justice, which normally constitutes a large portion of government budgets in other systems, is placed squarely on the shoulders of the individuals with the financial and economic capability to meet it. Not only does *Shariah* specify who must pay, but it also designates explicit categories of recipients.

To summarize, in an Islamic economy, the role of the state is to ensure five goals:

1. Everyone has equal access to natural resources and means of livelihood.
2. Each individual has equal opportunity—including education, skills, and technology—to utilize these resources.
3. Markets are supervised in such a manner that justice in exchange can be attained.
4. Transfer takes place from those more able to those less able in accordance to the rules of *Shariah*.
5. Distributive justice is done to the next generation through the implementation of the laws of inheritance.

The state is empowered to design any specific economic policy that is required in order to guarantee the attainment of these objectives. To meet the necessary expenditures associated with the performance of its duties, *Shariah* has given the control, utilization, and management of a portion of a society's natural resource endowment (e.g., mineral resources) to the state. The consensus of opinion among jurists is that the state is also empowered to impose taxes whenever there is a gap between the resources it can command and its expenditures. Borrowing by the state, when it does not involve paying interest, is permitted when and if necessary.

The state (as further elaborated in Chapter 9) is seen as indispensable for the orderly organization of social life, the achievement of legitimate objectives, and the creation of material and spiritual prosperity. The state is assumed empowered to use, within the limits of the law, all available means at its disposal to achieve the objectives and duties prescribed for the collectivity, including the synchronization of individual and public interests and especially ensuring that justice prevails in all facets of social life. Thus, existence of a judiciary system, with all apparatus necessary to carry out the verdict of the courts free of charges and available to all, is regarded as an indispensable duty of the state. Similarly, the guarantee of equal liberty and opportunity in terms of access to and use of resources is another duty specified for the state and requires provision of education, skills, and technology available to all. Once both equal liberty and equal opportunity are provided, then production of wealth and its possession and exchange become matters of equity.

SUMMARY

The Quran and the life of the Prophet (sawa) provide both the immutable and adjustable (as required by the prevailing circumstances and times) rules to develop a vibrant economic system that is based on justice. Economic justice embodies the equality of liberty and opportunity for all humans to pursue their dreams, having equal access for all generations to gifted resources of Allah (swt), justice in exchange (in all economic transactions), and distributive justice. A just economy is part and parcel of a just, healthy, and moral society.

Divine rules that were implemented by the Prophet (sawa) frame the scaffolding of the Islamic economic system. Humans are to be guided by material and spiritual incentives. They are trustees on this plane of existence and must preserve the rights of all humans and other living creatures. They must work hard (almost at the level of duty) and receive remuneration according to their level of productivity.

Humans must limit their wants, live modestly, refrain from hoarding wealth, and share with the less fortunate and the disabled. Allah (swt) has provided sufficient resources to satisfy the needs of all humans as long as they share. Wealth is the lifeblood of the economy and must be invested and circulated as opposed to hoarded.

KEY TERMS

Work ethic	Interest (*al-riba*)
Equal opportunities	Risk-sharing finance
Modest living	Distributive and redistributive justice
Limiting wants	Role of the state
Sharing with the less fortunate	

QUESTIONS

1. What is the importance of work in Islam?
2. What does distributive and redistributive justice in Islam mean?
3. Is Islam close to a socialist system?
4. What is the role of markets in Islam, and how does that role differ from the role of markets in a capitalist system?
5. How is the role of the state in Islam different from that in the capitalist system?
6. What is the essence of justice in Islam?
7. How do the building blocks of the Islamic financial system differ from the building blocks of the conventional system?
8. What are the benefits and costs of a risk-sharing financial system?

CHAPTER 5

Key Microeconomic Concepts

Learning objectives:

1. *How consumers and producers form their decisions.*
2. *How these decisions differ in Islam from those in the conventional system.*
3. *How supply and demand functions are determined and how price equilibrium is reached in markets.*
4. *The role and importance of markets in efficient resource allocation.*
5. *Role of the state and its policies in an economic system.*
6. *Difference between needs and wants.*
7. *Determinants of supply and demand curves.*

Though much has been written about the differences between Islamic and conventional finance, little attention has been paid to the differences in the realm of microeconomics that may in fact run even deeper. Microeconomic considerations in Islam are based on a different paradigm with answers to core economic questions that are in sharp contrast to those from conventional economics. Conventional microeconomics has been developed on the basis of hypothetical assumptions about the behavior of individuals and firms. These assumptions, though unrealistic, have continued to be largely unquestioned even though they are contradicted by prevailing facts. Moreover, conventional economics does not consider needed changes in individual and social behavior to realize its macroeconomic objectives, such as steady economic growth, full employment, and the like. This is a direct result of the dismissal by conventional economics of value judgments and its commitment to unrestrained individual freedom and choice.[1]

---

[1] Chapra (2011, p. 42).

Redefining the assumptions of microeconomics to bridge the gap with macroeconomics and achieve societal goals is not a small task. Construction of microeconomic theory under the Islamic principles is challenging for theoreticians and researchers in Islamic economics. However, Islamic economics does have the advantage of benefiting from the tools of analysis developed by conventional economics. In this chapter, the focus will be to explain the Islamic microeconomic perspective by introducing the key conventional microeconomic theories and discussing how these theories and ideas are different in the Islamic paradigm.

At the outset, it may be appropriate to highlight the fundamentals of the contrasting conventional and Islamic paradigms. First, let us begin by highlighting the commonalities. As previously mentioned, the subject matter of all economics is the allocation and distribution of scarce resources. Both paradigms play a role in facing the problems of humankind, which include poverty, lack of need fulfillment, unemployment, inequitable distribution of income, and others. Another commonality is that both paradigms seek to realize maximum human well-being, though this has "become vague, ambiguous, even protean"[2] in conventional economics. However, despite having similar goals, the point of difference lies in this question: Among the alternative uses of scarce resources, what is considered the most acceptable allocation and distribution of these scarce resources for society? As a result of differing worldviews, the two paradigms have different social visions, different thoughts as to what constitutes true well-being, and thus different means of achieving well-being. These differences in paradigm and approach are most evident in the sphere of microeconomics.

The worldview of mainstream economics has been inherited from the Enlightenment movement of the seventeenth and eighteenth centuries. Although the Enlightenment had the objective of freeing humankind from state and church despotism, it ended up declaring all revealed truths of religion as designs "to keep men ignorant of the ways of Reason and Nature."[3] It denied revelation of any role in the management of human affairs and instead placed an emphasis on the power of reason to distinguish right from wrong and to manage all aspects of human life in a manner that ensures human well-being. This removed the sanctity religion assigned to moral values and left them to the private domain of individuals. However, moral values are not concerned only with the private lives of individuals; they are also concerned with social, economic, and political dimensions of human life, which affect the well-being of all. The loss of sanctity left a void, which

---

[2] Kristol (1981, p. 215).
[3] Brinton (1967, p. 520).

was filled by philosophies of social Darwinism, materialism, determinism, and existentialism in economics as well as in other social sciences.[4]

The outcome of the Enlightenment is a worldview that discusses the nature of existence and attempts to answer questions about how the universe came to exist, the meaning and purpose of life, the ultimate ownership and objective of scarce resources, and the relationship of human beings toward each other and their environment. This secularist paradigm adopted by mainstream economics has led to an unrealistic view of individuals and their behaviors, an anathema to value judgments, and an insistence on individual freedom to pursue whatever is considered to be in his or her self-interest. The assumptions highlighted earlier, such as utility maximization and rationality, are a result of this worldview, no matter how unrealistic the assumption that individuals perform complicated utility calculations every time they undertake any economic decision. The primary purpose of mainstream economics has become to describe, analyze, and predict, not to make value judgments or adopt realistic assumptions.

This worldview has left economics in a self-contradictory position. There is commitment to the goals of reducing poverty and realizing full employment, but it is recognized that these goals require policies that cannot be defined without value judgments. Since value judgments are excluded, policies that help utilize scarce resources in a manner that realizes the goals are not implemented. Value neutrality has left conventional economics to the whims of its own idealized economic players.[5]

DEFINING MICROECONOMICS

Microeconomics is focused on how consumers and producers (businesses) make choices. It attempts to study human behavior by using a "scientific" approach. For economic actors to make a choice, it means that a selection was made among alternatives, and this involves two ideas central to conventional economics: scarcity and opportunity cost.

On one hand, resources are limited. There is only so much oil, land, and people available at any one time, and it is because of this that resources are not free and command a price. On the other hand, according to neoclassical microeconomics, human wants and desires for goods and services are unlimited. We always want more national security, food, and healthcare. Had our resources been infinite, we would not have to make choices. We would simply say yes to all of our wants and desires. However, economic

---

[4]Chapra (2011, pp. 70–71).
[5]Ibid.

actors must make choices to cope with scarcity. It is the constraint of scarcity that makes us choose among alternatives. This is the basis of conventional microeconomics.

The choices we face as a result of scarcity result in three fundamental economic questions that all economies must answer:

1. **What should be produced?** Using a nation's scarce resources to produce a good requires giving up producing another. Should the wilderness area be preserved as a national park or used for factories? Should farmers produce agricultural goods or livestock, and which goods and which livestock?
2. **How should goods and services be produced?** There are many different ways (technologies and combinations of factor inputs) to produce goods and services. Should the goods be produced locally or in foreign plants?
3. **For whom should goods and services be produced?** Along with the production of the goods comes the question of to whom the goods should go. Should food produced be sold to the highest bidder, or should poorer people have the chance to purchase these goods?

These questions are faced by all economies every day and are considered to be the three broad microeconomic questions.

Given the constraint of scarcity, it is necessary to define opportunity cost: the value of the next best alternative in making a choice. Opportunity cost should not be confused with the purchase price of the item chosen. Consider the cost of attending postsecondary education. School fees, living expenses, and books are all a part of that cost. However, the most important cost is the value of forgone alternative uses of the time spent at postsecondary school. Students could have worked, volunteered, or practiced a hobby instead of attending postsecondary school. Economists argue that understanding opportunity cost is crucial to studying individual choices. Assuming that we always choose the most beneficial option among the available set, the expected benefits of the alternatives affect our decision. As the alternatives change, choices individuals make also change. A sunny day can change the opportunity cost of going for a run. We can expect highly paid individuals to work long hours, as a high income changes the trade-off between work and play, which is opportunity cost of taking time off.

The concepts of scarcity and opportunity cost are central to the study of how economic actors make choices. Scarcity forces us to make choices among alternatives, and the opportunity cost of our choice is the next best forgone alternative. An economy cannot produce an unlimited quantity of goods and services; it has to decide what goods to produce and how best to

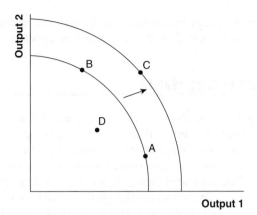

FIGURE 5.1 Expanded Production Possibilities Frontier

use its resources of labor, land, other natural resources, capital, and
technology to produce these goods. Figure 5.1 broadly shows the trade-
offs involved in what is called a production possibility frontier. The curved
frontier represents the trade-off between producing good 1 and good 2; the
frontier is curved because of diminishing returns in production. Points A
and B on the smaller frontier represent efficient and full employment of
available resources, whereas point D is a production level denoting lots of
unemployed resources (excess capacity) and/or inefficient (such as technology) production practices. The economy cannot produce outside (in excess)
of this frontier, but over time, with investment, education, and technical
progress, the production possibilities could expand to a new and larger
frontier that includes a level of output such as point C.

The three basic assumptions of conventional microeconomics include:

1. **Individual economic actors make choices that create a maximum value of
   some objective, given the constraints they face.** Consumers' objective is
   their own satisfaction, and they make choices (in reality very difficult
   calculations) in pursuit of maximizing their own satisfaction; in economics jargon, this is maximizing "utility." The objective of business firms is
   to maximize profits.
2. **Individuals maximize by making choices "at the margin," and maximization occurs when the marginal benefit equals the marginal cost.** At this
   point, the net benefit of an activity is maximized.
3. **Individuals behave rationally.** This means that individuals indeed act
   in their own interest as if they are making decisions that will maximize
   their utility.

These assumptions are fundamental to the way conventional economists approach microeconomics and will help frame concepts later in this chapter.

ISSUE OF NEEDS VERSUS WANTS

The conventional assumption is that individuals behave rationally and maximize some objective, given their constraints. Neoclassical economists assume that the economic objective of individual consumers is to satisfy their unlimited needs and wants. Economists are careful to distinguish between needs and wants. Humans need shelter; however, they do not need mansions. A mansion is a want. Economists emphasize that once humans have achieved the bare subsistence level of consumption of food, shelter, and clothing required to live, they can abandon all reference to needs and speak only in terms of wants. With our boundless appetites for things, we are challenged to fulfill our desires to the maximum, given the constraints we face, primarily our budgets. The problem we face is this: How do we go about allocating our income among the available goods and services?

When it comes to defining needs in Islam, the Prophet (sawa) explained in a *hadeeth*, or saying, what constitutes "subsistence level," which is considered a right of all humans and includes the right to bread, water, clothing, and shelter. The Prophet (sawa) also mentioned a "sufficiency level," which includes the financial ability to marry and to have suitable housing and a means for transportation.[6]

In the mind of an economic human who is *rasheed* (i.e., a rational Muslim consumer who is making progress on the path to perfection, and as a result applies sound judgment in line with the *maqasid-al-Shariah* [the goal of *Shariah*]), the needs of others are considered more important than the wants of the individual himself. This is in line with the teachings of the Prophet Mohammad (sawa), who would partake in public borrowing to feed those whose subsistence level was not being met by society.[7] Such unselfishness shows the importance of meeting the need fulfillment of all humanity as one of the biggest economic goals in Islam. It is important to note that human needs, according to a *hadeeth*, are not equal for everyone. Part of *rushd* (individual self-development) is to know what personal needs are and to act accordingly.[8] It is important to note that Allah (swt) does not prohibit the betterment of life in terms of the material (Quran 7:32). However, He dislikes

---

[6] Ahmad (2011, pp. 6–7).
[7] Siddiqui (1995).
[8] Ahmad (2011).

opulent, extravagant, and wasteful behavior. Allah (swt) addresses all of humanity in a verse of the Quran (7:31) that says:

> O Children of Adam! Wear your beautiful apparel at every time and place of prayer: Eat and Drink: but waste not by excess, for Allah loves not the wasters.

From the Quran and the example of the Prophet (sawa), economic needs have been defined, both in an absolute and a relative manner. In light of the teachings of the Prophet (sawa) and the *maqasid*, after one has satisfied both his "subsistence" and "sufficiency" levels, then the individual *must* seek to allocate a portion of his budget to those in need.

Given the concept of scarcity, an important question is whether resources are scarce relative to needs. This is referred to as "relative scarcity," meaning that the means of satisfaction (i.e., goods and services) are scarce in relation to people's needs at a point in time. Essentially, it means that though there may be sufficient physical quantities of the resources (or goods and services produced), scarcity exists because of problems in the distribution of available goods and services. This is different from "absolute scarcity," which means there are simply insufficient quantities of a resource to produce the required goods and services.

Some scholars, such as Masri, do not agree with the premise that in the context of Islamic economics, there can be no scarcity of resources relative to needs. He argues that scarcity will remain, and, as a result, the economic problem of how to meet unlimited wants with limited resources will remain in the Islamic economic system.[9] Others argue that the concept of relative scarcity cannot be rejected from an Islamic perspective and that, in fact, the logic behind the concept has been indicated in the Quran (15:19–21). The point concerning relative scarcity from a Quranic perspective is that the stock of natural resources have been created in abundance to meet the needs of humanity; however, the distribution of these resources is not abundant by Allah's (swt) will. This is His wisdom.[10] This position is based on the belief that the Almighty created the world with sufficient resources to fulfill the needs of all humans as long as humans learned to share. In a sense, the Almighty created a world in which at the macro or global level, there was no scarcity to satisfy human needs. This is true even at the micro or local level as long as humans worked hard and shared with the less fortunate. The Almighty also did not create humans with equal abilities; He created the world and humans in this way as a test for humans on this plane of existence. Furthermore, as we explain later, while conventional

---

[9]Khan (2011, p. 192).
[10]Ahmad (2011).

economics takes unlimited human wants and the desire for opulence as a given, Islam preaches the need for humans to suppress their wants, avoid opulence, and share (a moral activity that brings its own rewards and happiness).

CONSUMER BEHAVIOR

Francis Edgeworth, one of the earliest and most important contributors to the theory of conventional consumer behavior, imagined a device called a hedonimeter (from the word "hedonism") that measures pleasure:

> Let there be granted to the science of pleasure what is granted to the science of energy; to imagine an ideally perfect instrument, a psychophysical machine, continually registering the height of pleasure experienced by an individual, exactly according to the verdict of consciousness, or rather diverging therefrom according to a law of errors. From moment to moment the hedonimeter varies; the delicate index now flickering with the flutter of the passions, now steadied by intellectual activity, now sunk whole hours in the neighborhood of zero, or momentarily springing up towards infinity.[11]

The motivation behind consumer behavior according to neoclassical economics is satisfaction, or what economists call utility. The concept of utility cannot be measured on its own in the abstract. A person who consumes a good gains utility from it; however, this utility cannot be measured on its own. Utility is defined as an ordinal measurement, not a cardinal one. Thus, utility gained from a good can be ranked vis-à-vis an alternative good. For example, an environmentalist likely derives more utility from a low-carbon-emissions vehicle than a large gas-guzzling truck.

In the pursuit of utility, conventional economics assumes consumers act as if they can measure utility and make decisions such that their utility is as high as possible. As such, the total utility is the number of units of utility that a consumer gains from consuming a given quantity of a good, service, or activity during a particular time period. Upon reflection, it is hard to imagine that there is even a single human who constantly makes economic decisions in this way, let alone that all humans do so. Total utility rises with an additional unit of the good, service, or activity, and *ceteris paribus*, the last unit of utility is called the marginal utility. An important law, evident in most dimensions of life, is the law of diminishing returns. The utility derived

---

[11]Edgeworth (1881).

from the first slice of pizza consumed would be significant. However, with each additional pizza slice consumed, the marginal utility decreases (as you are becoming full, the utility derived from the last slice of pizza becomes less and less). An important assertion is that the marginal utility approaches zero as consumption of the good approaches infinity; however, marginal utility never really is zero. According to mainstream economics, in the pursuit of satisfying our unlimited wants and desires, when offered a free pizza after having consumed a dozen, we will accept it, as the marginal utility is still positive. Or more realistically, we will still consume other goods even though we are full.

To understand how consumers maximize utility, we introduce the marginal benefit rule. First, it is important to realize consumers have budget constraints. To simplify the analysis, economists often assume that consumers do not save or borrow. Their available budget is simply their income. Given that consumers are expected to spend their budget, we can expect consumers to spend their budget in a way that maximizes utility. This is done through the marginal benefit rule, which states that a good would be consumed as long the marginal benefit of its consumption exceeds the marginal cost. The marginal benefit of the good or activity is the utility gained by spending an additional $1 on the good. The marginal cost is the utility lost by spending $1 less on another good. They are both calculated by taking the marginal utility (MU) and dividing by its price (P):

$$\frac{MU}{P} \qquad (5.1)$$

Let's consider two goods, good X and Y. The marginal utility of good X is 10, and its price is $5. This means that an extra $1 spent on good X buys 2 units of utility. Good Y has a marginal utility of 5; however, it also costs $5. This means that an extra $1 spent on good Y buys 1 unit of utility. The decision between spending the next dollar on good X or Y is made simple by seeing which good will buy more utility per dollar spent, or marginal benefit:

$$\frac{MU_x}{P_x} > \frac{MU_y}{P_y} \qquad (5.2)$$

In this case, it is clear the consumer would buy good X. However, as the consumer buys more of good X relative to good Y, the marginal utilities of the goods will change due to the law of diminishing marginal returns. The marginal utility of good X will decline relative to that of good Y as the consumer purchases more of good X. As consumption increases, according to the marginal decision rule, the value of the left- and right-hand sides of the equation will approach equality. When both sides are equal, total utility has been maximized:

$$\frac{MU_x}{P_x} = \frac{MU_y}{P_y} \tag{5.3}$$

This result can be extended to all goods, services, and activities consumed:

$$\frac{MU_a}{P_a} = \frac{MU_b}{P_b} = \frac{MU_c}{P_c} = \frac{MU_d}{P_d} \ldots = \frac{MU_z}{P_z} \tag{5.4}$$

Equation 5.4 is a simple expression of the rational spending rule, which solves the problem of allocating a fixed budget across different goods while maximizing utility. In conventional economics, utility is all that matters and there is no room for value judgments. This utility maximization reflects rational behavior in conventional consumer theory. Interestingly, the words "utility" and "rational" have linguistic meanings that are different from their economic concepts. The concept of utility is developed as "good morality" as perceived by the individual. What constitutes "good" is not universal but is relative to what the individual thinks in achieving self-interest. These definitions and concepts do not conform to Islamic values.

Though Islamic economists should be interested in studying the actual behavior of consumers, it is also important to study and define the behavior of an idealized Muslim consumer. To do so, the correct approach would be to transform some relevant *Shariah* principles and guidelines into axioms. For starters, certain materials and business dealings prohibited by *Shariah* must be excluded from the consumer's feasible set of commodities and transactions, such as alcohol and interest. Some other matters are less clear and have to be treated on the basis of *ijtihad* (independent reasoning). For example, a *rasheed* must not be either opulent or a miser, as the Almighty says in the Quran (25:67):

> *Those who, when they spend, are not extravagant and not niggardly, but hold a just balance between those (extremes).*

Unlike conventional economics, where rational consumers allocate their budgets across goods such that utility is maximized, Islam challenges and encourages humans to maintain a just balance between extremes and to control their wants. The budget of a Muslim consumer is subject to taxes, such as *zakat* (the practice of charitable alms giving based on accumulated wealth), *kharaj* (tax on land), and *khums* (the obligation to give one-fifth of certain types of income to charity). Even after all these taxes are paid, the income of a Muslim does not determine consumption, as it must be shared

BOX 5.1 CONSUMER BEHAVIOR IN CONVENTIONAL AND ISLAMIC ECONOMICS

There is a stark divide between Islamic and conventional economics as to consumer behavior. Conventional economics makes assumptions in order to model consumer behavior, but it does not develop a model of how consumers actually behave or ought to behave. This is because conventional economics has no room for either realism or value judgments. It simply postulates that the pursuit of one's utility maximization is "rational" and goes on to explain that, in fact, when each individual seeks to maximize his or her utility, this in turn maximizes the benefits of society as a whole. In contrast, Islamic economics begins with values and goals based on *Shariah* to shape ideal consumer behavior. It still has work to do in the area of formulating postulates that must be adhered to when analyzing behavior of a *rasheed* Muslim consumer. In essence, in an Islamic system, microeconomics can be modeled by changing human and firm behavior to comply with Islamic principles of justice, sharing, awarding factors of production their just reward, or by imposing a number of constraints to human and firm behavior that reflect Islamic requirements.

further if income disparities and poverty continue. Regardless of whether resources are absolutely scarce, the safest route is to not consume beyond one's needs, as the welfare of others in society and those of future generations matters. The differences in assumed consumer behaviors in the conventional and the Islamic systems are distinct (see Box 5.1).

THEORY OF THE FIRM

Firms are important entities that bring together factors of production to produce goods and services that are demanded by consumers. In a market economy, the firm's role is significant and remarkable: Besides managing and combining factors of production efficiently, a firm also plays an important role in enhancing the market mechanism. According to conventional economics, like consumers, firms also use the marginal decision rule. However, conventional economists assume firms function in order to earn profits, which they try to maximize. Given this assumption, economists can predict how firms will behave in response to changes in demand, factor input prices, and other changing conditions. For example, it was no surprise to economists that firms moved some of their operations overseas as the cost of labor rose in the United States relative to that abroad. A question remains: How do firms go about maximizing profits?

Total revenue is simply the price per unit of a good multiplied by the quantity of the good sold. Marginal revenue is the revenue received for the last good sold, and in the case of a perfectly competitive market, the marginal revenue is simply the price of the good; that is, the cost of producing the last unit of a good determines its unit price. Marginal cost is the cost of making an additional unit of the good. To maximize profits, the quantity produced by a firm should be such that the marginal revenue equals the marginal cost. In a perfectly competitive market, this means that marginal revenue and marginal cost equal the price of the good. This is consistent with the maximizing condition observed with consumers: To maximize the objective function, the marginal benefit rule is used to make the decision to expand an activity until the marginal benefit, in this case marginal revenue, equals the marginal cost. To produce more than this, the increase in revenue would be less than the increase in cost, thus reducing profits. This is what economists mean by making decisions at the margin.

Production Cost

Two periods are invariably identified in production analysis: the short run and the long run. Let's first consider the short run: that is a planning period where at least one factor of production is a fixed, or does not vary. For example, for a factory, the building is a fixed factor of production for at least a year. This limits the firm's range of choices among its factors of production. A factor of production whose quantity can be changed during a period is called a variable factor of production. An example in the case of the factory would be labor, which can be increased and decreased anytime. As the firm expands the use of a factor of production (while holding all other factors of production as fixed), it will experience increasing, then diminishing, then negative marginal returns. For example, consider a hypothetical firm called BestShoes. Let's assume its fixed factor of production is its capital equipment, and its only variable factor of production is labor. As the units of labor per day are increased, the total number of shoes produced will increase. However, according to the law of diminishing marginal returns, the marginal return from each additional unit of labor decreases until it eventually becomes negative.

A firm's production costs in the short run are dependent on the quantity produced and the prices of its factors of production. The production costs are composed of fixed costs, the costs associated with the fixed factors of production, and variable costs, which are the variable factors of production. Total variable costs vary with the level of output, while total fixed costs do not vary with output. The total cost (TC) is the sum of total variable costs (TVC) and total fixed costs (TFC).

$$\text{TVC} + \text{TFC} = \text{TC} \qquad (5.5)$$

From a total cost curve, marginal cost, the total cost of making an additional unit, can be found simply by deriving the total cost curve.

The long run is a planning period over which a firm can consider changing the quantity of all of its factors of production. To maximize profits in the long run, firms must select the combination of factors of production for their chosen level of output that minimizes costs. To determine the cost minimizing factor mix, the marginal decision rule will again be used. Let's consider the marginal benefit of an additional dollar spent on a factor of production. Of course, the benefit in this case is not utility, as was the case with consumers, but product output. The marginal product (MP) per dollar spent on a factor of production (P), or the marginal product factor price, is simply calculated as shown in equation 5.6:

$$\frac{\text{MP}}{\text{P}} \qquad (5.6)$$

Similar to the outcome of maximizing consumer utility, to choose the combination of factors (n) that will maximize profits, the firm must seek a combination of factors wherein the marginal product price to factor price is equal:

$$\frac{\text{MP}_1}{\text{P}_1} = \frac{\text{MP}_2}{\text{P}_2} = \frac{\text{MP}_3}{\text{P}_3} = \frac{\text{MP}_4}{\text{P}_4} \cdots\cdots = \frac{\text{MP}_n}{\text{P}_n} \qquad (5.7)$$

Equation 5.7 is the same outcome of utility maximization. A simple and intuitive explanation of this equation at work is in the case of labor cost increases, the firm will shift to a factor mix that uses relatively less labor and more capital.

As shown earlier, there are parallels between consumer utility maximization and firm profit maximization. Aside from the mathematical similarities, another similarity is that neither firm nor consumer behavior makes room for value judgments. The theoretical model of the firm is generally based on purely economic variables. The construction of the objective function primarily emanates from the maximization of profit and minimization of cost.[12] Seldom does the objective function include social, ethical, and moral components. Opportunity cost is a pure economic phenomenon and does not include moral or social dimensions. In Islam, this is not the case.

Early Muslim scholars discussed the behavior of firms and their responsibilities toward society and the community. The Islamic system of governance works on the principle of no injury (the principle of *maslahah*).[13] It is established that worldly goods ultimately belong to Allah (swt) and are for the advantage of all. No one has the right to use these goods to cause a loss to the other members of society. According to Islamic economists, it is the moral and social responsibility of the firm to care for all stakeholders while it earns a profit. The main objective of the Muslim entrepreneur is to promote justice: to earn a reasonable profit, charge a just price, pay just wages, and enhance the welfare of society. In other words, Islam calls for socially responsible businesses. In many ways, Islam expects firms to behave in a similar manner to consumers when it comes to using *rushd* to make sound judgments for society.

Islamic economists debate whether conventional firm behavior and profit maximization is a useful and allowable theoretical construct in Islamic economics. The general answer, due to reasons such as the predictive power of firm behavior theory, is yes. However, Islamic economists argue that some modifications are needed. In particular, the profit maximization postulate of conventional economics has been touted for the applicability of conventional economic theory in Islamic economics. Thus far, two views have emerged. The first view holds that the profit maximization postulate is a useful theoretical construct but has to be modified before it is applicable to a firm operating in an Islamic system. An example of this view was articulated by Metwally, who first modified the profit maximization objective by introducing "charity" as an additional element in the objective function.[14]

The second view, which will be the focus of our discussion, has two components. First, it argues that an Islamic economy operates on the basis of rules, derived from the Quran and *Sunnah*, which constitute its institutional and normative structure.[15] Once these rules are in place, positive theories of firm behavior, among other theoretical constructs, can yield valuable insights as guides to policy. Second, this view argues that the profit maximization postulate is an efficiency criterion, and, as such, it is

---

[12] Azid, Asutay, and Burki (2007).
[13] Ibid.
[14] Metwally (1981).
[15] Iqbal (1992), Junaid (1992), Mirakhor (2009), and Mirakhor and Askari (2010).

applicable to an Islamic economy, provided that the normative structure represented by the institutional framework, derived from the Quran and *Sunnah*, is in place.[16] This view has gained traction as Islamic economists over the past few decades have argued: "We cannot tame markets with the cane of legislation. Hence, firms cannot be forced to act morally in such a market. We need to transform the market into an ethicized market by means of endogenizing the moral elements in all socioeconomic menus, preferences, institutions and interactions."[17] In other words, if the institutional structure is in place and the rules are internalized, positive theory can and will serve useful purposes.

Hasan argues that while the profit maximization postulate has been heavily criticized even in conventional economics, it continues to survive because, without it, the process of price formation in different markets and under different conditions would be difficult to explain, and because no other theoretical construct having the same degree of explanatory and predictive power has been offered as its replacement.[18] Hasan asserts that theoretical constructs such as profit maximization "constitute minimal tools needed to explain and investigate economic phenomena to help formulate theories with predictive ability needed to guide economic policy."[19]

Risk and Profit-Sharing Feature

Though Hasan acknowledges the power of the profit maximization postulate, he introduces the notion of profit sharing as part of the second view as an important additional element of the theory.[20] It can be argued that compliance with the rules prescribed by the Quran and *Sunnah* will ensure that in the long run there is no excess profit, as a firm in an Islamic economy is perceived "as a cooperative-competitive organization."[21] The term "cooperative" derives from the direct imperative of the Quran that commands cooperation while "competitive" derives from the necessity of efficiency in use of resources and their preservation.[22] It is argued that conditions specified for markets in an Islamic economy yield results that mimic those of perfect competition.[23]

---

[16] Iqbal (1992) and Junain (1992).
[17] Azid et al. (2007).
[18] Hasan (2011).
[19] Ibid.
[20] Sugema, Bakhtiar, and Effendi (2010).
[21] Azid et al. (2007).
[22] Ibid.
[23] Islahi (1982) and Islahi (1986).

If that is the case, then straightforward application of profit maximization leads to allocative efficiency, at least in the long run. However, in the case of excess profits, the notion of profit sharing would act as a means to maintain a very important principle between factors of production: *justice*.

How did the profit-sharing construct become an important element in an Islamic economy? In conventional economics, it was not until the 1970s that concerns with economic and social justice found their clear theoretical expression and gained the attention of economists.[24] To date, however, no operational propositions have resulted from the justice criteria developed in the substantial and growing literature on socioeconomic justice. In Islam, however, the criterion of justice and conditions under which it obtains are *ex ante*, simple and operational. The criterion contains two principles, each of which can be stated as the corollary of the other. The first is positioning all things in their rightful place. The second principle is giving each their rightful due. Both conditions would be met and justice will be obtained if and when the economy and its participants become compliant with rules prescribed by the Quran and the *Sunnah* of the Messenger (sawa). The second principle is perhaps what prompts Hasan,[25] Sugema, Bakhtiar, and Effendi,[26] and others to suggest that when applied to firm behavior, justice is served when each factor of production receives the value of its marginal product. This objective, these scholars suggest, is best achieved through profit sharing. This proposition is employed later in the chapter to derive a sharing rule that potentially can ensure both allocative efficiency and equity as understood from the second principle of justice.

The principle of profit sharing has attracted attention in the conventional theory of the firm since the 1970s. Much of this literature deals with the question of how best to elicit the maximum productivity from labor given that, it is argued, hired labor on fixed wages has an incentive to shirk working hard. A good part of this literature, therefore, is focused on the search for "incentive-compatible" labor contracts. Some form of profit sharing, in addition to fixed wages, is incorporated in the theories of "incentive compatibility." Because, it is asserted, "it is the separation of ownership and labor that creates the characteristic motivation problem of the capitalist enterprise" that profit sharing "will be incentive compatible." Theoretical research in the 1980s and 1990s on this issue concluded that "the problem of eliciting effort from workers may be fundamentally transformed by profit sharing."[27] The theory suggested, moreover, that a

---

[24]See, for example, Buchanan (1984), Nozick (1974), Rawls (1971), and Sen (2009).
[25]Hasan (1992).
[26]Sugema, Bakhtiar, and Effendi (2010).
[27]Putterman (1993).

possible incentive-compatible contract would be a linear combination of fixed wages and a share of the profit of the firm.[28]

More important, empirical research on actual profit-sharing arrangements in place in market capitalism suggests that favorable incentive effects accrue to firms that implement these arrangements. Hasan suggests, "Islam would prefer the whole value product minus depreciation and a minimum maintenance wage as profit to be shared between labor and capital on some agreed equitable basis."[29] It can be shown that, even with market imperfections assumed in models suggested by Hasan and by Bendjiali and Tahir, allocative efficiency with equity is possible without the necessity of adding anything, such as a minimum wage, to the neoclassical profit maximization other than requiring that all of the profit is shared between labor and capital.[30]

As noted earlier, an Islamic economy is a rules-based system defined by an institutional structure—a network of rules of behavior. It is argued that compliance with these rules results in efficient and equitable outcome.[31] In particular, production will be efficient because it is subject to the binding rules that induce economizing in producer behavior (in addition to the usual cost-saving behavior that is part and parcel of theory of the firm).[32] Furthermore, equity will be obtained because the principle of justice requires each factor to receive the full value of its contribution to production, and the profit-sharing arrangement ensures that excess profit is shared between factors of production. These results would imply that efficiency and equity criteria require that the firm operate on its production function, that the marginal rate of substitution among factor inputs equal the ratio of their prices, and that there be no excess profit.

A case can be made that this efficiency-equity result is a logical consequence of rule compliance that leads to the satisfaction of perfectly

---

[28] Weitzman (1984, 1986) and Weitzman and Kruse (1990).

[29] Hasan (1992, p. 240).

[30] Ibid., p. 248 and Bendjilali and Taher (1990).

[31] Hasan (1992).

[32] Such as no waste (*israf*), no destruction (*itlaf*), and no opulence (*itraf*). Note that these binding rules modify the conventional notion of "economic efficiency." The price of a product plays an important role in the conventional conception of economic efficiency. While this would also find application in a theory of the firm in an Islamic economy, practical implementation subject to the binding rules of no waste, no destruction, and no opulence render the results different in the two systems. For example, a dairy farmer in the conventional system may find it economically efficient to destroy an excess supply of milk because the price is too low. Similarly, cattlemen may destroy a herd because beef prices are too low. Such practices are not permissible in an Islamic economy.

competitive conditions. However, a more interesting case would be to demonstrate these results in the case where there is market imperfection, as is assumed by Bendjiali and Tahir.[33] This is illustrated later in this chapter.

DYNAMICS OF DEMAND AND SUPPLY

Demand captures a consumer's desire and ability to pay a price for a good or service. The demand for a good or service is made up of the demand of each individual consumer who made the choice to consume the good or service as part of maximizing its utility. All goods and services have their own special attributes that determine people's willingness and ability to consume. For example, when estimating how many tons of rice people will buy this year, there are many variables to consider. One major variable is price.

Before introducing the relationship between price and demand, it helps to state up front the law of demand: The law of demand holds that, for goods and services, a higher price leads to a reduction in the quantity demanded while a lower price leads to an increase in the quantity demanded.

The quantity demanded of a good or service is the quantity buyers are able and willing to buy at a particular price during a particular period, *ceteris paribus*. The law of demand is considered a law because of the results of countless studies that support it. A change in price causes a movement along the demand curve, which is a change in quantity demanded due to change in price. Figure 5.2 is a demand curve along with its demand schedule to illustrate the relationship between demand and price. Demand curves represent the total demand for a good or service.

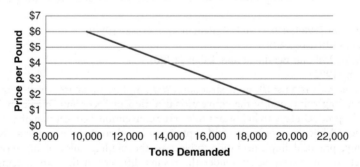

FIGURE 5.2 Demand Curve for Rice

---

[33] Bendjiali and Tahir, "Zero Efficiency Loss Monopolist."

When dealing with the relationship between price and demand, it is important to assume all else—especially income and the price of complementary and competitive goods—remained unchanged. However, in reality, price is not the only variable that determines the quantity of a good or service demanded. Other independent variables that are determinants of demand are income, consumer preferences, price of complementary and competitive goods and services, and buyer expectations. For example, as income rises, a person's consumption of many goods and services increases, thus increasing the quantity demanded. Changes in preferences can increase or decrease the demand of goods and services. Changes in prices of related goods and services (substitutes) can drive consumers toward or away from particular goods and services. Demographic changes, such as a declining birth rate, can decrease the demand for tutors and school supplies. If buyers expect the price of corn to increase in the future, the demand for corn in the current period would increase. When a change in one of these variables (such as income) increases demand, the demand curve shifts to the right, and vice versa.

Supply is the amount of a good that producers are willing to produce and sell at a particular price at a given time. The total supply of a good or service is the sum of the outputs of individual businesses that used the marginal decision rule to produce the good or service to maximize profits. What determines the quantity of goods or services firms are willing to produce? As was the case with demand, price is an important factor. In general, when there are many sellers, an increase in price results in an increase in quantity supplied, *ceteris paribus*. Though there are exceptions to this rule, this is often referred to as the law of supply. A change in price causes a movement along the supply curve, which is a change in quantity supplied due to a change in price. Figure 5.3 is an example of a supply curve along with its supply schedule. Supply curves include all the sellers of a good or service.

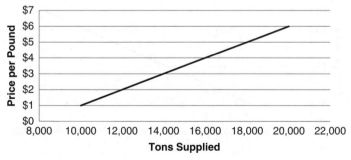

FIGURE 5.3 Supply Curve for Rice

As with demand, variables aside from price affect the willingness of sellers to supply a good or service. Variables that can change the quantity of a good supplied are the cost of production, returns from alternative activities, seller expectations, technology, natural events, and the number of sellers. For example, if the costs of producing rice rise, the quantity of rice supplied for a given price would decrease. When the return from producing other goods, such as tea, rises, it reduces the quantity of rice supplied. If oil producers expect the price of oil to rise in the future, the quantity supplied in the current period will decrease as they expect higher profits in the future. As technology improves, the cost of production decreases, which increases quantity supplied of a good or service. Natural events, such as droughts and storms, affect agricultural production and decrease the supply of agricultural goods. When the number of sellers of a good or service increases, the quantity supplied also increases. When a change in one of these variables increases the quantity supplied, the supply curve shifts to the right, and when a change in variable decreases the quantity supplied, the supply curve shifts to the left.

Equilibrium

How do we explain the market price and the quantity of a good produced? Though the interplay between the different variables that affect the quantities demanded and supplied of a good is complicated, the logic of the demand and supply model is simple. When the two curves are put together, we are able to find a price and a quantity at which the buyers and sellers are willing to settle. Figure 5.4 is a combination of both the demand and supply curves that together determine the equilibrium of price and quantity.

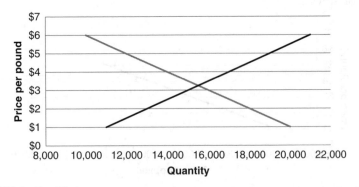

FIGURE 5.4 Equilibrium

Thus, a change in one of the variables that shift the supply and demand curves will change the equilibrium price and the quantity demanded and supplied of the good. An increase in demand shifts the demand curve to the right, which raises the equilibrium price, while a decrease in demand will have the opposite effect. An increase in supply shifts the supply curve to the right, which lowers the price, while a decrease in supply has an opposite effect. These are intuitive effects.

Role of Markets

Markets are where (though not necessarily a physical place) parties engage in exchange, where sellers offer their goods at a price to consumers. Adam Smith wrote:

> *He [an economic actor] generally, indeed, neither intends to promote the public interest, nor knows how much he is promoting it. By preferring the support of domestic to that of foreign industry, he intends only his own security; and by directing that industry in such a manner as its produce may be of the greatest value, he intends only his own gain, and he is in this, as in many other cases, led by an invisible hand to promote an end which was no part of his intention. Nor is it always the worse for the society that it was no part of it. By pursuing his own interest he frequently promotes that of the society more effectually than when he really intends to promote it. I have never known much good done by those who affected to trade for the public good. It is an affectation, indeed, not very common among merchants, and very few words need be employed in dissuading them from it.*[34]

Smith's idea was simple yet powerful: When individuals selfishly pursue their own interests to maximize their own net benefit, they unknowingly maximize society's net benefits with the help of the "invisible hand" that allocates resources to their best uses is the marketplace. When the allocation of resources is such that net benefits of all activities are maximized, economists say the allocation of resources is efficient. In simple terms, efficiency is when the maximum possible trades are made that make both parties better off. Sellers sell because they make a profit. Consumers consume because they gain utility worth more (consumer surplus) than their expenditures under perfect competition. For efficiency to be achieved, two conditions are required: The market must be competitive and must have transferable property rights.

---

[34]Smith (1776).

The Islamic economic system is a market-based system. But in contrast to some visions of market-based systems, free and unfettered markets are not conceived as an ideology but are instead embraced as an instrument for *efficient* resource allocation.

EFFICIENCY VERSUS EQUITY

In a free market that satisfies the efficiency condition, how is equity preserved? For example, if consumers indeed behave rationally and according to the marginal benefit rule, then the market will efficiently allocate a larger share of production to consumers with larger incomes. Is this fair? This is considered a normative judgment in neoclassical economics and leads to a debate of efficiency versus equity. Regardless of society's judgment, an efficient allocation of resources is preferred to an inefficient one. An efficient allocation maximizes net benefits, and these gains in net benefits could then be distributed in a way that leaves everyone better off than they would have been in an inefficient allocation. If something is unfair, it is not a result of efficient allocation of resources. Instead, it must be from the distribution of income, or in other words from distributive justice.

Islamic thinking is a total shift in paradigm, enabling us to move away from the abstract mainstream definition of efficiency and equity to a more down-to-earth definition in conformity with normative goals.[35] An economy may be classified as having attained optimum efficiency if it has employed the total potential of its scarce human and material resources to produce the maximum feasible quantity of need-satisfying goods and services with a reasonable degree of economic stability and a sustainable rate of future growth. An economy may be said to have attained optimum equity if the goods and services produced are distributed in such a way that the needs of all individuals are adequately satisfied and there is an equitable distribution of income and wealth, without adversely affecting work incentives, savings, investment, and enterprise activities.[36]

Some Islamic economists argue that, even according to the mainstream definition of efficiency and equity, the tension between efficiency and equity can be relieved. A compelling case can be made that this efficiency-equity result is a logical consequence of rule compliance that leads to perfectly competitive conditions being satisfied. However, a more interesting case

---

[35]Chapra (1992, p. 3).
[36]Ibid., p. 31.

would be to demonstrate these results in the case where there is market imperfection as assumed by Bendjiali and Tahir.[37]

MARKET MODELS

Market models vary greatly and span the spectrum from low to high level regarding market competitiveness. The most competitive model is the highly idealized form of competition called "perfect" by economists. It is this model that is assumed to achieve an efficient allocation of resources. The central characteristic of the model is that both buyers and sellers take the price as determined by the market through the interaction of demand and supply. No one firm and no one buyer can affect the equilibrium price. The assumptions of the model are that there are a large number of firms producing identical products, a large number of buyers, easy entry and exit, and complete information about prices in the market. In the short run, firms maximize profits by producing an output level at which marginal revenue equals marginal cost. In the long run, if firms are earning an economic profit, it is assumed that other firms will enter the market and will drive the price down until economic profit achieves long-run equilibrium of zero. If firms are suffering economic losses, firms will exit, which drives prices up.

At the other extreme, the least competitive model is the monopoly, where an industry is composed of a single firm and the price of entry for new firms is prohibitive. The firm in this model chooses a price and output to maximize profits, earning monopoly profits. Sources of monopoly power include high sunk costs associated with entry (very large capital requirement), restricted ownership of key inputs, government restrictions (patents, licensing, etc.), and economies of scale. To maximize profit, a monopoly firm produces at the quantity at which marginal revenue equals marginal cost. A problem with monopolies, however, is that the firm produces an output that is less than the efficient level and charges a higher price in comparison to a perfectly competitive firm. As a result, an equity issue is generated: The higher price reduces consumer surplus in comparison to the perfect market model, and the difference is transferred to the monopolist. Monopolies are typically regulated to prevent inequity and high prices.

In reality, all economies operate between the idealized extremes of perfect competition and monopoly. This situation is referred to as imperfect competition, where there are a number of sellers and at least one seller has some degree of market power. There are two types of imperfect competitive

---

[37]Bendjiali and Tahir (1990).

markets: monopolistic competition and oligopoly. Monopolistic competition is characterized by a number of firms producing similar but differentiated products in a market with easy entry and exit. Few firms dominating an industry and producing either standardized or differentiated products characterize oligopolies. There may also be substantial barriers to entry and exit in oligopolies. Strategic decision making is important for oligopolists to determine the best output and pricing strategies.

An important class of literature specifies appropriate binding rules for the operation of markets in an Islamic economy. While predating development of conventional economics by centuries, this economy resembles the defined characteristics of perfect competition. For example, Islahi, writing on the "economic concepts" of Ibn Taymiah, suggests that the latter, based on his understanding of the Quran and *Sunnah*, "had at least some of the conditions of perfect competition in mind" when expressing his views on the functioning of the market and "had a clear conception of a well-behaved, orderly market, in which knowledge, honesty and fair play, and freedom of choice were the essential elements."[38] The implication is that if there is rule compliance in an economy, results similar, and potentially even more beneficial, to those achieved in the ideal model of a perfectly competitive economy will be obtained.[39]

Given that markets in an Islamic economy mimic perfect competition, the profit maximization postulate can be applied directly to determine necessary and sufficient conditions for allocative efficiency. Under perfect competition, the distribution rule requires that each factor receives the value of its marginal product, a result that converges to the concept derived from the Islamic principle of justice, namely that each factor of production receives its just due. Benjiali and Tahir raise another interesting question under conditions similar to perfect competition: Is there any loss of efficiency if markets are not perfect.[40] Specifically, they consider the case of a monopoly operating in an Islamic economy.

Bendjiali and Tahir address the question of whether in an Islamic economy the operations of a rule-compliant firm with monopoly power result in loss of efficiency in resource allocation. Their answer is that it need not.[41] They suggest three things:

[38]Islahi (1982), Islahi (1986), Chapra (2010), and Siddiqi (2010, pp. 15–17).
[39]Mirakhor and Askari (2010).
[40]Benjiali and Tahir (1990).
[41]Bendjiali and Tahir (1990) assume that the Muslim entrepreneur maximizes utility as a function of profit and social welfare. They assume social welfare is "a function of the firm's output" but social welfare enters the utility function in a functional form only directly as output. Since profit as the other argument of the utility function is also dependent on output, utility becomes a function of output.

1. Profit maximization as an efficiency criterion is useful in an Islamic economy.
2. Profit maximization does not mean a sacrifice of equity.
3. These assertions hold even if there are market imperfections.

In conventional economics, more often than not, it is thought that there is a trade-off between equity and efficiency. Market imperfections, it is argued, exacerbate the trade-off. While it can be demonstrated that in a rule-compliant Islamic economy without market imperfections both efficiency and equity are achieved, we address a more challenging issue. Following Bendjiali and Tahir, it can be demonstrated that even in case of a monopoly, allocation efficiency with equity is possible provided that the monopolist is rule compliant.

Realistically, even in a fully rule-compliant Islamic economy, existence of factors that can lead to monopoly power cannot be ruled out. These factors include technological ones, innovation, economies of scale, and external economies (location and economics of agglomeration), among others. The question is: How will a rule-compliant firm with monopoly power behave to ensure that both allocative efficiency and equity criteria are satisfied? The next theoretical construct provides a tentative answer to this question by assuming that a firm produces an output (Q) with two inputs, labor (L) and capital (K). It hires labor at the wage rate (w) prevailing in the rule-compliant market. It raises capital through an *ex ante* (before production and sale of output Q) profit-loss-sharing arrangement. The funds thus raised and the amount of capital purchased with these funds give the price per unit of capital (r). Being rule compliant regarding distribution, the firm knows that all profits must be distributed among factor inputs, including entrepreneurial effort subsumed under one or the other inputs.

There are three possible cases during the postproduction and sale of output:[42]

1. Profits are exhausted by payments to inputs as agreed in the preproduction phase, $\pi = w\text{L} + r\text{K}$
   where

   π = profit of the firm

2. There are losses: $\pi < w\text{L} + r\text{K}$. In this case, the loss is shared among the equity holders based on preproduction profit-loss sharing arrangements.
3. There are excess profits: $\pi > w\text{L} + r\text{K}$.

---

[42] For complete derivation of the model, see Mirakhor (1992).

The focus is on the third case, as the other two pose no particular challenge. Specifically, we ask: Is there a rule that a firm can follow in distributing excess profits that ensures allocative efficiency and equity? It is envisioned that there are two sets of factor prices: r and w in the preproduction and sale phase, and $\hat{r}$ and $\hat{w}$ in the postproduction and sale phase, respectively. The production function of the firm is assumed to be $Q = f(L, K)$. $L, K, \frac{\partial f}{\partial L}, \frac{\partial f}{\partial K} > 0$. The firm's demand function is given by $p = P(Q)$ and its revenue function (concave) is $R(Q) = P(Q)Q$. Its cost function is $C(L, K) = wL + rK$. The firm's profit function is thus $\pi(Q, L, K) = P(Q)Q - (wL + rK)$. While the firm is committed to distribute all profits among factor inputs, capital (equity) has a prior claim arising from the preproduction profit-loss-sharing arrangement. Therefore, if there is any excess profit, capital has a prior claim to a share. The firm then operates under the constraint that:

$$p(Q)Q - \hat{w}L - rK \leq 0 \qquad (5.8)$$

In the preproduction phase, the funds available to the firm to pay labor are $P(Q)Q - rK$. However, if there are excess profits, the firm, based on its commitment to the rule of justice, knows that a share must be allotted to labor, thus ensuring that $w > \hat{w}$. Hence, the firm has an additional constraint that:

$$P(Q)Q - rK \leq wL \qquad (5.9)$$

Subtracting wL from both sides of this constraint and taking all terms to the left-hand side yields

$$\pi(Q, L, K) - (w - w)L \leq 0 \qquad (5.10)$$

The allocative efficiency issue arises because distributing more than a fair share to either input tilts resource allocation in favor of that input in violation of justice and the no-waste rule (i.e., more of that input will be used than necessary). What is needed is a distribution rule that ensures justice and allocative efficiency; that is, the right amounts of inputs are used in production. To search for such a rule, the next problem can be formulated:

$$\text{Maximize } \pi(Q, L, K) = P(Q)Q - (rK + wL) \qquad (5.11)$$

Subject to the constraints that:

$$Q - f(L, K) \leq 0 \qquad (5.12)$$

$$\pi(Q, L, K) - (r - r)K \leq 0 \qquad (5.13)$$

$$\pi(Q, L, K) - (w - w)L \leq 0 \qquad (5.14)$$

With this formulation, the constrained optimization problem can be solved to arrive at simple rules governing distribution. As is demonstrated in Mirakhor, the rule requires $\frac{\hat{r}}{r} = \frac{\hat{w}}{w}$, meaning that so long as the firm distributes profits such that this equation is satisfied, equity and allocative efficiency are ensured.[43]

ROLE OF THE STATE

Some believe that when governments intervene, markets are prevented from achieving equilibrium and maximum efficiency. However, government intervention plays an important role when markets fail, there are monopolies, and firms collude to abuse their market power. In these cases, regulations and enforcement are required to achieve socially desired goals.

Antitrust policies, designed to prevent oligopolistic collusion and excessive market power, assess how firm behavior and market structures affect social welfare and the public interest. The rule of reason guides most antitrust policies today in the United States, as many laws are left open for interpretation. There is considerable debate concerning the appropriate reasoning in specific cases.

There are different schools of thought when it comes to regulation. Often the differences in opinion between the schools of thought lie in whether there should be more or less regulation. For example, one group believes that regulation serves the public interest and should be increased. Another group believes that the regulated firms are always ahead of the regulators and that the regulation is fruitless. Though it may seem obvious that governments are needed to regulate industries to protect consumers, some industries have seen improvements in consumer welfare from deregulation, such as airlines and natural gas. Examples of federal regulatory agencies in the United States include the Securities and Exchange Commission, which regulates the securities markets, and the Food and Drug Administration, which regulates food and drug products.

Establishing a comprehensive socioeconomic restructuring to incorporate desired Islamic goals and minimize existing imbalances may not be

---

[43] Mirakhor (1992).

possible without the intervention of the state.[44] This is because, even in an environment where values have been endogenized, it still may be possible for individuals to be simply unaware of the urgent and unsatisfied needs of others or be oblivious to the problems of scarcity and compromised social priorities. The Islamic state may therefore have to play a significant role in the economy. It may have to go beyond the generally recognized roles of providing internal and external security, removing market imperfections and failures, and devising comprehensive rules and regulations and monitoring their supervision. It may have to help create a proper environment for removing injustice in all its different forms and for realizing society's normative goals. This may have to be done without resorting to regimentation and the use of force or to owning and operating a substantial part of the economy. The state may have to determine social priorities in the use of resources and to educate, motivate, and help the private sector to play a role that is consistent with goal realization. It may accomplish this by inculcating moral values among individuals; by accelerating social, institutional, and political reforms; and by providing incentives and facilities. It may have to create a proper framework for the interaction of human beings, values, institutions, and markets for the realization of goals. In the end, it is preferable that rule compliance and enforcement come from individuals and not through state intervention.

The role of the state in an Islamic economy is not one of intervention, which is an unsavory term and smacks of an underlying commitment to laissez-faire capitalism. It is also not in the nature of the secularist welfare state, which, through its dislike of value judgments, accentuates claims on resources and leads to macroeconomic imbalances. It is also not in the form of collectivization and regimentation, which suppresses freedom and saps individual initiative and enterprise. It is, rather, a positive role: a moral obligation to perform a mission in compliance with *Shariah* to preserve and promote morality and justice in all economic decisions, keep the economic train on the agreed track, and prevent its diversion by powerful vested interests. The test of the Islamic state would be its performance in upholding the desired principles in a way that allows maximum possible freedom and initiative for the private sector. The greater the motivation people have in implementing Islamic values and the more effective socioeconomic institutions and financial intermediation are in creating the proper environment for a just equilibrium between resources and claims, the lesser will be the role of the state. Moreover, the greater the accountability of the political leadership to the people, and the greater the freedom of expression and the success of the news media and the courts in exposing and penalizing inequities and

---

[44]Chapra (2007, p. 30).

corruption, the more effective the Islamic state may be in fulfilling its obligations.[45]

SUMMARY

The study of microeconomics is crucial for any economic system. Regardless of the fact that normative goals in both Islamic and conventional macro-economic systems are in general agreement, without a sound microeconomic foundation, these goals cannot be achieved. It is clear that problems such as poverty and obscene income disparity have not been solved in even the richest economies. The unrealistic assumptions of the conventional economic model and its distaste for value judgments have failed to achieve the well-being of all. It is for these reasons that conventional microeconomics needs serious reformulation.

Islamic economics is a rule-based system based on *Shariah* and has an alternate worldview to that of conventional economics. At the center of Islamic economics is socioeconomic justice, which makes the study of concepts more goal oriented than in conventional economics. Islamic economics argues that values are necessary and must be considered and that they are instrumental in achieving the *maqasid*. Though its precise formulation is still nascent, Islamic economics has already made valuable contributions to microeconomic thought and has provided alternate ways of thinking about the goals and behavior of the ideal consumer and firm.

According to Chapra, four steps are needed to complete the study of Islamic economics on a theoretical level to a point where it can be operationalized:

1. Study the actual behavior of individuals, groups, firms, markets, and governments.
2. Define the ideal behavior needed for goal realization.
3. Identify the reasons for the divergence of actual and desired behavior.
4. Suggest measures to bridge the gap between the actual and desired behavior in order to translate *maqasid* into a reality.[46]

In an Islamic system, microeconomics can be modeled by changing human and firm behavior to comply with Islamic principles of justice, sharing, awarding factors of production their just reward, and so on, or by imposing a number of constraints to human and firm behavior that reflect

---

[45]Chapra (2007, p. 30).
[46]Ibid., p. 33.

Islamic requirements. In the next chapter, we turn to key macroeconomic concepts in both Islamic and conventional economics.

KEY TERMS

Consumer behavior	Utility maximization
Theory of the firm	Risk and profit sharing
What, how, for whom	Supply
Production possibility frontier	Demand
Decisions at the margin	Market equilibrium
Needs versus wants	Efficiency versus equity

QUESTIONS

1. Define "demand curve." What is the law of downward-sloping demand? Why is there an inverse relationship between P and Q?

2. Define "supply curve." Show that an increase in supply means a shift in the curve. What is the difference between this and an upward shift in the demand schedule?

3. What is the difference between a movement along the demand cure and a shift of the demand curve?

4. What factors determine the demand for rice in the conventional system? What additional factors come into play in the Islamic system?

5. What factors determine the supply of rice in the conventional system? What additional factors come into play in the Islamic system?

6. Describe why the equilibrium price settles at the intersection of the supply and demand curves (and movements away from equilibrium lead to a return to equilibrium)?

7. Why is a stable equilibrium important in any market?

CHAPTER **6**

Key Macroeconomics Concepts

Learning objectives:

1. *How economic output is measured.*
2. *Why economic output from the depletion of natural resources is not the same as other output of goods.*
3. *How economic output is determined.*
4. *Determinants of consumption and investment functions.*
5. *What unemployment and inflation are.*
6. *Why there is unemployment and inflation.*
7. *Impact of government expenditures and taxes on economic activity, employment, and national debt.*
8. *Why countries trade and the role of exchange rates.*
9. *Why government policies have an important role in achieving full employment and stable prices.*

Macroeconomics is focused on the overall, or aggregate, economic performance of a city, a region, a country, or a group of countries such as the European Union, all Muslim countries, or the countries of the Middle East and North Africa. Why do some countries have a high level of income relative to other countries? Why are some countries rich while others are poor? Why do some countries exhibit fast economic growth and others do not? What causes recessions and depressions? Why do some countries have to suffer from high unemployment and poverty? What are the reasons for inflation? What determines national income and consumption, savings, investment, and trade balance? Macroeconomists collect data, build macroeconomic models to explain aggregate economic conditions such as those just listed, make predictions, and recommend policies to governments. Policy makers use the output of macroeconomic models to assess current policies and to formulate and suggest appropriate economic policies to remedy adverse developments. Governments around the world use macroeconomic data to design and evaluate long-term programs, as do international organizations, such as the United Nations, to compare economic performance and needs of nations around the world.

In the earlier chapters, we have tried to convey how and in what ways Islamic economics is different from conventional or Western economics. The Islamic system is a market-based system, but it is not a pure capitalist or socialist economic system. While Western economists treat capitalist and socialist economic systems as polar opposites, they are but two sides of the same coin. Although it is evident that scarcity is the core question of all economic systems, we have tried to explain that, in Islam, scarcity should be a major issue only at the country, state, or local level. At the world level, there should be no scarcity in the Islamic paradigm as long as humans work hard, share, and avoid opulence. Allah (swt) designed and created the world with sufficient resources *if* humans limited their wants, shared His bounty, and managed their society's economy (macroeconomy) efficiently and in line with the Islamic vision. The perceived burden of scarcity is a test for all humans to develop their spiritual dimension. In other words, while capitalist and socialist systems are solely focused on the materialistic side of things, the Islamic market-based system also incorporates spiritual and moral dimensions of life (including a fair market system) and stresses the importance of the life to come.

PRINCIPAL ECONOMIC AGENTS

In every economic system, four distinct and principal groups interact at the macro level: households, firms, government, and the foreign sector. All macroeconomic activities fall into one of these four groups:

1. **Households** own the factors of production, such as land, labor, and capital. Households sell these factors to firms, to the government, and to foreigners to earn income. They exchange labor and capital for wages, profits, and rents. Households use their income to pay tax to the government, to consume goods and services, and to save. (In an Islamic economy, there are no debt instruments that carry a fixed and predetermined rate of interest.)

2. **Firms** employ the factors of production and produce and sell goods (in an Islamic economy, excluding pork and other forbidden foods, alcohol, drugs, and, more generally, any goods that are harmful to humans and to society) and services (excluding interest-bearing financial assets,

gambling, sex trade, and any services harmful to humans and to society). Firms' earnings are derived from selling permitted goods and services to households, to other firms, to governments, and to foreigners. In the process firms make investments in their line of activity and earn profits for their stockholders and pay dividends (share their profits) and taxes.

3. **Governments** collect taxes (and may have other income, such as royalties) to provide government services for households and firms, which include national defense, physical and social infrastructure (including the legal system and regulatory and supervisory administration of markets, businesses, and a number of other institutions), public education, health services (in order to afford equal opportunities for all members of society to succeed in their lives in an Islamic economy), supervision and corrections of excessive income and wealth inequality, and a number of essential social programs. (See Chapter 13.)

4. **Foreign countries** buy (import) and sell (export) goods and services and make equity investments in other countries or afford investment opportunities.

If an economy has no relations with other countries, it is called a *closed economy*, while if it trades or borrows from other countries or invests in other countries it is called an *open economy*. In this chapter, we begin by considering a closed economy, and add the possibility of trade and capital flows later. We begin by discussing these principal concepts: national income, consumption/saving, investment, national income determination, inflation, unemployment, national income and output determination, and trade, capital flows, and open economies.

NATIONAL INCOME

A popular index and method for measuring the value of the economic activity is the *gross domestic product* (GDP). The idea behind GDP is to present aggregate economic activity of all groups (households, firms, government, and foreigners) in a single number for a given period of time. GDP, or more correctly a sister measure called net national product (NNP), essentially measures the largest level of sustainable aggregate consumption (called the "golden rule" in economics) without considering distribution of consumption among the members of society. Some may have vast incomes while others may not even have enough to eat. There are two ways to view GDP. One is as total income of everyone in the economy; and the other is as total expenditures on goods and services. The reason that GDP can show both the economy's income and expenditures is because every transaction in the economy has a buyer and a seller. What consumers spend on goods and services is income for the sellers. As a result, GDP shows the *national income* and expenditures on goods and services.

There is little correlation of GDP or GDP/capita to human happiness or welfare. The conventional GDP measure falls short on many counts. Externalities are excluded; if pollution from a factory ruins the air we breathe, the pollution is not included as a negative contribution to economic output. This issue is especially important in Islam because the Creator has given the world and all that is in it to all humans of all generations; the rights of all future generations must be protected. In the same vein, conventionally measured GDP does not account for the fact that the production of a depletable natural resource (oil, gas, coal, etc.) is not comparable to the production of goods from a sustainable base (corn, wheat, and other agricultural products, and most other goods) and services. If a country's total output is oil, then with the depletion of oil, its GDP goes to zero. Thus depletable resources have to be accounted for in a different way in GDP, especially for countries that rely heavily on depletable resources and for Muslim countries because such resources receive special treatment because they belong equally to all humans of all generations. This means that depletable resources are a part of the society's stock of capital. Their depletion must be accompanied by creation of alternate capital of equal value. But the conventional measure of GDP values a dollar of oil output the same as a dollar of wheat.

Thus three adjustments must be made to conventional GDP to derive Islamic GDP (IGDP).

1. All prohibited goods and services must be excluded; these include drugs, alcohol, pork, certain fish, gambling, prostitution, all activities that are vulgar, all activities that are based on fixed and predetermined interest rates, and all activities that are deemed illegal by society and cause harm.
2. All negative externalities (pollution, environmental degradation, etc.) must be assessed and subtracted from GDP to get IGDP. (Extensive data collection is required before this can be implemented in the Islamic system.) When these fallouts (negative externalities) are remedied, then improvement can be included in IGDP.
3. The value of the production of any depletable resources cannot just be included in IGDP (like other goods that come from a sustainable base), as is the current practice in conventional GDP derivation. Depletable resources are the Almighty's gifts to humans of all generations. Their depletion cannot be considered contributions to economic output. This issue requires further explanation, as it is very important for assessing the GDP of a number of Muslim countries, especially those that depend heavily on oil and natural gas output.

In economies that do not rely heavily on a depletable resource, such as oil, economic output, or NNP, does not diminish with time but normally can be expected to increase with time. In an oil-based economy, if the income from oil is consumed (and, as is the practice, if oil output is counted as a part of NNP), then NNP declines as oil reserves are depleted. So at least a part of current oil revenues must be saved and invested, domestically or abroad, to even out NNP and avoid a decline in national output in the future.[1] Put differently, the normally or conventionally measured NNP in an oil-producing country diverges from the "theoretically correct" measure of NNP for a country that has no depleting resource such as oil. In a sense the conventionally measured NNP for a depletable resource-based economy usually overstates theoretically correct NNP because at some point in the future, the depletable resource will run out and will no longer contribute to NNP.[2] The ratio of conventionally measured NNP to "theoretically correct NNP" (for a country whose total output is based on depletable resources) is:

$$Y/Y^* = 1/RT \tag{6.1}$$

where

  Y = conventionally measured NNP
  Y^* = theoretically correct NNP
  R = real rate of return on investment
  T = life of oil reserves (in years)

The result is intuitive. The higher the return on investments (i.e., the more compensation made for resource depletion) and the higher the T (i.e., the longer the resource will last at the current rate of extraction), the closer (more comparable) the conventionally measured and theoretically correct NNP.

---

[1] The conceptual interpretation of NNP in an economy is that it represents the highest level of sustainable consumption. In the development of the conceptual framework of national income accounting, extractive industries were treated as any other source of national product. As a result, the value of the extracted resource was added to the national product at the point of extraction. This method of valuing the contribution of extractive industries, as is now widely recognized, is ill conceived and results in significant distortions. For the derivation of the required rate of savings, see Askari and Dastmialtsch (1990). For a calculation of the savings rate for individual oil-exporting countries, see Askari Nowshirvani and Jaber (1997).

[2] It is possible that conventionally measured NNP understates theoretically correct NNP for a country that has lots of oil and a low extraction rate (very high T) and a high R.

For a country where only a part of its output is based on natural resources:

$$Y/Y^* = (1 - P)1/RT + P \qquad (6.2)$$

where

P = proportion of national output that is not based on depletable
resources

An alternative way of looking at the problem is that depletable resource-based economies need a higher savings rate during the period that the depletable resource is contributing to the national output. The indicated savings rate (to compensate for oil depletion) is lower the higher the life of reserves (in the extreme, no savings from oil revenues are needed if oil revenues were to last forever), the higher the return on investments (if the rate of return were infinite, then a minuscule amount of savings would compensate for oil depletion), the lower the current generation's concern for future generations (if the current generation did not care if future generations starved, then there would be little need for savings), and the lower the share of oil in a country's aggregate NNP. In other words, if a country has many years of oil output, it has less to worry about in comparison to a country whose oil will soon run out. But if society cares for future generations, it is important to save and above all to make investments that count (namely, with a high rate of return) to afford future generations the same benefits that current generations derive from oil. This can be put into a simple equation. For an economy that is based 100% on depletable resources, the required savings rate to compensate for resource depletion is:[3]

$$S = 1 - RT(1 - S') \qquad (6.3)$$

where

S = required savings rate
S' = desired post-resource (when the resource is depleted) savings rate
R = real rate of return on investment
T = life of oil reserves in years

This result is for an economy that derives 100% of its NNP from oil. For such an economy, it is conceivable that today's indicated savings rate could even be negative. The reason for this seemingly perverse result is essentially this: Imagine a region or country that has many years of oil reserves left at

---

[3] Askari et al., *Economic Development in the Countries of the GCC*, pp. 12–15.

current depletion rates (such as Abu Dhabi, a part of the United Arab Emirates) and wants a modest savings rate when oil is projected to run out. Today it can afford even to dissave (negative saving). This result is clearly the exception and is not indicated when we account for the fact that, in reality for most countries, there is a significant percentage of non-oil NNP (see the adjusted equation next) and that countries want to have a high savings rate when oil runs out.

For an economy that is *not* 100% resource based, the equation is:

$$S = PS' + (1 - P)[1 - RT(1 - S')] \qquad (6.4)$$

These three changes must be made to GDP to derive IGDP; the only word of caution is the needed data for calculating negative externalities. But there is more. The GDP or IGDP index would be indifferent to two very different situations: one where nearly all of the national income accrues to one person and the rest of society lives in poverty, and the other where everyone had at least comparable incomes. In the GDP calculation, it is assumed that humans live to acquire material wealth and that the higher the GDP, the better off they are. In other words, GDP is the indicator of choice and captures everything that matters. In an Islamic economic system, we would ideally like to have a measure of an Islamic gross social product of goods and services (IGSP) as a measure of an economy's aggregate output of goods and services. But this may be technically beyond reach and also may present other problems in devising macroeconomic policies, as GDP is the focus of policies that governments adopt. We have very little data on all dimensions of individual happiness and well-being and on the interaction and impact of individual circumstances on society. Moreover, items such as income distribution and poverty cannot simply be added to the value of output of goods and services; GDP is a dollar figure whereas income distribution is some sort of an index.

Fundamentally, well-being means different things to different observers. When well-being is defined as spiritual and humanitarian goals as well as material goals, other values such as justice, brotherhood, peace, happiness, solidarity, importance of family, and so forth intentionally come into play. Umar Chapra writes:

> *One of the tests for the realization of these goals may be the extent to which social equality, need-fulfillment of all, full employment, equitable distribution of income and wealth, and economic stability have been attained without heavy debt-servicing burden, high rates of inflation, undue depletion of nonrenewable resources, or damage to the ecosystem in a way that endangers life on earth.*

*Another test may be the realization of family and social solidarity,
which would become reflected in the mutual care of members of the
society for each other, particularly the children, the aged, the sick,
and the vulnerable, and absence, or at least minimization, of
broken families, juvenile delinquency, crime, and social unrest.*[4]

In this sense, the scope of the Islamic economics would be wider than in
conventional economics and would include social, political, environmental,
and historical issues. In the other words, well-being in this approach needs a
more comprehensive framework than satisfying self-interest. Thus, different visions and definitions for well-being make for different approaches
toward policies, mechanisms, and methods that are used in an economic
system.

However, none of the predominant worldviews is either totally materialistic or totally humanitarian and spiritual. The emphasis they put on
material versus spiritual goals is significantly different. The different level
of emphasis on each of those goals might result in different economic policies.
Moreover, in conventional theory, well-being is treated as a positive rather
than a normative concept. This means that it is value neutral and is defined in
terms of unrestricted individual freedom. Neglect of material needs or
spiritual needs may destroy the true meaning of well-being and lead to
undesirable results. The Islamic worldview is not value neutral, secularist,
and materialist. Some concepts are at the heart of the Islamic economics. It
insists on moral values, human brotherhood, and socioeconomic justice. It
relies on the role values play, market, family, society, and state to provide for
the well-being of all. The core of Islamic belief is that the universe and
everything in it has been created by the One God, and all humans are equal
brothers and sisters to each other. There is no superiority because of race, sex,
nationality, wealth, or power. Also, life in this world is ephemeral, and the
ultimate destination is the Hereafter. Allah (swt) will judge who has fulfilled
their obligations toward others.

As we have discussed earlier, there is little evidence to connect GDP to
happiness and well-being.[5] A number of studies recommend including at least
the quality of life, social progress, and sustainable development in a refor-
mulated index of national output. Although a general agreement has not
emerged among nations for a better criterion to measure well-being, the
Organization of the Islamic Conference signed the Istanbul Declaration in
2007, which emphasizes the need to go beyond GDP, specifically to incorporate the spiritual needs of humans. But little progress has been made in this

---

[4]Chapra (2000, p. 4).
[5]Easterlin et al. (2011).

regard. Thus, the best that can be done is to develop the data for IGDP as modified from GDP and make the social issues (such as eradication of poverty, a more equal distribution of income, etc.) an absolute constraint on economic management.

GDP or IGDP is determined by the quantity of inputs that are called *factors of production* and by the ability to convert these inputs to outputs, which is commonly called the *production function*. Main production factors are labor, including human capital, and capital, including technology embodied in machines. Labor is the time people spend working, and capital is the machinery and equipment workers use. The production function describes how much output can be produced by a given amount of capital and labor. The factors of production and the production function determine the total output of goods and services and also represent national income. What households earn in wages and rents go into the national income. What firms pay for wages and rents are called *factor prices*. Hence, the factor price for workers is wages; for owners of capital, it is rent/real rate of return. The demand for each factor affects its price. Factor prices are one of the important determinants of income distribution. In sum, a firm's output needs two inputs: labor and capital. The production function can be written as:

$$Y = F(K, L) \qquad (6.5)$$

where

Y = production or firm's output
K = amount of capital
L = amount of labor

The firm sells outputs at price (P), pays wages (W) to workers, and pays rents (R) to capital's owners in a profit-loss-sharing mode of partnership. Households own labor and capital and are paid by firms for these inputs. The assumption that households own the capital input is a simplification, but it does not undermine our results because in the real world, firms own capital and households own the firms.

A couple of questions immediately come to mind: How much do firms produce in an economy? Who gets the income from production? How much of the income will go to workers and how much will go to capital owners? To answer these questions, initially we assume that firms face competition from other firms in the market; this means that one firm cannot set market prices as prices rise and fall in the market because there are many sellers. Also, a firm cannot set wage or rental rates for factors of production because households can sell their labor and capital to other firms that offer higher wages or rents.

We further assume that firms maximize their profits. The profit for firms can be defined as:

$$\text{Profit} = \text{Revenue} - \text{Labor costs} - \text{Capital costs}$$

$$= PY - WL - RK \tag{6.6}$$

Replace Y with F (K, L):

$$\text{Profit} = PF(K, L) - WL - RK$$

This equation shows that profit depends on the price and quantity of the output, factor prices, W and R, and the quantity of factors of production, L and K, used. In a perfectly competitive market, firms cannot determine price (P) and are in fact price takers so that firms have to choose the combination of capital and labor to maximize their profits. The productivities of the factors of production determine this combination.

The marginal product of labor and marginal product of capital explain the productivity of the capital and labor. *Marginal product of labor* (MPL) is defined as the additional amount of output that is gained as the result of employing one more unit of labor. If we assume the amount of capital is constant, adding one more unit of labor increases the firm's revenue by P × MPL, where P is the price of output and MPL is the extra output of labor by using one more unit of labor. Change in cost for adding one more unit of labor is the wage (W) that firms pay. The next equation shows the change in profit for the firm (note that the amount of capital used has not changed):

$$\text{Change in profit} = \text{Change in revenues} - \text{Change in cost}$$

$$= (P \times MPL) - W \tag{6.7}$$

According to the equation, when P × MPL exceeds the wage rate, the addition of an extra unit of labor is profitable. Therefore, a firm continues to employ labor until P × MPL equals what is paid as wage:

$$P \times MPL = W \tag{6.8}$$

We can write this equation in another format:

$$MPL = W/P \tag{6.9}$$

W/P is called real wage and shows that labor is paid in units of production rather than with money.

Similarly, *marginal product of capital* (MPK) is an additional amount of output as the result of employing one more unit of capital while keeping the amount of labor employed a constant. If we assume the amount of labor is constant, adding one more unit of capital results in an increase of the firm's revenue by $P \times MPK$, where P is the price of output and MPK is the additional output. Change in cost for adding one more capital is the rent (R) that firms pay. This equation shows the change in the firm's profit:

$$\text{Change in profit} = \text{Change in revenues} - \text{Change in cost}$$

$$= (P \times MPK) - R \qquad (6.10)$$

Accordingly, when $P \times MPK$ exceeds the rent, adding an extra unit of capital is profitable. Therefore, the firm continues to rent capital until $P \times MPK$ equals the rental rate on capital: $P \times MPK = R$.

We can write this equation in another format as:

$$MPK = R/P \qquad (6.11)$$

R/P is called real rental price of capital and shows what capital is paid in units of production rather than in money.

In sum, in maximizing profits, a competitive firm hires each factor of production until the factor's marginal product is equal to the real factor price. In other words, productivity of capital and labor (marginal products of capital and labor) determine the proportion of the economy's income that go to labor and capital.

While Islam endorses the market system just described (for affording incentives and enhancing efficiency), firms cannot simply have as their sole objective the maximizing of profits. They must provide good working conditions, supplement healthcare provisions, and pay a living wage to all workers. Moreover, there are postmarket considerations for individuals. After receiving profits and incomes, they must make religious contributions in the form of *zakat* and *khums* (a flat income tax), pay taxes to finance needed public expenditures (including social infrastructure, to correct for unequal opportunities and poverty that continue to exist), and make further contributions to correct for large inequalities of wealth and income.

CONSUMPTION, SAVINGS, INVESTMENT, AND NATIONAL INCOME DETERMINATION

Up to now, GDP has been discussed as the total output of goods and services and IGDP as the same total with three major adjustments for Islamic morality considerations and concern for the welfare of future generations. GDP/IGDP can be also interpreted as the allocation of goods and services among different uses. GDP (from here on, we use "GDP" to mean IGDP as well, unless stated otherwise) is divided into four main categories: consumption (C), investment (I), government purchases (G), and net exports (NX). GDP or total output is equal to sum of these four parts:

$$Y = C + I + G + NX \qquad (6.12)$$

Each unit of GDP, for example, each dollar, falls into one of these categories.

Consumption is the amount of goods and services purchased by households. Consumption normally is further divided into three subgroups: *nondurable goods*, *durable goods*, and *services*. Nondurables goods are goods that deplete after a short time, such as food and clothing. Durable goods are goods that last for a long time, such as cars and refrigerators. Services are produced by individuals or firms, such as teaching, haircuts, and financial products.

Investments are goods and services that are purchased to produce future output of goods and services. Investments are made in order to increase future output and provide a higher standard of living in the future. There are three types of investment spending. A person makes a *residential investment*, which includes a new house to live in or rent to others. Businesses make a *business fixed investment*, which includes the equipment and structures used in production, and they also place some goods in storage as an *inventory investment*, which includes materials, semiprepared goods, and finished goods.

Government purchases are goods and services acquired by the government. For example, governments buy guns, build roads and bridges, build schools, and hire teachers. Governments also provide a number of social programs, such as healthcare especially for the less fortunate, food for the poor, or payments to the elderly in the form of income transfers and education.

Net exports depend on trading with other countries. Net exports are exports minus imports. Exports are the value of goods and services sold to other countries. Imports are the value of goods and services that a country buys from the rest of the world.

The first three are components in a closed economy, and the fourth belongs to an open economy (an economy that has trade with other countries). Here, we assume a closed economy. Thus, the NX is zero and three components constitute GDP:

$$Y = C + I + G \qquad (6.13)$$

As mentioned, households consume some of the economy's output; firms and households use some output for investment; and the government buys some outputs for its programs.

Households receive payments from firms for labor and capital and then pay a percentage of this as taxes to the government (to finance government expenditures). From their income, households pay *zakat* and *khums* (and land taxes [*kharaj*]). If the amount of these Islamic payments is *insufficient* to meet social needs and if income and wealth disparities are still too great, households are encouraged to pay more. If conditions are still unacceptable then the government may impose further taxes to meet social needs. What households have as income (*after* all of these various postmarket corrections) could be correctly labeled as *Islamic disposable income* in an Islamic economic system; households save a portion of this and consume the rest. The level of disposable income is an important determinant of consumption. A higher level of disposable income results in a higher level of consumption. In an Islamic system, the consumption function can be written:

$$C = C(Y - T - IP) \tag{6.14}$$

where

T $=$ taxes
IP $=$ direct Islamic-mandated payments (which become disposable income for others if completely passed through)

Thus for the economy as a whole, IP is akin to a deduction from the income of the well-to-do and income for those that are less fortunate. Since consumption is usually a substantial part of the GDP, macroeconomists invariably pay more attention to this part of the GDP. But it should be again emphasized that people must avoid ostentatious lifestyles and large disparities in lifestyles of the rich and the poor.

Government is the second component of the aggregate demand for goods and services. The government purchases goods and services for different purposes. For example, government buys guns, builds schools, and hires teachers. Programs such as welfare for the poor or payments to elderly persons that transfer income and are not exchanged for goods and services do not count as government purchases. Government income for most countries is largely from taxes. When purchases by governments and taxes are equal, G = T, a government has a balanced budget. If government's income or taxes are less than its expenditures, it incurs a budget deficit. If income exceeds expenditures, the budget is in surplus. Persistent budget deficits translate into a growing national debt. In a number of Muslim countries, nearly all of the government income comes from the depletion and sale of oil and natural gas reserves (something that cannot last forever).

The third component of output is investment. Investment is the most volatile component of GDP (in part because of the volatility of interest rates and economic activity in the conventional economic system). Firms and households purchase investment goods; for example, households buy new houses, and firms buy new machinery and equipment to replace old machinery and equipment. Also, households save their money in a number of ways, including stocks, other forms of investment partnerships, cash, and real estate that is used productively. (In the Islamic system, land not used productively for a period of time may be acquired by others.) Firms can use their own savings and raise money from investors (savers) to buy new investment goods. The quantity of investment goods demanded by firms is in part dependent on the demand for the output produced by the new investment, business expectations about economic conditions and the general business outlook, the real rate of return in the economy, and, more generally, the cost of capital (the interest rate in the conventional system) and taxes that affect the cost of financing. The larger the economy, the brighter the business expectations. The higher the real rates of return adjusted for investment tax incentives, the larger investment is. The amount of businesses borrowing from financial markets depends on the expected profitability of projects. When a project is profitable, earnings from it exceed the cost of money. As a result, in the Islamic system, when households want a larger share of the profits, fewer investments are generally profitable, and the demand for investment goods falls. The investment is what remains from the output after consumption by households and government expenditures:

$$I = Y - C - G \tag{6.15}$$

$Y - C - G$ is also called *national savings* or simply savings (S). National savings is divided into two parts: private savings (output minus tax and consumption) and public savings. Private savings $= Y - C - T$ (IP is a wash because it is a deduction from income for some households and an addition to income for others) and public savings (taxes minus government purchases) $= T - G$.

As the result, total savings *by definition* would be equal to investment:

$$S = (Y - T - IP - C) + (T + IP - G) = I \tag{6.16}$$

Equation 6.16 shows that national savings depends on national income Y, consumption, and the variables G, T, and IP (to the extent that different income groups would have different savings rates, IP affects national savings). By changing taxes and government expenditures, government fiscal policy can impact savings and investment. Consider the increase in government spending. When the total output is fixed and disposable income, Y – T, is unchanged, the rise in government spending must be met by an equal decrease in investment. Now consider a reduction in taxes; it increases disposable income and consumption. In this case, when government purchases are fixed and the economy's output is fixed by factors of production, then an increase in consumption must be met by an equal decrease in investment.

Household consumption decisions impact the economy in both the short run and the long run. The way that households decide between consuming and saving is a microeconomic question because it is an evaluation about individual decision makers, but in the aggregate, the combined behavior of consumers has important macroeconomic consequences. We explained earlier how consumption relates to disposable income: $C = C(Y - T)$. This approximation gives us a simple model to analyze consumer behavior in the short and the long run, but it is too simple to give us a complete explanation for consumer behavior. Since consumption is the largest component of aggregate demand and GDP, the consumption function has received the most attention and should be further explained. There are three prominent theories of consumption.

John Maynard Keynes developed a theory of consumption that plays a central role in his theory of economic fluctuation, which is discussed later. He had three assumptions for the consumption function. First and most important, he postulated that an increase in income would result in an increase in consumption, but not by as much as the increase in income. Thus when a person earns extra income, he or she spends some of it and saves some of it. Keynes defined the *marginal propensity to consume* (MPC), which is the additional amount of consumption as the result of an additional unit of income. He assumed MPC is between zero and 1 because people consume some part of their additional income and save the remaining part. Second, Keynes explained that the ratio of consumption to income, called the *average propensity to consume*, falls when income rises. He believed that saving is a luxury so that rich save a higher part of their income than the poor. Third, Keynes believed that income is the main determinant of consumption, and the interest rate (real rate of return in an Islamic economy) does not have an important role in consumption. (Classical economic theory taught that higher interest rates encourage people to save more and consume less.)

The Keynesian consumption function could not explain a number of observed facts. Keynes assumed that as income grew over the time, households would consume a smaller and smaller part of their income. As a result, there would be inadequate demand for goods and services, resulting in recession and unemployment. After the end of World War II, as incomes increased, these higher incomes did not lead to large increases in the rate of saving. In other words, Keynes's assumption that the average propensity to consume would fall with rising income did not hold. A second anomaly emerged as Simon Kuznets discovered that the ratio of consumption to income was quite stable over a long period of time. Thus, Keynes's assumption that the average propensity to consume would fall with rising income did not hold. In fact, economists believed that there were two consumption functions. For the short run, the Keynesian consumption function seemed to work pretty well, but for the long run, the average propensity to consume appeared to be a constant. Different behavior between short-run and long-run consumption functions made it necessary to explain why the consumption decisions were different.

The Keynesian consumption function relates current consumption to current income. Other economists hypothesized that the consumption decision was dependent on both current and expected future income. More consumption today affects the amount consumers can consume in the future. Irving Fisher introduced a model that determines how the constraints consumers face, the preferences that they have, and the interaction of constraints and preferences affect choices about consumption and saving. Keynes postulated that a person's consumption is largely related to current income; Fisher's model says that consumption is based on the income that the consumer expects over his or her entire life. Modigliani and Friedman separately tried to address this issue and provide the other two major theories of consumption.

Franco Modigliani argued that income varies over a person's lifetime and saving allows consumers to smooth out their consumption pattern by saving income during the high earning years for the low earning and retirement years. Thus the consumption decision today is based on wealth and current and future earnings in order to smooth out consumption over a lifetime. The shape of consumer behavior is called the *life-cycle hypothesis*; individuals save during years of high income and dissave during retirement. Retirement is one of the important reasons for variations in consumption. People save and invest during their working years to maintain the level of consumption during retirement. Consider a person who lives for another A years. This consumer has initial wealth (W) and expects to earn income (Y) until retirement (R) years from now. We want to know how much he would consume during a lifetime to smooth his consumption. Equation 6.17 shows the smoothed path of consumption for him:

$$C = (W + RY)/A \qquad (6.17)$$

Equation 6.18 tells us he consumes his wealth, W, and his lifetime earnings, RY, over A years. Also, we can write this equation as shown next:

$$C = (1/A)W + (R/A)Y \qquad (6.18)$$

Replace 1/A with α and R/A with β in the previous equation and the consumption function can be restated:

$$C = \alpha W + \beta Y \qquad (6.19)$$

where

α = marginal propensity to consume out of wealth
β = marginal propensity to consume out of income

Milton Friedman suggested the *permanent-income hypothesis* as an alternative to Modigliani's model. He used Irvin Fisher's theory that argues consumption does not depend on current income alone. Friedman emphasized that current income, Y, is made up of two parts: *permanent income*, Y^P, and *transitory income*, Y^T. Permanent income is the part of income that people expect to continue into the future. Transitory income is the part that people do not expect to continue into the future. In the other words:

$$Y = Y^P + Y^T \qquad (6.20)$$

Friedman believed that consumption would depend on permanent income, not transitory income. He reasoned that since consumers use savings and borrowing to smooth consumption during their lifetime, they would not spend all of their transitory income. Friedman concluded that the consumption function is approximately a function of permanent income:

$$C = \alpha Y^P \qquad (6.21)$$

where

α = a constant that determines the fraction of permanent income consumed

Fahim Khan argues that (theoretically) devout Muslims in an Islamic economy would make two types of consumption decisions (as opposed to one in all conventional economic systems): (1) to meet their own household needs, and (2) to meet the needs of others as mandated by the Islamic faith, with the allocation between these a matter of personal choice. Khan goes on to add:

Without specifying how much of one's income should be spent for others in the way of Allah, great emphasis has been placed on such spendings. The more one spends for others (for the sake of Allah) the better for him in this world and the hereafter.[6]

In all decisions, Khan argues that the Muslim consumer must be rational (learn and acquire the trait) and that this differs from the case of conventional economics, where it is assumed. And importantly, Khan adds that Muslims should save for future consumption, not by hoarding but by investing (along the lines of Modigliani). He sums up a Muslim's consumption behavior in this way:

1. *A Muslim consumer's total spending can be classified into the following major categories:*
   a. *Spending to achieve satisfaction in this world (E1). This includes (i) present (immediate) consumption (let us denote it by C1) and (ii) savings/investment for consumption in future (let us denote it by S1).*
   b. *Spending for others with a view to earn reward in the hereafter (E2). This includes (i) what is immediately consumed by the recipients (let this be C2) and (ii) what is invested for social purposes or community benefits or what is saved by the recipients for their own investment (S2).*
2. *The consumption basket of a Muslim is likely to be smaller than that of a secular consumer as it includes only permissible things and excludes prohibited things.*
3. *The allocation between E1 and E2 and between C1 and S1 within E1 or between C2 and S2 within E2 has been left to rational consumer behavior which should be dominated by God-consciousness.*
4. *The degree of God-consciousness is an essential parameter in determining consumer behavior of a Muslim.*
5. *The only limit that has been specified is the minimum limit of E2 for those who are obliged to make these types of spending.*
6. *A Muslim is allowed to save, a major part of which will have to be invested in order to earn at least a return that would prevent his savings from being depleted by zakah.*[7]

In sum, Keynes proposed that consumption is a function of current income. Other conventional economists argued that consumers take into

---

[6]Khan (1984, p. 6).
[7]Ibid., p. 10.

account their wealth and also look ahead to their expected future income, thus requiring a more complex model to explain consumption. Modigliani and Friedman suggested adding wealth and expected income to this function. Economists continue to argue over the theory of consumption. For example, some argue about the importance of the interest rate, and others focus on psychological effects. Consumption function seems to remain important in economists' debates because it has the dominant role in national income (a large share of aggregate demand, especially in the United States) and in economic fluctuations. In Islam, the major differences from the Modigliani hypothesis are that Muslims are required to spend in the Way of Allah (swt) for the less fortunate and for society, to limit their wants and live modestly, and to invest (not hoard) wealth to foster prosperity. But we must emphasize that while the Modigliani hypothesis is generally supported by data in most countries, the Islamic model (which also includes spending for the welfare of others) does not appear to be supported, even in Muslim countries. Essentially, Muslims do not appear to consume as recommended by the Quran and the *Sunnah*; they may be Muslims, but they behave as conventional consumers.

NATIONAL INCOME AND OUTPUT DETERMINATION

Most economists believe that the time horizon is an important dimension when it comes to analyzing macroeconomic models. They divide the time horizon into the short run and the long run because they believe economies behave differently in each horizon. The main point here is that in the long run, prices are flexible and can respond to change in supply and demand, but in the short run, many prices are sticky. Flexible prices are an important assumption of the classical economic theory. The theory assumes the prices adjust to ensure that the quantity of output demanded equals the quantity of output supplied; however, the economy behaves differently when the prices are sticky. In the short run, the output of the economy also depends on the economy's demand for goods and services, and demand depends on many other factors, such as monetary and fiscal conditions and policies.

Aggregate demand depends on monetary policy (quantity of money and real rate of return in the economy), fiscal policy (taxes and public expenditures), expectations, business confidence, foreign incomes, asset values, and demographic factors. Aggregate supply depends on the economy's potential output or its capacity to produce (especially in the long run), and on wage price relationships. (Price and wage stickiness give short-run aggregate supply an upward slope, but the long-run supply is a vertical line as all costs and prices adjust by roughly the same amount.)

In the short run, the interaction of aggregate demand and aggregate supply determines the economy's price level and the quantity of national output, or GDP. Since the firms that supply goods and services face flexible prices in the long run but sticky prices in the short run, the aggregate supply relations depend on the time horizon. Long-run aggregate supply (output), according to classical theory, does not depend on the price level (a vertical function). This long-run level of output, Y, is called *full-employment* or the *natural level* of output. This would be the level of output if the economy's resources are fully employed or unemployment is at the *natural rate*.

The state has a crucial role in ensuring economic activity and prosperity. As the world witnessed during the Great Depression and more recently in the Great Recession, there is no reason to believe that the economy will be operating at full employment (the natural rate, restated as NAIRU, the nonaccelerating rate of unemployment, by Modigliani and Papademos).[8] In fact, it is highly unlikely that the economy will be humming along at NAIRU for any length of time. There will be periods when aggregate demand is too low (aggregate supply is high) and others when it is too high (supply is low), requiring government intervention to nudge the economy back to the NAIRU level of activity. Stabilization policies—monetary and fiscal—are crucial in moderating economic fluctuations and in maintaining employment, something that is crucial to prevent economic hardships for families and for society in general. But government's role in stabilization goes beyond monetary and fiscal policies to include industrial policies, trade policy, exchange rate policy, and income policies. While government can adopt policies to support economic activity and nudge the economy toward its NAIRU level, it may have as important a role to enhance growth.

In the short run, most prices are stuck at predetermined levels. At these prices, firms want to sell as much as their customers are willing to buy, and they hire enough labor to answer the customers' needs. The fall in aggregate demand in the long run does not impact output (remember the classical theory) and adjustment is made by rising price levels. In the short run (prices are sticky), falling aggregate demand is compensated for by falling output. In sum, over the long run, prices are flexible, aggregate supply is vertical (output is fixed), and changes in aggregate demand affect only the price level, not output. Over a short period of time, prices are sticky, the aggregate supply has a slope (prices are fixed), and changes in aggregate demand affect the output of the economy. Since the prices are not fully flexible in the short run, reduction in aggregate demand reduces output.

---

[8]Modigliani and Papademos (1975).

After falling aggregate demand, firms are stuck with prices that are too high. As a result, firms sell less of their product so they reduce production and lay off workers. This is how an economy enters a recession. Monetary policy gives an important tool to policy makers to control aggregate demand. By reducing and increasing the velocity of money, central banks can play a vital role in aggregate demand.

Economists have developed different models over the years to explain the operation of the economy and different policies to avoid shocks and to stabilize economic conditions. What we have discussed so far regarding the determination of national income is largely the position of the *classical economic theory*. According to this theory, national income depends on factor supplies and available technology (potential output). The classical view has two main assumptions. First, it is assumed that supply creates its own demand in a macroeconomy. Thus someone will buy everything that is produced in the economy. Hence, the economy operates at full employment and production. The second assumption of the classical theory is that wages and prices are flexible, and they will adjust to ensure that the economy operates at full employment.

During the 1930s, many parts of the world experienced vast unemployment and significantly reduced incomes, namely the Great Depression. Since neither the factors of production nor technology had changed, economists questioned the capability of classical theory to explain the Great Depression. Hence, many economists believed that a new explanation was needed for the global economic meltdown. The British economist John Maynard Keynes proposed a new model as an alternative to the classical theory; it was called *Keynesian economics*. Keynes criticized classical theory for assuming that aggregate supply, including labor, capital, and technology, determine national income. He suggested that low aggregate demand is the reason for the low income and high unemployment. Keynes proposed that the economy's total income in the short run is determined by spending plans of households, government, and businesses. The logic of his statement is that when more people want to spend money on goods and services, firms provide more goods and services. In turn, to provide more goods and services, firms will have to hire more workers. As a result, Keynes believed that the problem during recessions and depressions is related to an inadequate level of spending or insufficient aggregate demand. To better understand this issue, we define actual and planned expenditures. *Actual expenditures* are the amount households, firms, and the government spend on goods and services, namely, GDP. *Planned expenditures* are the amount households, firms, and the government would like to spend on goods and services. The difference between actual and planned expenditures might come from unplanned inventory investment by firms. When firms sell less of their product than they planned, their stock of inventories rises. When firms sell more than they planned, the stock of inventories falls. Since these unplanned changes in inventories are taken into account as investment spending by firms, actual expenditures can be either above or below planned expenditures. Denote planned expenditures as PE and rewrite the output equation for a closed economy:

$$PE = C + I + G \qquad (6.22)$$

Equation 6.22 shows planned expenditures as the sum of consumption, C, planned investment, I, and government expenditures, G. Recall the consumption function, $C = C(Y - T)$, and replace it in the last equation:

$$PE = C(Y - T) + I + G \qquad (6.23)$$

Equation 6.23 determines that planned expenditures are related to the level of income, Y, the level of planned investment, I, and fiscal policy variables, G and T. (Again, it should be noted that the Islamic mandated payments, IP, are transfer payments between consumers and are omitted but their size does affect aggregate consumption as different income groups have different MPC.) In the Keynesian model, the economy is in equilibrium when actual expenditures are equal to planned expenditures, that is, the same as when *planned savings equals planned investment.* (By definition, actual savings always equals actual investment.):

$$Y = PE \qquad (6.24)$$

If output is greater than the equilibrium level, planned expenditures are less than production; hence, firms are selling less than what they are producing. In other words, firms are adding goods to their inventories. This unplanned rise in inventories causes firms to lay off more workers and reduce production, resulting in lower GDP and a higher unemployment rate. The process of falling output and rising unemployment will continue until Y falls to the equilibrium point. Similarly, if output is below the equilibrium point, planned expenditures are above production so that firms are shedding inventories. A lower level of inventories induces firms to increase employment and increase production to the point when Y equals planned expenditures. In sum, the Keynesian model determines how output, Y, is determined for a given level of planned investment and fiscal policy variables, G and T.

Having explained how planned investment can influence expenditures, we now examine briefly how fiscal policy affects the economy. For example, if we assume that government purchases rise by ΔG, it leads to an increase in income, ΔY. The change in income is bigger than change in government purchases. The ratio of ΔY/ΔG is called *government-purchase multiplier*. This ratio tells us how much income rises as the result of one unit increase in government purchases. This fiscal policy measure in turn has a multiplier effect on income because higher income leads to higher consumption according to the consumption function $C = C(Y - T)$. Hence, an increase in government purchases raises income and also raises consumption. The rise in consumption in turn also raises income, and this process will continue. The government can also decrease taxes. A reduction in taxes raises disposable income, $Y - T$. Hence, planned expenditures will be higher at any level of income. Therefore, in contrast to the classical theory that assumes that the economy can adjust by itself and that government intervention (stabilization policies) is useless or even counterproductive, the Keynesian school believes that government intervention in the short run can adjust the spending gap that is responsible for recession and unemployment. (See Figure 6.1.) The equilibrium level of national output, E, given by the level of C, I, and G, may entail a significant level of unemployment and unemployed resources. Here is when discretionary fiscal

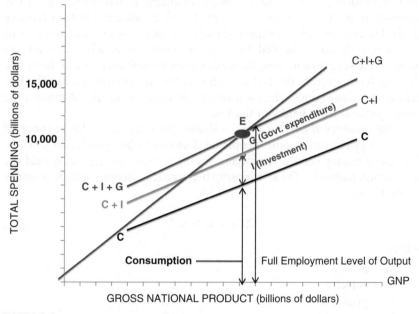

FIGURE 6.1 National Income Determination

and monetary policy come into play—increasing C, I, or G. This we take up in Chapters 12 and 13.

The Chicago School, pioneered by Milton Friedman, introduced the *monetarist view*. Proponents of the monetarist view challenge the Keynesian fiscal policy prescriptions. They believe that fiscal policy is ineffective, all government stabilization efforts are counterproductive, and a simple rule for the growth of money in the economy is the best form of monetary policy. Chapter 11 presents a more detailed discussion of monetary policy and its workings in an Islamic system.

INFLATION

Economists call the increase in prices inflation. Inflation is an increase in the average level of prices. An important source of inflation is too much demand chasing too few goods. As money in circulation impacts demand for goods and services, understanding money and its role in inflation plays a vital role in understanding inflation.

The quantity of money available in an economy is the *money supply*. The printing of money is under the control of government. Government's control of the money supply is called *monetary policy*. Usually a partially independent institution called a *central bank* is in charge of monetary policy. For example, in the United States, the central bank is called the Federal Reserve (Fed). The Fed controls the supply of money through the sale and purchase of government bonds. The Fed buys government bonds when it wants to increase the supply of money; the money goes to banks (in turn to the public through lending) from the Fed in exchange for government bonds. The Fed sells government bonds when it wants to decrease the supply of money; the money returns from banks to the Fed.

The *quantity theory of money* shows the relation of the quantity of money to prices and income. People need money to buy goods and services. The more money needed for buying results in more money being held for transaction purposes. The relationship between transactions and the quantity of money is:

$$M \times V = P \times T \qquad (6.25)$$

where

M = money
V = velocity
P = price
T = transactions

On the right-hand side of equation 6.25, T is the total number of transactions in a period of time (e.g., a year). In other words, T shows the number of times in a year that goods or services are exchanged for money. P is the number of units of money exchanged (e.g., dollars). As a result, PT is the number of dollars exchanged in a year. On the left-hand side of the equation, M is the quantity of money, and V is the *transaction velocity of money*. V measures the number of times that a unit of money changes hands in a given period of time. For example, if the quantity of money (M) increases and the velocity of money (V) remains constant, then price (P) or the number of transactions (T) has to rise.

The problem with the quantity equation is that the number of transactions is difficult to measure. To solve the problem, the total output of the economy, Y, could replace the number of transactions; this would indicate that when an economy produces more, we could expect that more goods and services are bought and sold. Therefore, equation 6.25 can be written as:

$$M \times V = P \times Y \qquad (6.26)$$

where

Y = output of the economy

If we add an assumption that the velocity of money, V, is constant, the quantity equation becomes a useful theory that shows the effect of money supply on output. This theory is called the *quantity theory of money*. Recalling that Y represents GDP, we also call Y real GDP. When the price level is introduced for accounting GDP, Y is called nominal GDP, which shows the dollar value of the economy's output. As a result, PY shows nominal GDP, and the quantity of money determines the nominal GDP.

Recalling that inflation is the percentage change in the price level, the quantity theory of money can be treated as one theory for explaining inflation. Rewrite the quantity equation in this form:

$$\% \text{ change in M} + \% \text{ change in V} = \% \text{ change in P} + \% \text{ change in Y} \qquad (6.27)$$

If we assume that the change in the velocity of money or demand for money is zero, then, if the percentage change of the quantity of money changes, the percentage change in the price level, P, or the rate of inflation or the percentage in output, Y, must also change. The change in output depends on growth in the factors of production and on technological progress. As a result, this theory explains that the growth in money supply determines the rate of inflation. Thus, if the central bank increases the money supply rapidly, the price level will rise rapidly; in other words, inflation is seen as a purely monetary phenomenon.

The question is often raised if money is lent without *riba* (interest), should the amount of the loan be adjusted for any decrease or increase in the value of money (real purchasing power) over the period of the loan. The indexation of financial obligation refers to an adjustment in value over a period of time to compensate for the change in value due to inflationary or deflationary pressures. Indexing wages to inflation is a very common practice, but indexing investments or financial obligations is also growing quickly in conventional financial markets. In the case of financial assets, inflation-linked securities link the returns to the consumer prices index or to the cost of living index. The adjustments are often in the form of *ex post facto* adjustments, and the objective is to guarantee a return equal to the real interest rate instead of the nominal interest rate.

Indexation is justifiable in the eyes of *Shariah* for wages, salaries and pensions, social security payments, and so on, but *Shariah* does not support indexation of financial assets. Some scholars argue that Islam's notion of justice is a ground for compensation when lending without *al-riba*; others argue that the prohibition is absolute and any compensation or indexation would amount to interest. Opponents of any adjustments base their arguments on moral, legal, economic, and financial grounds. Some of the arguments against indexation are based on finding solutions to the sources of fiscal imbalance and price instability rather than making any adjustments through indexation. Common arguments against indexations are briefly discussed here.

First, it is argued that the verses of Quran (2:275) clearly protect only the principal amount of the loan and consider anything in excess of it as *al-riba*. It is understood that this prohibition covers all transactions that may make any adjustments similar to *al-riba*, such as deferred exchange of currency, devaluation or revaluation, and change in the unit of currency at the time of repayment of loans. Since lending of money is a currency transaction that is treated as similar to exchange of a commodity, any compensation for the fall in the value of money is not justifiable.

Second, Muslim scholars also argue that by virtue of inflation in the economy, an investor's or lender's purchasing power would be at stake irrespective of whether money is lent as a loan on a non-*al-riba* basis or is invested in a return-bearing security. In either case, the net loss to the lender is a real interest rate or real return. Even if money was not lent but was kept for consumption purposes, the same loss of purchasing power will occur. Therefore, it seems unreasonable to expect the borrower to bear all the loss, a loss that the lender would likely incur even if he or she had not made the loan.

Third, it is argued that even if some form of indexation is allowed, it may not be in consonance with the notion of justice and therefore may not serve its intended purpose. While it is recognized that inflation is the loss of purchasing power and indexation is a compensation for such a loss, the problem is how to clearly identify and hold a certain party responsible for its share. There are several contributing factors leading to inflation, and the contributing magnitude of each factor and party cannot be determined. Therefore, it is unjust to ask one party to take the entire burden while others are burden-free. For example, if only the borrower is asked to compensate for the loss, which was caused by factors beyond the borrower's control (e.g., irresponsible policies of the government), it would imply that a person who is not responsible for inflicting the loss is made to compensate for it while the responsible party is not held responsible.

Fourth, some scholars have also discussed the practice of indexation by arguing that there is no perfect index that can fully capture the loss of the value. The constituents of the index representing the cost of living may not serve as a good proxy for the loss in purchasing power. Also, the cost of living index represents the consumption habits of an average person in an economy. Since the cost of living may differ from region to region and from city to city, it is not possible to measure it accurately. This inaccuracy can lead to an unjustified transfer of wealth from the borrower to the lender or vice versa. Similarly, inflation indices are based on a lag and therefore are not readily available to be used in daily financial transactions. All these factors make indexation less practical and prone to biases, which may open a back door for unjustified charges.

Finally, *Shariah* scholars and economists raise the issue that indexation is not the answer. Rather, price stability and fiscal discipline are to be achieved to combat inflation. In this respect, the role of the state in causing inflation leading to disequilibrium in the economy should receive serious attention. Some economists argue that it is the responsibility of an Islamic state to take effective steps to check inflation in order to minimize the depreciation in the value of money. When the government policies are the source of inflation, the government should compensate the borrower.

Irrespective of the causes and sources of inflation, indexation is not accepted by scholars; however, other remedies have been suggested. For example, if the lender and the borrowers are concerned about inflation, then the loan can be denominated in terms of a commodity (e.g., gold). The lender can lend a certain quantity of gold to the borrower who is obligated to return the same quantity at the expiry of the loan. It is also pointed out that the partnership and profit-and-loss-sharing instruments of the Islamic economic system provide a built-in compensation for inflation because the profit is shared in the agreed ratio whereas the losses are borne in the ratio of respective capitals.

UNEMPLOYMENT

Unemployment is a key macroeconomic indicator because it affects individuals and families directly and sometimes severely. Unemployment, especially for an extended period of time, means a lower standard of living and emotional hardship for most individuals and families. It also has a highly deleterious effect on the social fabric of society. In Islam, having a job and working hard (for those who physically can) is an important part of a Muslim's economic and social obligation. Thus, being close to the natural rate of employment (or full employment) must be an overriding goal of public economic policy. Thus, the provision of jobs becomes crucial.

If L is the labor force, E is the number of those employed, and U is the number of the unemployed, then the labor force is the sum of the employed and the unemployed:

$$L = E + U \qquad (6.28)$$

The unemployment rate is the ratio of unemployment to the labor force, U/L.

There are two types of unemployment: frictional unemployment and structural unemployment. *Frictional unemployment* is a result of the time invariably needed for workers to move from one job to another. Workers have different skills and preferences, and jobs have different skill requirements. Thus the provision of education and skills training becomes an important policy in an Islamic society. Moreover, the information about vacancies is not easily available, and labor mobility is not instantaneous. Therefore, matching workers to jobs consumes time and effort. Some frictional unemployment is thus inevitable and due to the fact that the types of goods that firms and households demand changes over time. When demand for goods shifts and changes, so does the demand for labor of different skills. For example, the invention of computers decreased the demand for typewriters and the demand for labor in the manufacturing of typewriters. Economists call a change in demand among industries a sectoral shift. Sectoral shifts invariably increase frictional unemployment because it takes time for workers to change sectors and acquire the skills in demand. Therefore, as long as demand and supply among firms for labor are changing, frictional unemployment is inescapable.

The other category of unemployment is *structural unemployment*. In this case workers are unemployed not because they cannot find suitable jobs for their skills but because there is a mismatch between the number of people who want to work and the number of jobs that are available. A major cause of structural unemployment is *wage rigidity*, which refers to the failure of wages to balance the supply and demand for labor so that there is no structural unemployment. This occurs when at the going wage rate the quantity of labor supplied exceeds the quantity of labor demanded. There are three common explanations for causes of wage rigidity:

1. Minimum wage legislation is one cause of wage rigidity.
2. Unions can push firms to raise wages and create wage rigidity.
3. Efficiency-wage theories suggest that firms may find it profitable to keep wages high for various reasons, such as enhancing worker morale and productivity.

In Islam, it is our view that employers must pay a wage that at least supports a minimum lifestyle. But beyond this minimum, individuals, through mandated Islamic payments (IP), and the government, through social programs, must elevate the economic well-being of the less fortunate. Moreover, given Islamic teachings in support of hard work and available jobs for all those who can work, it is incumbent on the state to afford employment a high priority in its economic policy objectives. Thus full employment and a wage that affords a minimum living standard to humans to develop and contribute to society should be fixtures of a well-functioning Muslim society. Reducing the unemployment rate may not be easily achieved for either frictional unemployment or structural unemployment. Unemployment is in the end a wasting of resources because those people who cannot find jobs cannot contribute to raise national output despite having the potential to do so. Economists and policy makers monitor the unemployment rate because fluctuations in employment are closely related to fluctuations in aggregate output and human welfare.

The economy is said to be in *recession* when it experiences a period of falling output (for at least two consecutive quarters) and rising unemployment. Economists call short-run fluctuations in output and employment the *business cycle*. Fluctuations in GDP and in the unemployment rate are the result of business cycles. Fluctuations in the economy come from changes in aggregate demand and aggregate supply. *Aggregate demand* determines the quantity of goods and services that people want to buy at any given level of price. *Aggregate supply* shows the relation between the quantity of goods and services that are supplied and the given price level. Economists call shifts in aggregate supply and demand *shocks*. A shock that changes aggregate demand is called a *demand shock*; a shock that changes aggregate supply is called a *supply shock*. Most economies have what are called automatic stabilizers—income transfers and programs that automatically kick in to increase demand when demand is insufficient (such as unemployment benefits and social programs) and vice versa. Automatic stabilizers should be most significant in the Islamic system as Islam places significant importance on individual, societal, and state support of those with insufficient income (unemployed, disabled, etc.), as discussed in Chapter 8. Policy makers attempt to develop policies that reduce the severity of shocks and economic fluctuations, called *stabilization policies*. In other words, policy makers try to maintain output and employment close to their natural levels in the long term. To this end, policy makers use appropriate monetary and fiscal policies as an important component of stabilization policy.

OPEN ECONOMY: TRADE IN GOODS AND SERVICES WITH OTHER COUNTRIES

Up to now, for simplification we have assumed that the economy is a closed economy and does not trade with other countries. In the real world, most countries have open economies. They export and import goods and services from abroad. Also, in an open economy, countries borrow and lend in financial markets. Recall the equation for output in the society:

$$Y = C + I + G \qquad (6.29)$$

I can be split into domestic and foreign components—I_d and I_f. The rearranged equation is

$$I_f = Y - (C + I_d + G) \qquad (6.30)$$

I_f is foreign investment, is referred to as the current account, and is equivalent to exports minus imports of goods and services plus net transfer payments (workers' remittances and foreign aid). The current account is the most comprehensive measure of a country's transactions with the rest of the world. A positive current account signifies that a country was a net creditor (investor abroad) to the world in that period of time. In an open economy, financial markets and the goods and services markets are thus closely related. The key difference between an open and a closed economy is that, in an open economy, a country can spend more than it produces by borrowing (foreigners lending or investing) from abroad, or consume less than it produces and lends (or invests) to foreigners. Therefore, contrary to a closed economy, in an open economy, a country's consumption is not necessarily equal to its total output—it can lend (invest) or borrow from the rest of the world. Thus global economic activity becomes an important determinant of local economic activity because it adds to demand and supply.

Islam clearly endorses free trade as it prohibits interferences that inhibit commerce. But an important question that must be addressed is how much sharing is mandated across national borders, especially when it comes to depletable natural resources. Namely, what God has given humans is for all humans of all generations. Thus, do countries need to share only domestically (equal access to all), or with Muslim countries or with all countries regardless of their religion and whether they in turn share their natural resources?

Now we will consider the prices that apply to transactions between international flows of capital and international flows of goods and services. Prices that residents of countries pay to trade with one another are determined by domestic prices and the *exchange rate* between the currencies of countries. Exchange rate is the price of one currency relative to another. Economists define a number of exchange rates, including the nominal exchange rate and the real exchange rate. The *nominal exchange rate* is the relative price of the currencies of two countries. For example, we can buy 55 Indian rupees to 1 U.S. dollar. A rise in exchange is called an *appreciation* or a *strengthening* of the currency, and a fall in the exchange rate is called *depreciation* or a *weakening* of the currency. For example, if the number of Indian rupees needed to buy a dollar rises from 55 to 60, an American can buy more rupees with a dollar and an Indian can buy fewer dollars with a rupee. It is an appreciation of the dollar and a depreciation of the Indian rupee.

The *real exchange rate* is the nominal exchange rate adjusted for the relative prices of goods. The relationship between the nominal and the real exchange rates is:

Real exchange rate = Nominal exchange rate * Ratio of price levels

If we denote e as a nominal exchange rate (the number of Indian rupees per dollar), P the price level in the domestic country (e.g., in United States), P^* the price level in the foreign country (e.g., India), and ε the real exchange rate, then the equation can be written as:

$$\varepsilon = e^* \left(\frac{P}{P^*} * \right) \qquad (6.31)$$

The higher real exchange rate signals that foreign goods are relatively cheap and domestic goods are relatively expensive. Clearly the real exchange rate, as opposed to the nominal rate, is the important determinant of trade.

In sum, the real exchange rate is an important determinant of net exports. When the real exchange rate is low, domestic goods are cheaper relative to foreign goods, and net exports will be high *ceteris paribus*. The current account is the indicator of a country's global savings position; it is positive if the country is a net lender to the rest of the world and negative (a current account deficit) if the country is a borrower—in other words, a country with a current account surplus in a given year is a lender to the rest of the world and one with a deficit is a net borrower.

WHY INTERNATIONAL TRADE IS SO CENTRAL TO ISLAM

The conventional theory of international trade is built on the theory of comparative advantage. The message of comparative advantage is profound and is not intuitively obvious. Namely, even if a country has an absolute advantage in the production of every good, it can benefit by specializing in production and engaging in trade. Trade affords a country the opportunity to exchange goods at a different price ratio than that available in the closed home market (increasing the consumption possibility frontier for the country, sometimes referred to as the static gains from trade), and specialization will over time increase productivity growth and output (expanding the production possibility frontier, sometimes referred to as the dynamic gains from trade).

Empirically, while gains from trade are important in economic growth, the dynamic gains are the more significant benefit. Economists, recognizing the gains from trade, almost universally recommend free trade. In addition to the direct economic gains, international affairs specialists focus on the importance of international trade and economic integration (such as common markets and customs unions, the free flow of labor and capital across national borders) for reducing conflicts and wars between countries; two countries that trade extensively and/or are members of a common market recognize that conflict will invariably reduce trade and take a bigger economic toll than for countries that do not trade with each other. In other words, trade and economic integration (free flow of labor, capital, and technology) promote political and social cooperation. It is a unifying factor in human relations, an important goal for any society that professes Islam.

Classical Theories of International Trade

There are two standard models for international trade: Ricardian and the Heckscher-Ohlin models. In the Ricardian model, assuming two countries, two goods, one factor of production (labor), constant returns to scale, and no transportation cost, the underlying reason for trade is different labor productivities in the production of each good (technology) across the two countries. Free trade results in the same price ratios in the two countries. Trade can only benefit (it cannot hurt) the two countries; the countries' production possibility frontier does not change, but their consumption possibility frontier expands and the extent of their gain from trade depends on the relation of the posttrade price ratio to the pretrade price ratio. It should, however, be noted that labor's income in the country with an absolute comparative advantage (higher labor productivities) will be higher after trade in comparison to the lower labor productivity country (as it was before trade). And over time, specialization and more rapid productivity growth will expand the output and the production possibility frontier of all countries.

In the Heckscher-Ohlin model, assuming two countries, two goods, two factors of production, the same production functions in the countries (technology), constant returns to scale, diminishing marginal product of factors of production, similar tastes, and no transportation cost, the underlying reason for trade is different endowments of factors of production. Trade results in the equalization of prices across countries and importantly in the price of factors (wages for similar labor, and rates of return to capital as the second factor). Although wage rates for the same labor become the same across countries, per capita incomes can be very different. The country that has the higher per capita endowment of the nonlabor factor of production (in the normal model assumed to be capital but it could be land, oil, or any other natural resource) will have the higher per capita level of income. When a country has a relatively large supply of a resource, that resource is the abundant factor in the country. Conversely, when a country has a relatively small supply of a resource, that resource is the scarce factor. Owners of a country's abundant factor gain from trade, but owners of a country's scarce factors lose. These are all intuitive outcomes and can be best understood by noting that the movement of goods across borders is a substitute for the movement of factors of production. Hence, some people lose real income from trade, but society as whole will be better off with free trade, namely the real national income goes up (or at least does not go down). Most conventional economists would not limit trade because of its impact on income distribution. They believe potential overall societal gains from trade are more important than the probable loss incurred by some groups and instead recommend other policies to address income distribution. Over time, the expectation would be that increased specialization would again increase productivity and thus economic growth.

Besides the impact on income distribution, trade also affects employment. Production in some sectors will increase (exports) and decline in others (imports). Moreover, as trade is a dynamic activity, comparative advantage changes over time. Some will lose their employment and must seek employment in other sectors. As a result, there is a strong case and a need for retraining and compensating those who are adversely affected by international trade. Again, we should emphasize that while the static gains from trade are important and are the usual point of emphasis in classroom discussions, most economists believe and the empirical evidence suggests that the dynamic gains from trade are much more significant.

Islam is a market-friendly religion. The Prophet (sawa) was himself a trader and grew up in a family of traders. The early history of the Muslims is a history that flourished from trade. The Quran states: "Eat not up your property among yourselves in vanities: but let there be amongst you traffic and trade by mutual good-will" (4:29). The Prophet's (sawa) own personal experience with trade and the many verses in the Quran dealing with trade give explicit guidelines for such economic activities. According to Islamic history, traders were known as knowledgeable individuals because they traveled to trade and gained knowledge from around the world. There is a great deal written in history indicating the depth of Muslim society's involvement in trade around the world. Hefner gives a picture of economic activities of Muslims in their early history:

> The first three centuries of the great Islamic expansion are recognized as having been an age of unprecedented commercial growth. By the tenth century, Muslim merchants and jurists had developed credit and investment institutions that were among the most advanced in all of Eurasia. Although the late Middle Ages (1250–1500) saw a decline in the Middle East's economic dynamism, the period was followed by a commercial boom in the Muslim-dominated Indian ocean. There Muslim merchants created the world's largest and most lucrative trade emporium, a vast network that tied coastal East Africa, southern Arabia, South Asia, and Southeast Asia into a vast trading zone. In the South-east Asian wing of this [trading community], the fifteenth and sixteenth centuries saw the development of an independent merchant class that, like its counterpart in Renaissance Europe, patronized the arts, promoted individualized styles of religiosity, and even sought to curb the authority of rulers.[9]

Notably, trade and comparative advantage are mentioned in the writings of Muslim scholars such as Ibn Khaldun. He is known as the first person to have systematically analyzed an economic system and develop the laws of

---

[9]Hefner (2006).

supply and demand. Ibn Khaldun explained mutual dependence and the impact of cooperation on efficiency that raises economic output, noting:

> *It is well-known and well-established that individual human beings are not by themselves capable of satisfying all their economic needs. They must all cooperate for this purpose. The needs that can be satisfied by a group of them through mutual cooperation are many times greater than what individuals are capable of satisfying by themselves.*[10]

As an aside, Krugman in a different context says that Ibn Khaldun "was a 14th-century Islamic philosopher who basically invented what we would now call the social sciences."[11]

Understanding and interacting are essential for effective integration of humans from different artificial groups, such as societies or nations. Mutual understanding helps members solve problems peacefully with the least amount of conflict. The economic path, of which trade is a critical component, is a powerful channel to enhance mutual understanding because economic conditions play a vital role in the life of all individuals and societies. Economic integration is necessary because it increases interaction, understanding, and cooperation among nations. Increasing dependency reduces the probability of conflicts and wars. Hence, trade liberalization among nations provides for the free movement of goods, capital, labor, technology, and information and in turn increases understanding. It supports communication among people and mitigates misunderstanding and conflicts. It strongly supports the ideals of Islam to reach integration of humankind and brotherhood. Hence, all activities that erect barriers toward integration must be seen as un-Islamic and are at odds with the core message of the religion. The Quran is emphatic on the importance of cooperation and mutual support: "cooperate in piety and goodness but do not cooperate in evil and transgression" (5:2). The Prophet (sawa) said: "God keeps on helping a person as long as he helps other human-beings." Some 600 years ago, Ibn Khaldun concluded, "There can be no development without justice." Injustice undermines development and is harmful for cooperation.

In sum, Islamic teachings support and encourage free trade and economic cooperation and integration as ways to increase economic prosperity, reduce conflicts, and integrate humanity. Thus all economic barriers to trade and sanctions, especially those that are initiated by one country and are preemptive, are discouraged.

---

[10]Chapra (2001).
[11]Krugman (2013).

Implications of Islamic Teachings for International Trade and Economic Integration

Islam encourages free trade for its direct economic benefits as well as for its unifying attributes to humankind. But as we have seen, while trade is beneficial for countries in the aggregate, it creates winners and losers. Given the Islamic emphases on economic justice, equal opportunities for all, the importance of hard work, and the availability of employment for all and the elimination of large income disparities, governments must develop policies to redistribute income between the winners and losers of trade and to retrain labor in sectors where they have lost comparative advantage. This is the policy requirement within Muslim countries (intrastate), but what about between countries (interstate)?

Combining the Islamic vision for humankind, Islamic rules of property rights, and the Islamic requirement to share and to eradicate poverty, it could be concluded that wealthy countries that have abundant natural resources should share the benefits of these resources with those who are deprived. Although the form and implementation of this policy can be debated, its applicability is undeniable, both on economic and on societal grounds. Allah (swt) gave these resources to all humankind, not to modern states with artificial boundaries; resources must be shared and in the process humans would step onto the path of unity.

Four questions come up with the form and implementation of sharing Allah's bounty:

1. Is a Muslim country duty-bound to share the benefits of its natural resources (oil, gold, etc.) with the rest of the world, with other Muslim countries only, only with countries that recognize the same principles, or with no foreign entity?
2. If a Muslim country's per capita income is lower than the world average or the average of other Muslim countries, is there a compunction to share the benefits of its natural resources (oil, gold, etc.) with the rest of the world, with other Muslim countries, or only with countries that also uphold the same principles?
3. What if a Muslim country has a higher per capita income because of better economic management and hard work, but no natural resource advantage; does it have to share its higher income with the rest of the world, with other Muslim countries, or only with countries that also uphold the same principles?
4. If some income sharing is called for, how should this be achieved, and can the country expect reciprocity?

These are questions that require answers when countries are opened to trade in the Islamic framework.

Moreover, Islam goes further than merely encouraging free trade. Islam encourages the movement of people, knowledge, technology, and ideas as an important channel for reintegrating humankind as originally created by the Almighty. Such exchanges would in turn increase understanding among humans, reduce disputes and conflicts, and promote justice. Although sharing natural resources with other nations is a far-fetched idea in the current state of the world, the core message of Islam supports it and much more. In its absence, there can only be more poverty, conflict, and wars for the future of our planet because of gross inequality and injustice.

Trade and the free flow of people and other factors of production would enhance welfare, promote integration of humankind, and mitigate conflicts and wars. Needless to say, unfortunately, Muslim countries have deviated from the Islamic vision of free trade as in other areas of Islamic teachings. One study shows trade among members of the Organization of the Islamic Conference (OIC) trade in 2009 was only 17% even though these countries are geographically close to each other and have diverse natural resources, agricultural goods, and manufacturing products that could raise trade among them. The study shows that the 57 OIC member countries had 7.2% of global GDP and 10.3% of global merchandise exports, but with a significant portion of this 10.3% in the form of exports of minerals, such as oil and natural gas.[12] In another empirical study, Mehanna found that a sample of 33 Muslim majority countries traded less than all other religions.[13] Naqvi writes:

> Our discipline must shed all traces of rejectionist romanticism and the excess baggage of anachronistic ideas to bring economic prosperity and spiritual happiness to the Muslim societies. It must be frankly admitted that success on this score has eluded our grasp. Still, it is important to persevere in our effort to raise a "unified" economic discipline, on testable foundations, in a typical Muslim society and not in some Islamic Utopia.[14]

All this is ironic for a religion that preaches the importance of economic prosperity; economic ethics; effective economic institutions; the best business practices; free markets with effective rules, supervision, and enforcement; poverty eradication; economic sharing; and, above all, economic and social justice.

---

[12] Alpay, Atlamaz, and Bkimli (2011).
[13] Mehanna (2005).
[14] Naqvi (2002, p. 520).

SUMMARY

The most commonly used measure of national economic output is the GDP. There is, however, increasing evidence that GDP does not closely track the level of human and social welfare. In Islam, attaining the highest level of conventional GDP cannot be society's economic goal. Human well-being and social justice are of paramount importance. Thus adjustments must be made to conventional GDP to account for negative externalities (such as environmental degradation), the depletion of nonrenewable resources as well as the output of prohibited goods to derive the Islamic GDP. But even the adjustments that could be made (requiring some new data collection) are insufficient because economic justice is of paramount importance. However, the creation of a level playing field, prevention of large income and wealth disparities, provision of essential social programs, and poverty eradication cannot be integrated into the GDP index of output to arrive at a broad measure of social economic output and social economic performance. Thus the measure of Islamic GDP must be accompanied by strict constraints that any level of output must also provide for these other social and societal objectives.

In the Islamic economic system, the aggregate demand function (consumption, investment, and government expenditures) has a number of differences from that in the conventional economic system. In the case of consumption, Muslims must limit their personal wants, incorporate the needs of others and those of society in their consumption-saving decision, and smooth out their consumption pattern through risk-sharing investments; businesses must incorporate social needs, the negative externalities of their business and investment activities, be motivated by the real rate of return, and raise capital through risk-sharing capital contributions; and government expenditures must provide for the social and infrastructure needs of society, create an economic environment where humans flourish, and manage an economy (through macroeconomic policies) that supports sufficient job creation for all those that can work. It would, however, appear that consumers in Muslim countries do not behave in such a way as to support these expectations, because income and wealth disparities are large, poverty is significant in a number of countries, and opportunities to develop and succeed are highly unequal.

Aggregate demand and aggregate supply interact to determine national economic output. On one hand, classical economics postulates that national economic output cannot be affected by government stabilization policies and is determined by potential output or the economy's capacity to produce (labor, human capital, capital, technology, etc.) as wages and prices are flexible and equate aggregate supply and demand. On the other hand, the Keynesian school argues that in the short run, wages and prices are inflexible and thus aggregate demand may be below or above aggregate supply, resulting in unemployment or in inflation. Thus the Keynesian school recommends stabilization policies (monetary and fiscal) to correct the short-run imbalance, whereas others argue against fiscal policies to adjust economic output and employment and recommend abandoning discretionary monetary policy for a simple monetary rule.

In a truly Islamic system, as long as the state provides efficient institutions, supervision, and rule enforcement, individual Muslims and businesses in caring for the welfare of others in society should provide a number of effective stabilizers that should limit economic fluctuations and large swings in employment and income. Moreover, the fact that real rates of return, instead of highly volatile interest rates, would motivate investment should afford further stability in the Islamic system. Still, in both the conventional economic system and the Islamic system, automatic stabilizers at times will be insufficient to restore economic balance. Thus the state should step in on both the supply side and the demand side through fiscal and monetary policy (see Chapters 12 and 13) to restore balance.

KEY TERMS

National income

Gross national product

Net national product

Consumption

Savings

Investment

Marginal product

Wage rate

Profit

Income determination

International trade

Exports

Imports

Exchange rate

Government expenditures

Taxes

Marginal and average propensity to consume

Keynesian economics

Ricardo's Theory of Comparative Advantage

Inflation

Velocity of money

NAIRU

Unemployment

Structural and frictional unemployment

QUESTIONS

1. Is GDP a good measure of a country's economic output and social welfare? How do you account for economic output from a depletion of a resource (oil) as compared to output from a sustainable base (agriculture)?

2. How would you modify GDP to measure output in the Islamic system?

3. Is GDP per capita a good measure of individual welfare?

4. List some of the reasons people save in Western capitalist economies. Would this list be different for the ideal Islamic economic system?

5. How and why are individual consumption decisions different in the Islamic system from in Western capitalist economies?

6. What is the multiplier? What is its relevance for government economic policy?

7. Why is an economy not always at full employment with stable prices?

8. Do Keynesian economic policies lead to full employment and stable prices?

9. Is a change in taxation and/or government expenditures always helpful in restoring employment and restoring price stability?

10. Why do countries benefit from international trade?

11. Why is the exchange rate an important factor in determining exports and imports? What other variables affect trade?

CHAPTER 7

Macroeconomic Equilibrium: Characteristics of an Islamic Economy[1]

Learning objectives:

1. *The prohibition of fixed interest-bearing debt instruments and economic management.*
2. *Islamic-endorsed assets and the needed range of financial instruments for macroeconomic analysis.*
3. *In the Islamic system, the return on financial instruments and its link to the real sector.*
4. *In the Islamic system, the link between the real and the financial sectors and its one-to-one mapping.*
5. *Stable economic equilibrium without interest-bearing debt instruments.*

In an Islamic financial system, all financial arrangements are based on sharing risk and return. Hence, all financial assets are contingent claims, and there are no debt instruments with fixed and/or predetermined rates of return. This characteristic makes the Islamic model ripe for the application of an Arrow-Debru-Diamond type analysis of a stock market economy under uncertainty. A fundamental principle that emerges from theoretical studies of such a system is that the returns to financial assets are primarily determined by the rate of return in the real sector. This principle implies that the rate of return of capital is the mechanism through which the demand and supply of lendable funds is equilibrated. This follows from

---

[1]This chapter is based on Mirakhor (1993).

the fact that the source of profit in such an economy is the addition to total output. Once the labor is paid its distributive share, the residual is then divided between the entrepreneur and the investor (saver). Since this residual is an *ex post facto* variable, it follows that the return to investors cannot be determined *ex ante*. In a system where the only assets that exist are those representing ownership claims to equity shares, a fundamental question is: What is the nature of equilibrium? In this chapter, the equilibrium conditions are derived for the case of a closed economy, an open economy with trade in goods only, and one with trade in both goods and equity shares. It is shown that the rate of return to capital equilibrates savings and investment, that the differential between domestic and foreign rates of return to equity determines the direction of capital flows, and that under a fixed exchange rate system, adjustments induced by exchange rate changes are channeled through the asset accounts. A stable equilibrium is achieved without a fixed and predetermined rate of interest.

MODELS OF AN INTEREST-FREE ECONOMY

While several models have been developed that rely on existence of a system-wide predetermined interest rate, these models cannot be applied to an Islamic economy, as such a system does not allow existence of a predetermined interest rate. We present a model that does not rely on a predetermined fixed interest rate. For sake of completeness, we present a model for a closed economy—with no trade with other economies—followed by a model for an open economy subject to international trade.

Closed Economy Model

We begin by assuming that the economy produces output described by a linear homogenous production function:

$$Q = f(K, L) \tag{7.1}$$

where

    L = quantity of labor services employed
    K = index of real capital[2]

---

[2]Uzawa (1969).

Per capita output $q = Q/L$ is then a function of capital-labor ratio $k = K/L$:

$$q_t = f(k) \tag{7.2}$$

where

$$f'(k) > 0$$
$$f''(k) < 0, \text{ for all } k > 0$$

Under full employment conditions, the rate of return to capital (the rate of profit of business firms), r, and the wage rate, w, are given by:

$$r = f'(k) \tag{7.3}$$

$$w = f(k) - kf'(k) \tag{7.4}$$

The macroeconomy is made up of firms and households. Equity shares to all capital stock represent the ownership claim of households. In Islamic profit-sharing arrangements, business firms exercise direct control over capital by employing it with labor. Households receive income in the form of wages for labor and returns on their equity shares. They divide their income between consumption and savings (to increase their equity holdings). Aggregate demand is composed of household consumption and the level of investment planned by business firms. National income is equal to the returns of the factors of production, which in turn determines the level of actual aggregate demand, consumption, and investment. When planned and actual aggregate demands are equal, the economy is said to be in short-run equilibrium, and a level of aggregate demand corresponding to such an equilibrium level determines the rate of capital accumulation.

Assuming homogenous quantities of labor and capital and that the aggregate behavior of households and business in the economy can be explained in terms of a representative household and business firm, aggregate income, Y, is given by:

$$Y = W + D + G \tag{7.5}$$

where

W = wages bill (total wage payments)
D = dividends
G = expected capital gains

The value of the equity shares held by households is:

$$V = P^e E \tag{7.6}$$

where

P^e = price of shares
E = number of shares

The rate of return to equity is expressed as:

$$r^m = \frac{D + G}{V} \tag{7.7}$$

Demand for new equity shares (i.e., the number of new shares desired by households) is given by:

$$E^D = \frac{S - G}{P} \tag{7.8}$$

where

$E^D = dE^D$
S = savings of households, which is given by:

$$S = s(r^m)Y \tag{7.9}$$

where

$s(r^m)$ = average propensity to save and is a positive function of the rate of return

Aggregate output is distributed as:

$$Q = W + D + R \tag{7.10}$$

where

R = portion of profits retained by firms for additional investment

The supply of new shares to be issued by firms is given by:

$$E^s = \frac{I - R}{P^e} \tag{7.11}$$

where

$E^S = dE^S$
I = desired investment by firms

Investment is determined by a marginal efficiency schedule (Lucas-Treadway-Uzawa type) and the Penrose function

$$i = i(z) \tag{7.12}$$

where

z = growth rate of total capital
I = I/K

The Penrose function can be interpreted in terms of the marginal cost of investment. The relationship between the investment-capital ratio and the rate of capital accumulation—that is, $i = i(z)$—requires that

$$\frac{di}{dz} > 0 \text{ and } \frac{d^2i}{dz^2} > 0 \text{ for all } z > 0 \tag{7.13}$$

The conditions in equation 7.13 reflect the scarcity of entrepreneurship, investment increases as the real rate of return to real capital increases, and the fact that the marginal cost of investment is increasing.

The optimum level of z, the rate of increase in capital, is a function of the marginal product of capital (the rate of profit), r, and the market rate of return to equity, r^m, prevailing in the equity market. Since $i = i(z)$ and $z = z(r, r^m)$ then:

$$z = z(r, r^m) \tag{7.14}$$

$$i = i(r, r^m) \tag{7.15}$$

$$\text{where } \frac{\partial z}{\partial r} \text{ and } \frac{\partial i}{\partial r} > 0 \text{ and } \frac{\partial z}{\partial m} \text{ and } \frac{\partial i}{\partial m} < 0 \tag{7.16}$$

Equations 7.14 and 7.15 are graphically represented in Figure 7.1 for a given rate of profit r. The rate of capital accumulation $z(r, r^m)$ can be positive or negative, depending on whether the market rate of return is smaller or larger than the rate of profit, r. Also, at a given rate of profit, firms undertake additional investment depending on the magnitude of the market rate of return to equity relative to the rate of profit. In an efficient equity market, no firm will be able to attract financing for its investment projects that do not promise to yield a rate of return at least as large as the prevailing market rate of return on shares.

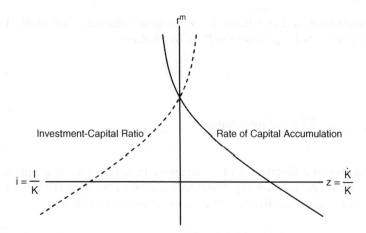

FIGURE 7.1 Relationship between Investment-Capital Ratio and the Market Rate of Return and between the Market Rate of Return and the Rate of Capital Accumulation

In an economy just described, the equilibrium condition for the goods market is:

$$Q = C + I \qquad (7.17)$$

The labor market is in equilibrium when there is full employment, that is:

$$L = N \qquad (7.18)$$

where

N = quantity of labor employed

The labor force is assumed to grow at a rate n and capital accumulation at a rate z, defined relative to the investment-capital ratio i through the Penrose curve. The equity market is in equilibrium when:

$$E^D = E^S \qquad (7.19)$$

and per capita output is given by equation 7.2 as $q = f(k)$. National income is defined as:

$$Y = W + r^m V \qquad (7.20)$$

Dividing equation 7.20 by N to convert into per capita terms yields:

$$y = w + r^m v \qquad (7.21)$$

If we assume that capital gains, G, always reflect retained profits, output will equal national income, as in:

$$y = q = f(k) \qquad (7.22)$$

The short-run equilibrium for this economy requires that:

$$I = S \qquad (7.23)$$

In terms of investment-capital ratio and savings per unit of capital (as well as in per capita terms):

$$i(r^m, r) = s(r^m)\frac{y}{k} \qquad (7.24)$$

In other words, planned savings must equal planned investment. Equilibrium is attained at a market rate of return, r^m, that equates the level of investment per unit of real capital desired by the firms and the amount of savings per unit of real capital that households are willing to save at the market rate. Figure 7.2 is a graphic representation of investment and saving schedules of equation 7.24. The vertical axis shows the market rate of return, and the horizontal axis shows the desired investment or desired saving per unit of capital. The intersection of the two curves II and SS determines the equilibrium market rate of return. While a change in the market rate of return causes a movement along the curves, a change in the rate of profit, r, causes a shift of the curves. An increase in the capital-labor ratio, k, reduces the marginal product of capital, r (the rate of profit), resulting in a shift of II downward and to the left. The same increase in k reduces average product y/k of capital, causing an upward shift in the SS curve. As a result, investment declines but the market rate of return may or may not decline, depending on the way the two curves shift.

The long-run equilibrium of the system depends only on the rate of growth of the labor force, n. The system will remain at a steady state if, and only if, the rate of investment per unit of capital is at a level i(n), which corresponds to the exogenously given rate of growth of labor, n. The dynamics of the economy is described by the differential equation:

$$\frac{k^*}{k} = i(r^m, r) - n \qquad (7.25)$$

Designating the steady-state level of capital-labor ratio as k^*, whenever k is lower than its long-run equilibrium level k^*, then the capital-labor ratio increases; that is, $k > 0$. If k is at a higher level than k^*, then $k < 0$ and the

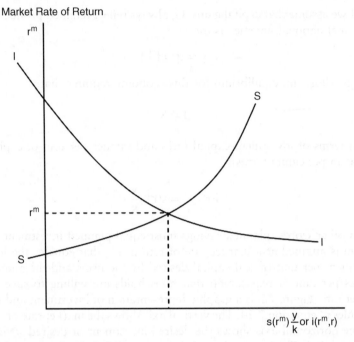

FIGURE 7.2 Relationship between Savings (and Investment) per Unit of Capital and the Market Rate of Return to Equity

capital-labor ratio declines. The long-run equilibrium level of the capital-labor ratio k* is determined by the long-run equilibrium levels of investment and savings from the equations 7.26 and 7.27:

$$i\left(\overset{m}{r^*}, r^*\right) = i(n) \tag{7.26}$$

$$s\left(\overset{m}{r^*}\right)\frac{y^*}{k^*} = i(n) \tag{7.27}$$

where

r*	= long-run equilibrium market rate of return
y* = f(k*) and r* = f'(k*)	= long-run equilibrium levels of income and profit rates respectively
i(n)	= equilibrium rate of investment corresponding to the rate of growth of labor, n

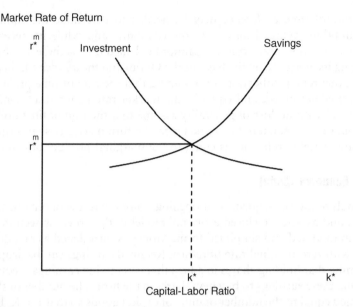

FIGURE 7.3 Long-Run Equilibrium Levels of Capital-Labor Ratio and the Market Rate of Return to Equity

Equations 7.26 and 7.27 state that there is a pair of rates of return, $\overset{m}{r^*}$ and r^*, that equate the long-run desired levels of investment and savings per unit of capital. As shown in Figure 7.3, the intersection of desired savings per unit of capital and desired investment per capita determines the long-run equilibrium market rate of return and the capital-labor ratio. The equilibrium conditions (7.26) and (7.27) convey the fact that for any market rate of return (r^*) above its long-run equilibrium level, $\overset{m}{r^*}$, the rate of profit (r^*) must also increase (thus k^* must decrease) in order for investment to be maintained at its long-run equilibrium level i(n). Also, an increase in the market rate of return above its long-run equilibrium level must be accompanied by a higher capital-labor ratio (k^*) and thus a lower average productivity of capital (y^*/k^*) in order for savings to equal the long-run equilibrium level of investment i(n). The long-run equilibrium of the economy can be determined once the production function, consumption-saving behavior, investment function (the Penrose curve), and rate of growth of labor (n) are specified.

The important implication of this analysis is that the assumption of a fixed and predetermined rate of interest is *not* necessary either for the determination of savings-investment behavior or for the existence of a long-run equilibrium for the economy. While it is true that the existence of a rate of time preference may be needed to determine the equilibrium consumption-savings behavior in the economy, and while its necessity or existence in an Islamic economy cannot be denied (nor is there any basis for rejecting its existence on the basis of the Quran and the *ahadeeth*), there is no strong theoretic justification for assuming that the rate of time preference is fixed, predetermined, and equal to the market rate of interest.[3] One could easily and without loss of generality assume that the rate of time preference (discount rate)is equal to the market rate of return on equity shares (in which the rate of time preference is equal to the marginal product of capital).[4]

Open Economy Model

To analyze the consequences of opening a noninterest economy to trade in goods and assets, the closed economy model in the previous section can be used in modified and simplified form. Money is introduced as an additional asset with zero nominal rate of return. Retained earnings can be dropped by assuming that holding shares in a firm that is retaining earnings is equivalent to using these earnings to buy new shares in the firm. The number of shares is assumed equal to the number of units of capital goods so that E = K. Because of our interest in the effects of trade in equity shares, the aggregate supply is assumed to be a function of capital, that is,

$$Q = F(K) \text{ where } F' = \frac{\partial F}{\partial K} > 0 \text{ and } \frac{\partial^2 F}{\partial K^2} < 0 \qquad (7.28)$$

The rate of return to equity shares is now defined as $r = \frac{F'P}{P_E}$ where

P = price level
P_E = nominal price of shares
F'P = value of marginal product of capital

Defining the real price of shares as $P^e = \frac{P_E}{P}$ becomes the rate of return in real terms:

$$r = \frac{F'}{P_E} \qquad (7.29)$$

which along with assumptions on capital gains and profits modifies equation 7.15 to become i = i(r). Since by definition $i = \frac{I}{K}$ and capital stock is given

[3]Knight (1971) showed that the neoclassical notion of time preference can also produce either a negative or a zero rate of discount. See also Olson and Bailey (1981) and Epstein and Hynes (1983).
[4]Montiel (1986).

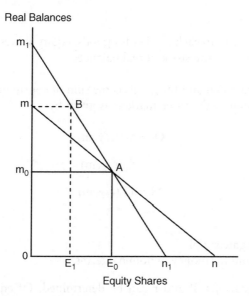

FIGURE 7.4   Optimal Portfolio Mix

in the short run, investment becomes a function of r and K as:

$$I = I(r, K) \text{ where } \frac{\partial I}{\partial r} < 0 \text{ and } \frac{\partial I}{\partial K} < 0 \tag{7.30}$$

Real wealth is defined as $(P^e E + m)$, where $m = MP$ is the stock of real balances. In searching for an optimal portfolio, individuals adjust their holding of real cash balances and equity until the actual and desired mix of the two assets is equal. Such an equilibrium is represented in Figure 7.4. If the wealth constraint is $m_1 n_1$ instead of mn, the desired mix will be at point B where individuals will attempt to increase their holding of money balances by reducing their equity holdings. Given equation 7.29, as the price of shares decreases, r increases and the slope of $m_1 n_1$ declines, causing it to rotate around point A downward to the right, until it coincides with mn and the original equilibrium is established at point A.

Demand equations for goods, equity, and money are assumed, in real terms, to have the following form[5]:

$$D_i = D_i(r, y, m) \tag{7.31}$$

---

[5]Patinkin (1965). See also Chapters 9 to 11 in this book for further explanation on the functional forms of the demand equations.

where

i = 1, 2, 3 refer to each market for goods, equity shares, and money
m = real income and stock of real balances

The aggregate demand for goods is the sum of consumption and investment. Equilibrium in the three markets is given by:

$$Q = AD(r, y, m) \qquad (7.32)$$

$$K = E_d(r, y, m) \qquad (7.33)$$

$$M = PL(r, y, m) \qquad (7.34)$$

where

Q = aggregate supply
PL = demand for money in nominal terms

From these equations, P and r can be determined. Of equations 7.32 to 7.34, only two are independent, given the constraint indicated by the Walras law:

$$y = AD + p^e(E - K) + (L - M) \qquad (7.35)$$

Given the money supply and the level of real capital, and assuming the existence and stability of the system, the price level of goods and the rate of return on equity shares can be determined.[6] The long-run equilibrium is attained when real capital and money supply do not change. The conditions for long-run equilibrium can be given as when $y = AD$, $E = K$, and $I = 0$. These conditions are satisfied when $m = m^*$, $r = r^*$ and $K = K^*$. An asterisk next to the variable designates its long-run equilibrium value.

Assume that the economy is small relative to the rest of the world, that it faces a world price of goods P_f, and that the exchange rate is given by

$$e = PP_f \qquad (7.36)$$

where

P = domestic price level

---

[6]Patinkin (1965). See also Chapter 10 in this book.

Concentrating first on trade in goods only, the domestic money supply will increase or decrease corresponding to the balance of trade. The short-run equilibrium is given by

$$Q = AD\left(r, y, \frac{M}{eP_f}\right) + T \qquad (7.37)$$

$$K = E\left(r, y, \frac{M}{eP_f}\right) \qquad (7.38)$$

where

T = trade balance

From these equations, T and r can be determined. The dynamic structure of the adjustment process is determined by the following pair of differential equations:

$$\dot{M} = eP_f T \qquad (7.39)$$

$$\dot{K} = I(r, K) \qquad (7.40)$$

If the initial (before trade) domestic price level P is lower than P_f when trade takes place, there is an immediate increase in real balances, which leads to portfolio adjustment in favor of domestic equity shares. There is also a positive trade balance. Recalling portfolio adjustment described in Figure 7.4 and considering equation 7.38, in the first phase of adjustment M becomes positive and K becomes negative, thus lowering the rate of return and increasing investment. Increases in M and K reduce T and K, and the system moves toward its long-run equilibrium position. Once there, all variables attain their steady-state values with new money supply M* and $P^* = P_f$. Under a flexible exchange rate system, the exchange rate adjusts to attain an equilibrium balance of trade and the same pretrade long-run equilibrium will be achieved.

When trade in assets as well as goods is allowed, the short-run equilibrium conditions (7.37) and (7.38) become:

$$Q = AD\left(r_f, y, \frac{M}{eP_f}\right) + T \qquad (7.41)$$

$$K = E_d\left(r_f, y, \frac{M}{eP_f}\right) + E_f \qquad (7.42)$$

where

r_f = world rate of return to equity

E_d = domestic holding of domestic equity

E_f = foreign holding of domestic equity and equals the difference between domestic capital and the equity claims held by domestic residents

Given K, M, and P_f, then T and E_f can be determined from equations 7.41 and 7.42. If E_f is positive, it means that the country is a debtor; if it is negative, it represents domestic residents' holding of foreign equity claims and the domestic economy is a creditor. It is assumed that the equities being traded internationally are homogenous. If the marginal product of capital is higher in the domestic economy, its equity shares will have a higher price and adjustment in the rate of return to equity shares takes place through adjustment in their prices.

If the domestic rate of return on equities is higher than the world rate, then upon opening of trade, there will be an excess demand for domestic equity, which raises the price of equity and the wealth of domestic households and, along with a reduction in the rate of return, induces an instantaneous portfolio adjustment of the type described in Figure 7.4, where the increase in real value of assets changes the wealth constraint from mn to $m_1 n_1$. The new short-run equilibrium, with a new rate of return equal to r_f, domestic holdings of real cash balances and equities become m and E_1, respectively. Thus the economy exchanges $E_1 E_0$ units of equity for $m_0 m$ of real balances with the rest of the world, and the new portfolio equilibrium moves from point A to point B.[7] With a domestic rate of return greater than r_f, the foreign holding of domestic equities increases initially, that is, E > 0. A lower domestic rate of return and positive M will mean a positive K and a worsening trade balance, but the balance of payments will be positive because of increased demand for money, M > 0. Given a nonoscillating adjustment mechanism, if the initial shock from capital movements is not very strong, the adjustment process will proceed.[8] An increase in real capital and in payments of return to foreign holdings of domestic equity, which in real terms equals $F E_f$, will lead to positive trade accounts.

Considerations of payments for return on foreign holdings of domestic equities, that is, $y = F(K) - F E_f$, modifies equations 7.41 and 7.42 to become[9]

---

[7] Frenkel and Rodriguez (1975) and Frenkel and Fischer (1972).

[8] See Dornbusch (1971), Dornbusch (1976), Frenkel (1971), and Frenkel (1976).

[9] Since $Q = F(K)$, $dQ = F dK$ and $y = F(K) - F E_f$, then $dy = F dk - F' E_f dK + F dE_f$.

$$Q = E_d\left(r_f, [F(K) - F'E_f], \frac{M}{eP_f}\right) + T \qquad (7.43)$$

$$K = E_d\left(r_f, [F(K) - F'E_f], \frac{M}{eP_f}\right) + E_f \qquad (7.44)$$

Equations 7.43 and 7.44 yield the following simultaneous equation system:

$$\begin{bmatrix} 1 & -\dfrac{\partial AD}{\partial y}F' \\[2ex] 0 & 1 - \dfrac{\partial E_d}{\partial y}F' \end{bmatrix} \begin{bmatrix} DT \\[2ex] dE_f \end{bmatrix} = \begin{bmatrix} F'(K) - \dfrac{\partial AD}{\partial y}(F' - F''E_f) \\[2ex] 1 - \dfrac{\partial E_d}{\partial y}(F' - F'E_f) \end{bmatrix} dK + \begin{bmatrix} -\dfrac{\partial AD}{\partial M} \\[1ex] eP_f \\[2ex] -\dfrac{\partial E}{\partial M} \\[1ex] eP_f \end{bmatrix} dM$$

$$(7.45)$$

The effects of changes in M and K on the short-run equilibrium values of T and E_f can be determined using equation 7.45, which yields:

$$\frac{dT}{dK} = \frac{1}{D} \begin{vmatrix} F' - \dfrac{\partial AD}{\partial y}(F' - F''E_f) & -\dfrac{\partial AD}{\partial y}F' \\[2ex] 1 - \dfrac{\partial E_d}{\partial y}(F' - F''E_f) & 1 - \dfrac{\partial E_d}{\partial y}F' \end{vmatrix} > 0 \qquad (7.46)$$

$$\frac{dE_f}{dK} = \frac{1}{D} \begin{vmatrix} 1 & F' - \dfrac{\partial AD}{\partial y}(F' - F''E_f) \\[2ex] 0 & 1 - \dfrac{\partial E_d}{\partial y}(F' - F''E_f) \end{vmatrix} > 0 \qquad (7.47)$$

$$\frac{dT}{dM} = \frac{1}{D} \begin{vmatrix} -\dfrac{\partial AD}{\partial M}eP_f & \left(-\dfrac{'AD}{\partial y}F'\right) \\[2ex] -\dfrac{\partial E}{\partial y}eP_f & \left(1 - \dfrac{\partial E_d}{\partial y}F'\right) \end{vmatrix} < 0 \qquad (7.48)$$

$$\frac{dE_f}{dM} = \frac{1}{D} \begin{vmatrix} 1 & -\dfrac{\partial AD}{\partial M}eP_f \\[2ex] 0 & -\dfrac{\partial E}{\partial M}eP_f \end{vmatrix} < 0 \qquad (7.49)$$

and the determinant D is

$$
D = \begin{vmatrix} 1 & \left(-\dfrac{\partial E_D}{\partial y} F'\right) \\ 0 & \left(1-\dfrac{\partial E_d}{\partial y} F'\right) \end{vmatrix} < 0 \tag{7.50}
$$

The results attained in equations 7.46 to 7.49 can be explained as follows: an increase in real capital increases the supply of goods and equity shares, but, because the income effect is normally positive and less than 1, the increase in demand is less than the increase in supply; therefore, foreign demand for goods and equities must increase to restore equilibrium in the market. Thus, the trade balance and foreign holdings of domestic equity respond positively to changes in capital. However, equations 7.48 and 7.49 are negative. The reason is that an increase in money supply increases real balances, and this in turn raises the domestic demand for goods and equity shares. Since the supply of goods and equity do not change, the foreign demand for goods and foreign equity holdings of domestic assets must decline for the markets to clear.[10] Reductions in foreign holdings of domestic equity, of course, lower return payments to foreign holders of equity shares.

The dynamic adjustment equations are:

$$
\ddot{K} = I(r_f, K) \text{ where } \frac{\partial I}{\partial r_f} < 0 \text{ and } \frac{\partial I}{\partial K} < 0 \tag{7.51}
$$

$$
\ddot{M} = eP_f L\left(r_f, y, \frac{M}{eP_f}\right) - M \tag{7.52}
$$

[10] Here we have not suggested how the stock of money is increased. The adjustment process depends on whether the change in money supply has "inside" or "outside" sources and whether it is in the form of once-for-all change or in the form of continuous open-market operation in which the government buys and sells equities in order to change the money supply. Moreover, the adjustment process depends also on the way in which the government disposes of earnings from its equity holdings and how households view the government holdings of equity shares. Nonetheless, results obtained in equations 7.48 and 7.49 are general and should hold under various assumptions. For further discussion, see Frenkel and Rodriguez (1975), Metzler (1951), Metzler (1952), Mundell (1960), and Waud (1970).

Equation 7.52 expresses surplus or deficit balance of payment and is the familiar monetary approach to balance of payments. Linearization of differential equations 7.51 and 7.52 yields the following coefficient matrix:

$$A = \begin{bmatrix} \dfrac{\partial I}{\partial K} & 0 \\ eP_f \dfrac{\partial L}{\partial y} \left(F' - F''E_f - F' \dfrac{dE_f}{dK} \right) & \dfrac{\partial L}{\partial M} - 1 \end{bmatrix} \qquad (7.53)$$

The determinant of this matrix is:

$$|A| = \frac{\partial I}{\partial K} \left(\frac{\partial L}{\partial M} - 1 \right) > 0$$

As the trace of equation 7.53 is negative, the equilibrium is locally stable, as shown in Figure 7.5.

The system is also globally stable if the a_{21} element of equation 7.53 is positive everywhere and its a_{22} element is negative everywhere. The discriminant of equation 7.53 is (trace)$^2 - 4\,|A|$, that is,

$$D = \left(\frac{\partial I}{\partial K} + \frac{\partial L}{\partial M} - 1 \right)^2 - 4 \left[\frac{\partial I}{\partial K} \left(\frac{\partial L}{\partial M} - 1 \right) \right] = \left(\frac{\partial I}{\partial K} - \frac{\partial L}{\partial M} + 1 \right)^2 \geq 0$$

Both roots are real and there are no oscillations in the adjustment process.

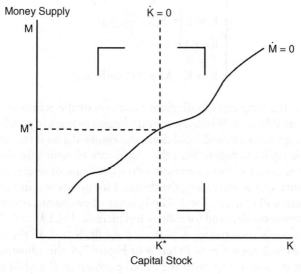

FIGURE 7.5 Dynamic Adjustment Path

Given an initial position and the fact that the adjustment path is non-oscillating, the properties of the adjustment process can be explained. The long-run equilibrium is obtained when $\ddot{K} = 0$ and $\ddot{M} = 0$. By the Walras law we have

$$eP_f(y - AD) + P_E(\ddot{K} - E) + \ddot{M} = 0 \tag{7.54}$$

Substituting $\ddot{M} = 0$ and $\ddot{K} = 0$ in equation 7.54 with given P_f and r_f and the short-run equilibrium conditions, the long-run equilibrium of the economy with trade in goods and assets is

$$\begin{cases} F(K) = AD\left(r_f, [F(K) - F'E_f], \dfrac{M}{eP_f}\right) + T \\[2mm] K = E_d(r_f, [F(K) - F'E_f], \dfrac{M}{eP_f}; +E_f \\[2mm] I(r, K) = 0 \\[1mm] F'E = T \\[1mm] K = K^*, M = M^*, E = E^*, \text{ and } T = T^* \end{cases} \tag{7.55}$$

To compare equation 7.55 with the initial position of the economy before trade, we recall the long-run equilibrium without trade, which is as follows:

$$\begin{cases} F(K) = AD\left[r, F(K), \dfrac{M}{P}\right] \\[2mm] K = E\left[r, F(K), \dfrac{M}{P}\right] \\[2mm] I(r, K) = 0 \\[1mm] T = 0 \\[1mm] K = K^*, M = M^* \text{ and } r = r^* \end{cases} \tag{7.56}$$

Clearly, the long-run equilibrium positions of the economy before and after trade are different. When the country begins to trade in goods and equity claims, foreign investors will hold domestic equity shares if the rate of return on domestic equity is higher than the world rate of return on similar assets, and E_f will be positive. But as investors do so, the rate of return declines (and price of equity shares increases), the demand for goods will increase, and the trade account will worsen, $T < 0$. The balance of payments, however, will be positive because the demand for money has increased and $\ddot{M} > 0$. Lower rates of return increase investment, $\ddot{K} > 0$; as a result, $\ddot{E} > 0$. In the long run, as $\ddot{K} = 0$ and $\ddot{M} = 0$, then $\ddot{E} = 0$. In terms of Figure 7.5, the adjustment process implies that if $r > r_f$ ($r < r_f$), then the initial position of $\ddot{K}$ and $\ddot{M}$ are the area below (above) the line $\ddot{M} = 0$ and to the left (right) of the line $\ddot{K} = 0$. The

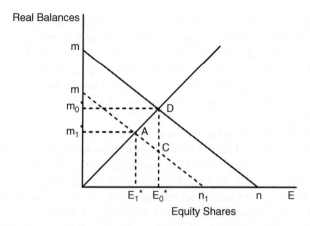

FIGURE 7.6 Portfolio Adjustment Induced by Changes in Exchange Rate

adjustment process is reversed if the domestic rate of return on equities is lower than the foreign rate of return on similar assets.

The adjustment process just described can be used to analyze the effects of changes in the exchange rate. Since in the open economy case the quantity of real balances is defined as $m = M/eP_f$, then any change in the exchange rate will have results analogous to those following changes in the nominal quantity of money.[11] Thus, a devaluation is analogous to a one-time reduction in the nominal money supply. Interpreted in this way, no additional derivation is required for examination of the effects of changes in the exchange rate. Equations 7.48 and 7.49, for example, can be used to show the effects of a devaluation on short-run equilibrium values of the trade balance and capital flows. As can be seen from these equations, a devaluation should increase capital inflows, through an increase in foreign ownership of domestic equity, and improve the balance of trade.

Equations 7.48 and 7.49 also imply that the channels through which these effects are transmitted are the asset markets (equity shares and money). A devaluation raises the price level $P = eP_f$ and thereby reduces the value of real balances (therefore, real wealth), inducing an instantaneous portfolio adjustment. Figure 7.6 illustrates the portfolio adjustment triggered by a devaluation. With the initial equilibrium at point D, a devaluation leads to a reduction in real wealth to a point such as C, which then induces an instantaneous portfolio adjustment from C to A when the asset drawdown is divided between equity shares and money so as to achieve portfolio balance. Recall that the system is homogenous of degree zero in the nominal

---

[11] Frenkel and Rodriguez (1975).

money stock, M, and in the exchange rate, e, and also that the aggregate asset holders' demand for real cash balances, L, is assumed proportional to the value of their equity holdings. As the domestic equity holders reduce their stocks of equities, the price of equities is reduced, thus making them more attractive for exports. However, devaluation reduces aggregate consumption expenditures relative to income, thus leading to an improved balance of trade.

A currency revaluation has the opposite effects since it is as if real balances were raised. There is an excess demand for equity shares, and as a result of an instantaneous portfolio adjustment, part of the increase in real cash balances is exchanged for additional equity holdings. The monetary change, however, does not affect the capital stock, hence the level of output is fixed, but aggregate consumption expenditure increases.[12] Additional equity holding by foreigners of domestic equities leads to an improvement in the capital account (by the amount of the rate of return multiplied by a change in foreign holdings of domestic equities). But at the same time, due to increased consumption, the surplus (deficit) in the balance of trade is reduced (increased). These changes in the capital account reflect the once-and-for-all stock adjustment needed to restore portfolio balance. Much of the adjustment in the short run is channeled through the asset accounts. As the adjustment proceeds, there will be a gradual deaccumulation of assets, which will be reflected in a surplus in the capital account and a deficit in the monetary account. There will also be a gradual improvement in the trade account until the adjustment process comes to an end and the long-run equilibrium is reestablished.

SUMMARY

An Islamic macroeconomy has a number of distinguishing features. Here we have focused on two principal characteristics: There are no fixed-return assets and, by implication, the rate of return to financial assets must be determined by the return in the real sector of the economy. We have tried to determine whether equilibrium can be achieved without a predetermined fixed rate of interest. An open economy model has demonstrated the effects of trade in goods and assets on the macroeconomic equilibrium of the economy. It is argued that the only assets that can exist in an Islamic economy are those that represent ownership claims to real capital. One asset that satisfies the Islamic requirements is an equity share in the form of a common stock. In the model presented, it is assumed that only equity shares can be

---

[12]Metzler (1951) and Frenkel and Rodriguez (1975).

traded internationally. Considerable emphasis has been placed on the developments in the real sector to show how the rate of return in this sector determines the macroeconomic equilibrium in the economy *without* the assumption of a fixed rate of interest.

Three sets of long-run equilibrium conditions are derived: for a closed economy, for an open economy with trade in goods only, and finally for an open economy with trade in goods and equity shares. For the most general case, it is shown that the direction of capital flow depends crucially on the differential between the domestic and foreign rates of return to equity shares and ultimately on differentials in the marginal product of capital. Moreover, it was shown that trade in goods does not, in and of itself, change the long-run equilibrium of the economy, but when trade in equities is also allowed, the long-run equilibrium is affected. Consequently, whereas in the first instance policy must concentrate on the adjustment process alone, in the second case additional policies must be adopted to consider welfare effects of capital movements and to reflect a desirable adjustment process. It was also shown that under a fixed exchange rate regime, much of the adjustment process induced by changes in exchange rate will be channeled through the asset accounts. The main conclusion is that the absence of interest-bearing assets does not hamper macroeconomic analysis or the workings of the economic system in closed or in open economy models. Standard macroeconomic analysis can be carried out to determine the conditions that must exist for a noninterest economy to reach its equilibrium.

KEY TERMS

Open and closed economies

Equilibrium

Stable equilibrium

Interest-bearing assets

Risk-sharing assets

Capital flows

QUESTIONS

1. Why is the existence of a stable equilibrium important in any economic system?
2. Does the absence of interest-bearing debt instruments impair economic management?
3. Do you feel disadvantaged if you cannot acquire fixed interest–bearing debt instruments?

CHAPTER 8

The Financial System

Learning objectives:

1. *The essential role and functions of a financial system.*
2. *The link between the real and the financial sector.*
3. *The notion and implications of risk sharing in finance.*
4. *The contrast between conventional and Islamic banking.*
5. *The menu of permissible and prohibited instruments and the nature of risk-sharing financial assets.*
6. *The form of Islamic insurance.*
7. *The nature of Islamic capital markets.*
8. *The importance of vibrant stock markets in the Islamic system.*
9. *The stability and growth implications of the Islamic financial system.*

The primary role of a financial system is to create incentives and mechanisms for an efficient allocation of financial and real resources for competing aims and objectives across time and space. A well-functioning financial system promotes investment by identifying and funding the best business opportunities; mobilizes savings; monitors the performance of managers; enables the trading, hedging, and diversification of risks; and facilitates the exchange of goods and services. Within a financial system, financial markets and banks perform the vital functions of capital formation, monitoring, information gathering, and facilitation of risk sharing. An efficient financial system is expected to perform four functions.

1. The system should facilitate efficient financial intermediation to reduce information and allocation costs.
2. It must be based on a stable payments system.

3. With increasing globalization and demands for financial integration, it is essential that the financial system offers efficient and liquid money and capital markets.
4. The financial system should provide a well-developed market for risk trading, where economic agents can buy and sell protection against event risks as well as financial risks.

These functions ultimately lead to the efficient allocation of resources, rapid accumulation of physical and human capital, and faster technological progress, which, in turn, stimulate economic growth.

An interest-based financial system invariably creates a phenomenon known as financialization that results in a divergence between the real sector and the financial sector of the economy. The conventional fractional banking system allows multiple amounts of money to be created out of a given amount of deposits received, facilitating and enhancing the process of debt creation. The development of complex financial derivatives has resulted in credit expansion outpacing the growth of the real sector of the economy. As layer upon layer of securitization decouples the connection between the financial and the real sectors, an inverted credit pyramid is created: Liabilities of the economy become a large multiple of real assets needed to validate them.[1] Additionally, such a system is characterized by mismatched maturity and values of asset and liability structure of balance sheet of banks. These institutions borrow short and lend long. When subjected to asset price shocks, the liability side of the balance sheet is very slow to adjust, while the asset side adjusts rapidly. Both mismatches create a potential for instability that can spread rapidly through contagion. The result can be an increase in the frequency, contagion, and severity of financial and economic crises.[2]

Research on financial intermediation and financial systems in the past two decades has enhanced our understanding of why the financial system matters and the crucial role it plays in economic development and growth. For example, studies have shown that countries with higher levels of financial development grow by about an additional 0.7% per year. Between 1980 and 1995, 35 countries experienced some degree of financial crisis. These were essentially periods during which their financial systems stopped functioning. Consequently, the real sectors were adversely affected, leading to economic downturns and recessions. Although strong evidence points to the existence of a relationship between economic development and growth and a well-developed financial system that promotes efficient financial intermediation

[1] Mirakhor (2011).
[2] Askari et al. (2012).

through a reduction in information, transaction, and monitoring costs, this linkage and the direction of causation is not as simple and straightforward as it may at first appear. The form of financial intermediation, the level of economic development, macroeconomic policies, and the regulatory and legal framework are some of the factors that can complicate the design of an efficient financial system (see Box 8.1).

BOX 8.1 FUNCTIONAL VIEW OF A FINANCIAL SYSTEM

A financial system may be better understood when viewed as the set of functions it performs in an economy. Although the most fundamental role of a financial system is still financial intermediation, the following are its core functions:

- **Efficient capital mobilization.** The core or central function of a financial system is to perform efficient resource allocation through capital mobilization between savers and users of capital. Access to capital has to be easy, transparent, and cost effective, with minimal transaction costs and free of information asymmetries.
- **Efficient risk allocation.** Under uncertainty and volatile market conditions, the functions of risk sharing, risk transfer, and risk pooling become critical in a financial system. The function of insurance is vital in any financial system, and availability of efficient risk-sharing facilities promotes diversification and allocational efficiencies.
- **Pooling of resources and diversification of ownership.** A financial system provides a mechanism for the pooling of funds to undertake large-scale indivisible investments that may be beyond the scope of any one individual. They also allow individual households to participate in investments that require large lump sums of money by pooling their funds.
- **Efficient contracting.** A financial system should promote financial contracting that minimizes incentive and agency problems arising from modern contractual arrangements among owners, managers, regulators, and other stakeholders.

(continued)

BOX 8.1 (*Continued*)

- **Transparency and price discovery.** A financial system should promote efficient processing of information such that all available information pertaining to the value of an asset is available at the lowest cost and is reflected in the value or price of the asset.

- **Better governance and control.** A financial system should facilitate transparency in governance and promote discipline in management through external pressures or threats, such as takeovers, so that misallocations and misappropriations are minimized.

- **Operational efficiency.** A financial system should provide smooth operation of financial intermediaries and financial markets by minimizing any operational risk due to failure in processes, settlement, clearing, and electronic communication.

NOTION OF RISK SHARING

Islamic finance is basically a financial system structured on risk sharing. Islamic finance encourages risk sharing in its many forms but generally discourages risk shifting or risk transfer, in particular interest-based debt financing. It is in part so designed to promote social solidarity by encouraging finance to play an integrating role between humankind. This form of finance would be inclusive of all members of society and all entities, especially the poor, in enjoying the benefits of economic growth, and to bring humankind closer together through the sharing of risk. Since risk sharing is the foundation and a basic activity in Islamic finance, it is governed by rules that, if and when observed, lead to lower transaction costs than in conventional finance. Risk sharing is a contractual or societal arrangement whereby the outcome of a random event is borne collectively by a group of individuals or entities involved in a contract or by individuals or entities in a community. In a company, all shareholders share in the risk inherent in the operations of the company. At the community level, a family or a nation shares in the risks affecting the well-being of the family or the nation. In finance, risk sharing is an essential feature of equity financing, where risk of loss and gain are shared, as opposed to interest-based debt financing, where the lender does not share in the risk of losses and thus all the risk of loss is shifted to the borrower.

The sharing of risk has many possible meanings, depending on how risk sharing is organized. All forms of organized risk sharing have a mutuality dimension in their activities. The most familiar are cooperatives of various forms to share risk faced by their members. Producer, consumer, and farm cooperatives allow members to share risks of production, consumption, crop output, and related activities. In the case of Islamic insurance such as *takaful* (mutual care), a group pools its resources to ensure its members against risk. Ordinary insurance, where a person buys an insurance contract for a fee (indicated by a premium), is not an example of risk sharing but of risk transfer, where for a fee the insured transfers part of his or her idiosyncratic risks to a firm willing to provide protection against possible contingencies. What is missing here is the element of mutuality.

BUILDING BLOCKS OF THE ISLAMIC FINANCIAL SYSTEM

A financial system comprises different subsystems, such as the banking system, financial markets, capital markets, insurance, and derivatives, and is underpinned by legal and commercial infrastructure. When compared to the conventional system, the Islamic financial system has two distinct features: (1) the prohibition of *al-riba* (interest) results in the elimination of debt from the system, which ultimately removes leveraging; and (2) the financial system promotes risk sharing through modes of transactions that are designed to share risks and rewards on a more equitable basis.

The Islamic financial system is based on a banking system that operates without debt and promotes the financing of the real economy. Due to the risk-sharing nature of the system, stock markets play a vital role and are expected to represent a large segment of the financial system. Researchers have argued that an active and vibrant market of securitized assets, which has some resemblance to the conventional asset-based debt market but has its own distinct features, replaces the debt market and behaves and operates differently.

Islamic Banking System

The banking system in the Islamic finance paradigm uses a set of *intermediation contracts* that facilitates efficient financial intermediation and is sufficiently comprehensive to provide a wide range of typical intermediation services, such as asset transformation, payment system, custodial services, and risk management. Box 8.2 briefly describes key intermediation contracts. Both *mudarabah*, a principal/agent profit-sharing contract, and *musharakah*, equity partnership, are cornerstones of financial intermediation in the Islamic financial system.

BOX 8.2 KEY FINANCIAL INTERMEDIATION CONTRACTS IN THE ISLAMIC FINANCIAL SYSTEM

Although Islam prohibits interest-bearing debt instruments, it sanctions a wide variety of instruments and arrangements that do not entail an interest-bearing debt security but entail risk sharing and asset-based financial asset. Financial intermediation takes the form of pass-through asset management and is based on some of next types of contracts.

Mudarabah (Principal/Agent Profit-Sharing Asset Management)

In a *mudarabah* contract, an economic agent with capital develops a partnership with another economic agent who has expertise in deploying capital into real economic activities with an agreement to share the profits. *Mudarabah* partnerships perform an important economic function by combining the three most important factors of production—capital, labor, and entrepreneurship. Typically, the contract of *mudarabah* involves an arrangement in which the capital owner entrusted capital or merchandise to an agent (*mudarib*) to trade with and then return to the investor the principal plus a previously agreed on share of the profits. As a reward for the agent's labor and entrepreneurship, the agent receives the remaining share of the profit. Any loss resulting from the exigencies of travel or from an unsuccessful business venture are borne exclusively by the investor. More formally, a *mudarabah* contract is a contract of partnership between the investor (principal) and the entrepreneur who acts as an agent of the investor to invest the money in a fashion deemed suitable by the agent with an agreement to share the profits. This contract usually is limited to a certain period of time at the end of which the profits are shared according to preagreed profit-sharing ratios.

Musharakah (Equity Partnership)

The *musharakah* contract is a versatile contract with different variations to suit different situations. *Musharakah* is a hybrid of *shirakah* (partnership) and *mudarabah*, combining the act of investment and management. *Musharakah* or *shirakah* can be defined as a form of partnership where two or more people combine either their capital or their labor to share the profits and losses and where they have similar rights and liabilities.

Wikala (Principal/Agent Representation)

The contract of *wikala* is the designation of a person or legal entity to act on one's behalf or as one's representative. It has been a common practice to appoint an agent (*wakil*) to facilitate trade operations. A *wikala* contract gives a power of attorney or an agency assignment to a financial intermediary to perform a certain task. In case of *mudarabah*, the *mudarib* has full control and freedom to utilize funds according to professional knowledge, as opposed to the case of *wikala*, where the *wakil* does not have similar freedom. A *wakil* acts only as a representative to execute a particular task according to the instructions given.

Amanah (Trust) and *Wadia* (Deposits)

Amanah (trust) and *wadia* (deposits) contracts are all concerned with placing assets in trust with someone. These contracts are utilized in facilitating a custodial relationship between investors and financial institutions. *Wadia* arises when a person keeps his or her property with another person for safekeeping and also allows the other person to use it without the intention of receiving any return from it. The term *amanah* (trust contract) is a broad term used when one party is entrusted with the custody or safekeeping of someone else's property. In the context of intermediation, *amanah* refers to a contract where a party deposits assets with another for the sole purpose of safekeeping. Unlike *wadia*, where the keeper of the asset is allowed to use the asset, an *amanah* deposit is purely for safekeeping and the keeper cannot use the asset. Demand deposits of an Islamic bank are offered through *amanah* contracts.

Kifala (Suretyship)

The contract of *kifala* (suretyship) refers to an obligation in addition to an existing obligation in respect of a demand for something. In the case of financial obligation, it refers to an obligation to be met in the event of the principal debtor's inability to honor the obligation. In financial transactions, under the contract of *kifala*, a third party becomes a surety for the payment of a debt or obligation if it is not fulfilled by the person originally liable.

(continued)

BOX 8.2 (*Continued*)

Jo'ala (Service Fee)

The contract of *jo'ala* (service fee) deals with offering a service for a predetermined fee or commission. A party undertakes to pay another party a specified amount of money as a fee for rendering a specified service in accordance with the terms of the contract stipulated between the two parties. *Jo'ala* allows contracting on an object not certain to exist or come under a party's control.

Although committed to carrying out their transactions in accordance with the rules of Islam, Islamic banks are expected to perform the same essential functions as banks in the conventional system. That is, they act as the administrators of the payments system and as financial intermediaries. They are needed in the Islamic system for the same reason that they are needed in the conventional system. That is, generally, their raison d'être is the exploitation of the imperfections in the financial markets. These imperfections include imperfect divisibility of financial claims; transaction costs with the search, acquisition, and diversification by the surplus and deficit units; and the existence of expertise and economies of scale in monitoring transactions.

The contracts available to trade and the exchange of goods and services permitted by Islamic law, coupled with the intermediation contracts, offer a comprehensive set of instruments with varying financing purposes, maturities, and degrees of risk to satisfy the needs of diverse groups of economic agents in the economy. This set of instruments can be used to design a formal model for an Islamic financial intermediary (IFI) or an Islamic bank that can perform the typical functions of resource mobilization and intermediation. By utilizing this set of intermediation contracts, an IFI will be able to offer a wide array of commercial and investment banking products and services.

Formally, three theoretical models have been suggested for the structure of Islamic financial intermediation and banking. The first model is based on *mudarabah* and is commonly referred to as the two-tier *mudarabah* model, while the second model is known as the two-windows model. A less used model is known as a *wikala* (agent/representative; see Box 8.2 for detail) model, which is based on the principal/agent model but with defined restrictions. As mentioned earlier, a *mudarabah* is a principal/agent contract, where the owner of the capital (investor/depositor) forms a partnership with the holder of a specialized skill (professional manager or bank) to invest capital and to share profits and losses from the investment.

Two-Tier *Mudarabah* This model is called two-tier because the *mudarabah* contract is utilized on each side of the balance sheet of the bank. The first model, relying on the concept of profit sharing, integrates the assets and liabilities sides. This model envisages depositors entering into a contract with a bank to share the profits accruing to the bank's business. The basic concept of this model is that both fund mobilization and fund utilization are based on the same profit sharing among the investor (depositor), the bank, and the entrepreneur or users of the funds. The first tier of the *mudarabah* contract is between the investor and the bank, analogous to a depositor and the bank, where investors act as suppliers of funds to be invested by the bank as *mudarib* on their behalf. Investors share in the profits and losses earned by the bank's business related to the investors' investments. Funds are placed with the bank in an investment account.

The liabilities and equity side of the bank's balance sheet thus shows the deposits accepted on a *mudarabah* basis. Such profit-sharing investment deposits are not liabilities (the capital is not guaranteed, and investors incur losses if the bank does) but are a form of limited-term, nonvoting equity. In this model, in addition to investment deposits, banks accept demand deposits that yield no returns and are repayable on demand at par and are treated as liabilities. This model, though requiring that current deposits must be paid at the demand of the depositors, has no specific reserve requirement.

The second tier represents the *mudarabah* contract between the bank as supplier of funds and the entrepreneurs who need funds and agree to share profits with the bank according to a certain percentage stipulated in the contract. The bank's earnings from all its activities are pooled and are then shared with its depositors and shareholders according to the terms of their contract. Thus the profit earned by depositors is a percentage of total banking profits. A distinguishing feature of the two-tier model is that, by design, the assets and liabilities sides of a bank's balance sheet are fully integrated, which minimizes the need for active asset-liability management, which, in turn, provides stability against economic shocks. The model does not feature any specific reserve requirements on either the investments or the demand deposits.

Two-Windows Model The two-windows model also features demand and investment accounts but takes a different view from the two-tier model on reserve requirements. The two-windows model divides the liabilities side of the bank balance sheet into two windows, one for demand deposits (transactions balances) and the other for investment balances. The choice of the window is left to depositors. This model requires a 100% reserve for demand deposits but stipulates no reserve requirement for the second window. This is based on the assumption that the money deposited as demand deposits is placed as *amanah* (safekeeping) and must be backed by 100% reserves, because these balances belong to depositors. The bank does not have a right to use these deposits as the basis for money creation through fractional reserves. Depositors know that money they deposit in investment accounts will be invested in risk-bearing projects, and therefore no guarantee is justified. Also in this model, depositors may be charged a service fee for the safekeeping services rendered by the bank. In this model, the provisions of interest-free loans to those who may need them are limited to depositors who believe that the bank may be better equipped to channel such loans. No portion of the deposits in current accounts or investment accounts has to be used for this purpose.

Wikala **Model**   A third but less known model for an Islamic bank has also been suggested. This model is based on the contract of *wikala*, where an Islamic bank acts purely as a *wakil* (agent/representative) for investors and manages funds on their behalf for a fixed fee. The terms and conditions of the *wikala* contract are to be determined by mutual agreement between the bank and its clients. An Islamic bank is typically a hybrid between a conventional commercial bank and an investment bank, and thus resembles a universal bank. Table 8.1 constructs a conceptual balance sheet of an Islamic bank based on different functions and services to give us an overview of its structure, operations, and capabilities of intermediation.

Liabilities   On its liabilities side, an Islamic bank offers current, savings, investment, and special-investment accounts to depositors. Unlike conventional commercial banks, which accept deposits with the promise to return the principal amount in full with a fixed and predetermined return, an Islamic bank would not be able to offer such explicit guarantees of principal and fixed return. Rather it would assure depositors that it would select the best opportunities that minimize risk of loss for depositors but still provide

TABLE 8.1   Stylized Balance Sheet of an Islamic Bank

Assets	Liabilities
Trade financing (*salaam, murabahah*)	Demand deposits (*amanah/waad*)
Leasing/Rentals *(ijarah/istisna)*	Investment accounts (*mudarabah*)
Profit-sharing/Loss-sharing investments (*mudarabah)*	Special investment accounts (*Mudarabah*)
Equity investments (*musharakah)*	Capital
Fee for services	Equity
	Reserves

attractive market-competitive returns. Using the techniques of portfolio management and diversification, an optimal portfolio of trade-related and asset-linked securities can be financed using depositors' funds. By deploying funds in this fashion, the intermediary will be able not only to offer short-term time deposits with minimized financial risk and sufficient liquidity but also to facilitate a system-wide payment system backed by real assets.

Current accounts are demand accounts kept with the bank on custodial arrangements and are repayable in full on demand. Current accounts are based on the principle of *wadia* or *amanah*, creating an agency contract for the purpose of protecting and safekeeping depositors' assets. The major portion of the bank's financial liabilities would consist of *investment accounts* that are, strictly speaking, not liabilities but a form of equity investment, generally based on the principle of *mudarabah*. Investment accounts are offered in different forms, often linked to a preagreed period of maturity, which may be from one month on and can be withdrawn if advance notice is given to the bank. Profits and returns are distributed between depositors and the bank according to a predetermined ratio (typically 80:20, but this may vary considerably from bank to bank).

A bank may also offer *special-investment accounts* customized for various types of investors: ordinary householders, high-net-worth individuals, or institutional clients. These accounts also operate on the principle of *mudarabah*, but the modes of investment of the funds and distribution of the profits are customized to suit client needs. In general, these accounts are linked to special investment opportunities identified by the bank. These opportunities have a specific size and maturity and result from the bank's participation in a pool of investment, private equity, a joint venture, or a fund. To some extent these accounts resemble specialized funds to finance different asset classes. The maturity and the distribution of profits for special-investment accounts are negotiated separately for each account, with the yield directly related to the success of the particular investment project. Funds for special-investment accounts can be designed and developed with specific risk–return profiles to offer customers and clients opportunities to manage portfolios and to perform risk management. In addition to deposits, an Islamic bank offers basic banking services, such as fund transfers, letters of credit, foreign-exchange transactions, and investment management and advice, for a fee, to retail and institutional clients.

The last item on the liabilities side is typically equity capital and reserves accumulated over the time. It should be noted that given the prohibition of debt, Islamic banks do not carry any debt capital, which is a significant source of capital for conventional banks. Rather, Islamic banks are capitalized through equity. It has been argued that since the mode of intermediation is based on a pass-through profit-sharing/loss-sharing agreement, Islamic banks do not need to keep significant equity capital. This notion may be theoretically correct but as we will see later, Islamic banks are still required to maintain a certain minimum level of capital. They can also set aside a portion of the profits each year as reserves to be used during times of economic slowdown.

Assets   While the liabilities side of the bank has limited ways to raise funds, the assets side can carry a more diversified portfolio of heterogeneous asset classes, representing a wider spectrum of the risk and maturity profile. For short-maturity, limited-risk investments, there is a choice of investing in short-term trade financing. Such assets originate from trade-related activities, such as *murabahah*, *bay' al-muajjil*, or *bay' salám*, and are arranged by the bank, which uses its skills, market knowledge, and customer base to finance the trading activity. In addition, the bank can provide short-term funds to its clients to meet their working capital needs. The short-term maturity of these instruments and the fact that they are backed by real assets minimize their level of risk. The bank considers these securities highly attractive and gives them preference over other investment vehicles.

For medium-term maturity investments, the bank has several choices. The funds can be invested in assets based on *ijarah* (leasing) and *istisna* (construction/manufacturing contract). A benefit of these contracts is not only that they are backed by an asset but that they can also have either a fixed- or a floating-rate feature that can facilitate portfolio management. The common features of Islamic and conventional leasing provide additional investment opportunities for the bank since investing in conventional leases with appropriate modifications can be made consistent with *Shariah* principles. However, leasing has its own overheads, which a bank may not like to accept. For example, leasing requires a bank to deviate from its primary role as a financial intermediary, in that it involves purchasing an asset and retaining ownership of it until the asset is disposed of, with the responsibility of maintenance and associated costs over the life of the contract. Disposing of the asset requires not only bearing all risks resulting from price fluctuations but also having some marketing expertise. All this will require the bank to engage in activities beyond financial intermediation.

In addition, an Islamic bank can set up special-purpose (customized) portfolios to invest in a particular asset class and sector and can finance these portfolios by issuing special-purpose *mudarabah* investment accounts. In some way, this segment of the assets side represents a fund of funds, where each fund is financed by matching *mudarabah* contracts on the liabilities side through special-investment accounts. For longer-term maturity investments, an Islamic bank can engage in venture-capital or private-equity activities in the form of *musharakah*.

An Islamic bank can attract depositors/investors either by inviting them to share profits and losses on a general pool of assets maintained by the financial intermediary itself or by acting as a dealer/broker for third-party products. The general pool could be in the form of various funds specializing in specific sectors or geographical regions. In this case, investors/depositors will be placing funds with the bank in a fund of funds, a collection of diversified portfolios of financial assets. The relationship between the bank and the depositors/investors could be on the basis of a *mudarabah*, where the bank manages assets for a fee, or a *musharakah*, where the bank shares profits and losses with the depositors/investors. In either case, there is risk sharing between the financial intermediary and depositors/investors. Or the Islamic bank can act simply as a dealer/broker and help the investor to select and place funds in portfolios of independent fund managers who specialize in specific asset classes, investment styles, sectors, and maturity terms. In this case, the bank facilitates the purchase/sale of third-party products and has no liability regarding the outcome or the performance of those products. However, the bank may perform due diligence on the funds and their managers before making any recommendations to customers. Typically, the assets are divided into banking and trading books. The banking book consists of old-fashioned investments and financing of real-sector activities, whereas the trading book contains financial securities such as bonds.

Banks in the Islamic financial system can be reasonably expected to exploit economies of scale, as do their counterparts in the conventional system. Through their ability to take advantage of these imperfections, they alter the yield relationships between surplus and deficit financial units and thus provide financing at a lower cost to deficit units and a higher return to surplus units than would be possible with direct financing. Just as in the conventional financial system, the Islamic depository enables financial intermediaries to transform the liabilities of business into a variety of obligations to suit the preferences and circumstances of the surplus units. Their liabilities consist of investments/deposits, and their assets consist mainly of instruments of varying risk-return profiles. These banks are concerned with decisions relating to such issues as the nature of their objective functions; portfolio choice among risky assets; liability and capital management; reserve management; the interaction between asset and liability sides of their balance sheets; and the management of off-balance sheet items, such as revolving lines of credit, standby and commercial letters of credit, and bankers' acceptances.

Moreover, as asset transformers, these institutions become risk evaluators and serve as filters to evaluate signals in a financial environment with limited information. Their deposit liabilities serve as a medium of exchange, and they have the ability to minimize the cost of transactions that convert current income into an optimal consumption bundle. One major difference between the two systems is that, due to the prohibition against taking interest and the fact that they have to rely primarily on profit sharing, Islamic banks have to offer their asset portfolios of primary securities in the form of risky open-ended "mutual fund"–type packages for sale to investors/depositors. In contrast to the Islamic system, banks in the conventional system keep the title of the portfolios they originate. The banks fund these assets by issuing deposit contracts, a practice that results in solvency and liquidity risks, since asset portfolios and loans entail risky payoffs and/or costs of liquidation prior to maturity while deposit contracts are liabilities that often are payable instantly at par. In contrast, Islamic banks act as agents of investors/depositors and, therefore, create pass-through intermediation between savers and entrepreneurs. In short, Islamic financial intermediaries are envisioned to intervene with an embedded notion of risk sharing. Intermediation is performed on a pass-through basis such that the returns (positive or negative) on the assets are passed to investors/depositors. The intermediary applies financial engineering to design assets with a wide range of risk-return profiles to suit the demands of investors on the liabilities side.

Distinctive Features of the Islamic Mode of Intermediation and Banking   Financial intermediation and banking in the Islamic financial system differ from conventional banking in a number of important ways.

Socially Responsible and Ethical Financing   Compliance with rules prescribed by Islam forces banks and financial intermediaries to engage in socially responsible and ethical financing by declining financing of harmful activities for the society and by encouraging financing of social welfare and expending access to finance.

Nature of Fiduciary Responsibilities   With financial intermediation in Islam, the intermediary simply passes through the performance of its assets to investors/depositors on its liability side. There is an element of risk-sharing present in the contractual agreement between the financial intermediary and depositors/investors. Assets on the asset side of the balance sheet could be in form of over-the-counter assets financed by the Islamic bank or direct investments in marketable securities of *Shariah*-compliant assets (i.e., equities or asset-linked securities). In the case of Islamic banks, there is more diversity of contractual agreements as the banks may be acting as trustees in one mode of intermediation and acting as "partners" in another. Islamic banks also enter into a principal/agent model on both sides of the balance sheet.

Profit/Loss Sharing The profit-sharing/loss-sharing concept implies a direct concern for the profitability of the physical investment on the part of the creditor (the Islamic bank). Conventional banks are also concerned about profitability of a project, because of concerns about potential default on the loan. However, conventional banks emphasize receiving the interest payments according to set time intervals, and so long as this condition is met, the banks' profitability is not directly affected by whether the project has a particularly high or a low rate of return. In contrast, Islamic banks have to focus on the return on the physical investment, because their own profitability is directly linked to the real rate of return.

Enhanced Monitoring Islamic financial contracting encourages banks to focus on the long term in their relationships with clients. However, this focus on long-term relationships in profit-sharing/loss-sharing arrangements means that there might be higher costs in some areas, particularly in regard to the need for monitoring the performance of an entrepreneur in any business arrangement. Conventional banks are not obliged to oversee projects as closely as Islamic banks are, because the former do not act as if they were partners in the physical investment. To the extent that Islamic banks provide something akin to equity financing as opposed to debt financing, they need to invest relatively more in managerial skills and expertise in overseeing different investment projects. This is one reason why there is a tendency among Islamic banks to rely on financial instruments that are acceptable under Islamic principles but are not the best in terms of risk-sharing properties, because in some respects these financial instruments are closer to debt than to equity.

Asset/Liability Management Theoretically, Islamic banks offer their asset portfolios in the form of risky open-ended mutual funds to investors/depositors. By contrast, banks in the conventional system finance their assets through issuing time-bound deposit contracts. This practice results in solvency and liquidity risks, since their asset portfolios and loans entail risky payoffs and/or liquidation costs prior to maturity, while their deposit contracts are liabilities that often are payable instantly at par. In contrast, Islamic banks act as agents for investors/depositors and, therefore, create a pass-through intermediation between savers and entrepreneurs, eliminating the risk faced by conventional banks. One of the most critical and distinguishing features of financial intermediation by Islamic banks as compared to that by conventional banks is the inherent design by which the assets and liabilities sides of the Islamic bank's balance sheet are matched. Conventional banks accept deposits at a predetermined rate irrespective of the rate of return earned on the assets side of the bank. This instantaneously creates a fixed liability for the banks without the certainty that they would be able to earn more than they promised or committed to paying to depositors. Since the return on the asset depends on a bank's ability to invest the funds at a higher rate than the one promised on the liability side, and since this rate is unknown, it can lead to the classic problem of mismatch between assets and liabilities. In contrast, there is no predetermined rate on the deposits/investments and depositors' share in profits and losses on the assets side of the Islamic bank; therefore, the problem of asset–liability mismatch does not arise. It has been argued that because of this pass-through nature of the business and the closely matched assets and liabilities, financial intermediation by Islamic banks contributes to the stability of the Islamic financial system.

Stability of the Banking System   The conventional banking system is a fractional reserve banking system that is predominantly based on debt financing and, by its structure, creates money and encourages leveraging. The embedded risk of such a system is that its money and debt creation and leveraging could be excessive. Safeguards, such as deposit guarantee schemes by the Federal Deposit Insurance Corporation in the United States and the classification of some banks as too big to fail are the implicit government subsidies that reduce funding cost and create moral hazard, encouraging mispricing and excessive assumption of risk by financial institutions. The mispricing of loans and assumption of excessive risk, in turn, threaten the liquidity and solvency of financial institutions. Systemic risks that are inherent in the system, such as linkages and interdependencies of institutions as well as the prominence of institutions that are too large to fail, create financial instability and threaten the financial and the real economy. To enhance financial stability, regulators would have to adopt policies and practices that eliminate moral hazard and excessive debt creation and leveraging.

One way to ensure the stability of the financial system is to *eliminate* the type of asset–liability risk that threatens the solvency of all financial institutions, including commercial banks. This would require commercial banks to restrict their activities to cash safekeeping and investing client money as in a mutual fund. Banks would accept deposits for safekeeping only (e.g., as in a system with 100% reserve requirement) and would charge a fee for providing this service and for check-writing privileges. In their intermediation capacity, banks would identify and analyze investment opportunities and would offer them to clients; banks would charge a fee for this service, much as traditional investment banks do. The bank would not be assuming any asset–liability risk on its balance sheet; instead, gains or losses would accrue directly to client investors. In other words, there would be very little debt financing by banks, only equity financing, and no risk shifting, only risk sharing. Banks would not create money, as under a fractional reserve system. Financial institutions would be serving their traditional role of intermediation between savers and investors but with no debt on their balance sheets, no leveraging, and no predetermined interest rate payments as an obligation. Proposals along these lines are not new. Financial systems in some such form have been practiced throughout recorded history. Such an approach was recommended in the Chicago Plan, formulated in a memorandum written in 1933 by a group of renowned University of Chicago professors and forcefully advocated and supported by Professor Irving Fisher in his book titled *100% Money*. More recently, Laurence Kotlikoff has made a proposal along similar lines, calling it limited purpose banking.[3]

Capital Markets

Conventional capital markets can be broadly divided into three categories: (1) debt markets; (2) equities or stock markets; and (3) market for structured securities, which are hybrid of either equity or debt securities. Debt markets dominate the conventional capital markets, and debt is considered the major source of external funding for the corporate and public sectors. As a result of financial innovations and the application of financial engineering, large numbers of financial products have been developed for resource mobilization. Most of these innovations are variations of plain-vanilla debt or equity security with added optionality or customization.

In comparison, Islamic capital markets would have two major categories: (1) stock market and (2) securitized "asset-linked" securities. Due to the prohibition on interest, the financial system is free of any pure debt market, and there is a clear preference for risk-sharing securities, such as an exchange-traded stock market. After the stock market, a market for securitized securities issued against a pool of assets, which carry risk-return characteristics of underlying assets, is be the major source of capital.

Stock Markets With the prohibition on interest and the preference for partnerships to share profits and losses, equity markets hold a significant place in the Islamic financial system. Therefore, Islamic scholars have pointed out the necessity, desirability, and permissibility of a stock market in the Islamic financial system in which transactions in primary capital instruments such as corporate stocks can take place. The conditions of the operations of these markets, in accordance with the rules of *Shariah*, are much like those that must prevail in markets for goods and services. For example, in such markets the rules are intended to remove all factors inimical to justice in

---

[3]Kotlikoff (2010).

exchange and to yield prices that are considered fair and just. Prices are just or equitable not on any independent criterion of justice but because they are the result of bargaining between equal, informed, free, and responsible economic agents. To ensure justice in exchange, *Shariah* has provided a network of ethical and moral rules of behavior for all participants in the market and requires that these norms and rules be internalized and adhered to by all. Given that a proper securities underwriting function is performed by some institutions in the system (e.g. the banks), the firms could then directly raise the necessary funds for their investment projects from the stock market, which would provide them a second source of funding other than the banks.

If we assert that Islamic finance is all about risk sharing, then the first best instrument of risk sharing is a stock market, "which is arguably the most sophisticated market-based risk-sharing mechanism."[4] Developing an efficient stock market can effectively complement and supplement the existing and to-be-developed array of other Islamic finance instruments. It would provide the means for business and industry to raise long-term capital. A vibrant stock market would allow risk diversification necessary for management of aggregate and idiosyncratic risks. Such an active market would reduce the dominance of banks and debt financing where risks become concentrated and lead to system fragility.[5]

A stock market operating strictly in accordance with Islamic rules is envisioned to be one in which the disposal of investible funds is based on the profit prospects of enterprises, in which relative profit rates reflect the efficiencies between firms and in which profit rates (as signals coming from the goods market) are not distorted by market imperfections. Such a market might be expected to allocate investible funds strictly in accordance with expected investment yields (i.e., resources would be allocated in order to finance higher-return projects). Stock markets would also be capable of improving allocation of savings by accumulating and disseminating vital information in order to facilitate comparisons between all available opportunities, thus reflecting the general efficiency in resource allocation expected from a system that operates primarily on the basis of investment productivity.

Securitized—Asset-Linked Securities—Markets In addition to the standard stock market, there is another capital market that provides a platform for structuring and trading asset-linked securities. The notion in Islamic finance of binding capital and financing closely and tightly to the real asset that is financed encourages the issuance of marketable securities against such portfolios of assets.

---

[4]Brav (2002).
[5]Sheng (2009).

Securitization involves the collection of homogeneous assets with a known stream of cash flows into a pool, or portfolio, which is independent from the creditworthiness of the financier. This pool or portfolio of assets is used to issue securities, which can be marketed to different classes of investors. The securities are structured in such a way that all payoffs in terms of risks and returns are passed through to investors or holders of the securities. As a result, this is similar to a direct ownership by the investor in the underlying assets; he or she shares the returns from the assets and is exposed to all associated risks. The securities can be traded on organized exchanges or over the counter.

The main structural difference between the Islamic securitization process and that of conventional securitization is, however, the way in which returns and risks are shared with investors; in the conventional system, the buyer and the holder of the security is exposed to a number of risks that are passed on to him or her (including credit risk, market risk, and interest rate risk,) but he or she enjoys some protection given by the underlying assets that "back" the security ("asset-backed security"). This structure does not transfer any rights or control or ownership over these assets to investors. The function of the asset backing is credit enhancement: In the case of a default, the assets will be seized and the proceeds from foreclosure will be used to repay investors.

In contrast, the Islamic finance structure suggests the establishment of a link between the security ownership and payoffs and the underlying assets. This "asset-linked" structure leads to (1) an ownership interest by investors (i.e., Islamic bank) in the underlying asset and (2) uncertainties in the security's cash flows to investors. Investors' returns will depend on the performance of the underlying asset. The repayment of principal will not be necessarily guaranteed but would be limited to the market value of the asset at the time of repayment. Additionally, the holder of the security establishes an ownership claim against underlying assets (whereas in a conventional securitization structure, the holder of a security establishes a claim against a pool of assets).[6]

Figure 8.1 depicts a simplified model of securitization as used in a *ijarah*-based securitization, which is commonly known as *sakk* (certificate of ownership). The core legal entity in the securitization is a special-purpose *mudarabah* (SPM) or special-purpose vehicle (SPV), which is bankruptcy remote and has *Shariah*-compliant assets on the asset side against liabilities of *sukuk* or marketable securities. Although fund mobilization, pooling of assets, setting up of SPMs or SPVs, placement, and servicing are structured

---

[6]Zöngür (2010).

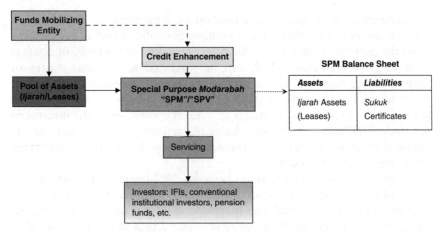

FIGURE 8.1 Anatomy of a *Shariah*-Compliant Securitization
Source: Iqbal and Mirakhor (2011).

similar to those of conventional securitization, credit enhancement, which gives the certificates an investment grade rating, is complex to replicate. It is difficult to provide financial guarantees and credit enhancement because Islamic finance is risk sharing and passing through the return on assets to investors. This is particularly critical in the case where the underlying assets are exposed to high risk, similar to that of microfinance portfolios.

Table 8.2 shows the main differences between conventional and *Shariah*-compliant securitized assets. The comparison is with a conceptual view of *Shariah*-compliant securitization and may be different from the actual securitized product practiced in the market. In a conventional asset-backed or mortgage-backed security, the typical pricing model uses variables such as the probability of prepayment or refinancing, which depends on the expected interest rate levels in the future, the loan-to-debt ratio, the credit score of the borrower, and other considerations. Since the principal of the security is guaranteed through credit-enhancing mechanisms, the security is priced in the same way as a coupon-bearing debt security with an early prepayment option.

In the case of an Islamic security, however, the price will depend on variables determining the expected periodic cash flows in the future. In addition, it will have to take into consideration the expectation of future market values or the residual values of the underlying assets. In the absence of any guarantee of the principal, the redemption value of the security will depend on the expected market value of the asset at the time of maturity of the security. Another factor that influences the pricing of an Islamic security is the underlying risk-sharing agreement. In an asset-linked security, the price of

TABLE 8.2 Comparison between Conventional and Islamic Securitized Securities

	Conventional Asset-Backed Security	Shariah-Compliant, Asset-Based Security
Type of security	Fixed income (debt based)	Hybrid structure depending on contract and underlying asset
Intended risk allocation	Risk transfer	Risk sharing
Ownership	No ownership in underlying assets	Security owner has ownership interest in underlying asset
Linkage with asset value	No direct link to market value of underlying asset	Final or other payoffs may be linked to market value of underlying asset
Principal protection	Principal is protected irrespective of the value of underlying real estate	Principal is linked to market value of underlying asset
Pricing variable	Based on expected yields, current interest rates, creditworthiness of asset owner and issuer or guarantor	Based on expected yields, current levels of return, market value of underlying asset, expected value of underlying asset at maturity
Recourse	No recourse of security holder in case of distress	Recourse to underlying asset in case of distress
Principal-agent problem	May exist	Moral hazard should be minimized

Source: Iqbal and Mirakhor (2011).
The table highlights the differences from a theoretical perspective. At present, in most cases *sukuk* issues resemble conventional securitization structures.

the security will also incorporate the riskiness of the underlying assets, and investors will be sharing the risk through fluctuations in the price of the security. Investors will be exposed to the risks associated with the portfolio of assets and will share the losses. This will put greater emphasis on the need for prudent selection of the underlying assets and close monitoring of the assets' performance, and should motivate securitization specialists to structure good-quality securities that offer valuable and secure investment opportunities.

Principal–agent problems are treated in a different way in the Islamic system. In a conventional securitization, securitization can create considerable agency costs if agents (borrowers, originators, issuers, arrangers, investors, servicers, credit-rating agencies, and third-party guarantors) are tempted to pursue their own economic interests. For example, uncertainty about the future value of the securitized assets could lead to moral hazard by originators if default risk is completely passed on to the investors. The advantage of the originator with regard to information about the quality of borrowers and the historical performance of individual asset exposures could also give rise to adverse selection when security selection favors the originator rather than the investor. In a *Shariah*-compliant securitization, moral hazard should be minimized by *Shariah*-compliant contract structures. For example, the *musharakah* arrangement with predetermined profit-loss-sharing ratios aims to regulate incentive structures.[7] Additionally, *Shariah* requirements to maintain high moral values and ethics by the stakeholder would discourage practices such as predatory lending or walking away.

Derivative Markets

No discussion of financial systems can be complete without a mention of derivative markets. Derivative markets perform the three main functions in a financial system:

1. **Risk reduction and redistribution.** It is widely accepted that the primary function of the derivatives market is to facilitate the transfer of risk among economic agents. Financial derivatives unbundle the risks associated with traditional domestic and cross-border investment vehicles, such as foreign exchange, interest rate, market, credit, and liquidity risks. Derivatives facilitate the decomposition of risks and the redistribution of these risks from those who do not want or are not capable of hedging them to those who are in a better position to do so.
2. **Price discovery and stabilization.** The existence of derivatives markets for futures and options is expected to increase information flows into the market and is known to lead to a price-discovery function in the financial sector.
3. **Completeness of markets.** Another critical function of the derivatives market is that it can enable individuals and firms to customize and monetize payoffs that might not otherwise be possible without considerable transaction costs.

Research on the scope of derivative securities and trading of risk in an Islamic financial system is in its early stages. *Shariah* scholars are working on assessing the permissibility of derivatives such as forwards, futures, options,

---

[7] Jobst (2009).

and swaps. Unlike financing and investment instruments, which have been in existence for several centuries and therefore have been studied by *Shariah* scholars, financial derivatives as independent financial contracts that can be traded have no precedents in classical Islamic jurisprudence. As a result, the research in this area is still evolving. While there have been a number of studies, these have not resulted in any concrete conclusions and consensus.

The majority view of *Shariah* scholars is that an option is a promise to sell or purchase a thing at a specific price within a stipulated time, and such a promise cannot be the subject of a sale or purchase. The Islamic Fiqh Academy, Jeddah, asserts:

> *Option contracts as currently applied in the world financial markets are a new type of contract which do not come under any one of the Shariah nominate contracts. Since the subject of the contract is neither a sum of money nor a utility nor a financial right which may be waived, the contract is not permissible in Shariah.*[8]

These objections are based on the prohibition of *maysir* (speculative risk) and *gharar* (exposure to excessive risk). The Quran prohibits *maysir*, warning the faithful to avoid games of chance with asymmetrical probabilities (i.e., those in which the probability of a loss is much higher than the probability of a gain). Conventional finance asserts that speculators play an important role in price discovery and price stabilization, but it omits the fact that excessive and large-scale speculation can become a factor for instability in the system. In Islam, all gambling is strictly discouraged on the grounds that it does not create value in society and an addiction to gambling is detrimental to economic growth.

In short, debate on derivatives will continue in Islamic finance. At present they have very limited acceptability, and it is unlikely that the practice of derivatives will be as widespread as seen in conventional markets any time soon. However, as Islamic finance grows, its own version of hedging mechanisms and financial products with embedded options will emerge. Prohibition of derivatives, however, does not preclude an Islamic financial intermediary from designing a risk-sharing or risk-mitigating scheme. This can be achieved through the creation of a risk-mitigating instrument synthetically using existing instruments. As shown earlier in this chapter and in Chapter 7, Islamic financial instruments promote risk sharing, which implies that there will be risk sharing across the system while there will be opportunities for financial intermediaries to utilize these

---

[8] IRTI (2000).

contracts and the freedom to contract in designing products and services to hedge against exposures.

TAKAFUL (ISLAMIC INSURANCE)

The closest Islamic instrument to the contemporary system of insurance is the instrument of *takaful*, which literally means "mutual or joint guarantee." See Box 8.3 for the important features of *takaful*. Table 8.3 compares different features of *takaful*, conventional, and mutual insurance.

BOX 8.3 DISTINCTIVE FEATURES OF *TAKAFUL*

Insurance in Islam, or *takaful*, has its own distinctive features and is compatible with the concept of risk sharing.

Cooperative Organization

Takaful is based on principles of mutual assistance and therefore is similar to conventional cooperative insurance whereby participants pool their funds together to insure one another. The customers (policy holders) of the *takaful* business agree to pool their contributions and share the liability of each. Claims are paid out of the combined pool of contributions and assets.

Risk Sharing

In the risk-sharing aspect, *takaful* is closer to the essence of Islamic finance than the Islamic banks are. The policy holders share in the profits and losses of the business through sharing each other's insurance risk as compared to conventional insurance, where there is no sharing of risk across policy holders. For example, in the case of a typical *takaful* model, a surplus or profit made at the end of a financial year after satisfying all claims and reserves is shared between the *takaful* operators and their policy holders. If at the end of the financial year the policy holders' fund suffers a loss, the deficit is funded by an interest-free loan (*qardh hassan*) from the shareholders' fund. Any future surpluses are used to repay the loan. The shareholders' access to the capital from the fund is restricted until the loan is repaid.

Shariah-Compliant Investments

One of the most distinguishing features of *takaful* is the requirement that all investments and assets under management be invested in accordance with the principles of Islam. Therefore, they have to be fully compliant with *Shariah*. Where conventional insurance companies invest funds in debt-based, fixed-income securities, derivatives, government securities, and hedge funds, a *takaful* asset manager cannot invest in these products. Similarly, any investment in stock markets is required to be compliant with *Shariah*. With the continued expansion of Islamic financial markets, there are more opportunities to find *Shariah*-compliant investment products, and this requirement is becoming much less of a constraint.

Mutual Guarantee

Takaful is based on cooperative principles that spread the liability among the policy holders, and all losses are shared. This mutuality results in the policy holders guaranteeing the performance of each other. In other words, policy holders are both the insurer and the insured.

TABLE 8.3 Comparative Features of Conventional Insurance, Mutual Insurance, and *Takaful*

	Conventional Insurance	Mutual Insurance	*Takaful*
Responsibility for providing protection	Risk is transferred from the insured to the insurer	Mutual risk sharing among members	Mutual risk sharing among participants
Governing law	Secular law and regulation	Secular law and regulation	Secular law and regulation and *Shariah* law
Ownership	Shareholders of insurance company	Members	Participants
Contract forms	Bilateral insurance policy	Bilateral insurance policy	*Wikala/ mudarabah* agreement and unilateral contracts based on principles of *tabarru* (donation)

(*continued*)

TABLE 8.3 (*continued*)

	Conventional Insurance	Mutual Insurance	*Takaful*
Investment	No restrictions on equity/debt investments	No restrictions on equity/debt investments	All investments to be in accordance with *Shariah* principles—excludes all debt and some equity investments
Liability of operator	Insurance company (and ultimately its shareholders) is responsible for any claim payments	Members of the mutual fund are collectively responsible for payment of claims and may be asked to contribute in the event of shortfall	Participants are collectively responsible for payment of claims and may be asked to contribute in the event of shortfall if *takaful* operator does not provide *qardh hassan* (interest-free loan)
Surplus in operational income	Ultimately for shareholders' accounts	For members' accounts	For participants' accounts

Source: Peter Hodgins, *Middle East Insurance: Takaful Q & A* (London: Clyde & Co., 2009).

At present, *takaful* has very limited application in Islamic financial markets, with very few institutions offering insurance services on a large scale. Although the application of *takaful* is for the most part indemnity based and limited to the loss of physical property, a growing number of products in the market target family and medical coverage based on *Shariah* principles.

There is no standard operating model for *takaful* companies, as each country may decide on a particular model. Primarily, *takaful* models can be *mudarabah* based, *wikalah* based, or a hybrid of the two. Typically, implementation of *takaful* is carried out in the form of solidarity *mudarabah*, where the participants agree to share their losses by contributing periodic premiums in the form of investments. They are then entitled to redeem the

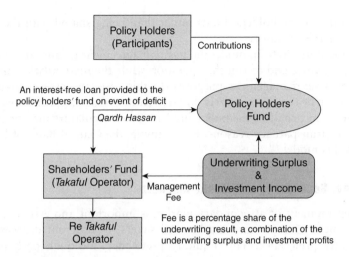

FIGURE 8.2 *Mudarabah*-Based *Takaful* Model
Source: E&Y (2009).

residual value of profits after fulfilling the claims and premiums.[9] One of the critical differences between contemporary insurance models and *takaful* is participants' rights to receive surplus profits. While the participants in a given *takaful mudarabah* have the right to share the surplus profits generated, at the same time they are liable for additional amounts if the initial premiums paid during a period are not sufficient to meet all the losses and risks incurred during that period. *Takaful* companies can constitute reserves (like conventional mutual insurance companies), which allows for the need of the insured to make supplemental contributions if claims exceed premiums (insurance claim payouts exceed insurance premiums paid in). Figure 8.2 shows a *takaful* setup based on a *mudarabah* contract.

In the *wikalah* model, the policy holders and the *takaful* operator enter into a principal (policy holder) and agent (operator) agreement whereby the operator becomes the representative (*wakil*) of the policy holders. The operator is paid an agreed fee to operate and manage the policy holders' assets. Technically, there is not much difference between the *mudarabah*-based or *wikalah*-based models except that the underwriting surplus goes

[9]For instance, under the Malaysian *Takaful* Act 1984, the legal definition of a *takaful* scheme is based on the concept of solidarity and brotherhood, which provides mutual financial aid and assistance to participants in cases of need, whereby participants agree mutually to contribute for that purpose.

back to the policy holders' funds rather than being shared with the share-holders or the operator.

In the third, hybrid, model the *wikalah* agreement is utilized for under-writing activities and to run the operation while the *mudarabah* contract is used for asset-management purposes. In this case, the asset-management business can be run by an entirely different entity—that is, a professional asset manager—on behalf of the policy holders. Some regulators may prefer this model for transparency reasons. For example, the Central Bank of Bahrain prefers this model.[10]

Primary, Secondary, and Money Markets

The development of a secondary market is important and essential to the development of a primary market. All savers, to different degrees, have a liquidity preference. This liquidity preference, although perhaps to a different extent and magnitude, can exist in an Islamic system or in any other system. To the extent that savers can, if necessary, sell securities quickly and at low cost, they will be more willing to devote a higher portion of their savings to long-term instruments than they would otherwise. Since the probability is high that primary securities in the Islamic system would be tied to the projects and management of particular enterprises, there are various risks that must enter into the portfolio decisions of savers. Examples of these types of risks concern the earning power of the firm and the risk of its default.

Another class of risk is closely tied to the secondary market for a given security issued by firms. If two securities are identical in all respects except that one has a well-organized secondary market while the other has a poor one, an investor in the latter runs the risk of liquidating security holdings at depressed prices as compared to the prices offered for the security with the well-organized secondary market. Moreover, the degree of this mar-ketability risk is directly related to factors such as the extent of participants' knowledge as well as the number of traders in the market, which determine the depth and the resilience of secondary markets.

In an Islamic system, perhaps more than in any other, both the primary and secondary markets require the active support of the government, the central bank, and regulators, not only in their initial development and promotion but also in their supervision and control, in order to ensure their compliance with the rules of *Shariah*. Particularly in the case of the secondary markets, traders and market makers need the support and supervision of the

---

[10]Ernst & Young (2009).

central bank if these markets are to operate efficiently. For secondary markets to transform an asset into a reliable source of cash for an economic unit whenever the latter needs it, they must be dealer markets in which there is a set of position users who trade significant amounts of assets. In the traditional interest-based system, these position takers are financed by borrowings from banks, financial intermediaries, and other private cash sources. Since in the Islamic system refinancing on the basis of debt is not permitted, reliable and adequate sources of funds must be provided by the central bank. There will have to be arrangements through which the central bank and the financial regulator can, at least partially, finance secondary markets and supervise them fully.

In a conventional interest-based system, the money market becomes a means by which financial institutions can adjust their balance sheet and finance positions. Short-term cash positions, which exist as a result of imperfect synchronization in the payment period, become essential ingredients for the presence of the money markets. The money market, in this case, becomes a source of temporary financing and a repository of excess liquidity in which transactions are mainly portfolio adjustments, and no planned or recently achieved savings need be involved. In an Islamic financial system, the liabilities that an economic unit generates are, by necessity, closely geared to the characteristics of its investment. The liabilities that financial intermediaries generate, in contrast, are expected to have nearly the same distribution of possible values as the assets they acquire. Hence, given that debt instruments cannot exist, money market activities will have different characteristics from their counterparts in the conventional system. As stated earlier, the existence of a poorly organized money market combined with a poor structure of financial intermediation leads to a situation where money becomes more important as a repository of wealth than would be the case with more active financial intermediation.

The existence of broad, deep, and resilient markets where assets and liabilities of financial intermediaries can be negotiated is a necessary feature of supportive money markets. Additionally, to the extent that money markets lower the income elasticity of demand for cash and finance investment projects, their importance in an Islamic financial system cannot be overlooked. Even in this system, money markets will enable financial units to be safely illiquid, provided they have assets that can be efficiently exchanged for cash in the money market. In this system, too, the basic source of the money in the market is the existence of pools of excess liquidity. One main activity of money markets in this system is to make arrangements by which the surplus funds of one financial institution are channeled into profit-sharing projects of another. It is conceivable that, at times, some banks may have excess funds, but no assets to invest in, or at least assets sufficiently attractive in their risk–return characteristics. Yet there may be banks with insufficient financial resources to fund all available opportunities or with investment opportunities requiring commitments of what the banks may consider excessive funds in order for them to take a position and for which they may prefer risk sharing with surplus banks. In such a case, the development of an interbank funds market is a distinct possibility. It may also be possible for some banks to refinance certain positions that they have taken by agreeing to share their prospective profits in these positions with other banks in the interbank funds market. Finally, since most bank investment portfolios will contain equity positions of various maturities, it is also possible that a subset of their asset portfolios comprising equity shares can be offered in the money market in exchange for liquidity.

Here, too, effective and viable money markets in an Islamic system will require active support and participation by the central bank, particularly at times when the investment opportunities and/or the risk–return composition of projects and shortages of liquidity in the banking system may require a lender of last resort. Such money markets must be flexible enough to handle periods of cash shortage for individual banks, based on some form of profit-sharing arrangement. The challenge for money markets, as well as for the secondary markets, in an Islamic financial system is the development of instruments that satisfy the liquidity, security, and profitability needs of the markets while, at the same time, ensuring compliance with the rules of *Shariah* (i.e., provision of uncertain and variable rates of return on instruments with corresponding real asset backing).

SUMMARY

The functions of the Islamic financial system in the economy are similar to that of the conventional system. However, because of the prohibition against interest and debt in Islam, the Islamic system is based on *risk sharing* as contrasted with *risk shifting*, which is the case with debt. As such, Islamic finance relies heavily on equity finance. In turn, this calls for well-developed stock markets and other secondary capital markets for equity finance, where the asset holder has direct access to the underlying asset, to motivate savers to provide financing and to supply entrepreneurs with sufficient resources for their projects. Islam endorses a different form of insurance whereby risk is shared and not shifted. The building blocks of the Islamic financial system are readily identified and require important government regulations and supervision to be effective and efficient.

KEY TERMS

Al-riba (interest)

Takaful (insurance)

Mudarabah (investor-investment manager contract)

Musharakah (partnership)

Shirakah (partnership, akin to *Musharakah*)

Wikala (principal agent)

Ijarah (lease)

Qardh hassan (interest-free loan)

Risk sharing

Vibrant stock market

Asset-linked securities

Socially responsible finance

Asset-liability management

Money markets

QUESTIONS

1. What is the difference between fractional reserve and 100% reserve banking?
2. How do conventional banks create money?
3. What is the asset–liability problem of conventional banks?
4. Why is a 100% reserve banking institution not exposed to asset liability management and risk of default?
5. Do Islamic banks need deposit insurance?
6. Is the notion of "too big to fail" important in Islamic finance?
7. How does the investment activity of Islamic banks avoid the risk of default?
8. Describe the range of Islamically sanctioned financial assets.
9. Are government regulation, supervision, and enforcement important in the Islamic system?
10. How does insurance in Islam differ from conventional insurance?

CHAPTER 9

Role of the State and Public Policy

Learning objectives:

1. *The importance of rules and their supervision and enforcement.*
2. *The need for government intervention if individuals don't adhere to rules.*
3. *Important government functions to keep the economy, especially markets, functioning smoothly.*
4. *The importance of rules (institutions) as the foundation of economic prosperity, with government monitoring and enforcement.*
5. *The importance of the rule of law for sustained economic and social prosperity.*
6. *The government's programs for the disabled.*
7. *The government's preservation of the right of all individuals in all generations to natural and depletable resources.*
8. *The government's provision of an environment where free individuals have equal opportunity to pursue their dreams.*
9. *The government's provision of defense and safety.*
10. *The government's intervention to restore economic activity, employment, and price stability, especially with market failure.*

A ll mixed market systems, whether the capitalist system as adopted in the West or the Islamic system, depend on the intervention of the state to ameliorate the economic life of a community, region, and country. Governments strive to develop appropriate policies (so that social and private interests converge) and supervision incentives (where rules and regulations are followed and cooperation and coordination are enhanced) for a thriving economy where all citizens can find good jobs and those who cannot work are provided for. The major difference among capitalist economies is the extent of state participation and intervention and the degree of social concern. But in the Islamic system, while the role of the state is similar in many areas of economic life to the Western capitalist model, there are important differences of nuance. In some areas, the roles are even diametrically opposed.

BASIC ROLES OF THE STATE IN ALL ECONOMIC SYSTEMS

Broadly speaking, the state has seven roles in the economic life of a country:

1. Establishing the legal framework and the rules and regulations of a market economic system
2. Supervising and enforcing its rules and regulations
3. Affecting the allocation of resources in order to enhance economic efficiency, widespread participation and prosperity, safeguard the environment and natural resources, and generally reduce negative economic externalities
4. Replacing the market in areas of natural monopolies (infrastructure and national defense)
5. Developing programs that increase social welfare by providing social services such as education, addressing gross income and wealth inequalities, and providing a social safety net
6. Formulating and implementing macroeconomic policies to maintain economic activity and a high level of employment while keeping inflation in check
7. Negotiating international economic and financial agreements with other countries

While there can be differences in the extent of government involvement in the economic areas just mentioned, they are generally accepted government activities that require at least a little elaboration before we turn to the role Islam advocates for the state in managing the economic affairs of the community.

From the writings of Adam Smith over two centuries ago, Western societies realized that without laws and regulations and their supervision and enforcement, an economy becomes akin to a jungle. Individuals and businesses will invariably be overly selfish and take the easy way, no matter what the negative fallouts for the society at large, to satisfy their own ambitions and goals. In the absence of laws and regulations and their enforcement, confidence in the economy evaporates. As a result, savings and investments decline. Economic participation becomes limited. Technological progress slows to a trickle.

Imagine how savings would be affected if there was no protection that contracts for the safekeeping of savings and their management would be honored. What incentive would there be to save? Why would a business invest to develop a new product or to increase output if its assets could be randomly confiscated? Why would anyone go through formal markets if they afforded no protection and transparency? Why would a business invest in developing new technologies or products if there were no enforceable patent laws? Why would anyone undertake any activity that was time or resource intensive (such as acquiring a formal education) if there was nothing that could be counted on about the future? What about product liability laws? What if a product is not what it claims to be and kills consumers? One could write a whole book made up of such questions. Similarly, what about laws to protect workers in case of injury? Would they get healthcare and time off? A flourishing economy needs laws, rules, and regulations in a multitude of areas. Laws and their enforcement provide a necessary foundation for business confidence and economic prosperity. Thoughtful rules, regulations and enforcement, and transparency essentially reduce uncertainty and the costs associated with business transactions. Moreover, a legal system is effective to the extent that everyone in society is equal before the law. This is an absolute requirement. A regulatory and supervisory structure must be established and the laws enforced uniformly and without exception.

While some may recommend a pure market system, no matter its shortfalls, the government has an undeniable role to reduce risk and uncertainty, improve resource allocation and business and economic efficiency, and to minimize the fallout of negative externalities and safeguard the interests of future generations. Markets do not always work perfectly and can fail for many reasons. Markets can fail because of information asymmetries that lead to adverse selection and moral hazard.[1] In perfect competition—where there are many buyers and sellers so that no market participant is big enough to set the price—the market mechanism can be undermined by monopolists (or oligopolies) who prevent competition, drive out some buyers, and then set the price to the detriment of all consumers. Thus, a government may want to break up large firms, prohibit collusion among firms, and adopt antitrust policies. In a similar way as the case of a single seller, a single buyer can also cause market failure.

Although perfect competition is generally desirable, it may be the wrong solution in cases where efficient production requires a few large firms. Here the government would have to monitor these firms to ensure that producers are not engaged in otherwise harmful activities. The government's role in addressing negative economic externalities is multifaceted. Businesses will not voluntarily clean up their harmful environmental discharges (such as into

---

[1] Akerlof (1970).

the air and waters) as they seek to maximize profits. While the current generation may be adversely impacted, the effect on future generations could be much more ominous; in addition to environmental degradation, resource depletion is another facet of neglecting the right of future generations, especially as they have no vote. In regard to depletable natural resources, such as oil, countries in the capitalist system take polar positions: Some grant private ownership of all minerals on private lands while others mandate public ownership of most minerals but without adequately protecting the rights of future generations. We have largely focused on the government's role in the market for goods and services, but we should note that the government has an equally important role in labor markets. Employers may discriminate against some workers by gender, religion, race, and ethnicity; treat workers in inhumane ways; and short-circuit labor markets to pay a below-market wage. Besides the injustice, these adverse actions may deprive the economy of its best workers and misallocate resources away from their best possible use.

There are natural monopolies in a number of areas of economic activity, such as public health, public safety, electricity and water transmission, roads and bridges, airports, and the like. For efficiency, the government may want to provide such services directly or regulate such monopolies. In other words, there are areas where the government could use its "visible hand" to improve resource allocation, economic efficiency, and economic performance. In capitalist economies, these activities fall into the area of public choice, namely the government's decision to take collective action on behalf of all consumers in the economy. If governments represent the collective will of the people (through elections or other forms of representation), undertake such projects, and implement them efficiently, then an economy moves closer to the frontier of its production possibility. Although not directly connected to economic performance but in the same vein, governments almost always provide for national defense.

Modern economic growth stresses the importance of education (human capital) as an input. Employment considerations also confirm the importance of education in securing good-paying jobs and improving a family's social condition. From a social standpoint, education makes individuals better citizens and more productive members of society. It is for this reason that in most countries, education is mandatory up to a certain level. While private education thrives in many countries around the world, it can be expensive and impossible to afford for most families. Thus most governments (at the national or local level) supply free primary and secondary education for all; some countries even supply free (or at least subsidized) university education. For many of the same reasons why education is provided, many countries provide free or subsidized healthcare, especially for the less fortunate members of society. While governments have provided education and in some cases healthcare and used the progressive tax system for income redistribution, the earnings and wealth gap in most countries (as discussed in Chapter 2) between social classes has become increasingly pronounced since the 1970s. Equal access to quality education is an important element in addressing economic and social disparities. Countries see wealth and income inequities very differently. Social preoccupations are different. Still, addressing such disparities is best implemented through collective public action and equitable access to education.

As further discussed in Chapters 6, 8, 10, 11, and 13, modern economic theory envisions an important role for government macroeconomic policies when the economy dips significantly below its natural rate of employment (recession) or experiences rapid price increases (inflationary pressures). As a general rule, there is a low likelihood that the economy would operate at the natural (or full) employment level with limited inflationary pressure, thus necessitating government intervention. In an idealized model, macro-economic policies create inducements that elicit desired responses from sectors of the economy reflecting the desired level of income, prices, and employment. The two main policy tools to achieve these are monetary policy (to increase or reduce the supply of money and thus spending and production in the economy) and fiscal policy (government taxation and spending as means of indirectly and directly influencing aggregate demand and the level of economic activity). Whenever there is a shock to the economy, these tools are used, independently or in combination, to stabilize it. An important conse-quence of the global financial crisis has been the increasing challenge in managing the macroeconomy and sustaining economic growth. In this context, uncertainty has been growing about the adequacy of current policy regimes, whose central anchor is the interest-based debt system. While monetarists recommend a simple monetary rule and neo-Keynesians see a role for both fiscal (short-run) and discretionary monetary policy, govern-ments have important roles in economic management. These roles become ever more important in a globalizing world where economic and financial shocks are more frequent and significant.

Finally, we should note that the economies of nearly all countries are open economies—they trade and interact in many ways with the rest of the world and require representation at the international economic and financial level. There are memberships in international organizations—United Nations, World Trade Organization, International Monetary Fund, World Bank Group, G-24, G-8, bilateral trade agreements (North American Free Trade Agreement, European Union), and so on. Governments offer the best means for a community collective membership and participation in these important international organizations and agreements.

No matter one's political or social inclinations and beliefs, it is clear that governments have an important role to play in a country's economic life. While the extent and the degree of government involvement and intervention may be open for discussion, the importance of its role cannot be denied.

ROLE OF THE STATE IN THE ISLAMIC ECONOMIC SYSTEM

In all economic systems, the state plays a role in the economy. Only the extent of the state's involvement differs, depending on the common values and belief system shared by the individuals who make up the particular society. The role of the state in an Islamic economy is to ensure that everyone has equal access to resources and means of livelihood, that markets are supervised so that *justice* is attained and transfers take place from the more able to the less able, and that distributive justice is ensured for the next generation.[2] As mentioned throughout this book, Islam is a rule-based system. In such a system, the state regulates, supervises, and provides an incentive structure for rule compliance, all within the framework (rules) prescribed by the Quran and *Sunnah*.

Islam uses the market as an efficient mechanism to solve part of the coordination problem within the economy. The state enters the market as the supervisor/regulator of economic activity. It is the combination of state supervision/regulation and free enterprise that is used to maximize social welfare. The state must actively complement market forces to ensure that individual initiative does not degenerate into a private greed for gains, especially when the gains are nonproductive. The capstone rule in Islam is urging compliance with the rules and discouraging rule violation. Compliance with this rule is required of all members of society and for the self, and to ensure that others comply. When humans individually fail, the state is required to step in.

The role of the government is only that of a trustee to society, and it is to act according to the rules prescribed in the Quran and *Sunnah*. Therefore, the foundation for legitimacy of the government is rule compliance. In Islam, legitimacy of a government is initiated through a contract of *mubayaá*—a contract of exchange between the government (the ruler) and the people. The government makes a commitment to strict adherence to rules prescribed by the Quran in exchange for the loyalty of the people, so long as that government remains rule compliant. Repeatedly, both the Quran and the Beloved Messenger emphasize that members of the society must remain vigilant in exercising their duty of "urging rule compliance and discouraging rule violation" (*al-amr bil-ma'ruf wa Al-nahy 'an il munkar*) with respect

---

[2] Al-Hasani and Mirakhor (2003).

to one another and to the government. In earlier times, the act of *mubayaá* was performed directly between those who were to rule and the people or between the ruler's representatives and the people, where distance prohibited direct contact between rulers and the people. It is presumed that this function is performed by election in contemporary times. If so, then it is the responsibility of the people in society to participate fully in government elections. Hence, the duty of electing and voting out a government is given to society, where every individual has equal political rights and the responsibility of participation.

The government's role is broadly divided into two functions: a policy function that ensures that private interest does not diverge too far from public interest; and a supervisory function that is to design and implement an incentive structure to encourage rule compliance, coordination, and cooperation. The presence of market failures can impair economic relations and transactions. In such situations, government intervention is justified to protect the public interest. The state, through the government, is empowered to use all available means permitted by law to achieve the objectives and duties prescribed for the society, including synchronization of individual and public interests. An important function of government is to reduce uncertainty for members of society to allow them to overcome the obstacles in decision making caused by lack of information. The rules prescribed specify what kind of conduct is most appropriate in achieving just results when individuals face alternative choices. The effectiveness of rule enforcement is determined by the degree to which members of society internalize the objective of social justice.

The foremost task of the state in Islamic economy is to strive for achieving objectives of *Shariah* (*maqasid-al-Shariah*) to ensure preservation of the wealth, property, safety, and life of its citizens irrespective of their race, color, or belief.

At the outset, we must stress that Islam requires much of Muslims. They must be moral and honest and uphold justice (and confront injustice and oppressors) in everything that they do, including their participation in the economy. The goal of human participation in the economy is not to maximize individual earnings and wealth, as is basically the case in the conventional or Western system. Economic participation has a more important spiritual dimension. Economic participation provides humans another means to cooperate and grow spiritually toward becoming a part of Allah's (swt) unity. At the same time, the economic behavior of humans is a test of their spiritual growth and their becoming Allah (swt) conscious. If individuals follow the Almighty's rules, then the role of the state becomes limited. If they deviate from Allah's (swt) path, then the state must more actively enforce the rules to bring society back to its designated path. In a sense, the need for extensive state interference in the community and in human behavior is a sign of individual failure as a collective in internalizing and adopting Allah's (swt) rules.

In the Islamic conceptualization of humans' ultimate goal and destination, economic life occupies a purely instrumental role. Even in this role, economic affairs are to provide institutions and mechanisms necessary to satisfy humans' economic needs while allowing people's essence as Allah's (swt) supreme creature to be manifested in this world. Thus, the economic system is designed in accordance with Islam's fundamental principles to assure that humans can exercise their eminent dignity, freedom, responsibilities, and rights in the conduct of economic affairs. The economic system must be ordered such that it does not assign to humans purely instrumental roles in achieving the goals of the economy or the state. Islam seeks to guide humans to direct individual actions and responsible participation in economic affairs in a manner that commits them to spiritual progress and purification and to community solidarity and cooperation, resulting in a dynamic and growing economy. Thus, individuals are made accountable for the moral effects of their social actions, including those in economic affairs, such that their own inner personal-spiritual transformation and growth is bound to the progress of the community. Hence, Islam utilizes cooperation and competition in structuring the ideal society through harmonization and reconciliation between these two opposed but equally primeval and useful forces at every level of social organization.

From this perspective, one can argue that one of the greatest distinguishing characteristics of Islam is its forceful emphasis on the integration of human society, as a necessary consequence of the Unity of Allah (swt). To this end, the personality of the Prophet (sawa) is absolutely inseparable from what the Quran considers as the optimal approach necessary for the emergence of solidarity in the human society. Every dimension of the personality of the Prophet (sawa), manifested in His various social roles in the community, was directed toward maximum integration and harmony in the society. Moreover, every rule of behavior, including those in the economic area, is designed to aid the process of integration. Conversely, all prohibited practices are those that in one way or another lead to social disintegration. Although Islam stresses individual human development, it is uncompromising in its focus on social cohesion and the development of society and the community. If a significant number of humans deviate from the indicated path, then society and all its members in turn fail. Put differently, no Muslim can pursue his or her own path and ignore the rest of society. The failure of society is a failure of all humans. When this happens, the state must step in to reset society's path.

In the Islamic economic system, the state supports the market as the supervisor/regulator of economic activity to maximize social welfare. The state complements market forces to ensure that individual interest does not lead to private greed and exploitation and that rules are followed. Again, we repeat: *The overarching rule in Islam is rule compliance and standing up to rule violators.* Compliance with this rule is required of all members of society. In a sense, *the government's role is akin to that of a trustee of society and a referee to make sure that rules are followed for the good of society.* Thus, the foundation for a legitimate government is its rule compliance. The government makes a commitment to strict adherence to rules prescribed by the Quran in exchange for the loyalty of the people, so long as that government remains rule compliant. But members of the community must be engaged also and support rule compliance.[3]

The Quran and the traditions of the Prophet (sawa) make clear references to the dual nature of competition and cooperation; that is, human beings can cooperate and compete for good or evil, which leads to the integration or disintegration of human society. The fundamental sources, however, emphasize that competition and cooperation must be utilized in probity and piety rather than evil and enmity. Thus, the Quran declares:

> *Cooperate with one another unto righteousness and piety. Do not cooperate with one another unto sin and enmity. (5:2)*

Muslims are urged to compete with one another in beneficial and righteous deeds.[4] There is no evidence in these sources that would allow suppression of one of these forces in favor of the other when they are used within the framework of the rules specified by *Shariah*. Rather, all of the regulatory and supervisory authority invested in the legitimate political authority is directed toward a balanced and constructive utilization of these forces. An example of such balance is *Shariah* rules regarding market structure and the behavior of market participants.[5] Although the rules of *Shariah* regarding economic affairs demarcate limits and boundaries of desirable competitive and cooperative behavior necessary for the provision and preservation of solidary characteristics of the society, the individual always remains the identifiable agent through whose action (and on whose behalf) economic activities takes place.

---

[3] It would seem that this function is performed by election in contemporary times. If so, then it is the responsibility of the people in society to participate fully in the election of the government. Hence, the duty of electing and voting out a government is given to society, where every individual has equal political rights and the responsibility of participation.

[4] See Quran 23:61 (Pickthal's translation), for example.

[5] The development of guilds whose initial intent was the self-regulation of various professions is another example of attempts to harmonize the utilization of cooperation and competition.

Islam considers economic relations and behavior as a means of integration of the society and the integration of humans into a higher order of reality. For this purpose, humans are asked to consider their economic attainments as means and not as ends in themselves. All the rules of behavior regarding economic matters are addressed to individuals and their collectivity. This collectivity is organized into a polity, which is represented by the state. The state is considered as a basic institution, indispensable for the orderly organization of social life, the achievement of legitimate objectives, the creation of material and spiritual prosperity, and the defense and propagation of faith. Hence, all responsibilities directed at the collectivity are assumed by *Shariah* to be incumbent upon the state, which is primarily a vehicle for implementing *Shariah*; its legitimacy is derived from enforcing its rules. When and where individuals fail, the state steps in to correct the course.

POLICY INSTRUMENTS OF THE STATE IN ISLAM

The state is assumed empowered to use, within the limits of the Law (*Shariah*), all available means at its disposal to achieve societal objectives. Foremost among the collective duties is to ensure that justice prevails in all facets of social life. Thus, a judiciary system, with all apparatus necessary to carry out the verdict of the courts free of fees and available to all, is regarded as an indispensable duty of the state. The guarantee of equal liberty and opportunity in terms of access to and use of resources, identified by *Shariah* for the use of individuals, is another duty specified for the state. This requires provision of education, skills, and technology to all. Once both equal liberty and equal opportunity are provided, then production of wealth and its possession and its exchange become matters of equity.

All infrastructures and other public goods and their provision have been traditionally a responsibility of the state. The state can tax the community in a just way to provide needed services. The state can use a flat income tax and a flat land tax (*kharaj*) as envisaged in Islam to finance its expenditures.[6] A pure (regardless how the land is used) land tax is one of the most efficient (least distortionary) forms of taxation that there is:

> *Since the amount of land is fixed, taxing it cannot distort supply in the way that taxing work or saving might discourage effort or thrift. Instead a land tax encourages efficient land use. Property developers, for instance, would be less inclined to hoard undeveloped land if they had to pay an annual levy on it. Property taxes that include the value*

---

[6]For further details on Islamic taxes, see Askari, Cummings, and Glover (1982).

of buildings on land are less efficient, since they are, in effect, a tax on the investment in that property. Even so, they are less likely to affect people's behavior than income or employment taxes. . . . Property taxes are a stable source of revenue in a globalized world where firms and skilled people can easily move. They are also less prone to cyclical swings. In the financial bust America's state and local governments saw smaller declines in property taxes than other forms of revenue, largely because the valuations on which tax assessments are based were adjusted more slowly and less dramatically than actual prices. Property taxes may even restrain housing booms by making it more expensive to buy homes for purely speculative purposes.[7]

If taxes are insufficient to fund public sector projects, the state can also borrow. Due to the prohibition of interest, in an Islamic economy the policy instrument for public sector borrowing should be based on risk sharing. Instead of borrowing, the government could issue equity participation shares (papers) to finance development projects and issue papers that carry a return that is tied to the real rate of return in the private sector. These would mobilize higher private sector savings in many countries to support productive public sector investment projects. By issuing risk-sharing instruments to fund development expenditures, the burden of debt could be reduced. At the same time, the household sector would be able to enjoy a higher rate of return on its savings because the rate of return would be driven by the return to the real sector.

As mentioned, the government could also issue equity participation papers, instead of debt-based borrowing, to fund its general expenditures in case of shortfalls in tax collection. Equity participation shares would have a rate of return that would be tied to the real growth of the national income or to the actual rate of return in the real sector of the economy. The issues should be in small enough denominations and traded on the secondary market so they would be more accessible and affordable to the general public. This would unlock the revenue potential hidden in idle resources. At the same time, it would provide investment opportunities at a higher rate of return for the public than that currently earned in savings deposits. By tapping these resources, the government would not only avail itself of a source of funding for its expenditures but would also provide a more equitable opportunity for the public to have access to the wealth of the nation. The economic pie could now be shared among a larger segment of the economy, not only by the more financially able few. The distributional implication of this policy instrument

---

[7] *Economist* (2013, p. 70).

would further strengthen social solidarity. The cost to the government of raising financing through equity participation shares would not be much higher than the current rate of interest paid on debt instruments, but it would provide a better impetus to the growth of the economy by mobilizing funds otherwise sitting in deposits. At the same time, these papers could also serve as ideal instruments for monetary policy measures. To expand the money supply, the papers could be bought from the open market, thereby increasing the amount of money in circulation to increase consumption. At the same time, if the voluntary payment of *zakat* (directly paid by the better off members of society) is underpaid, the state can take measures to enforce *zakat* payments; and if these are insufficient to meet the basic needs of the disadvantaged, state tax revenues from *khums* (literally, a "one-fifth" charge levied on war booty during the earliest period in Islamic history) and *kharaj* (the tax on land, with additional taxes levied as necessary) can be used to meet this important social need.

The first market for the Muslim community was built in Medina at the direction of the Prophet (sawa), who required that trade be allowed to take place in that market freely, without any charges or fees imposed on market participants, and appointed supervisors for the market. On this basis, jurists have recognized market supervision, and its control, only when necessary, as a duty of the state.

ECONOMIC JUSTICE AND PUBLIC POLICY

As stated earlier, while Islam recognizes equity on the basis of effort and rewards, it declares an inviolable right for those unable to actualize their potential equal liberties and opportunities in the wealth of those more able. Thus Islam, as a practice for the believer, requires a balance between libertarian and egalitarian values. The libertarian principle of the inviolability of the right of individuals to their property and wealth is respected so long as individuals remit claims specified earlier. This is the concession of libertarianism to egalitarianism and of enterprise to distributive justice. Islam leaves no doubt that the preference is for voluntary actions of individuals in payment of levies incumbent upon them. The larger the extent of shirking on the part of the individual, the heavier becomes the duty of the state to correct the resulting skewed distribution of income and wealth. The more individuals conform their behavior in production, exchange, and distribution to the rules of *Shariah*, the weaker is the state's justification to interfere. When these rules are violated, interference becomes the duty of the state.

In contrast to the mixed capitalist economic system, the pursuit of economic justice is part and parcel, and at the heart, of the Islamic system.

In Islam, economic justice cannot be seen as an appendage. It is of prime importance in the Islamic economic objective function. While economic justice has different meanings to different peoples and societies, its brief Islamic definition is centered both on the means and the opportunities available to all humans and the end results or outcomes. In Islam, economic justice would be assured if all humans followed the rules conveyed in the Quran and by the *Sunnah*. It should be noted that Islam affords all living creatures certain rights also; while a major criticism of the most famous Western concept of justice (the theory of justice proposed by John Rawls) is the neglect of animal rights, Islam acknowledges the rights of all of Allah's (swt) creation. In the case of humankind, all humans must be afforded the freedom and similar opportunities (education, healthcare, and basic necessities of life) to follow their dream goals. These are not handouts but the means to develop and grow. If these are made available to all but still glaring inequities arise, then they must be addressed individually, and if this fails the state must step in and use all means possible (taxes and expenditures) to correct the imbalance. Again, to emphasize, economic justice in Islam covers both the means available to all humans and the resulting outcome. But Islam goes even further than this and affords all generations of humans the same. To this end, Islam emphasizes the preservation of the environment and Allah's (swt) gift of natural resources intended for all humans (and other living creatures). Humans must not in any way diminish Allah's (swt) gift intended for all generations. Pollution and environmental degradation of any sort cannot be tolerated.

The treatment of depletable resources in Islam (e.g., oil, gas, copper, all other minerals, and underground water) deserves repeating. As mentioned a number of times earlier, in Islam, underground minerals belong to all humankind of all generations. No individual or generation has special access. Minerals are thus akin to capital stock for all generations. As such, this in-ground capital must be efficiently transformed into other forms of capital (note: not consumed) and an *equal* real benefit (real income) must be afforded to every human of every generation. No ruler and no generation have special access to these gifts of God. The most straightforward way to achieve this end is to create a fund that issues the same real annual benefit to all humans of all generations.[8] The management and transformation of depletable minerals is clearly assigned to the state. But there is a clear point of contention of ownership. Do the minerals discovered in a Muslim country belong to all humans, to all Muslims on earth, or only to the citizens (residents) of a country? There is no recognition of nation-states and divisions between Muslims and non-Muslims in the Quran. More practically, how would

---

[8] For details see Askari (2006).

one country share its resources when others do not reciprocate? The problems for meaningful sharing appear insurmountable. But sharing and preserving the rights of all, if we could somehow do it, would clearly increase cohesion and unity among all humans. At the least, resource depletion should be accompanied by a fund that affords equal benefits to all citizens of every generation of a Muslim country (if not of all Muslims or all humanity).

Eradication of poverty is undoubtedly one of the most important of all duties made incumbent upon the state, second only to the preservation and propagation of faith, whose very existence is considered threatened by poverty.[9] Islam regards poverty primarily as a result of shirking on the part of the more able and wealthy members of society to perform their prescribed duties. Hence, commitment to distributive justice, which normally constitutes a large portion of the government budgets in other systems, is placed squarely on the shoulders of individuals with the financial and economic capability to meet it. Not only does *Shariah* specify who must pay, but it also designates explicit categories of recipients. But again, if individuals fail in this important test, then the state must step in and correct prevailing inequities.

Given the importance of hard work, jobs, economic prosperity for humans, and societal cohesion, the state should do all it can to support economic progress when collective action is required but be careful not to impinge on other important societal goals. The state should consider all necessary macroeconomic and microeconomic policies to restore full (the natural rate of) employment. In an increasingly global economy where countries are exposed to external economic (and financial) shocks, individuals are powerless. Collective action is called for. The government must use its macroeconomic arsenal to deflect adverse external economic shocks and restore economic activity.

Finally, we should note that national defense is an area where only one entity, namely the state, can represent a country's collective interest. But in Islam, defense means defense, not offense. Such representation is not for aggression against another community or country but is justified only to defend against aggression from the outside. Thus military expenditures should be only for defensive purposes, to repel outside aggression, and not for attacking another community or country.

ROLE OF PUBLIC POLICY

Policies are decisions of the government to undertake certain actions directed toward achieving certain objectives. At a macro level, policies have been traditionally designed to achieve the objective of the economic system consistent

---

[9]M. Iqbal (1987) and F. Ahmad (1983).

with the worldview of the society. In most cases, the achievement of growth and development in the economy is seen as the primary objective of macro-economic policies.

Monetary and Fiscal Policy

Monetary policy is a process undertaken by the monetary authority in controlling the money supply and cost of money to achieve economic stability. It relies on the relationship between the rate of interest and the supply of money to influence economic growth, inflation, exchange rates, and unemployment. The central bank is normally the institution that manages the economy's money supply, currency, and interest rates. It has control over the country's monetary base and regulates the financial system through the operation of monetary policy. Monetary policy is conducted through open market operations, buying and selling financial instruments, and setting the reserve requirement and the discount rate. Central banks serve as the lender of last resort to the banking sector.

In undertaking an expansionary monetary policy, the central bank seeks to expand the monetary base—consisting of money in circulation as well as the banking sector reserve with the central bank—by injecting liquidity into the economy. This can be done by reducing the reserve requirements of the banking sector or through open market operations: either through large purchases of financial instruments, such as government bonds, or direct lending to the banking system with low discount rates, thereby increasing the amount of cash in the system. *In the conventional system, this mechanism works through the banking sector as the transmission agent for the expansionary monetary policy.* A reduction in the discount rate or reserve requirement signals a green light for the banking sector to expand balance sheets and increase lending, which in turn aims at increased spending by consumers. An illustration of this transmission mechanism is presented in Figure 9.1. It is important to note that monetary policy acts indirectly, in the sense that it relies on the banking sector to increase or decrease lending to the private sector and on the private sector to act in the way that the monetary authorities hope for.

Monetary policy must meet certain challenges, notably, dealing with the flexibility of the financial system to react and ensuring the timing and credibility of announcements. The latter depends on the success of the previously implemented monetary policies, as reputation is an important element in the implementation of a successful monetary policy. The success of this policy also depends on the effectiveness of the transmission mechanism and the independence of the central bank from the rest of government. The objectives of the government as policy maker and of the private banking

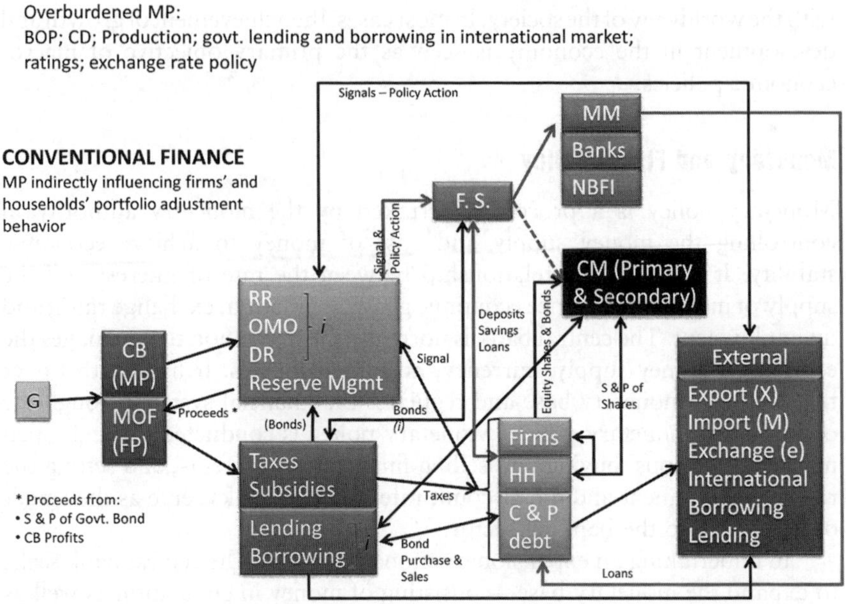

Overburdened MP:
BOP; CD; Production; govt. lending and borrowing in international market;
ratings; exchange rate policy

FIGURE 9.1 Fiscal and Monetary Policy Transmission Mechanism in a Conventional Economy

sector may not converge. When the banking sector does not transmit the increased liquidity to the rest of the private sector and consumers, but instead uses the liquidity to expand its own bottom line, the transmission mechanism has failed. In a fractional reserve banking system, the implementation of a central bank monetary policy makes the conventional financial system unstable and vulnerable to financial turmoil as a result of credit expansion out of thin air. Interest rates set by the central bank create a wedge between the money interest rate and the natural rate of interest.[10] It allows money capital to multiply independently of real or physical output. Creation of credits not backed by the real economy diverts real savings from productive activities to nonproductive ones that in turn weaken the process of real wealth expansion.

Fiscal policy is the use of the government's power to tax (an indirect effect) and spend (a direct effect) to influence economic activities. In most

---

[10]Thornton [1802] (1939) distinguished between a market (loan) rate of interest and the interest rate (the marginal rate of profit, or the natural rate of interest), which equilibrates savings and investment. According to Thornton's theory of two interest rates, inflation results from a divergence between the two rates.

situations, when government spending has increased and revenues have not increased commensurately, governments finance the resulting shortfalls (budget deficits) by increasing borrowing, raising taxes, or both. In theory, a stimulus to spur economic activity during slowdowns is supposed to be financed by subsequent growth. More often than not, current and prospective rates of economic growth are lower than the interest rate on the growing debt. Growth may not be large or fast enough to validate debt levels that may exceed 100% percent of gross domestic product, as is the case today in many advanced countries. The solution of austerity, higher taxes, and lower spending suggested by the dominant policy regime requires a strong political consensus. Increased borrowing by issuing bonds or long-term government borrowing also does not appear to be a desirable solution, as it increases vulnerability to shocks, creates a burden on future taxpayers, and has adverse distributional implications.

The current public sector borrowing policy in a conventional economy that is based on interest is putting countries in highly leveraged and precarious positions. As borrowing increases, the countries run the risk of producing income only to service the interest on debt. The problem of debt repayment must be passed on to the public, as tax revenue must increase in order to pay for the debt. As borrowing continues to fund increasing government spending, the problem will be passed on to future generations of taxpayers. When government borrowings are funded externally, the problem is exacerbated by the outflow of resources on debt servicing that will add pressure to the balance of payments. So far the solution to the problem has come in the form of providing more loans to help countries out of their debt problem. A question arises: Is solving a debt crisis with more debt the right solution?

While monetary policy in a conventional economy uses interest rates to regulate the money supply, in an Islamic economy, money supply is altered through asset market (such as the stock market) activities. The incentive structure intended by monetary authorities in the conventional system to induce portfolio adjustment may be distorted if signals are not transmitted to the private sector by the banking sector. For example, the banking sector may use the excess in reserves arising from a lowering of the reserve requirements to buy government bonds instead of lending to the private sector to increase consumption and investment. As a result, the effect of the monetary policy may not be fully achieved. The use of the interest rate as a tool for monetary policy creates incentives for financial decoupling. As can be seen in Figure 9.2, a distinctive feature of the Islamic financial system is that monetary policy influences portfolio adjustments of the private sector directly through the expansion and/or contraction of the money supply through the capital market investment rather than through the money market through the lending process, as in the conventional economy. Risk-sharing instruments

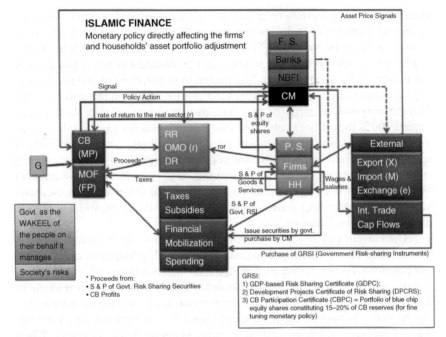

FIGURE 9.2 Fiscal and Monetary Policy Transmission Mechanism in an Islamic Economy

can avoid the problem whereby banks do not transmit the proper signal to the private sector. Such instruments, issued by the government to finance its operations and used by the monetary authority to affect portfolio adjustment by the private sector, can achieve the objectives of monetary policy while promoting greater resilience of the economy to shocks.

In the arena of fiscal policy, the high level of debt in the conventional system constrains government's ability to take on additional risk in its balance sheet. Apart from the threat of a credit rating downgrade, persistent fiscal deficits also impair the ability of the policy makers to respond effectively to future shocks. Additionally, increasing the debt burden could have adverse distributional impacts for current and future generations. This is due to the fact that the middle- and lower-income classes carry the burden of the taxes that are needed to service government debt held by either higher-income groups or foreign investors. The design of instruments for fiscal policy in an Islamic economy should reflect concerns, such as distributive justice. An alternative approach to the current policy dilemma would propose a two-pronged solution: reform of the tax system and a radical change in the way governments finance their spending. The tax system needs to be simplified to induce voluntary declaration from taxpayers and widened to include a tax on wealth. At the same time, financing of economic activities should move away from the current interest-based system to one based on risk sharing through utilization of funds available to the public at large.

A simple tax system can be designed around a flat tax, reflecting the structure of *zakat* and other charges prescribed in the Quran. As a matter of equity, taxes should be levied according to ability to pay. The current focus on taxing income may impose undue burdens on income earners who need the income for their day-to-day living. The possession of wealth adds to the capacity to pay tax, over and above the income yielded by that wealth. Taxing wealth means making those who are more financially able contribute more in tax. Wealth represents accumulated assets owned, not just income earned. Therefore, in the interests of equity, it is justifiable to tax wealth in addition to income. Moreover, as wealth generally represents a much larger tax base than income, the rate of taxation can be kept low but still raise substantial tax revenue. In addition, advocates of a wealth tax argue that such a tax may encourage the wealthy to transfer their assets from less productive uses to more productive ones and from idleness to income-producing ventures. The wealthiest segment of the population, which holds assets in the form of properties and stocks, will probably be paying a relatively low tax as a proportion of their wealth compared to those whose wealth consists mainly of their monthly salary. Collecting tax revenue from the segment of the population with the most wealth could promote equality, as the wealth that is currently concentrated in the hands of a few would become revenue for the government to be used for social development. Under an Islamic economic system, a flat tax system consisting of an income tax component and a wealth tax component has the potential to be ideal. It reflects the rate structure of *khums* (and *zakat* prescribed by the Quran and the *Sunnah*). The optimum flat tax rate may differ from country to country, depending on the unique economic situation. As a general guideline, it is proposed here that the tax structure be composed of a 20% income tax and a 2.5% wealth tax. When revenue is not sufficient to cover a budget deficit, the government must borrow. Due to the prohibition of interest, in an Islamic economy, the policy instrument for public sector borrowing should be based on risk sharing.

Public Policy and Societal Risk Management

Government is the ultimate risk manager in a society. It could well be argued that in contemporary societies, risk management is the central role of government. The span of this function ranges from risks to international and domestic security to the risk of contagion from communicable diseases. This spectrum of government risk management policy could be considered as a series of responses to shortcomings on the part of the market and nongovernmental sector to correct risk-related failures. If one considers a catalog of government risk management responsibilities, a great many would be responses to this kind of failures pervasive in a contemporary "free market" economy. As noted, neoclassical theory suggests that in a well-functioning free market economy—with complete contingent markets or with complete Arrow securities (see further on for more explanation)—risk optimally would be shared among market participants according to their ability to bear risks. Such an economy would develop markets where all kinds of risks would be traded. In a society with such a well-functioning economy, government would play a minimal role. In the absence of such an economy, however, risk-related failures can render economic relations and transactions dysfunctional. In contemporary "free market" economies, even in some of the richest, complete markets for risk do not exist. For example, while a home-owner can buy insurance against the risk of fire damage to a residential dwelling, there is no available market to trade the risk of decline in home prices. Nor is there a market to trade risk to allow purchasing of protection against unforeseen shocks to income and livelihood. The lack of well-functioning markets for these risks and others signal that the collective well-being of societies is much less than its full potential.

Understanding the distinction between risks that are specific to an individual consumer, household, or firm (idiosyncratic risks) and those that are highly correlated across all participants in the economy (systematic risk, aggregate risk) is crucial for risk management. Sometimes what is an idiosyncratic risk for an individual or a firm may be systematic risk for another. What would be an idiosyncratic risk to a major internationally active bank may become systematic for a small bank in a given locality in that country. For a firm operating in a local community as the only monopoly employer, its idiosyncratic risk will be systematic for the community. Various types of market failure make the private market for risk bearing less than optimal. In principle, government interventions could potentially increase market efficiency. In practice, however, there are cases where intervention in the form of insurance against risk raises the possibility of government (on behalf of the public) assuming the risk of losses and the private sector capturing the gains. Such is the case, for example, with deposit guarantees in a fractional reserve banking system. It is thought that aside from the famous moral hazard problem and the too-big-to-fail issue, there is also the distributional impact of such interventions. Deposit insurance, intended to reduce the risk of bank runs and protect the payment system, raises more questions about redistribution than its efficiency implications.

It has been argued that the owners and managers of institutions give incentives to politicians and civil servants to support deposit insurance that funds their risk-taking activities.[11] Moreover, deposit insurance may have an important benefit for the rich—owners of existing houses, land, and other capital assets—and powerful relative to ordinary taxpayers; it reduces the price of loans and thus affords a benefit to those that borrow, leverage, and invest in such capital assets.[12] Governments should not be protecting and subsidizing those who are well off when it comes to banking and finance but should do what it does in other areas in protecting the public—develop sound regulations, and monitor and enforce them on an equitable basis.

In most economies, governments play a major role in bearing risk on behalf of their citizens. For example, governments provided social safety net measures and insurance for a variety of financial transactions. The history of the economic explanation for government's role in the economy spans more than a century as economists attempted to justify the role as being necessitated by the divergence between public and private interests. Some six decades ago, Arrow and Debreu focused on finding precise conditions under which public and private interests would converge as envisioned in a conception of Adam Smith's "invisible hand."[13] The result was an elegant proof that competitive markets would indeed have a stable equilibrium, provided some stringent conditions were met. It was clear, however, that even under the best of actual conditions, markets did not perform as envisioned either by Smith or Arrow and Debreu. Considerations of violations of the underlying conditions spawned a voluminous body of literature on the theory and empirics of market failure. This concept became the starting point for analytic reasoning that justifies government's intervention in the economy to protect the public interest.[14] The reason that contemporary societies implement social safety nets, such as social security, healthcare, and public unemployment insurance programs, is that individual households face substantial risk over their life span, such as mortality risk, wage and other income risks, and health risks. Because private insurance markets do not provide perfect insurance against all risks, there is said to be a market failure, and government intervention is called for to correct it. What has become clear in the wake of the global financial crisis is that even in the most advanced industrial economies, existing social safety nets are incapable of coping with adverse consequences. Not only has the crisis shaken previous levels of confidence in markets, nearly all analyses of its causes attribute it to market

---

[11] Kane (1989, p. 177), quoted in Wright (1993).
[12] Wright (1993).
[13] Arrow and Debreu (1954).
[14] Stiglitz (1993).

failure in one dimension or another. This has intensified calls for government interventions to counter the adverse effects of the crisis on income and employment, to strengthen social safety nets, and to reform the financial sectors. The most important lesson of the crisis has been that people at large carry too big a risk of exposure to massive shocks originating in events that are beyond their influence and control. Hence, attention has been focused on ways and means of expanding collective risk sharing.

Heretofore, it has been assumed that government interventions, in the form of providing social safety nets, public goods, and deposit insurance, were solely for the purpose of addressing various kinds of market failures. While this is a crucial justification for intervention, there is an important dimension of government's role that has not attracted much attention. Much of these activities in the provision of a social safety net, from a minimal amount in some countries to substantial amounts in welfare states, are also about collective risk sharing. This dimension has been particularly neglected in the analysis of government provision of social insurance and services in which the sole focus has been the trade-off between equity and efficiency, the issue at the heart of state versus market debates. Relatedly, in these debates, the focus on distortions caused by taxation to finance these activities neglects to consider what taxes are financing in a particular society. One important risk-sharing use of taxes is in the area of transfer payments or automatic stabilizers intended to provide a cushion to citizens' consumption should they be affected by adverse consequences of shocks. Automatic stabilizers work without any discretionary government decisions. For this reason alone, these safety net measures cannot automatically differentiate between temporary and permanent or persistent shocks. While automatic stabilizers tend to help steady the economy in the short run, they can create fragility in the fiscal positions of government in the medium or long term. The risk to the government's fiscal position places emphasis on the appropriate design, eligibility criteria, and focus of alternative ways and means of addressing consequences of more permanent shocks.

Some have argued that government risk-sharing schemes intended to mitigate the consequences of adverse shocks to income are akin to insurance and as such they raise the issue of moral hazard. Additionally, it is argued, they have an adverse incentive effect in that they cause the labor supply to be inefficiently low. The standard argument is that while more equity can be achieved through redistribution, using taxes and transfers, it comes at the cost of reduced efficiency because it will adversely affect the incentive to work. A number of studies argue that this is too simplistic a view.[15] Consider a simple example where the tax system imposes a proportional tax on income. The tax

---

[15] Andersen (2008, 2010, 2011), Hoynes and Luttmer (2010), and Sinn (1995, 1996).

then is used to provide a lump-sum transfer. In this example, those earning high incomes are taxed to finance lump-sum transfers to low-income earners. This is an *ex post facto* redistributive system but *ex ante* it is an income risk reduction device to potential recipients. This implies that a tax-redistribution risk-sharing scheme has an insurance effect that runs counter to the incentive effect and raises the possibility that such a scheme may lead to a larger rather than a smaller labor supply effect, as the former may dominate the latter.[16] One of the strongest risk-sharing programs of existing welfare states is in the area of human capital through investment in free education financed by taxes. These programs allow society as a whole to share the risk involved in educating its younger members. Investment in human capital through education is known to have two important characteristics. First, since human capital is an important driver of growth, there is a substantial payoff to the society in the medium to long term in terms of tax payment and higher productivity. Second, it is also known that this payoff is at least as large as, if not larger than, investment in equity markets.[17] Since in the absence of free education some households, if not most, will be resource constrained to finance higher education, private financing may mean that the society's potential human capital is not utilized efficiently, leading to lower productivity and thus lower average incomes.

Theoretical literature suggests that in most economies, the potential of risk sharing within, between, and among countries remains underexploited, leading to a substantial loss of welfare. Many activities of the financial sector are interest rate based, thus forcing financial transactions into credit/debtor relationships with their own peculiarities, requirements, and constraints. Hence, a large portion of productive activities remain finance constrained; examples are small and medium-size enterprises (SMEs), rural poor and nonbanked communities everywhere, as well as individuals and very small firms in the informal economy. Largely due to the nonexistence or incomplete availability of insurance, these segments of the economy are exposed to idiosyncratic and systematic risks. Microfinance was discussed briefly earlier. In the case of SMEs, finance constraint is one among a number of others— such as access to markets, regulations that are mainly designed businesses that have access to capital markets, and tax codes. However, so long as the financial constraint is binding, resolving other issues, while important, would be of little help. The major source of finance for SMEs is the banking system that provides external funding for these firms.[18] Banks, however, prefer to deal with large transactions because of the high costs of risk appraisal,

---

[16] Andersen (2011).
[17] Judd (1997).
[18] Levitsky (1986) and World Bank (2010).

processing, and monitoring. It is also argued that because SMEs do not provide sufficient information and their operations tend to be opaque, there is a risk of moral hazard due to information asymmetry, which leads banks to charge a high risk premium.[19] However, substantial benefits are claimed for encouraging the relaxation of finance constraints for these firms. These benefits include social ones that accrue due to growth, entrepreneurship, private sector development, job creation, and improved income and wealth distribution.[20] A number of government policies and instruments have been used to create improved risk-sharing environments for SMEs. These measures have been targeted to the supply and demand side of the market as well as to the financial sector.[21]

In the course of the last three decades, concerns have been raised regarding the ability of governments to deal with severe fiscal constraints. Additionally, concerns have also been expressed regarding the relative efficiency of governments to provide public services. Pressure has been exerted on governments to find alternative ways and means of delivering public services through sharing governance functions with the private sector. Outsourcing is one example where government's traditional functions of procurement, provision of public goods, and provision of services have been relegated to the private sector. Public-private partnerships (PPPs) are risk-sharing instruments that have been popular with many governments over the last two decades. These are cooperative ventures between governments and the private sector in which risks and returns are shared through a long-term contract whereby the private sector develops one or every aspect of a project from conception to development, completion and administration, including ownership and management.[22] In every one of these functions, there are risks.[23] The effectiveness of a given PPP depends on the degree to which risks are shared. Case studies have demonstrated that in a number of projects throughout the world, risks have been shifted to one side, mostly to governments, or transferred rather than shared.[24] When there is no risk sharing and

---

[19] Beck (2007).

[20] Levy (1993) and Beck (2007).

[21] For details on these risk-sharing instruments, see Beck et al. (2006), Berger and Udel (2005), Duan et al. (2009), Helmsing (1993), Klein (2010), (Levy, 1993), Stephano and Rodriguez (2008), Tan (2009), WB (2008), and World Bank Group (2010).

[22] Hodge (2004).

[23] Hombros Bank (1995).

[24] See, for example, Ball et al. (2003), Berg et al. (2000), Bracy and Moldovan (n.d.), Canadian Council for PPPs (1997), Collin (1998), Greve (2003), Hodge (2002), Ishigami (1995), Jacobson (1998), Lawson (1997), Osborne (2001), Perrot and Chatelus (2000), and Savoie (1999).

there are losses, the government bears the costs, but the gains accrue to the private sector. Provided that risk-sharing contracts are designed such that risks are allocated consistent with both market conditions and expectations and the contracts are transparent and flexible to allow both government and private sector partners to deal with external shocks, PPPs have the potential to benefit the parties as well as society at large. These benefits may well include efficiency gains, improved value for money, and greater fiscal space for the government.

SUMMARY

In most areas of the economy, Islam advocates individual participation and responsible behavior with social welfare in mind. As long as Muslims follow the Quranic rules and the interpretations provided in the *Sunnah*, most of the socioeconomic issues of society would be addressed. But because individuals stray from the true path, the state must step in when and where there is failure. In an Islamic economy, the state has these roles:

1. Ensure that everyone has the freedom and equal liberty of access to natural resources and means of livelihood; equal access to natural resources (including a clean environment) is the right of all humans of all generations.
2. Ensure that each individual has an equal opportunity to acquire the needed skills, including education, and equal access to utilize these resources.
3. Ensure that transparent market rules are developed and supervised and that rules are enforced.
4. Adopt policies to prevent market failure and take action when market failure occurs.
5. Ensure that the legal framework and scaffolding for the economy is justice, with laws enforced (in all areas including business contracts) and equal justice for all.
6. Ensure that income and wealth transfer takes place from those more able to those less able in accordance to the rules of *Shariah*.
7. Adopt and implement policies, in particular macroeconomic policies, to bring about an environment of full (natural rate) employment and low inflation, because of the importance of gainful employment and poverty eradication.
8. Ensure that distributive justice is secured for the next generation through the implementation of the laws of inheritance and preservation of the capital provided by the Creator in the form of depletable natural

resources. The state is then empowered, especially when individuals fail to achieve society's intended goals, to design any specific economic policy that is required in order to guarantee the attainment of these objectives. To meet the necessary expenditures associated with the performance of its duties, *Shariah* has given the control, utilization, and management of a portion of natural resource endowment of the society (e.g., underground mineral resources) to the state. It has also empowered the state, according to a consensus of opinion among jurists, to impose taxes whenever there is a gap existing between the resources it can command and its expenditures. Borrowing by the state, when it does not involve the payment of interest, is also permitted when and if necessary.

9. Develop a national defense capability (not offensive) in case of outside threats and aggression.

KEY TERMS

Economic externalities

Market failure

Competition

Economic collusion

Environmental preservation

Rights of future generations

Resource allocation

Human capital

Macroeconomic policy

Private and public interest

Rule compliance, coordination, and cooperation

Risk and risk management

Monetary policy

Fiscal policy

QUESTIONS

1. What is market failure?
2. Describe instances of market failure.
3. What are economic externalities, and how do they adversely affect economic activity and social welfare?
4. How do private and public interests diverge?
5. What can the government do to prevent market failure and converge public and private interests?
6. What business regulations should governments develop?

7. How do governments manage risk for society?

8. What are the rights of future generations?

9. Why are the rights of each human being and those of future generations so emphasized in Islam?

10. Are the interests of society given more importance in Islam than in the Western capitalist system? Please explain your answer.

CHAPTER 10

Fiscal Policy

Learning objectives:

1. *The goals and objectives of fiscal policy in the conventional and the Islamic systems.*
2. *The role and importance of societal welfare in Islam.*
3. *The instruments of fiscal policy in the conventional system.*
4. *The instruments of fiscal policy in the Islamic system.*
5. *The financing (taxation and borrowing) of government expenditures in the conventional and in the Islamic system.*
6. *The workings of the multiplier.*
7. *The difficulty of achieving full employment and stable prices.*
8. *The implications of deficit financing and national debt.*
9. *The workings and limitations of fiscal policy in the longer run.*
10. *Waqf as a complementary fiscal instrument in Islamic finance.*
11. *The role of built-in stabilizers.*
12. *The arguments for and against different forms of taxation.*
13. *The concept of public-private partnerships.*
14. *National participation papers as a financial instrument.*

The state plays a key role in every economic system. Only the extent of the state's involvement differs, depending on the common values and belief system shared by the individuals who make up the particular society. The role of the state in an Islamic economy is to ensure that everyone has equal access to resources and a means of livelihood; that there are rewarding employment opportunities for all those who can work; that market rules, regulations, and supervision minimize business uncertainties so that justice is attained and transfers take place from the more able to the less able; and that distributive justice is ensured for the next generation. As has been emphasized in this book, Islam is a rule-based system. In such a system, the state regulates, supervises, and provides an incentive structure for rule compliance, all within the framework prescribed by the Quran and the *Sunnah*. The role of the government is broadly divided into two functions: a policy function that ensures that private interest does not diverge too far from public interest; and second, an institutional function to design and implement an incentive structure to encourage rule compliance, coordination, and cooperation.

In market economies when the markets fail to clear (i.e., when there is unmet demand or oversupply), it is said that there is a market failure. The presence of market failures can impair economic relations and transactions. In such situations, government intervention is justified to protect the public interest. The state, through the government, is empowered to use all available means permitted by law to achieve the objectives and duties prescribed for society, including synchronization of individual and public interests. An important function of government is to reduce uncertainty for members of society to allow them to overcome the obstacles in making decisions due to lack of information. In this sense, the state becomes the ultimate risk manager of society. The prescribed rules specify what kind of conduct is most appropriate in achieving just results when individuals face alternative choices. The degree of effectiveness of rule enforcement is determined by the degree to which members of society internalize the objective of social justice.

Policies are decisions of the government to undertake actions directed toward achieving certain objectives. At a macro level, policies traditionally have been designed to achieve the objective of the economic system consistent with the view of society. In most cases, the achievement of economic stability, full employment, growth, and development of the economy is seen as the primary objective of macroeconomic policies. In an idealized model, macroeconomic policies create inducements that elicit desired responses from sectors of the economy reflecting the desired level of income, prices, and employment. To achieve these objectives, two main policy tools are utilized: monetary policy and fiscal policy. Monetary policy aims at inducing adjustments in the portfolio of the private sector (producers and consumers) to fine-tune aggregate demand. It uses the instrument of the interest rate to increase or reduce the level of the supply of money and thus spending and production in the economy. Fiscal policy uses the power of the government to tax and spend as a means of influencing aggregate demand and the level of economic activity. Whenever there is a shock to the economy, these tools are used, independently or in combination, to stabilize the economy and nudge it toward a state of full employment and price stability.

Fiscal policy is the use of the government's power to tax and spend to influence economic activities. In most situations, when government spending has increased and revenues have not increased commensurately, governments have financed the resulting shortfalls (budget deficits) by increasing borrowing, raising taxes, or both. Printing money is always an option, but it is not a recommended one. In theory, a stimulus to spur economic activity during slowdowns is normally assumed to be financed by subsequent growth. More often than not, the current and prospective rates of growth of the economy are lower than the interest rate on the growing debt. Growth may not be large or fast enough to validate debt levels that may exceed 100% of gross domestic product (GDP), as is the case today in many advanced countries. The solution of austerity, higher taxes, and lower spending suggested by the dominant policy regime requires a strong political consensus. Increased borrowing by issuing bonds or long-term government borrowing also does not appear to be a desirable long-term solution, as it increases vulnerability to shocks, creates a burden on future generations of taxpayers, and has adverse distributional implications.

The government has a crucial role in ensuring economic activity and prosperity. There is no guarantee that the economy will be operating at full employment (NAIRU, the nonaccelerating rate of unemployment). It is highly unlikely that the economy will be humming along at NAIRU for any length of time. There will be periods when aggregate demand is too low (aggregate supply is high) and others when it is too high (supply is low), requiring government intervention to nudge the economy back to the NAIRU level of activity. Stabilization policies—monetary and fiscal—are crucial in moderating economic fluctuations and maintaining employment, something that is crucial in order to avoid economic hardships for families and for society in general. But government's role in stabilization goes beyond monetary and fiscal policies to include industrial, trade, exchange rate, and income policies.

The current public sector borrowing policy in a conventional economy that is interest based is putting countries in a highly leveraged position. As borrowing increases, the country runs the risk of producing income only to service the interest on debt. The problem of debt repayment must be passed on to the public, as tax revenue must increase in order to pay for the debt. Thus the risk of mismanaging the economy is shifted from the present to future generations. As internal borrowing continues to fund increasing government spending, the problem will be passed on to future generations of taxpayers. In addition, to the extent that the government borrows from the rich and taxes mostly the middle and lower income groups, income and wealth distribution skew in favor of the wealthier segment of the population. When government borrowings are funded externally, the problem is exacerbated by the outflow of resources on debt servicing that will add pressure to the balance of payments. As was experienced by the emerging markets in Asia and Latin America in the late 1990s, external borrowing exposes economies to "sudden stop" shock, whereby economies are prevented from any progress whatsoever. So far the solution to the problem has come in the form of providing more borrowing to help countries out of their recession. But is solving a debt crisis with more debt the right solution to the problem?

ROLE OF FISCAL POLICY

In Chapter 6, we discussed the form of the consumption (savings) and investment functions in an Islamic economic system and how national income is in turn determined. Importantly, we saw that there is no guarantee that the conventional economy would always operate at full employment and with stable prices. In fact, it is highly unlikely that the economy would operate at an equilibrium level that is characterized by full employment and stable prices. Fluctuations in investment, and to a lesser degree in consumption (savings) and external economic shocks, are the major cause of fluctuations in national income. Business conditions hardly ever stand still. Economic booms may be followed by economic panics and crashes. Invariably economic expansions lead to economic recessions with a fall in national output and employment; business profits fall; and an economic bottom is reached followed by economic recovery, which may be slow or fast and may lead to another economic boom with little inflation or with rapid inflation. The process of economic expansion and contraction, inflation and deflation, and rising and falling employment is captured under the umbrella term "business cycles." No two business cycles look exactly the same in their four phases—recession to a trough (bottom), expansion to a peak, recession, and expansion. Governments use macroeconomic policies to moderate business cycles.

Prior to the Great Depression of the 1930s, economists believed that the appropriate fiscal policy for a government was to maintain a balanced budget. But the Great Depression changed this widely held view. As we have mentioned, John Maynard Keynes put forward the idea that fiscal policy should be used in a countercyclical manner so that the government moderates the expansion and contraction phases of the business cycle in a process of leaning against the wind. Thus the government budget should be in deficit when the economy is in the doldrums and contracting and in surplus when it is booming with no excess capacity and inflation. But fiscal policy has not been an effective tool to smooth these cyclical movements because of political constraints and also because the economy has what are called built-in stabilizers, such as a progressive tax system and unemployment insurance. Politicians resist raising taxes when the economy is booming, as this is not a popular policy with the electorate; and automatic stabilizers cushion the impact of booms and busts, reducing the incentive for discretionary policies. (During a recession, incomes will be shrinking, but because of progressive taxation, the loss of income or purchasing power is cushioned, which will lead to a decline in government tax revenues. So long as the government does not reduce expenditures, the end result will be a moderation in the decline in the level of economic activity.)

The effectiveness of discretionary fiscal policy has been questioned on other grounds as well, primarily the policy's "inside lag" and its long-run impact on economic output. Inside lag is the time when the need for fiscal policy arises and when the policy makers actually implement it. In practice, the art of economic forecasting is such that forecasts are uncertain and policy makers realize the need for policy months after the need should have been recognized; and it takes policy makers (parliaments and parties) time to reach a political compromise and to take remedial action. In part because of these limitations, some economists argue that discretionary fiscal policy to counteract business cycle fluctuations may do more harm than good. Others prefer monetary policy and see little need for fiscal policy. Others argue that the longer-run impact of fiscal policy may be seriously limited because the higher aggregate demand resulting from a fiscal stimulus translates into higher prices, not into permanently higher output, as sustainable economic output is determined by the supply of the factors of production (capital, labor, and technology).

The supply of the factors of production determines a "natural rate" of output around which business cycles and macroeconomic policies can cause only temporary fluctuations. The fact that output returns to its natural rate in the long run is not the end of the story, however. In addition to moving output in the short run, expansionary fiscal policy can change the natural rate, and the long-run effects tend to be the opposite of the short-run effects. The basis of this argument is as follows. A short-term expansionary fiscal policy affects longer-run output because of its impact on the savings rate. Savings are made up of a private and a public component. A fiscal expansion results in government dissaving; with lower aggregate savings, either investment in plant and equipment will decline or external borrowing (for investment) would have to increase; the former (lower savings) would lead directly to lower investment and the latter could be sustained only if the return on investment is higher than the cost of foreign debt. In short, the argument is that expansionary fiscal policy will lead to higher output today but will lower the natural rate of output below what it would have been in the future.

As a final point, we should note that fiscal policy also affects the relative burden of future taxes. An expansionary fiscal policy adds to its stock of debt. But because of the government's obligation to pay interest on this debt or pay back debt in the future, expansionary fiscal policy may impose an additional burden on future generations.

Thus through fiscal policy and monetary policy there is a role, which is open to some debate, for the government to nudge the economy toward full employment and/or restore stable prices as needed. Additionally, the government uses fiscal and monetary policy to enhance economic growth and prosperity. In this chapter, our focus is the instrument of fiscal policy— changes in government expenditures and taxes. The government increases aggregate demand directly by increasing its expenditures and indirectly (through private sector consumption and investment) by decreasing taxes; the change in aggregate demand affects the level of national income. The process of fiscal policy (adjusting government expenditures and taxation) and its financing in turn affects the government's budgetary position. In the next chapter we examine how monetary policy also affects national income, employment, and prices. A US$1 change in investment leads to more than a $1 change in national income because of the multiplier effect.

We begin this discussion with a recapitulation of the standard income determination equilibrium diagram in Figure 10.1. As can be seen, government expenditures (G) can be directly added to the other two components of

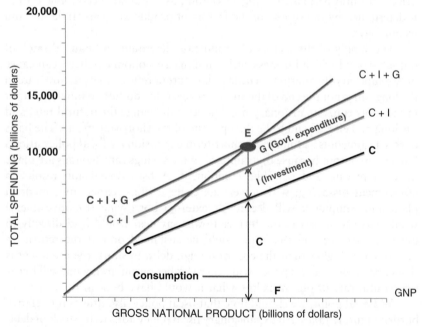

FIGURE 10.1   Effect of Government Expenditures on Income Determination

demand, consumption (C) and investment (I); G adds on to aggregate demand just like investment. An additional unit of G, like an additional unit of I, increases income by more than the increase in G (the multiplier) because one person's expenditure becomes someone else's income. That person spends a part of that increase in income and saves the rest and so on down the line with each additional expenditure less than the previous recipient's extra income because a portion is saved by each recipient. The equilibrium point (E) is stable in the sense that at any other point in the figure, the desired investment of business does not equal the desired savings of families; and as result, if the economy is not at E, it will tend to move or gravitate toward it. Moreover, if F is the full employment level of gross national product, then at point E there is significant unemployment of labor (and other resources). Increasing G could nudge the economy toward F directly or alternatively this could be done by adopting tax policies that increase private consumption or C (see Figure 10.2) and/or I. Alternatively, if there is unwanted inflation—an indication that the economy is operating too close to its capacity and excessive demand is pressuring price and wage increases to clear markets—then the government may be called to reduce G or adopt tax policies that reduce C and/or I. We should, however, note that to offset a US$200 billion upward shift in G, tax

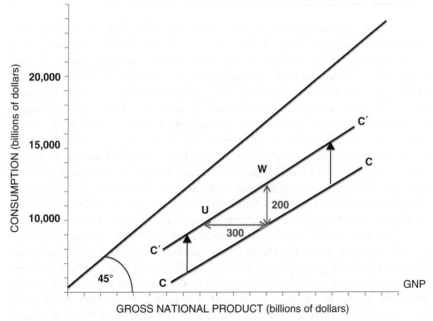

FIGURE 10.2 Effect of Taxes on Consumption Schedule

collection must increase by more than US$200 billion; if the marginal propensity to consume is two-thirds, then if C is to be lowered by US$200 billion, we need taxes of US$300 billion to balance the government budget and avoid an inflationary gap. We should add that a US$1 decrease in taxes has less of an impact on income than a US$1 increase in government expenditures and would lead to a larger budget deficit; in the former case, the private sector expands, while in the latter case, the public sector expands.

Recall two important points that have been made before. First, there is a continuing debate about the overall effectiveness and benefits of fiscal policy on employment and long-term economic growth. Second, the effectiveness of fiscal policy is further limited by two important lags—the time when the need for policy should have been recognized to the time that it is in fact recognized, and the time after the need for a change in fiscal stance is recognized to the time when the government is authorized to change its expenditure/tax policies (approval by the legislature, etc.). We also should note that a change in government expenditures directly affects aggregate demand, whereas a change in taxation is indirect, as it depends on the private sector to change its expenditures (consumption and investment).

FISCAL POLICY IN AN ISLAMIC ECONOMY

At the outset, we must emphasize that the goals of fiscal policy in the Islamic economic system are broader than those in conventional economics. Yes, while nudging the economy to full employment, limiting inflation, and supporting economic growth are all important, Islam demands more of fiscal policy: poverty eradication, tolerable gap between the rich and the poor, adequate safety net, and enhanced resource allocation to preserve the rights of individuals in every generation, and all under a general umbrella of rule compliance that achieves social justice. Fiscal policy, supported by other initiatives, would be conducted so that everyone has the bare necessities of life—food, shelter, and healthcare. This means that fiscal expenditures, while broadly addressing unemployment, inflation, and economic growth, must also directly alleviate poverty. Similarly, the tax system must be designed so that there is not opulent living alongside economic deprivation.

In an ideal Muslim society, individual Muslims, before or after they have paid levies or taxes mandated in Islam (*zakat*, *khums*, and *kharaj*), cleanse their wealth by helping the less fortunate members of society (especially those who cannot work or find work) in order to close income and wealth gaps to tolerable levels. In Islam, a great deal is expected from every member of society, and the intervention and the role of the state would be minimal if humans lived up to their obligations and commitments as rule-compliant

Muslims by complying with the rules of behavior prescribed by Islam. History is full of examples where Muslim societies developed sound institutions of social services based on Islam's instruments of redistribution. Research by Professor Murat Çizakça is evidence of this fact. (See Box 10.1.) If society fails to engage in social development as prescribed by Islam, then the state must levy taxes and focus fiscal expenditures to address societal shortcomings. At the same time, Islamic justice calls for a society where every member of the community has a reasonably equitable opportunity to develop and succeed in life; again, fiscal expenditures must address these concerns.

BOX 10.1 *WAQF* AS COMPLEMENTARY FISCAL TOOL

Professor Murat Çizakça has undertaken invaluable research in the area of the history of economics and finance in Islamic civilizations. With reference to fiscal responsibilities of Muslim communities, he makes an important observation that Islamic institutions of redistribution, particularly *waqf* (endowment), are critical social services provided by the private sector, which complemented fiscal responsibilities of the public sector by lessening its fiscal burden. He observes that:

> *Only a few taxes are mentioned in the Qur'an, leading some Islamic economists to wonder how additional taxes can be imposed. But this is missing the point. The message of the Qur'an should be obvious: in an Islamic economy, taxes should be few and the tax burden should be light. With government revenue thus limited, assuming a balanced budget, expenditures must be limited, as well. Since national defence constitutes the most important and inelastic government expenditure, which cannot be compromised, this means that the bulk of tax revenue must be earmarked for defence, leaving other important social services such as health and education inadequately funded. Ottoman budgets from the sixteenth century demonstrate that this was indeed the case.*
>
> *The resulting gap in the provision of services was filled by the waqf system. Known as charitable or philanthropic foundations in the West, waqfs were voluntary endowments provided by high net-worth individuals in order to finance,*

(continued)

BOX 10.1 (*Continued*)

organize, and maintain in perpetuity the most important services needed by the society. That this was not just a theory but found widespread application in the Islamic world is attested by the magnificent architectural monuments all over the Islamic world, from the shores of the Atlantic to the ends of the Indian Ocean. But architecture represents just the tip of the iceberg. The predominant role waqfs played in Muslims' lives has been explained by the historian Bahaeddin Yediyildiz, who argued that "a person could be born in a house belonging to a waqf, sleep in a cradle provided by that waqf, be educated in the school of the waqf and read the books provided by it, become a teacher in the waqf's school, earn a waqf-financed salary and at his death be placed in a waqf-provided coffin for burial in a waqf cemetery.

Source: Murat Çizakça, "Finance and Development in Islam: A Historical Perspective and a Brief Look Forward," in Zamir Iqbal and Abbas Mirakhor, eds., *Economic Development and Islamic Finance* (Washington, DC: World Bank, 2013), 134–135.

Similarly, we should note that the fiscal instruments that can be used in an Islamic economy are different from those in the conventional system. If expenditures are financed by taxes (pay as you go), there is clearly no issue, but when the state spends more than it collects in taxes and incurs deficits, then there are limitations on a Muslim government because of the prohibition of interest-bearing debt instruments. The state cannot use predetermined interest-bearing debt instruments to finance its deficit. However, it can use a number of other avenues to finance expenditures that exceed tax revenues. For example, the state can issue non-interest-bearing securities that the wealthier members of society may want to hold as one of their contributions to overall societal goals. But any debt, even non-interest-bearing debt, must be paid back. This would impose an unwarranted burden on future generations unless the state has used the proceeds to finance investments that will generate sufficient revenues to pay back only the debt (as there is no interest) in a reasonable period of time. But the state does not have to resort to deficit financing to the extent that modern governments have become accustomed to.

In short, fiscal policy in Islamic economy stands on two key pillars: taxation and public finance. The degree of reliance on taxation and/or public finance depends on how the society supplements social welfare programs through Islam's redistributive instruments and the developmental state of the economy.

Taxation

The focus of taxation is on increasing government revenue. *Zakat* in Islam and taxation in conventional terms are similar in that they ensure that resources of a country are more fairly enjoyed by all members of society. *Zakat* is imposed on the wealth of Muslims (in a sense on their surpluses) to redeem the rights of others in the society who are less able. The difference between *zakat* and taxation is that distribution of *zakat* is prescribed to only eight categories of people, whereas taxes are collected to support government spending for the provision of public goods and development.[1] *Zakat* is also compulsory according to divine law, while taxation is a policy imposed by the government. According to Muslim scholars, the state is authorized to collect additional taxes if *zakat* is insufficient to meet the needs of those requiring assistance and to produce public goods (such as social infrastructure).

While there are numerous reasons for tax avoidance in many countries and in different systems of government, including complex governance issues in general, a good tax policy is one that balances simplicity, efficiency, fairness, and revenue sufficiency. The tax structure needs to be reformed in such a way that the people will be willing to pay taxes without much enforcement, as they believe that they are giving away a fair amount of their income. The tax structure should also be easy to administer and capable of generating the revenue required. A complex system of taxation poses a challenge for taxpayers to comprehend and comply with. At the same time, a complex tax system provides incentives for shrewd taxpayers to identify loopholes to reduce tax payments or avoid taxes altogether. Simplifying the tax system will also reduce costs both to the government (of auditing taxpayers and enforcing compliance) and to taxpayers (of engaging tax consultants and tax lawyers to defend contentious tax positions). With a simple tax system, investors can be certain about the tax costs of doing business. A simple tax system based on the ability to pay also can bring more taxpayers into the tax net. This could reduce the perception that a tax system is unjust because it captures only a small segment of society net. A simple tax

---

[1] The eight categories are the poor; the needy; collectors and administrators of the *zakat*; those whose hearts lean toward the love for Allah (swt); freeing humans from worldly bondage; those who are overburdened with debts (e.g., those who have gone bankrupt); expenditure for removing obstacles in the path of humans toward their Creator; and wayfarers (see the Quran 9:60).

system can be designed around a flat tax, reflecting the structure of *zakat* and other charges prescribed in the Quran.

Flat Tax   A flat tax system is simple, as there is only one tax rate applicable to all income and to all taxpayers. A simple tax system would naturally lead to efficient tax collection. Implementing a flat tax system would increase compliance by taxpayers and thereby increase tax revenue. A flat tax system, because it is a fairer tax system than a progressive tax system, could lead to less tax evasion. To address the issue of the tax burden of the low-income earners who currently may be paying a low tax rate, a minimum exemption level of income could be determined before taxes would be payable. As mentioned before, Islam places a great deal of emphasis on human dignity. Therefore, the amount determined for the minimum bracket is one that could enable a person to live in the society with dignity. This usually translates into sufficient income to guarantee "basic needs." This minimum level is called the *nisab* limit. Two well-known proponents of the flat tax system, Hall and Rabushka, have developed a system that taxes income and eliminates double taxation by excluding taxes on investment.[2] It is advocated as a simple tax system that would generate greater tax compliance, as tax filing would become a less painful process. It would reduce tax evasion while raising high levels of revenue for the government. This is not a new tax system. A flat tax has been adopted in a number of countries.

Wealth Tax   As a matter of equity, most argue that taxes should be levied according to the ability to pay. The current focus on taxing income may impose undue burdens on income earners who need the income for their day-to-day living. Income alone may not be a sufficient measure of well-being or taxable capacity. Wealth adds to the capacity to pay tax, over and above the income yielded by that wealth. Taxing wealth means making those who are more financially able contribute more in tax. Wealth represents accumulated assets owned, not just income earned. Therefore, in the interests of equity, it is justifiable to tax wealth in addition to income. Moreover, as wealth generally represents a much larger tax base than income, the rate of taxation can be kept low but still raise substantial tax revenue. In addition, advocates of a wealth tax argue that such a tax may encourage the better off to transfer their assets from less productive uses to more productive ones and from idleness to income-producing ventures. The wealthiest segment of the population, which holds assets in the form of properties and stocks in companies and projects, will probably be paying a relatively low tax as a proportion of their wealth compared to those whose wealth consists mainly of their monthly salary.

---

[2]Hall and Rabushka (1995).

Collecting tax revenue from the segment of the population with the most wealth could promote equality, as the wealth that is currently concentrated in the hands of a few would become revenue for the government to be used for social development.

Under an Islamic economic system, a flat tax system consisting of an income tax component and a wealth tax component has the potential to be ideal. It reflects the rate structure of *khums* (literally, a one-fifth charge levied on war booty during the earliest period in Islamic history) and *zakat* prescribed by the Quran and the *Sunnah*. The optimum flat tax rate may differ from country to country, depending on the unique economic situation. As a general guideline, it is proposed here that the tax structure be composed of a 20% income tax and a 2.5% wealth tax (with an appropriate level of income and wealth exclusion to reflect the minimum necessities of life). The flat tax system of 20% on income may represent a reduction in the marginal tax rate from the tax rate prevailing in most countries. The reduction in marginal tax rate would incentivize people and firms to work and increase production. The reduction in tax rates also represents an increase in disposable income to individuals that would lead to increased consumption in the economy. With a simple tax system in force, tax administration would be much easier, and government resources could be released to attend to other matters more important and productive to the economy.

PUBLIC FINANCE

Capital markets play a critical role in Islamic finance for both private and public sector financing. The first best instrument of risk sharing is a stock market, which is considered the most sophisticated market-based risk-sharing mechanism.[3] It would provide the means for the business and public sector to raise long-term capital. In addition to the standard stock market, another capital market provides a platform for trading securitized asset-linked securities. The notion of "materiality" in Islamic finance of binding capital and financing closely and tightly to a real asset that is financed encourages the issuance of securities against a portfolio of assets. These "asset-linked" securities would be traded in the market through competitive bidding by a pool of investors, which includes individuals, Islamic banks (for their portfolios), institutional investors such as pension funds or insurance funds, and corporate treasuries. These investors trade these securities in primary and secondary markets.

[3] Brav et al. (2002).

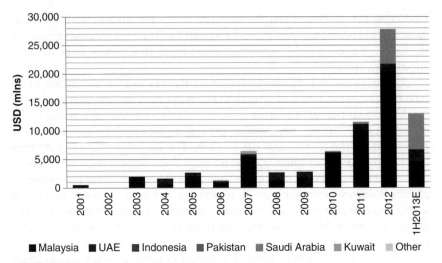

FIGURE 10.3 Infrastructure *Sukuk* Issuance by Country
Source: Kuwait Finance House Research.

Recent development of *sukuk* (Islamic bonds or ownership certificates) is an initial step in this direction.[4] *Sukuk* can play an important role in raising finances for public projects as *sukuk* could be structured in different flavors to match different needs. Government development projects could be financed through *sukuk*, which could give ownership stakes to investors during the financing period; in return, the investors share the risks and returns of the project. For example, government could issue *sukuk* against a single infrastructure project or against pools of several development projects with different maturities. Figure 10.3 and Box 10.2 provide some examples of *sukuk* used to finance infrastructure project by different Muslim countries.

In an Islamic society, the state pays for most, if not all, current expenditures (such as social programs) by taxes and finances, and all needed capital expenditures through private-public programs. The state should develop the project, whether it is a bridge, a power plant, or an airport, and sell either equity shares or ownership certificates; in other words, the state would use *sukuk* for financing, with stockholders or *sukuk* holders taking the risk and getting the income generated from the project as dividends or returns. Similarly, in what amounts to the same thing, a number of projects could

---

[4]The word *sukuk* (plural of the Arabic word *sakk*, meaning "certificate") reflects participation rights in preidentified pool of assets. The term is not new and was recognized in traditional Islamic jurisprudence.

BOX 10.2 LIST OF NOTABLE INFRASTRUCTURE
***SUKUK* ISSUED BY SOVEREIGN GOVERNMENT–**
RELATED ENTITIES

- General Authority of Civil Aviation: US$4.56 billion (Saudi Arabia)
- Pengurusan Air SPV Berhad: US$3.3 billion (Malaysia)
- Saudi Electricity Global Sukuk Co.: US$1.75 billion (Saudi Arabia)
- DanaInfra Sukuk: US$300 million (Malaysia)

Sources: Islamic Finance Information Service, Zawya, Kuwait Finance House Research. Data was provided by KFHR.

be combined and equity shares sold in the portfolio of projects; or, again what is essentially the same thing, the combined projects could be the assets that back a *sakk* (bond) that generates income with the *sukuk* holders who have access to the underlying assets. To our mind, the Islamic approach is in fact a better way for governments to finance their capital expenditures than the conventional approach in which interest-bearing debt is the instrument of choice and, invariably, with projects receiving less-than-full scrutiny, excessive debt crowds out the private sector (raising the level of general interest rates), governments incur higher funding costs, and the private sector (such as pension funds) are locked out of investments that could afford them interesting opportunities.

Even under conditions where there was no direct revenue from an infrastructure project, the government could resort to private sector financing with dividends paid by the government. But given that there are no fixed interest benchmarks in an Islamic system, the question becomes the appropriate rate of remuneration or dividend. Islam accepts public and joint ownership of assets as long as ownership claims can be priced in the market so that, in the event of dissolution, shareholders can sell and monetize their claims.[5] Therefore, capital expenditures can be financed via equity shares, provided there is a market for trading shares. The issue is then one of determining the appropriate rate of return that compensates shareholders in a market where there is no benchmark, such as a fixed rate government

---

[5] For the details of how a benchmark can be approximated, how such an instrument can be designed and developed, and how the market for these securities can be enhanced, see Ul-Haque and Mirakhor (1999).

security. But given that the rate of return in an Islamic economy is determined by the return in the real sector, it serves as a benchmark for investment decisions, and Mirakhor suggests that such a reference rate can be approximated by calculating the cost of capital using Tobin's q against which expected rates of return to private-public projects can be measured.[6] After these securities have been sold, market forces will determine their daily price.

Since the expected earnings of shareholders are derived from the expected returns, it can be argued that the discounted value of expected earnings at the prevailing rate of return is the market value of a security and the supply price of capital. In the case of government securities, this would also constitute the demand side of the market for these instruments. Moreover, the face value of securities, the length of maturity, and the expected dividend constitute the supply side of the market for government securities. At equilibrium, the social rate of return is such that the marginal benefit from public investment projects is equal to the opportunity cost of the provision of marginal services from these projects. But because of the public nature of these projects, the marginal benefits may not be truly measurable. It can be argued, however, that precisely because of this characteristic of infrastructural and development projects, their social rates of return must be greater than, or at least equal to, the rate of return in the private sector; otherwise, there is no financial justification for undertaking these projects.[7] As a result, the coupon on non-interest-based government securities can be issued and traded in equity markets that promise on maturity to pay a rate of return represented by an average rate of return on the underlying assets that is equal to the rate of return in the private sector. In addition to financing new projects, this approach can be used to retire government debt to the central bank that has financed previous projects since this debt can be securitized, providing the basis for the flotation of "national participation papers" to be traded on the stock market. These government securities are considered to be in consonance with Islamic law.

Financing a portion of the government budget through the stock market has advantages, 14 of which are summarized here.

1. It can energize a stock market—provided that all preconditions, in terms of human capital and the legal, administrative, and regulatory framework—are met and can help strengthen the credibility of the market.
2. It deepens and broadens the stock market.
3. It demonstrates that stock markets can be used as a tool of risk and financial management.

---

[6] Mirakhor (1996).
[7] Choudhry and Mirakhor (1997).

4. It reduces budgetary reliance on borrowing, thus imparting greater stability to the budget and mitigating the risk of "sudden stops."
5. It has a positive distributional effect in that the financial resources that normally would go to service public debt can now be spread more widely among the people as returns to the shares of government projects.
6. It enhances the potential for financing larger portfolios of public works projects without the fear of creating an undue burden on the budget.
7. It makes the task of monetary management simpler by limiting the amount of new money creation.
8. It promotes ownership of public goods by citizens. This should have a salutary effect on maintenance of public goods as it creates an ownership concern among the people and to some extent mitigates the "tragedy of the commons."
9. It has the potential of strengthening social solidarity.
10. It also has the potential to promote better governance by involving citizens as shareholders/owners of public projects.
11. It provides an excellent risk-sharing instrument for financing of long-term private sector investment.
12. It is also an effective instrument for firms and individuals to use to mitigate liquidity and productivity risks.
13. By providing greater depth and breadth to the market and minimizing the cost of market participation, governments convert the stock market into an instrument of international risk sharing as other countries and their people can invest in the stock market.
14. It will help demystify Islamic finance and will create an environment of cooperation and coordination with international finance.

It is not difficult for governments to design risk-sharing instruments for issue. These instruments can be traded in the secondary market if shareholders experience a liquidity shock. Their rate of return can be structured as an index of return tied to the rate of return to the stock market. If the domestic stock market is not deep, then an index of regional and/or international stock market returns can be included. The argument is that since the social rate of return to public goods is much higher than to privately produced goods and services, the rate of return for investments in public goods should be at least as high as the return to the stock market to promote efficient resource allocation. Of course, since governments are usually less risky, the rate of return to government-issued shares has to be adjusted downward to take account of the government's risk premium. Depending on the country and the interest rate the government pays on borrowed money, it is not likely that the rate of return it would pay to holders of equity shares it issues—adjusted for the credit rating of the government reflected in lower risk—would be any higher than the interest rate. Even in the unlikely event that a few basis points higher have to be paid, the trade-off is worthwhile, considering the positive contributions the instrument would make to the economy and the society.

Case for National Participation Paper

Haque and Mirakhor proposed an index-based security called a national participation paper (NPP) that can be used to issue government securities for public finance as well as instruments of monetary policy.[8] The concept of an NPP is based on the reasoning that such non-interest-based government securities can be issued and traded in equity markets that promise on maturity to pay a rate of return approximated by an average rate of return on the underlying assets equal to the rate of return in the private sector but adjusted for any reduction in risk due to the government's backing. In addition to financing new projects, this method can be used to retire government debt to the central bank that has financed previous projects since this debt can be securitized, providing the basis for flotation of an NPP that is to be traded on the stock markets.

In its most general form, the rate of return on the private sector may be written as follows:

$$I = w_1 \, WI + w_2 \, PPI + w_3 \, LSI + w_4 \, ROG$$

where

I = index growth of which will determine the uncertain (or the non-guaranteed) rate of return on the NPP

$w_1 \ldots w_4$ = weights that need to be determined

WI = international stock market index

PPI = weighted average of returns in commercial participation paper market as it develops

LSI = measure of market performance index in the country in which paper is being issued (stock index, earnings per share [EPS], dividends, return on equity [ROE], or average Tobin's q for the economy, where q is the ratio of value of a firm's assets to its market value)

ROG = measure of the rate of return on government investments that underlie the NPP

---

[8] Ul-Haque and Mirakhor (1999).

Using this general formulation, the next suggestions should be considered and investigated:

- **ROG only** (w1, . . . ,w3 = 0; w = 1). If the ROG could be estimated and reported by the central bank, this would be a simple solution.
- **LSI only (stock index based)** (w1, w2, w4 = 0; w3 = 1). Here, it should be borne in mind that the stock market is subject to speculative and other pressures. These should be excluded from the rate of return applied to the NPP.
- **LSI only (EPS, dividend, or ROE based)** (w1, w2, w4 = 0; w3 = 1). Given the difficulties with the stock market development, proxies of economy-wide rates of return can be derived from estimates of EPS, dividend yields, and ROEs.
- **PPI only** (w1, w3, w4 = 0; w2 = 1). A weighted average of NPP returns could be a useful indicator for the future when the NPP market develops.
- **More general index.** Weights can be derived for any and all w1 ($i = 1$). However, this will require considerable investigation and maintenance work. If desired, investigative efforts should be exerted to derive and maintain the appropriate index. Experimentation with weights and variables mentioned in the expression for I will allow a stable and realistic indicator to be developed for the rate of return.

The choice of weights should be dictated to a large extent by the need to derive a stable measure of the rate of return for the private sector. When local markets—the stock market and the participation paper market—are developed adequately, they should be given due weight in the index. Until then, their weight should be limited. The appropriate determination weights should be based on empirical investigation and then kept under constant review, although the weights should be changed only at discrete, preannounced intervals.

Because of market volatility, asymmetric information, and the possibility of speculative behavior, stock prices as well as market indexes include a risk premium that risk-averse investors require to hold risky assets. In most markets, government paper represents the most secure asset (often considered as the risk-free asset), and its rate of return is used as a benchmark for comparing all investments.[9] In equilibrium, the rate of return on government domestic paper would be equal to the rate of return on the stock market after adjustment for the risk premium. The index derived using the techniques discussed represents the rate of return to the private sector. Therefore, a risk premium should be subtracted from the private sector rate of return to obtain

---

[9] In particular, a government, unlike private firms, is considered to be free of default risk.

the rate of return that should be applied to government paper that is relatively free of market-based risk. The difficulty lies in finding an appropriate measure of the rate of return on assets that are similar in character to the government's to allow the system to begin. Any available bank deposit or loan rate (e.g., adjusted foreign rate, exchange rate, or rate on equity-based domestic transactions) would be a candidate if it were determined on market considerations. Any other reference rate that allows the establishment of a risk-free rate could also be used. This rate could be derived from any borrowing on a government project or a rate of return that has been obtained from such a project. When the NPP system is developed, its rates of return in the immediately preceding period could be used to estimate the risk premium. In this sense, the risk premium, like the index, will be updated on a regular basis. Using this rate, we can derive the risk premium as follows:

$$RP = \mu^I - R^{country}$$

where

RP = risk premium

μ^I = mean of the index I that has been derived earlier

$R^{country}$ = rate of return on bank deposits or government project

The risk premium can be calculated by applying data from the immediately past period. This formula, as well as the risk premium itself, can be revised periodically. But, given that stability of preferences has been observed around the world and through different time periods, there is little reason to assume large changes in this variable.

Payment on the NPP coupon will be made according to the growth of the I during the term of the paper. This RP should be subtracted from the growth of I to determine the final rate of return:

$$R_f = R_s - RP$$

where

R_f = final rate of return to be paid

R_s = rate of growth of I that has been suitably smoothed to correct for speculative and other behavior

The case of NPP is worth exploring for issuing government securities with varying maturities and for varying objectives. Once developed, the market of such paper could provide mechanisms for governments to finance development projects and to use for fiscal and monetary policy transmission and execution.

SUMMARY

The principal goal of fiscal policy is to nudge the economy toward full employment and/or restore stable prices as needed. Additionally, the government uses fiscal and monetary policy to enhance economic growth and prosperity. The government directly increases aggregate demand by increasing its expenditures and indirectly (through consumption and investment) by decreasing taxes; the change in aggregate demand affects the level of national income. In the Islamic economic system, the goal of fiscal policy is broader than in the conventional economic system. While nudging the economy to full employment, limiting inflation, and supporting economic growth are all important in Islam, Islam demands more of fiscal policy: It seeks poverty eradication, a tolerable gap between the rich and the poor, an adequate safety net, enhanced resource allocation to preserve the rights of individuals in every generation, and all under a general umbrella of social justice. The process of fiscal policy (government expenditures and taxation) and its financing in turn affect the government's budgetary position.

Rules governing an Islamic economy can address the persistent budget deficit and rising level of government debt. The high level of debt constrains government's ability to take on additional risk in its balance sheet. Apart from the threat of a credit rating downgrade, persistent fiscal deficits also impair the ability of policy makers to respond effectively to future shocks. Additionally, increasing the debt burden could have adverse distributional impacts for current and future generations. This is due to the fact that the middle- and lower-income classes carry the burden of the taxes that are needed to service government debt held by either higher-income groups or foreign investors. The design of policy instruments for fiscal policy in an Islamic economy should reflect concerns such as distributive justice.

Relatively stable fiscal revenue is essential for macroeconomics management and in turn for sustained growth.[10] A fiscal deficit is a common phenomenon in many nations, including the developed industrialized countries. This suggests that the policy prescriptions that had been put in place were not sufficient to create a sustainable fiscal position. This may have been due to either multiple structural weaknesses in the current tax system or a breakdown in fundamentals. In either case, a new policy configuration that

---

[10] Askari, Iqbal, and Mirakhor (2009).

would lead to a more sustainable and growth-supportive fiscal position would be in order.

An alternative approach to the current policy dilemma would propose a two-pronged solution: reform of the tax system and a radical change in the way governments finance their spending. The tax system needs to be simplified to a flat tax to induce voluntary declaration and compliance from taxpayers and widened to include a tax on wealth. At the same time, financing of economic activities should move away from the current interest-based system to one based on risk sharing through utilization of funds available to the public at large. Therefore, it is imperative that policies to increase revenue are put in place in tandem with a policy to mobilize debt-free public sector financing.

In Chapter 11 we examine how monetary policy also affects national income, employment, and prices, and in conjunction with monetary policy, we assess the transmission mechanisms of both monetary and fiscal policy in an Islamic economic system.

KEY TERMS

Goals and objectives	National debt
Taxation	Economic shocks
Income (flat, progressive)	Inside lag
Wealth (flat, progressive)	Automatic stabilizers
Sales and value added taxes	NAIRU
Public finance	Natural rate of employment
Expenditures	Multiplier
Budget deficit	National participation papers

QUESTIONS

1. Do you think fiscal policy is effective both in the short and in the long run and why? (Hint: Read the next chapter before answering.)
2. What would happen if the government just kept on spending to increase GDP? Would output just go on increasing?
3. Explain why $1 in government expenditures does not have the same effect on GDP as a tax cut of $1.
4. What form of taxation, if any, do you think is the most fair?

5. Do you think that the government's budget should be always balanced? Why or why not?

6. Do you think that fiscal policy should incorporate important social objectives (and which ones) or just stabilize and nudge the economy toward NAIRU?

7. Do you think that fiscal policy is more limited in Islam because of the prohibition against interest-bearing government bonds, and why or why not?

CHAPTER 11

Monetary Policy

Learning objectives:

1. *The goals and objectives of monetary policy in the conventional and Islamic system.*
2. *The instruments, channels, and impact of monetary policy in the conventional and the Islamic systems.*
3. *The different views regarding the effectiveness and track record of discretionary monetary policy.*
4. *The monetary policy role of commercial banks in the two systems.*
5. *Lags in monetary policy.*
6. *The complementary role of monetary policy to fiscal policy.*
7. *The short-run and long-run trade-offs between inflation and employment.*
8. *The role and monetary instruments of central banks in the conventional and the Islamic systems.*
9. *The non-interest-bearing securities of monetary policy in the Islamic system.*
10. *The potency and directness of monetary policy in the Islamic system.*

We have seen that economies rarely operate at full employment and at capacity. Instead, economies go through periods of high unemployment and excess capacity (idle factories, machinery, and equipment) followed by periods of low unemployment and little or no excess capacity. Thus, the government tries to nudge the economy upward when there is too much excess capacity and downward when there is little or no excess capacity with rapidly rising prices. The government has two broad sets of policies—fiscal and monetary—at its disposal. In Chapter 10, we considered fiscal policy; in this chapter, we look into monetary policy.

The most important objective of monetary policy is to influence the portfolio decisions of the private sector (consumers and producers). Monetary policy manipulates the incentive structure of the private sector in terms of credit availability to induce portfolio adjustment in the demand of this sector. Monetary policy is normally implemented by a country's central bank. In recent years, in most Western countries, the central bank is structured as an independent institution in order to be relatively free of political pressures so that it can focus on adopting the monetary policy (discretionary or rule based) that best suits the national interest as opposed to the career ambitions of politicians and the selfish interests of political parties. Monetary policy essentially boils down to controlling the quantity of money in circulation and also interest rates in order to affect private sector demand and promote economic prosperity with low inflation. The mandate for monetary policy varies from country to country. In some countries, the mandate of the monetary authority is simply to adopt a target (normally a narrow range) rate of inflation and to conduct its monetary policy in order to achieve the target or targeted range of inflation. In other countries, the central bank's mandate is to strive for full employment with moderate inflation. Monetary policy is expansionary when the monetary authority is increasing the money supply and lowering interest rates, and contractionary when it is doing the opposite. More money in the economy and lower interest rates encourage individuals to borrow more and spend more and, most important, businesses to borrow and invest more. This adds to aggregate demand, as we saw in Chapter 10, and nudges national output higher with a multiplier effect as with fiscal policy.

ROLE OF MONETARY POLICY

In the conventional economic system, there are essentially three forms of money: coins, bills, and bank deposits. In such a system, the central bank can pump money (bills and coins) into the economy through banks; banks in turn can lend the money to investors (and consumers); and when and if banks increase their lending, investment increases, lifting national output. But we need to explain in more detail the structure of the banking system in such an economy, why bank deposits are considered money, and in turn how banks create money.

When a person deposits $100 in a bank checking account, the bank issues that person checks; he or she can in turn write checks up to $100 and use them just as if he or she had cash. But the bank does not stand still; it lends as much of the $100 that person deposited to others and charges the borrowers interest; central banks limit the percentage of money deposits that banks can lend by requiring them to hold a proportion of the $100 as reserves (the reserve requirement). If the reserve requirement is, say, 10%, the bank can lend out $90; the borrower takes the $90 and deposits it in a bank and can write checks on it. The bank now lends $81 (90% of $90) to another borrower; and so the process continues. Of course, there may be some leakage from the system we have described—borrowers not depositing all the money they borrow and/or the bank not lending out all the cash that is deposited. But the story should be clear: The original $100 injected into the money supply does not stay as $100, but banks use it to *create more money* in the form of demand deposits; in fact, if the reserve requirement is 10% and if there is no leakage, $100 creates $1,000 ($100 × 1/1 – 0.9) in demand or bank deposits. Thus such a banking system, referred to as the fractional reserve system, creates money. In other words, the $100 is leveraged into $1,000 of demand deposits (through interest-based loans).

The central bank in the conventional system uses a number of tools to affect the money supply and interest rates. The primary instrument of a central bank's monetary policy is open market operations, which is buying and selling mainly government Treasury bills, corporate bonds, other securities, and foreign currencies. Secondary instruments are lending through the discount window (lender of last resort), the changing reserve requirement of banks, moral suasion, and changing market expectations through press conferences and other such means. Through open market operations, the central bank changes the money supply (increasing the supply by buying securities for cash and decreasing it by selling securities on the open market) by selling and buying securities in the market in order to achieve a short-term interest rate target, such as for the federal funds rate, the rate for overnight interbank lending. The central bank as a lender of last resort affects bank lending and interest rates by changing its discount rate, the interest rate at which it lends to member banks when they are temporarily caught short of funds. The money supply can be increased or reduced by reducing or increasing the reserve requirement of banks. Banks can be also "persuaded" to act in ways that the central bank wants, and money markets and expectations can be affected by targeted speeches and interviews. Central banks use announcements especially to affect expectations about inflation (and interest rates) as high inflationary expectations can become a self-fulfilling prophecy.

The upshot of monetary policy in the conventional system is summarized in Figure 11.1. The central bank can raise the money supply from point A to point B, lowering interest rates; this increases investment from C to D; and the higher level of investment raises gross national product (GNP) from E to F. We should note that the impact of monetary expansion is also reflected in what is called the quantity theory of money:

$$MV = PQ$$

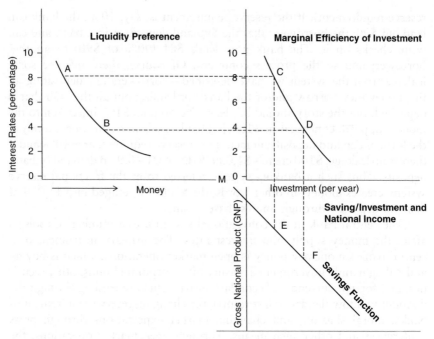

FIGURE 11.1 Monetary Policy and National Income Determination

where

M = Money supply
V = Velocity circulation of money or income velocity
P = Average price level
Q = Real GNP

V, the velocity of circulation of money, is the rate at which the money stock is turning over per year to enable income transactions. The crude version of this theory is that V is a constant so that a doubling of M leads to a doubling of P. But in real life V is not a constant. The more sophisticated view of this relationship is that an increase in M results in an increase in PQ, which is the dollar or money (nominal) GNP. Thus in Figure 11.1, the velocity, V, is a little lower from E to F, but not enough to keep the new MV and GNP from being higher.

An important consideration in the implementation of both monetary and fiscal policy has been the trade-off between unemployment and inflation. In 1958, William Phillips plotted historical data on wage inflation against

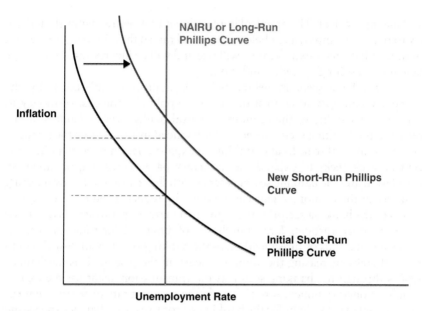

FIGURE 11.2 Phillips Curve

unemployment and found what appeared to be a trade-off: If the central bank wants to attain full employment, it may have to put up with more inflation, indicating a trade-off between unemployment and inflation. This relationship came to be known as the Phillips curve. (See Figure 11.2.) Economists generally accepted the relationship until the 1970s when the United States experienced stagflation (unemployment coupled with high inflation) and Milton Friedman and others questioned the validity of the trade-off portrayed in the Phillips curve. They argued that the Phillips curve was only a short-run relationship; in time, inflation would be taken into account by labor, and labor contracts would incorporate anticipated inflation. Thus, with monetary expansion, unemployment would go back to its original level but with higher inflation. The implication is that there are a series of short-run Phillips curves and, in the long run, there is no trade-off between unemployment and inflation. In other words, the long-run Phillips curve is vertical, as shown in Figure 11.2. In the long run, only a single rate of unemployment, the nonaccelerating inflation rate of unemployment (NAIRU), is consistent with a stable rate of inflation that can be attained. With unemployment rates below NAIRU, inflation accelerates. With unemployment above NAIRU, inflation decelerates. With the unemployment rate equal to NAIRU, inflation is stable. In other words, monetary policy affects prices but not real values like output and unemployment. The practical implication is that central banks should not try to reduce unemployment below its natural rate; if they do so for any length of time, inflationary expectations will rise and will be incorporated into wage demands, resulting in higher inflation.

As we have seen, monetary policy is a process undertaken by the monetary authority to control the money supply and the cost of money to achieve the stability of the economy. Central banks serve as lenders of last resort to the banking sector when and if financial institutions or the financial system is under threat. In undertaking an expansionary monetary policy, the central bank seeks to expand the monetary base—consisting of money in circulation and the banking sector reserve with the central bank—by injecting liquidity in the economy. This can be done by reducing the reserve requirements of the banking sector or through open market operations (as described earlier): either through large purchases of financial instruments such as government bonds or direct lending to the banking system with low discount rates, thereby increasing the amount of cash in the system. This mechanism works through the banking sector as the transmission agent for the expansionary monetary policy. A reduction in the discount rate or reserve requirement signals a green light for the banking sector to expand balance sheets and increase lending, which in turn aim at increased spending by consumers.

Monetary policy must meet certain challenges, notably, dealing with the flexibility of the financial system to react and ensuring the timing and credibility of announcements to affect market expectations. The latter depends on the success of the previously implemented monetary policies, as reputation is an important element in the implementation of a successful monetary policy. The success of this policy also depends on the effectiveness of the transmission mechanism and the independence of the central bank from the rest of the government, especially independence from personal and party political agendas. The objectives of the government as policy makers and the private banking sector may not converge. When the banking sector does not transmit the increased liquidity to the rest of the private sector and consumers, but instead uses the liquidity to enhance its own bottom line, then the transmission mechanism has failed. In other words, conventional monetary policy is indirect in that it relies on the banking sector to support and implement the wishes of the central bank. Moreover, within the context of a fractional reserve banking system, the role of the central bank in the course of implementing its monetary policy makes the current conventional financial system unstable and vulnerable to financial turmoil through the expansion of credit out of thin air, which in the end results in excessive leveraging and a debt crisis. Interest rates set by the central bank create a wedge between the money interest rate and the natural rate of interest. Monetary injection allows money capital to multiply independently of real or physical output. Creation of credits not backed by the real economy diverts real savings from productive activities to nonproductive ones that in turn weaken the process of real wealth expansion.

The challenge in an Islamic framework is to design instruments that satisfy the requirements of an effective monetary policy while meeting the rule of exchange-based transactions without resorting to the interest rate mechanism. The solution is to devise financial instruments that rely on the risk-sharing features of equity finance, as discussed in Chapters 8 and 9. Where monetary policy in a conventional economy uses interest rates to indirectly regulate the money supply, in an Islamic economy money supply is directly altered through asset market activities. The incentive structure intended by monetary authorities to induce portfolio adjustment may be distorted if signals are not transmitted to the private sector by the banking sector. For example, the excess reserves arising from a lowering of the reserve requirements may be used by the banking sector to buy government bonds instead of lending to the private sector to increase consumption and investment. As a result, the effect of the monetary policy may not be fully achieved. The use of the interest rate as a tool of monetary policy creates incentives for financial decoupling. Risk-sharing instruments can avoid this problem. Such instruments, issued by the government to finance its operations and used by the monetary authority to affect portfolio adjustment by the private sector, can achieve the objectives of monetary policy while promoting greater resilience of the economy to shocks.

MONETARY POLICY IN AN ISLAMIC ECONOMY

In an Islamic economy, the conventional tools normally available in a conventional modern economy are at the disposal of the monetary authorities with the exception of the discount rate and other policy tools that involve an interest rate (buying and selling of interest-bearing bonds). All other tools, namely open market operations (where equity shares rather than bonds are traded) and credit policies, can be as effective in an Islamic system as they are in the conventional Western system. The authorities in an Islamic system can utilize reserve requirements and profit-sharing ratios to achieve changes in the stocks of money and credit. Moreover, as we shall see, monetary policy could be considered to operate through a more direct channel in the Islamic financial system.

The principal goal of monetary policy is to ensure macroeconomic stability, characterized in the main by price-level stability and a viable balance of payments position. The establishment of a stable macroeconomic environment is a prerequisite for increased savings, investment, and foreign capital

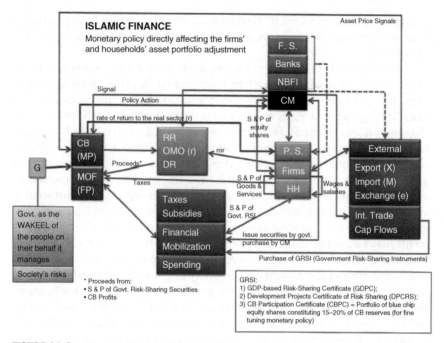

FIGURE 11.3 Monetary Policy in Islamic Finance

inflows—all of which are central to the growth process. Basically, without macroeconomic stability, economic growth can falter and not be sustained. Furthermore, without broad-based economic growth, the basic structural and social transformations that make up the process of Islamic development will not occur, and the other objectives of Islamic society, such as a more equitable distribution of resources and income, providing useful employment, improving living standards and the quality of life, and the alleviation of poverty, are unlikely to be met.

In Figure 11.3, we depict the transmission of monetary and fiscal policy in the Islamic financial and economic system. The central bank, by buying and selling risk-sharing securities, directly affects the financial portfolio of the private sector—households and firms—and indirectly affects the holdings of banks and conditions in capital markets that in turn affect real economic activity. The decisions of households and firms impact the real rate of return in the economy, which again affects economic activity, while financial signals to capital markets through central bank policies affect the availability of real resources for investment.

As discussed earlier, the Islamic banking system or financial intermediation is by design a 100% reserve banking system. Banks cannot create money as in the fractional banking system. Moreover, in the Islamic system, there are no interest-bearing debt instruments. Thus, a different set of instruments must be used to affect monetary policy. Monetary policy in the Islamic system has broader objectives than monetary policy in the conventional system. Yes, although nudging the economy to full employment with low inflation is important, Islamic principles expect more. They expect that monetary policy should also support preservation of the purchasing power of money, poverty eradication, a tolerable gap between the rich and the poor, and an adequate social safety net. As we have said throughout this book, the rights of individuals in every generation must be preserved, and all under a general umbrella of social justice where everyone has the bare necessities of life—food, shelter, and healthcare. While the focus in this chapter is on the acceptable instruments (in place of interest-bearing debt instruments) that can be used in open market operations, these broader objectives must be supported.

When revenue is insufficient to cover a budget deficit, the government must borrow. Due to the prohibition of interest in an Islamic economy, the policy instrument for public sector borrowing should be based on risk sharing or through asset-linked financing (i.e., *sukuk* [Islamic bonds or ownership certificates]). The benefits of risk sharing are manifold, as discussed. Instead of borrowing, the government could promote public–private sector partnerships to finance development projects. This would mobilize higher private sector savings in many countries to support productive public sector investment projects. By issuing risk-sharing instruments to fund development expenditures, the burden of debt could be reduced. At the same time, the household sector would be able to enjoy a higher rate of return on its savings because the rate of return on the papers would be driven by the return to the real sector.

The first best instrument of risk sharing is the stock market. With an active stock market, individuals can buffer idiosyncratic liquidity shocks by selling equity shares in the market. When risk is spread among a large number of participants through an efficient stock market, closer coordination between the financial and real sector is promoted. Moreover, the benefits of economic growth and financial system stability are better shared. Risk sharing through equity finance will ensure that Islamic finance is anchored to the real sector at all times. As discussed earlier, another segment of capital markets, securitized financing or asset-linked securities such as *sukuk*, play equally important roles in financing of the real sector. The market for asset-linked securities can also be an important instrument of monetary policy execution.

Using the same concept, liquidity in the economy through the monetary policy mechanism can be controlled through the issuance of financial instruments, such as equity participation shares or asset-linked securities, which enable investors to participate in financing government expenditures, such as in development projects. The papers must have low enough denominations and be traded in secondary markets so that ordinary citizens—not just institutional investors—can have access to them (enabling a more direct and predictable impact of monetary policy). To contract the money supply, these papers would be issued directly to the market to mop up excess market liquidity. The effect would be immediate, and leakages arising from intermediation would be reduced. Conversely, if the goal is to increase money supply, the monetary authority would buy these papers from the private sector.

The rate of return on these papers would be referenced to the rate of return to the real sector of the economy. The rate could be benchmarked against the average rate of return of the stock market or the market for securitized assets, which is generally higher than the interest rate in the economy, and hence this presents investors with a better return on their idle income. For example, in late 2012, the interest rate on government securities in Malaysia was approximately 6%, while the rate of return on bank deposits was 2%. If the rate of return on equity participation shares could be set to reflect the equity premium in the stock market (between 9% and 11%), it could potentially earn 7% to 9% (adjusted for the government's risk premium). An alternative could be that the rate of return to these papers could be benchmarked on the return to the real sector of the economy. Either way it would represent a better investment alternative for investors. In countries such as Malaysia, where private savings are high, resources that are earning 2% return could be mobilized to productive use in the economy for a higher rate of return. The effect of this policy measure would be not only to achieve a more potent monetary policy impact than in the conventional economy; it also would serve as a measure of improving income distribution by providing members of society better access to the benefits from the growth of the economy. It would also serve as a consumption-smoothing instrument (to mitigate idiosyncratic risk) for small investors.

These papers should be openly traded in the secondary market so that holders can redeem or liquidate them by selling them at prevailing market prices. This means that institutional investors, such as banks, would have to pay the market price to have access to this instrument for purposes of managing their asset portfolios. In this way, the same economic opportunity would be available to all; it would not be limited to the more financially able. At the same time, the opportunity (risk–reward profile) in economic activity would be available according to the financial capability of each investor. Such monetary policy instruments would also enhance governance, as the government would be more accountable to the general public regarding its investments in the risk-sharing instruments.

The cost to the government of raising financing through equity participation shares would be not much higher than the current rate of interest paid on debt instruments, but it would provide a better impetus to grow the economy by mobilizing funds that would be otherwise idle in deposits. At the same time, these papers could serve as ideal instruments for monetary policy measures ("ideal" in the sense that monetary policy signals would reach the private sector without being filtered by the banking system). To expand the money supply, the papers could be bought from the open market, thereby increasing the amount of money in circulation to increase consumption and investment. An illustration of the mechanism of the Islamic monetary and fiscal policy instruments is provided in Chapter 9.

The monetary instruments that can be used in an Islamic economy are different from those used in the conventional system. Open market operations can be used to buy and sell papers of a different sort because interest-bearing financial debts, such as bonds, are prohibited in the Islamic system. As mentioned, the state can use a number of other avenues to finance expenditures that exceed tax revenues, resulting in securities that can be bought and sold by the central bank to conduct monetary operations. The state can finance all needed capital expenditures through private–public programs, as mentioned: The state could develop the projects and sell equity shares (or national participation papers) for its financing, with stockholders taking the risk and getting the income generated from the project as dividends. Similarly, a number of projects could be combined and equity shares sold for the aggregate number of projects; or, again what is essentially the same thing, the combined projects could be the assets that back a bond that generates a fixed income with the bondholders having access to the underlying assets. Even under conditions where there was no direct revenue from an infrastructural project, the government could resort to private sector financing with dividends paid by the government at (or above or below) the rate of return in the real sector.

The central bank in the Islamic system has other instruments, in addition to our proposed equity shares or participation papers (securitized paper) in development projects, that it can buy and sell in the market to affect the money supply and thus attain its monetary objectives. The major objective of that bank is generation of market-oriented incentives to induce portfolio adjustments to stabilize the economy. These risk-sharing and interest-free instruments work as monetary policy tools to absorb and expand liquidity to and from the economy and at the same time match investors' intentions of investing in Islamic monetary instruments. The available instruments include a variety of Islamic bonds or *sukuk* (based on ownership in a debt, *sukuk al murabaha*;

in an asset, *sukuk al ijara*; on a project, *sukuk al istisna*; in a profit-sharing business, *sukuk al musharaka*; on an investment, *sukuk al istithmar*):

1. The state can issue non–interest-bearing bonds (*qardh hassan*) that the wealthier members of society may want to hold as one of their contributions to overall societal goals.
2. Securities that can be backed by trade-based financing or *tijarah* (fixed rates).
3. Securities can be backed by lease-based financing *ijara* (fixed rates).
4. Securities can be linked to real assets that are securitized and the security holder has access to the underlying asset (especially in the event of default). They are of two basic types:
   a. *Istisna* contracts can be securitized to raise funds based on assets that provide a rental income (such as buildings for fixed income or variables in the case of road tolls).
   b. *Salám* contracts entail the delivery of specific goods in the future, where the goods are sold to the public on a markup.

As we have elaborated, open market operations, the buying and selling (from the investment bank type of Islamic institutions, and not from the safekeeping category of institutions; more on this below) of equity or securitized assets in projects (participation papers) and asset-linked bonds (*sukuk*) are expected to be the main instruments of monetary policy, but the central bank can adopt additional tools to affect its monetary stance in the Islamic system. Before we elaborate on these other instruments, we must address two controversial and unsettled issues concerning the operation of central banks in Islamic finance. Are central banks permitted to print paper money, and can they act as lenders of last resort (LoLR)? We believe that the answers to both of these questions are yes. Let us explain.

While some argue that money and value cannot be created out of thin air in Islam, we believe that this proposition can be challenged if money is created to benefit particular members of the community. To our mind, there is nothing in the Quran or in the *Sunnah* that recommends or prohibits the state from creating money (of course, we realize that there was no paper money at the time of the Prophet (sawa). Yes, the state cannot issue interest-bearing bonds and paper money that earns interest. But if the state prints money in order to facilitate business transactions and enhance prosperity for the benefit of the community because the economy's output is below its potential, then money creation by the state should be permissible. Such a situation can be operationally defined as when there is unused productive capacity in the economy. Also, the central bank can print money to accommodate expected additions to productive capacity. This would mean that there is accurate estimation of full employment output and expected future growth of the economy.

And yes, the state gets the normal advantage of seigniorage, but again if this is used for the equitable benefit of all members of society, not rulers and privileged classes, then why should the central bank be barred from issuing paper money? It is in the interest of the community. Similarly, the central bank should be permitted to act as an LoLR as long as it does not charge interest in order to sustain economic growth. It could charge a financially sound investment bank in need of liquidity a rate consistent with the rate of return to the real sector of the economy *ex post facto* (thus an actual real rate of return). Alternatively, the central bank could purchase assets from the investment bank, which in the end is akin to acting as an LoLR.

Two things need to be clarified. The banks operate on 100% reserve basis, and there are no deposit guarantees, either for banks that handle the payment system (i.e., those that are allowed to accept demand deposits), or for investment banks (which, even though they are not permitted to take demand deposits, can take investment funds). Those who would not allow central banks to print money argue that the prohibition against money printing is necessary to tie the hands of authorities and monetary policy so it cannot fuel inflation through monetary expansion. But this power is very much limited once the 100% reserve system is the structure of the banking system. The most important point is that a responsible and accountable central bank under a 100% reserve system limits the liability of the government (printing money) to no more than the economy would allow in terms of expansion in productive capacity.

In Table 11.1 we list results of a survey conducted by the Islamic Financial Services Board (IFSB) of 24 regulatory and supervisory authorities

TABLE 11.1 Current Status of *Shariah*-Compliant Lender of Last Resort (SLoRL) Facilities

% of RSAs	Status
25%	The SLoLR facilities **have been developed** for the Islamic Finance Information Service in your jurisdiction, as your central bank distinguishes between conventional institutions and IIFS.
38%	The SLoLR facilities **have not been developed**, as your central bank has conventional LoLR facilities available, and it does not differentiate between conventional institutions and IIFS when it comes to providing LoLR facilities.
37%	So far, your central bank has not been required to use SLoLR but it is **considering the importance of developing SLoLR facilities.**

Source: Islamic Financial Services Board.

(RSAs) where Islamic financial institutions are active and operating. It is evident that the majority of jurisdictions do not have adequate arrangements for providing LoLR due to several factors, such as lack of instruments, lack of threshold of institutions requiring LoLR arrangements, and the relatively small market segment captured by Islamic banks (and thus providing a *Shariah*-compliant LoLR is not a priority for such RSAs).

A commercial banking system that is 100% reserve banking prohibits lending. The need for reserves and changes in the reserve requirements of these commercial banks as a policy instrument is eliminated. But investment banking affords important policy options: Investment banks channel investor funds into different investment projects (by risk, maturity, rent/dividend, etc.) and issue investors equity shares or bonds (backed by the investments) that are traded in the market. The central bank can affect the operation of these banks in two principal ways. First and foremost, the central bank can buy and sell the securities that it issues directly to investors and those that it issues on its account by investing its own capital. In the case of security purchases, the central bank injects cash into the hands of investors and the banks, resulting in investors and banks having cash to invest in new projects. Note the power of this instrument and compare it to open market operations in the conventional banking system. Here, the central bank puts cash directly into the hands of investors who decide on their investments. In the conventional system, the cash is put into the hands of bankers who *may* or *may not* lend. Open market operation is a much more potent policy instrument in Islamic banking than it is in the conventional system. Second, the central bank can change the reserve requirement of investment (mutual fund activities) banks. Investment banks essentially invest the capital of investors in projects of different sorts in a pass-through mode and invest their shareholders' capital in these or other projects. The central bank can require reserves of these investment banks, not because of exposure to risk but to influence investment banks' ability to channel funds into projects and in turn reduce the return to investors. Let us explain. By requiring reserves, these investment banks can invest less of the investors' assets (keeping a part as reserves) and thus reduce the attractiveness of investing (lower rate of return as a portion is kept as reserves and does not earn any return).

Such reserve requirements do raise a number of issues: Should reserve requirements be changed on existing equity investments or imposed only on new investments? Depending on the answer to this question, should these reserves be kept at the central bank and returned to the holder of the equity asset at the time of maturity? In addition to open market operations and reserve requirements for the central bank, we should note that the central bank could use its guidance advisories to form market expectations and thus affect the investment/saving decision, which in turn will affect economic activity. The impact and effectiveness of central bank guidance, including inflation targets, will be directly proportional to its credibility.

In addition to the implementation of monetary policy, central banks in an Islamic system could take the lead in evolving financial institutions and instruments that facilitate efficient mobilization of savings and allocation of resources consistent with the economic development objectives of the Islamic economy. The central bank, in particular, must initiate and foster the development of primary, secondary, and money markets. Mere adoption of Islamic rules of finance will not necessarily create the impetus for financial and economic development where the shallowness of financial markets and lack of attractive financial instruments have created impediments to the saving–investment nexus and for the process of financial intermediation.

There are reasons to believe that the relationship between financial deepening and real growth of the economy would be strong in an Islamic economy where profit sharing can be expected to have significant positive influence on the saving–investment process. The positive relationship between expansion of financial markets and financial development on one hand and between financial development and economic development on the other necessitates an active participation by the monetary authorities in evolving the economy's financial infrastructure. For example, monetization of transactions in rural areas requires a wider geographical and functional penetration of the banking system. Through provision of such facilities and expansion of financial markets, the central bank can both lower the cost and increase the availability of credit in the economy. Moreover, the prohibition against interest provides natural opportunities for the integration of financial markets. The monetary authorities, through the central bank, can take steps to foster competition between organized and unorganized markets on the basis of profit sharing and rates of return in order to enhance the process of integration.

The extension and enforcement of Islamic regulations concerning contracts and property rights to financial and capital markets is needed to reduce uncertainties arising from the present structure of rights, which tends to discourage private investment. Such actions would include imposition of legal sanctions on irresponsible behavior on the part of agent/entrepreneurs to the extent necessary to reduce moral hazard problems and to encourage lending on the basis of viability and profitability of investment projects rather than solvency, creditworthiness, or collateral strength of entrepreneurs. Uncertainty in contract and property rights combined with heavy costs, at least initially, of project appraisal, evaluation, and monitoring may lead to a significant reduction in investment. In fact, it can be argued that the risk of adoption of an Islamic financial system, particularly in the initial stages, is not lower savings but lower investment, if the Islamic rules regarding contracts and property rights are not enforced. In the absence of legal protection, risk-averse bankers and savers may simply refuse to provide funds on the basis of profit-sharing arrangements. Alternatively, principals and agents may engage in contrived contractual relationships that may be Islamic only in appearance. The enforcement of Islamic rules regarding contracts and property rights would increase public confidence in capital markets, financial institutions, and the process of financial intermediation. Only then will banks and other financial institutions, through their direct involvement in profit sharing with the real sector, become instruments of industrialization and development. This way the whole investment process would add to efficiency, as real entrepreneurs would utilize savings rather than those whose only claim to enterprise is based on ownership of savings. The increase in efficiency will, in turn, increase profits and afford a higher rate of return to savers.

The central bank in the Islamic system can be expected to perform the usual regulation, supervision, and control functions that central banks perform in the conventional financial system. The central bank can also control the banking system through its purchase of equity shares of banks and nonbank financial institutions. The necessity of the central bank's leadership role in initiating and evolving primary, secondary, and money markets has already been discussed. Through performance of these functions and its LoLR role, the central bank can exert greater influence in the financial system. Moreover, opportunities will exist for the central bank to directly invest in the real sector on a profit-sharing basis as well as to take equity positions in joint ventures with other banks. The opportunity for the central bank to buy and sell securities in the financial markets may enable it to influence further financial resource allocation, if that becomes necessary or desirable.

Choice of Islamic Monetary Instrument

An Islamic central bank has the primary responsibility of formulating and conducting monetary policy. Its auxiliary functions include assisting the banking system in the transition, promoting money market development, safeguarding the payments and clearing system, and performing bank regulation and supervision. Also, as the leading financing institution, it is concerned with the efficiency of intermediation between savers and investors, which takes place via the financial system and contributes to stable economic growth.

An Islamic central bank can operate directly through its regulatory and powers or indirectly through its influence on capital market conditions. Direct and indirect instrument operations can be distinguished in two ways: (1) direct instruments set or limit prices or quantities through regulation, while indirect instruments operate through market by influencing underlying demand and supply conditions; and (2) direct instruments are mainly aimed at balance sheets of commercial banks, while indirect instruments are aimed at the balance sheet of the central bank.

Using indirect instruments, the central bank can determine the supply of reserves. This affects the commercial banking sectors' liquidity position, as long as they have to settle their payment obligations across the books of the central bank and provided they do not have unlimited (with no penalties) access funding at the central bank. The effect on banks' liquidity positions results in adjustments to bank, interbank, and money market pricing that are expected to reequilibrate demand and supply of reserve balances.

Choice of Direct Instruments It is important to note that in an ideal Islamic economy, there are no money markets, since in these markets, money now is traded for money later. However, during the transition to the ideal economy, money markets do exist, although the rates of return in these markets are noninterest bearing. In this situation, the choice of direct instruments of monetary control is based on the variety shown in Table 11.2. The major instruments are bank-by-bank credit ceilings, statutory liquidity ratios, and directed credits. They are all linked with the assets side of banks and are one of the major factors affecting money supply. They provide effective control on allocation and distribution of bank credit at the discretion of the central bank and in line with the monetary program, taking into account other economic and social objectives. These instruments are particularly suitable at the initial stages of Islamizing and restructuring banking and financial institutions.

There are seven main advantages of direct instruments of monetary control:

1. These instruments are perceived to be reliable in controlling credit aggregates or the allocation of credit and its cost; they seem to have performed well for a period in many countries.
2. They are relatively easy to implement.
3. Their direct fiscal cost has been relatively low.
4. They are easy to quantify and link to a monetary program within an economic policy framework.
5. In countries with noncompetitive financial systems and less developed primary and secondary capital markets, direct instruments are the only feasible monetary instruments to operate effectively.
6. With other forms of credit scarce, bank-by-bank credit ceilings are effective regardless of the exchange rate regime.
7. Direct instruments can, at least temporarily, be attractive in situations of specific or general market failures in a severe financial crisis.

TABLE 11.2 Direct Instruments of Monetary Control Advantages, Disadvantages, and Operational Issues

Instruments	Advantages	Disadvantages	Issues in Design and Operations	Experience and Assessment
Interest rate controls (abolished under Islamic law)	Contain the effects of noncompetitive pricing when entry into banking is limited. Limit adverse selection problems, particularly when information on borrowers is scarce or banking supervision is weak. Often resorted to when authorities cannot achieve a target interest rate through market means or when long-term rates are a policy objective.	Interfere with price mechanism. Lead to rationing of credit and misallocation. Ceiling easily circumvented by shifting bank deposits into assets yielding market rates (such as foreign exchange) or into goods. Floors or ceilings encourage disintermediation or nonbank intermediation.	Design can involve fixing interest rates or spreads.	Increasingly ineffective as markets and financial instruments develop.
Bank-by-bank credit ceiling	Can deliver effective control over bank credit if reserve money creation is otherwise controlled. Can minimize loss of	Because credit ceiling are not market determined, they progressively distort the allocation of bank resources. Can	Quotas may depend on capital, existing credit, and existing deposits. Secondary trading of unused credit quotas	Still used in some African and Asian countries and in transition economies.

	monetary control during transition to indirect instruments when transmission mechanism is uncertain.	lead to disintermediation and ultimate loss of effectiveness. Difficult to implement if there are many banks and if there are capital inflows.	introduces elements of market allocation and mitigates distortions.	Supply of base money must be consistent with money demand; otherwise instrument leads to buildup of excess reserves; creates incentives for evasion.
Statutory liquidity ratios	By providing captive demand for qualifying assets (typically government debt), ratios reduce cost of borrowing for issuer of these instruments.	Distort competition by imposing constraints on banks' asset management. Distort pricing of securities and stifle secondary trading. Can lead to disintermediation, increase spread, and loss of effectiveness.	Design involves choosing eligible securities, eligible maturities, and averaging methods, of either requirement, base, or both.	Still used in many countries but mainly for prudential reasons and more recently to provide captive demand for government papers.
Directed credits	Method of distributing central bank credit mostly to finance particular sectors. Provide banks with direct control over aggregate central bank credit.	Credit allocation process is discretionary. Misallocation of resources is possible. May be used to direct credit to public enterprises, thus reducing direct budgetary impact.	Design involves setting a mechanism to allocate credit and to ascertain ultimate use of funds. Usually credit does not require collateral. Occasionally extended through special rediscount facility.	Used in many transition economies. Because of fungibility, are unlikely to be effective in directing resources. Costly in terms of resource allocation.

(continued)

TABLE 11.2 (*continued*)

Instruments	Advantages	Disadvantages	Issues in Design and Operations	Experience and Assessment
Bank-by-bank rediscount quotas * (abolished under Islamic law)	Place a floor under interbank rates and thereby improve transmission of interest rate changes. Otherwise, used mostly to rediscount (at preferential rate) paper of particular sectors and provide liquidity to particular banks.	Below-market discount rate can discourage development of inter-bank money market if use of facility is not limited. Fungibility undermines assessment and control of funds' destination if instrument is used primarily to direct credit.	Need mechanism to allocate refinance quotas and review quality of eligible paper.	Used to provide incentives to lend to particular sectors. Discount rate is a highly visible rate and can be effective in signaling policy changes.

Source: Nurun N. Choudhry and Abbas Mirakhor, "Indirect Instruments of Monetary Control in an Islamic Financial System," *Islamic Economic Studies* 4, no. 2 (May 1997): 27–65.

*Interest rate is replaced by expected dividend based on profit-sharing principle under Islamic law.

These perceived advantages must be weighed against the costs of utilizing direct instruments resulting in inefficient resource allocation as banks attempt to evade credit ceilings and ossify the distribution of credit. For example, banks would try to perpetuate these credit market shares, independent of their competitiveness, thereby reducing incentives for banks whose credit ceilings are constraining. In economies where state-owned banks dominate, as in a number of Muslim countries, state banks tend to limit the inroads that private sector can make in banking. The use of direct instruments tends to multiply and micromanage monetary conditions, which are likely to be particularly volatile in the transition to Islamic banking. Also, there is the possibility of liquidity overhang because of limits imposed on bank lending. Moreover, the overhang can be exacerbated by money financing of the deficit with added inflationary consequences.

The use of direct instruments often results in arbitrary allocations of credit. Moreover, the fungibility of money makes it difficult to ensure that the credit or credit ceiling will be used for intended purposes. Experiences of developing countries show that such instruments lose their effectiveness with the passage of time because they are circumvented by numerous means. There is evidence that banks themselves may attempt to undermine direct controls by introducing new financing techniques that are outside the boundaries of existing controls and divert funds into artificially profitable activities created by the controls themselves. Consequently, policy objectives are often defeated in practice, even if monetary targets are met. Thus, the perceived reliability of direct instruments can often be misleading.

Finally, like other forms of economic control, direct instruments hamper competition. For example, bank-by-bank credit controls protect inefficient banks from competition by limiting the growth of efficient banks. Also, if compliance is not uniform, financial intermediaries that comply with the controls may be placed at a disadvantage, further compromising the position of the formal sector. Clearly, use of direct instruments has considerable costs to the economy.

Choice of Indirect Instruments   The choice of indirect instruments is limited mainly to reserve requirements, public sector deposits, and foreign exchange swaps, as shown in Table 11.3. Reserve requirements and public sector deposits directly link the balance sheets of the central bank and commercial banks; foreign exchange swaps with the central bank directly link their asset sides. Indirect instruments involving open market–type operations with equity-based instruments, as discussed in the following section, provide more flexibility for effective monetary control by the central bank.

The advantages of indirect instruments are precisely the reason that direct instruments become ineffective over time. Indirect instruments can

TABLE 11.3 Indirect Instruments of Monetary Control: Advantages, Disadvantages, and Operational Issues

Instruments	Advantages	Disadvantages	Issues in Design and Operations	Experience and Assessment
Reserve requirements*	Help to induce demand for reserves and therefore enhance predictability of reserve demand. Useful in one-off sterilization of excess liquidity or otherwise to accommodate structural changes in demand for reserves.	Imposes tax on bank intermediation and can lead to spread between lending and deposit rates. Can be neutralized through reserve remuneration. Not convenient for short-term liquidity management, as frequent changes disrupt bank portfolio management.	Design includes definition and monitoring of requirement base, eligibility of assets, and averaging rules and rate of remuneration. Averaging provides banks with greater flexibility in portfolio management.	Used extensively in some countries, especially in Latin America. Active use for policy purposes has dropped significantly in industrial countries.
Rediscount window	Rediscount rate has announcement effect as a key rate.† Initial impact is wider than with open market operations. Develops demand for rediscountable paper. May also be useful when open market operations are limited due to lack of paper.	Not very convenient for precise base money targeting, since access to window is usually at initiative of banks. Criteria for rediscountable paper and for access to window have often been utilized to implement selective credit policy.	Rediscount rate can be above-market rate to discourage access. If rate is below market, nonprice rationing must be used. Elements of design include eligible paper and access criteria.	Used in many countries as standard instrument for monetary control. Effectiveness largely determined by provisions that regulate access. Also used for moral suasion.

Lombard window or overdraft window	Provides facilities for very short-term (collateralized) loans usually priced above any alternative source of funds. Can be key part of payments system arrangements.	See rediscount window above. Disadvantage of preannounced rate facility where access is at discretion of banks.	Lombard requires bank decisions to borrow from central bank with appropriate collateral. *Overdraft* occurs automatically and need not be collateralized.	Standard facilities in many countries. Lombard rate can be key rate in announcing changes in policy stance.
Public sector deposits	Given magnitude of daily flows in and out of government deposits between central bank and commercial banks, can be key instrument to offset short-term liquidity impact.	Lack transparency. Militate against the development of secondary market for government securities.	Allocation mechanisms needed to ensure equitable distribution among competing commercial banks.	Used in a few countries. Require close coordination of central bank and Treasury.
Primary-market sales of central bank paper (open market–type operations)	Flexible instrument for short-term liquidity management because issuance is at discretion of central bank. If Treasury not willing to accept sufficient expected dividend flexibility, central bank papers preserve its operational autonomy.	Central bank may incur losses if large primary issuance is needed to sterilize liquidity. If central bank bills are used in parallel with Treasury bills, problems may occur in absence of strong coordination between issuing agents.	Liquidity management can be achieved through staggered primary issuance. Procedures involve decisions on auction system, counterparts, frequency, maturities, and settlement rules.	Used by many countries, particularly when there is need to separate monetary policy objectives from public debt management objectives. Also used when secondary markets are insufficiently developed.

(continued)

TABLE 11.3 (*continued*)

Instruments	Advantages	Disadvantages	Issues in Design and Operations	Experience and Assessment
Primary market sales of government securities (open market–type operations)	Management similar to central bank bill. Encourage fiscal discipline on part of government if direct central bank financing is discontinued.	Debt management objective can conflict with monetary management if Treasury manipulates auction to keep funding costs below market. High frequency of auctions may hamper secondary market development.	Same as above. Sometimes when central bank portfolio contains government securities, reverse repo auctions can be used instead of outright sales in primary markets.	Used in many countries when secondary markets are insufficiently developed to conduct open market operations.
Foreign exchange (FX) swaps and outright sales and purchases	In case of deep FX market but inactive government securities market, swaps can substitute for repo operations in government paper. FX outright sales and purchases may be useful when FX market is more developed than money market.	Central bank can suffer losses if foreign exchange operations used in attempts to preserve unsustainable exchange rate.	Need to design appropriate risk-management procedures.	Swaps used on a regular basis by a few countries.

Secondary market operations (outright purchases and sales or repo operations)	Can be undertaken on continuous basis, hence provide flexibility. Transparent. Enhance market development. Immediacy of response in money market	Require liquid and deep secondary market, and central bank must have adequate stock of marketable assets.	Repos have advantage of being automatically reversible, especially well-suited for offsetting seasonal fluctuations.	Used by most countries with liquid and deep secondary markets.

Source: Nurun N. Choudhry and Abbas Mirakhor, "Indirect Instruments of Monetary Control in an Islamic Financial System," *Islamic Economic Studies* 4, no. 2 (May 1997): 27–65.

*Reserve requirements have elements of both a direct and an indirect instrument. This table follows conventional central bank usage and classifies them as indirect instruments.

†Rediscount rate or interest rate applies to expected dividend in Islamic context.

control fluctuations in liquidity on a short-term basis in line with monetary policy objectives. Reserve requirements and public sector deposits, through changes in requirement ratios and shifts in the allocation of government deposits between the central bank and commercial banks, directly influence the banks' reserve balances with the central bank. Foreign exchange swaps, instigated by the banks, change the composition between the foreign currency–denominated assets and domestic currency assets. Through outright sales and purchases of foreign exchange, the swaps can change the banks' reserve balance with that of the central bank. Open market–type instruments can provide more effective monetary controls than direct instruments because of their greater flexibility in use. Since these instruments work through, rather than around, markets, they can influence monetary conditions, even when specific monetary aggregates become economically less important (e.g., government borrowing can be offset or partially neutralized through open market–type operations). In policy implementation, frequent changes in the equity-based Treasury bills or central bank credit auctions to absorb or augment liquidity provide greater flexibility in timely responses that are difficult with direct instruments, particularly with credit ceilings, as they are often set on an annual or quarterly basis. Besides, frequent changes in credit limits place an undue burden on banks' portfolio adjustments.

In situations where the exchange rate is flexible, authorities can pursue their own inflation rate objective, which may differ from the international rate of inflation, by exercising their monopoly power as the supplier of high-powered money with indirect instruments to create liquidity shortages and to relieve them as necessary. In situations where the exchange rate is managed, although the domestic inflation rate will depend on international inflation, the central bank will have to set its instruments to influence monetary conditions in order to obtain a desired balance-of-payments objective.

Finally, in contrast to direct instruments, when direct instruments are the principal means of monetary control, the use of indirect instruments by the central bank can facilitate the development of financial markets. This is very important for Islamic countries that are undertaking economic liberalization and have begun Islamic restructuring of their banking systems.

The disadvantages of indirect instruments are that their use is inherently complex and the impact on monetary aggregates can be ambiguous. Simple correspondence does not hold in the case of indirect instruments, and policy may be difficult to implement. Only banks' reserves may be controlled in the short term by reallocation of government deposits since frequent changes in reserve requirements—particularly increases—would be disruptive and costly in terms of portfolio adjustment. Also, reserve requirements cannot be used to mop up excess liquidity if the latter is unevenly distributed among banks and there is no effective means for redistribution of reserve balances among the banks. Moreover, when demand deposits are subject to 100% reserve requirements, there is likely to be overexpansion of credit, as there might be little or no reserve requirements for investment deposits. Further, with 100% reserve requirements, these are reserves for safeguarding purposes, reserves that cannot be used for the banks' liquidity needs. An unintended consequence could be that financial disintermediation occurs as savings flow into unregulated or informal financial markets, such as fringe banks and informal lending as well as transfers of savings abroad through illegal means if there are external capital controls. Thus, depending on the model of banking chosen in an Islamic economy, the authorities may have difficulty in exerting effective monetary control.

Although public sector deposits can be very powerful indirect instruments, they lack transparency and militate against the development of financial markets. In the reallocation of government deposits between the central bank and the commercial banks in order to offset the impact of such flows on short-term liquidity via the banks' reserve balances, the use of this instrument provides less incentive for speeding up the development of financial markets as banks can easily replenish their reserves without recourse to the interbank and money markets. The preferred alternative involves short-term, low-risk, equity-based government securities. Transactions in these securities can be frequent and facilitate market growth by making the underlying securities more liquid without directly interfering with market force.

The use of foreign exchange swaps requires restriction-free capital account and a developed FX market. In most Islamic countries, capital accounts have restrictions and financial markets are not well developed. Often such swaps are discouraged by the central bank because of FX scarcity. If FX constraint is not binding, as in several Islamic countries, this can be used frequently to bolster banks' reserves in times of shortages in domestic liquidity.

Government Securities and Open Market Operations Equity-based government securities with variable yield based on the concept of profit sharing may be considered a viable substitute for traditional securities involved in open market operations. A similar idea involving issuance of commercial papers has been proposed by economists concerned with interest-free banking. Open market–type operations using such securities can be carried out in the primary market, and fully flexible two-way operations involving repurchases and reverse repurchases can be carried out as the secondary market develops.

Equity-Based Government Securities It is proposed that government securities must incorporate three prerequisites: credibility, liquidity, and low risk. Short-term securities, which have a range of maturity and corresponding yield, are suitable for any liquidity need. Their availability for frequent auctions makes them ideal liquidity instruments in the primary market, and they can speed up the development of the secondary market, where they can be actively traded. Longer-term government securities with maturities from two to five or more years are ideal for longer-term liquidity requirements, such as projected future increases in net loan demand or longer-range protective liquidity.

The yield of securities will depend on government operating surplus and is a policy parameter that is used as a price signal. The bases of yield depend on the face value, maturity, and outstanding number of securities and the distribution of the budget surplus among dividend, repayment of government issues of securities at maturity, and retention for capital outlays. At the time of issue, the yield is quoted as an expected dividend, which is adjusted on a quarterly basis (to accommodate the 91-day issue) according to the budgetary outcome for the quarter, and a declaration is made public. Once the face value is set, the market price of the securities will depend on the expected yield (the holders' stream of expected earnings), the length of time to maturity, and market supply–demand conditions. As the adjustment introduces an element of uncertainty in expected yield, the risk differentials among government securities and other marketable assets become an important factor affecting market conditions. Consequently, the adjustment process provides an incentive for the government to pursue fiscal prudence in order to preserve credibility, liquidity, and essentially risk-free status of the securities.

The expected dividend as a measure of yield of securities is rooted in the concept of social rate of return. The expected earnings of holders of government securities are derived from the expected dividend, and the market price of the security would be the discounted value of the stream of expected earnings at the prevailing rate of return in the market. The discounted value of the stream of expected earnings derived from government surpluses is the cost of equity capital in terms of the security, with the rate of discount being the social rate of return. The market price of securities is determined when the market value is equal to the cost of equity capital. If the public's expectation is for a higher dividend than the government expectations on budget surpluses, the demand for government securities will be greater than their supply. As a result, the market price rises when the expected dividend is higher than the expected surplus, and vice versa, until equilibrium is established. Fluctuations in the market price of securities with longer maturities will be more than those of the shorter-term securities with varying expectations on dividends and social rates of return.

At equilibrium, the social rate of return is such that the marginal social benefit from the consumption of public services is equal to the opportunity cost of the provision of such services. Because of the nature of public services, the marginal social benefits are difficult to quantify while user charges and fees for the provision of public services may fall short of their opportunity costs. As the former is analogous to marginal revenue and the latter to marginal costs, the government covers the actual cost of operation by revenue from taxation, taking into account receipts from user charges and fees. The payment of expected dividends on government securities is adjusted on the outcome of the budget surplus. The expected budget surplus may have to be altered periodically by raising or lowering taxation and/or user charges and fees so that the adjusted expected dividends on government securities are made competitive with expected dividends on private equity.[1]

In transactions with government securities, actual cash may change hands or cross the books, as when a central bank transacts in Treasury or central bank securities with banks to smooth out reserve balance fluctuations. For the duration the securities are held, the yield must accrue, and the market price reflects the supply–demand conditions, taking into account the uncertainty in adjustments of expected dividends. If the central bank undertakes monetary contraction through reserve absorption by the sale of securities, the market price of securities declines, taking into account the duration to maturity and the risk for adjustment of expected dividends. With longer-term securities, the market does provide an indication of the cost of equity capital in nominal terms and provides a yardstick to business of gauging the present value of future income streams (using expected rate of return), thereby permitting economically more meaningful judgments to investment plans.

Open Market–Type Operations   In conducting open market–type operations, the discount window and auctions of Treasury or central bank bills and central bank credit auctions are often used varyingly to achieve operating monetary objectives. The extent of such operations depends on the availability of equity-based government securities, the relative size of the primary and secondary markets, the existence of a competitive interbank market, and, more generally, the extent to which government is willing to deregulate and rely on market processes for channeling savings into investment. Since in many Muslim countries secondary markets are nonexistent or are in the early

---

[1]Even when governments do not generate operating surpluses, the concept of "expected dividend" still remains valid. This is because the marginal social benefit from government services is greater than the marginal revenue from taxation. If the level of taxation was raised to the level of opportunity cost of this provision of public services, which is equal to the level of marginal cost, then there would be surplus left over for distribution of dividends, repayment of government securities at maturity, and retention for funding capital projects. For economic and political reasons, the government could not raise taxation to a level high enough to generate operating surpluses. However, as circumstances permit and economic growth proceeds, the government raises the level of taxation so as to generate surpluses. Thus, the social rate of return implicitly justifies the concept of expected dividends.

stages of evolution, central banks would be limited to open market–type operations in the primary market to absorb or inject reserves through auctions of newly issued Treasury bills or credits.

When the central bank offers a new issue of Treasury security, this constitutes a monetary operation (not a government debt management operation) only if the incoming funds are sterilized and unavailable for government spending. If the central bank overestimated the reserve surplus when it initially issued the securities and subsequently needed to augment reserves temporarily, it could buy the securities back before maturity and credit banks' reserve accounts. Such repurchases before maturity and, if need be, subsequent resales would have the ancillary advantage of laying the basis for the development of a secondary market among nonbank private participants, in addition to strengthening a competitive interbank market for redistribution of reserves around the banking system. Since the securities are based on expected dividends, buying and selling prices between the parties will be negotiated, just as is done by premia and discounts on the fixed interest rate, thereby effectively market pricing on profit-sharing principle.[2]

Open market–type operations involving new issue of Treasury or central bank securities are used most effectively when excess liquidity piles up in the banking system from large capital inflows. However, if investment deposits have no reserve requirements, banks will tend to keep reserve balances when demand for loans is weak. In the absence of an active money and interbank market, the central bank may be deprived of information about actual and emerging liquidity conditions that are implied by such deposits. Thus, without reserve requirements on these deposits, it would be more difficult for the central bank to plan the timing and size of an open market–type operation, and the outcome of monetary control may be uncertain. The reserves needed to support expansion in money supply and credit for economic growth cannot be adequately provided with open market–type operations. In such circumstances, credit auctions and discount windows will be particularly suitable for monetary expansion for growth.

The auction of credit through the central bank's open market–type function can be distinguished from credit made available through the

---

[2]The cost to the government in terms of expected dividends from the sale of these securities for monetary purposes is roughly the same as occurs when the central bank sells securities from its portfolio, auctions new securities of its own, or reduces its loans to the banking system. The cost in terms of payments of dividend on these securities will be adjusted with the receipt of dividends from the auction of central bank credit. Dividends may be negative or positive and should be regarded as budgetary expenditures or revenues from these operations. Experience suggests that the central bank, on balance, comes out better than even, even after its own administrative costs are taken into account.

discount window. The central bank can use a credit auction to control the volume of reserves to be supplied. The banks, through the bidding process, determine the expected dividend they are willing to share with the central bank for the duration of the loan, thereby effectively determining the market price of securities. In contrast, at the discount window, the expected dividend in the form of the price of securities is set by the central bank while the amounts of borrowing and, therefore, reserves supplied are at the initiative of the banks, not the central bank. Moreover, the central bank might be able to resell commercial paper acquired in the auction as collateral at its initiative into a secondary market (if it exists). Also, loans at the discount window normally would be repaid on a schedule or renewed at the initiative of the borrowing bank. Generally, in contrast to a discount window, a credit auction gives the central bank more initiative on the timing, amount, and price at which reserves are supplied, thus providing some flexibility on reducing reserves for policy purposes in secondary markets.

In the absence of a significant floating supply of government debt, a special Treasury obligation with certain special features could be employed for the expansion of reserves. Special Treasury obligations or securities, once created, would remain on the asset side of the central bank balance sheet. To support the banking system reserve, the central bank would be given the right to transfer to the banks a corresponding special Treasury deposit liability. This deposit liability would not be controlled by the Treasury and would be created simultaneously with the special Treasury security at the time when the central bank wishes to expand reserves. At that point, the deposit liability would be transferred to the banking system either by a distribution based on bank size or through the auction of a predetermined amount.

An auction would be the preferable means, which in effect would be a primary market auction of bank reserves conveyed via Treasury deposit liabilities. The special Treasury deposit liability would be priced to yield a market return (linked to the banks' average profit sharing) to the Treasury, and this, in turn, would determine the return on the special Treasury security held by the central bank.[3] In fact, this return is akin to savings on expected dividends that the Treasury would have made if the central bank had been able to purchase securities in the open market in order to retire government debt. The special Treasury securities and deposit liabilities could have a range of maturity depending on the demand for reserves for short to medium term (from three months to two years), and the market price should be based on expected profitability of the banking system. Both special issues and deposits

---

[3]Actually, the return on special Treasury securities will be the market return on special Treasury liabilities (government deposits earmarked for this operation) less the administrative costs of the central bank for managing this operation.

could be marketable, though sales of securities in the secondary market should be limited to those consistent with the basic reserve-supplying function.[4] Banks could buy and sell the special deposits as the reserves situation fluctuates, effectively making these instruments of the interbank market. Thus, backed by special issues, the special Treasury deposit liabilities, which would create permanent reserves, could become a liquid and relatively low-risk instrument of monetary control.[5]

Open Market Operations   With economic growth and development of markets and with greater integration of the financial institutions with the real sector, an Islamic central bank will place greater reliance on fully flexible open market operations. In transition toward the latter, repurchase agreements (repos) and reverse repurchase agreements for financial instruments will tend to be used more frequently. Navigating the financial markets is a complex process. In addition to competitive financial institutions, substantial infrastructure must be developed, including a large-value transfer system, book-entry systems for recording ownership transfer (an important legal requirement in Islamic property rights), and a legal and regulatory framework. Once such a market is developed, open market operations can be highly effective and flexible tools of monetary policy.

Repos in government securities are most commonly used in industrial countries and countries that are successfully transforming their economic structure. As compared with direct purchase and sale operations, repos interfere less with the development of secondary market trading in outstanding securities since they essentially provide temporary financing of reserve fluctuations and do not directly influence the basic supply and demand conditions underlying securities that serve as collateral.[6] In fact,

---

[4]The central bank sells the special Treasury securities in the market to absorb excess reserves, although their basic purpose is to enable the central bank to create corresponding special deposit liabilities.

[5]In this case, the potential negative impact on the government's budgetary position if a bank with a special deposit were to fail would be no different than if the central bank held such a bank's commercial paper as collateral.

[6]The discussion is confined to repo transactions for domestic policy purposes with domestic securities as the underlying collateral. For insufficient domestic securities, FX swaps can be utilized to affect domestic liquidity. However, when swaps are used for influencing the exchange rate, the central banks' open market operations in domestic securities would be affected differently, depending on whether the central bank was being guided by the reserve aggregate or its net domestic assets. If the latter, it would not automatically sterilize the domestic market effect of an FX operation; if the former, it would.

they serve to enhance the liquidity of the underlying securities and in that way facilitate the development of a secondary market. While repo transactions are generally for short terms, the underlying collateral would comprise both short-term and longer-term government securities, thereby augmenting liquidity to all sectors of the market.

The use of repos with a short maturity also signals that the central bank is encouraging the market to develop alternative short-term instruments for borrowing or lending in order to redistribute the aggregate reserve around the banking system. Also repos are ideally suited to offsetting short-term fluctuations in factors affecting bank reserves that are the major influence on day-to-day operations. Because the maturity of repos can be set by the central bank, repos can be timed automatically to reverse themselves as circumstances change. Moreover, repos are useful for offsetting large shifts in liquidity conditions that might be caused by large capital inflows.

The establishment of repos as effective money market instruments would facilitate the widening of the money market among private sector participants facing temporary shortages and surpluses of funds. The central bank should make it clear that the availability of central bank financing would depend on monetary policy rather than strictly on market considerations. However, in the early stages of market development, the central bank might have to consider market needs, particularly in times of funds shortages. In general, in such situations, outright transactions by the central bank (open market type) could hamper market development, particularly in longer-term market sectors. Whether outright or repos, market development would be most encouraged by use of competitive bidding mechanisms. While a few large market makers for government paper may at times be useful, they are generally considered unfair practices by other participants and tend to slow the widening of the market.

SUMMARY

In the Islamic system, while the objective of monetary policy is broadly the same as that in the conventional system—to promote macroeconomic stability, characterized in the main by price-level stability, near full employment, and a viable balance of payments position, other more broad-based objectives must be kept firmly in sight. These broad-based objectives include a more equitable distribution of resources and income, providing useful employment, improving living standards and the quality of life, and alleviation of poverty, all under the umbrella of social justice. In addition to conducting monetary policy, the central bank in an Islamic system should take the lead in developing financial institutions and instruments that facilitate efficient mobilization of savings and allocation of resources consistent with the economic development objectives. Moreover, the central bank must assume a forceful role in adopting needed regulations and the supervision of banks and investment banks in the system.

There are three major differences in the conduct of monetary policy between the Islamic and the conventional system. In the Islamic system, the instruments of monetary policy are different; there are no interest-bearing debt instruments, and interest-bearing debt is replaced by a variety of equity-based securities (national participation papers, government securities tied to the real rate of return in the economy, etc.) for implementing and conducting open market operations. Moreover, the banking system in the Islamic system is 100% reserve banking as contrasted with fractional reserve banking in the conventional system; this difference eliminates the creation of money by banks and affords the central bank in the Islamic system better monetary control, resulting in a financial system that is more stable and less prone to frequent crises. Finally, monetary policy signals are more potent in the Islamic system because while the objective of both systems is to affect portfolio adjustment in the private sector, in the conventional system, the transmission mechanism of these signals is *indirect* through the banking system whose objective function is different from that of monetary authorities. Hence, the signals through this transmission mechanism may weaken the signals as they are transmitted through the banking system; namely, the central bank may inject cash into the banking system, but in the final analysis, it is the banks who decide whether to lend to the private sector. In the Islamic system, the transmission mechanism establishes a *direct* means of signal reception by the private sector through the retail security market. Thus the potency of the signals sent by the monetary authority is strengthened considerably.

KEY TERMS

Central bank	Central bank
Open market operations	Central bank advisories (indications)
Discount window	Central bank credibility
Reserve requirement	Inflation targeting
Jawboning or moral suasion	Commercial bank lending
Interest rates	Money creation

QUESTIONS

1. What are the instruments and channels of monetary policy in the conventional system?
2. What are the instruments and channels of monetary policy in the Islamic system?
3. What is the function and role of the central bank in the two systems?
4. Is an Islamic central bank handicapped because it is prohibited from buying or selling interest-bearing government securities? Why or why not?
5. Is an Islamic central bank handicapped because there is no financial interest that it can affect? Why or why not?
6. What do you see as the lags and bottlenecks of monetary policy in the conventional system?
7. Is monetary policy more direct and potent in the Islamic system? Why or why not?
8. In your opinion, can a central bank in the Islamic system issue paper money? Why or why not?

CHAPTER 12

Economic Development and Growth

Learning objectives:

1. *The evolving conventional thinking on development from Adam Smith to Mahbub ul-Haque, Amartya Sen, and Douglass North.*
2. *Islam's perspective on economic and social development.*
3. *Why rules and institutions are the keys to development and growth.*
4. *How cooperation, coordination, and trust are linked to development and growth.*
5. *Dimensions of economic growth and development in Islam.*

EVOLUTION OF WESTERN ECONOMIC THOUGHT: FROM SMITH TO NORTH AND SEN[1]

The concept of modern economic development in the Western economic literature owes its origin to the eighteenth-century writers of the Scottish Enlightenment, especially Adam Smith, who formulated the first systematic idea of economic development, beginning in his seminal work, *The Theory of Moral Sentiments* (1759).[2] Smith believed that through effort and cooperation, motivated by self-love tempered by the moral value of "sympathy" for others, there would be continuous material improvement. Sympathy is the quality that each individual would take to the market as a mechanism that would translate the self-love, or self-interest, of each market participant into love for others. If individuals entering the market were devoid of sympathy and cooperation, progress would be undermined. The dimension of the self

---

[1] This chapter is based on Mirakhor and Askari (2010).
[2] Smith (1759).

that is a reflective judge of a person's own actions and *sense of duty* would create an appropriate balance between the interests of the self and those of others. This guidance by an "invisible hand" in the marketplace would lead to positive economic and social change. The separate self-love of all individuals would be galvanized toward the benefit of all, leading to a stable social order.

Driven by self-love and regulated by sympathy, each individual would be directed to the most productive economic activity. Labor would be one of two major inputs for increasing the "wealth of nations." At the same time, the profit motive would increase capital accumulation, the other major input. Increasing labor productivity would finance investment in machinery and equipment, with increasing returns based on the division of labor providing the basis for Smith's optimism. Labor productivity could either be increased through the expansion of skills and dexterity or through the adoption of new technology and the deployment of new machinery and equipment. Smith emphasized the limited but critical role of the state to guarantee the sanctity of property, to create the conditions enhancing free and voluntary exchange, and to ensure that commitments generated from contracts of exchange are honored. Under such circumstances, the only limit to continuous material progress and growth would be the size of the market; this limit could be removed through trade among nations, which would in turn result in global peace and tranquility.[3]

In the latter part of the twentieth century, rediscovering Adam Smith, economists began to attribute some of the differential in economic performance to the quality of institutions. This explanation for economic performance had its more recent roots in the last decades of the nineteenth century and the first few decades of the twentieth century. This view of economic development is that in addition to factor endowment, human capital, and technological progress, institutional structure plays a significant role in development. The starting point of why institutions matter in economic development is why countries with considerable resource endowments and access to finance are nevertheless economically (and politically) underdeveloped. While differences in capital per worker, investment in human capital, and technology may explain differences in the level of per capita income across countries, these cannot be considered a fundamental reason for the underdevelopment of many countries. The assertion that there are more fundamental reasons for the state of development is particularly poignant in the age of globalization since capital is mobile and should move to countries where its rate of return is higher. Moreover, investment in human capital should have higher returns in countries with low investment in education.

---

[3]Smith (1759, pp. 128–150).

However, if the institutional structure of a country is weak, its ability to mobilize, organize, and finance growth is constrained.

Neoclassical growth theory implicitly assumed that economies have institutions that provide political stability, guarantee and enforce property rights, and protect and enforce private contracts and the rule of law. In addition to assuming that the countries had efficient markets, it was assumed they also had the financial, legal, accounting, and regulatory apparatus that ensure transparency, accountability, and good governance. Douglass North over the years argued that while the growth of advanced economies is explained by productivity increases from division of labor, specialization, technical progress, and the competitive market, the key to their performance is low transaction costs, resulting from the institutional structure that developed over the last 250 years.[4] Conversely, it is the existence of prohibitive transaction costs that is the main obstacle to development. A modern economy relies on impersonal relationships that, by their very nature, involve a great deal of uncertainty. Efficient institutions reduce uncertainties and related costs.

Much of the intellectual effort of major thinkers in the eighteenth and nineteenth centuries was focused on the search for appropriate ways of establishing social order in the face of rapid industrialization and resulting socioeconomic dislocations as disorder increases uncertainty, decreases confidence, and increases transactions costs.[5] North argues that after a period of disorder resulting from radical changes and crises, whether social order will be established quickly depends on the stability of the institutional structure of society, with those having such stable institutions recovering more rapidly. The collectivity of institutions provides society with the social capability to establish a stable order by reducing uncertainties or ambiguities. The institutional structure of a society is composed of constitutions, laws, and rules of governance; its government; its finances, economy, and politics; written rules, codes, and agreements that govern contractual relations and exchange and trade relationships; and commonly shared beliefs, social norms, and codes governing human behavior. The clarity of rules, social norms, and enforcement characteristics are important to the degree of compliance exhibited by the members of a society. The higher the degree of rule compliance, the more stable the social order and the lower the transaction costs in the society. For example, social norms that prescribe trust, trustworthiness, and cooperation have a significant impact on encouraging collective action and coordination.[6]

---

[4]North (1995) and North (2003).
[5]North (2003).
[6]Ibid., pp. 115–130.

While acknowledging that needed changes to improve economic growth may be slow to materialize because of cultural factors, North nevertheless envisions an ideal political-economic institutional structure that has potential for achieving good economic performance and societal well-being as a framework of:

1. An institutional matrix that defines and establishes a set of rights and privileges
2. A stable structure of exchange relationships in economic and political markets
3. A government that is credibly committed to a set of political rules and enforcement to protect individuals, organizations, and exchange relationships
4. Rule compliance as a result of internalization of norms as well as coercive enforcement
5. A set of economic institutions that create incentives for the members of society and organizations to engage in productive activities
6. A set of property rights and an effective price system that lead to low transaction costs in production, exchange, and distribution

Contrasted with this ideal institutional structure, North argues that the institutional framework of poorly performing economies does not provide the right incentive structure for activities that can improve productivity because of vested interests that resist change and because factor and product markets are ineffective in getting relative prices right. A prerequisite to successful actions to improve economic performance is "a viable polity that will put in place the necessary economic institutions and provide effective enforcement."[7]

On a parallel track, during the 1970s, the intellectual and practical field of development changed its focus to human beings, both as the means and the ends of the development process. In the late 1970s and early 1980s, economists, inspired by the contributions of Mahbub ul Haq and Amartya Sen, began to question the popular definition of economic development and the path for its achievement. They argued that development was much more than an increasing level of per capita income and a simple structural transformation. For the first time, human development—including education, healthcare, poverty eradication, a more even income distribution, environmental quality, and freedom—was seen as an integral component of the economic development process. Although people need bread to live, people do not live by bread alone.

[7]North (2003, p. 157).

In assessing human well-being in Sen's framework, capabilities represent the real opportunities individuals have to lead or achieve a certain type of life. Functionings, on the other hand, represent the actual life they lead. Defining development as a process that promotes human well-being would then mean expansion of capabilities of people to flourish. In this framework, freedom is "the real opportunity we have to accomplish what we value."[8] Consequently, progress is assessed primarily in terms of whether freedoms are enhanced. Ananta Kumar Giri argues that Sen neglects the development of the "self," maintaining that self-development is a crucial aspect of societal development, without which Sen's approach would not succeed. John Cameron criticizes Sen for focusing only on the poor and lower levels of income while ignoring or neglecting the upper levels of income and the impact of income inequality on the development of capabilities; he argues that in so doing, Sen deemphasizes the need for radical income redistribution that would correct the patterns of functionings in society. Thomas Pogge argues that affluent functionings damage human well being and that the behavior of the affluent is a direct cause of the underdevelopment of poor countries.

In short, the concept of economic development has progressed from a concern for social order, the role of civil society, culture, and state to development as material well-being, with ethics, freedom, development of the self, income equality, environmental preservation, and sustainability factored in. It should be stressed that Smith is the basis of Western thinking on development, but the author of *The Wealth of Nations*, stressing the self-interest motive that is the basis of utility and profit maximization for the individual consumer and producer at any cost to society, including the impoverishment and exploitation of fellow human beings, is very different from the author of *The Theory of Moral Sentiments*. Smith makes clear in his less cited book that while compliance with the rules prescribed by the Creator is a must, compliance with the market, an instrument for achieving the greatest good, is also a necessity. Smith succinctly and clearly shares some of the foundational scaffolding of Islam: belief in the one and only Creator; belief in the accountability of the Day of Judgment; belief in the necessity of compliance with the rules prescribed by the Creator; and belief that justice is achieved with full compliance with rules. To paraphrase Sen, no space need be made artificially for justice and fairness; it already exists in the rules prescribed by the Lawgiver. Smith considers the internalization of rules—being consciously aware of the ever-presence of the Creator and acting accordingly—as crucial to all human conduct, including economics. Rules reduce uncertainty and transaction costs and promote coordination, making collective action possible and promoting social solidarity. All of these

---

[8] Sen (1994).

elements have been directly emphasized or strongly implied by the Quran and in the traditions of the Prophet (sawa). Thus today, the Western concept of development is focused on efficient institutions; a political system that nurtures institutions and prohibits rent-seeking activities and the confiscation of legitimate wealth; and a social outlook that embraces human development, including education, healthcare, poverty eradication, a more even income distribution, sustainability, and freedom. This is akin to the Islamic view—with one big difference and one small one. Islamic teachings (not the practice of Islam today) embrace heavier doses of social and economic justice, morality, humanity, compassion, generosity, and charity; and Islam places more emphasis on rules and rule compliance.

FOUNDATION AND FRAMEWORK OF DEVELOPMENT AND GROWTH IN ISLAM

The Islamic concept of development has three dimensions: individual self-development; the physical development of the earth; and the development of the human collectivity, which includes both. The first specifies a dynamic process of the growth of the human toward perfection. The second specifies the utilization of natural resources to develop the earth to provide for the material needs of the individual and all of humanity. The third concept encompasses the progress of the human collectivity toward full integration and unity. Together they constitute the rules-based compliance system, which is intended to ensure progress on the three interrelated dimensions of development. Fundamental to all three is the belief that the Supreme Creator has provided the ways and means to facilitate the achievement of all three dimensions of development.

These three dimensions of development are closely interrelated to the point where balanced progress in all three is needed to achieve development. The four basic elements of the Western concept of development—namely, scarcity, rationality, and the roles of the state and of the market—are perceived somewhat differently in Islam. All three dimensions of Islamic development assign heavy responsibility to individuals and society—with both held responsible for any lack of development. Balanced development is defined as balanced progress in all three dimensions. Progress is balanced if it is accompanied with justice. The objective of such balanced development is to achieve progress on the path to perfection by humans, through rule compliance. Enforcement of the prescribed rules is accomplished by an internal and an external mechanism. The love of humans for one another is a part of their adoration of the Creator, and each human is responsible for ensuring that others are rule compliant. The governance structure envisaged in Islam requires full transparency and accountability by the state and the full participation of all members.

In recognition and acknowledgment of their dignity, the Supreme Creator has endowed humans with freedom of choice. The autonomy provided by the freedom of choice is exercised through compliance with rules (institutions). The agent-trustee office requires the activation of the nonmaterial gifts from the Creator that empower humans to perform their responsibility. To this end, however, a self-cleansing and purification process is required.

The importance of knowledge is also emphasized in Islam. The knowledge of rules describes the path from Islam to *iman* (belief) in its various stages and characteristics such as gratitude, patience, righteousness, honesty, justice, struggle, and forbearance. Much of becoming intimately and experientially familiar with the knowledge of just duty relates to the progress of the self. It empowers and strengthens the working of the spirit gifted to humans. For individuals, Islam is a process governed by "just duty," the second type of knowledge named by the Prophet (sawa). The knowledge of just duty—an intimate knowledge of the rules of behavior—and the implementation of that knowledge result in inner harmony.

Economic Growth in Islam

In Islam, economic growth is seen as helpful to the extent that it is focused on human spiritual and material needs and that humans are both its intended ends as well as its means. Economic growth cannot be for growth's sake. There must be a higher motive that improves human lives and brings them together in to the unity of Allah's (swt) creation. Economic growth in Islam is seen as a function of factor productivity, which, in turn, depends on the adoption of policies that promote efficiency in the use of resources. Enhancing human productivity is important for economic growth, but this becomes reality when the labor force is well nourished, skilled, and well educated. Technological progress that allows human societies to obtain the highest possible output from the resources provided by the Almighty must be supported. Economic prosperity is important because it provides the means by which humans can satisfy their material needs and thus remove the economic barriers on the path to their spiritual progress. Moreover, institutions (rules and norms plus their enforcement characteristics) have been found to play a crucial role in determining total factor productivity in the economy. Institutions (rules) proposed by Islam relating to governance, social solidarity, cooperation, and justice are designed to achieve economic development and growth. Additionally, the Quran emphasizes a particular consequence of rule compliance, *baraka* (blessings), a source of increase in total factor productivity. As part of its incentive structure to induce rule compliance, the Quran asserts that every righteous action brings multiple returns. A righteous action-decision can be operationally defined as any action-decision that is undertaken in full consciousness of the ever-presence of Allah (swt) and for the purpose of achieving His pleasure and approval; that is, any action-decision undertaken in compliance with the rules prescribed by the Lawgiver. Whosoever brings a good deed will receive tenfold of the like thereof (Quran 160:6).

This concept is particularly striking with respect to certain economic behaviors, especially those whose goal is to improve the economic well-being of other humans, such as providing loans to those in need without expecting a monetary reward. This type of loan is called *qardh hassan*, or a "beautiful loan," because the Quran (245:2) designates the borrower to be Allah (swt) and not the person who receives the loan: Who is it that will lend unto Allah (swt) a beautiful loan so that He may give it manifold increase? This act of righteousness is so important that providing it to those in need is placed at the same level as the required daily prayers, the cleansing of one's income and wealth, and the belief in and strong support of the messengers of Allah (swt), all of which lead to forgiveness by Allah (swt) of (previous) misdeeds:

> *Verily Allah made a covenant with the children of Israel and We raised among them twelve chieftains, and Allah said: Lo! I am with you. If you establish daily prayers and cleanse your income and wealth (pay the due portion) and believe in and support My Messengers, and lend to Allah a beautiful loan, surely I shall remit your transgressions, and surely I shall bring you into gardens underneath which rivers flow. Whoso among you disbelieves after this, will surely go astray from the path. (Quran 12:5)*
>
> *Establish the daily-required prayers, pay* Zakah *(cleanse your income and wealth from the rights of others in them), and lend unto Allah a beautiful loan. Whatsoever good you send before you for your selves you will surely find it with Allah better and greater in recompense. (Quran 20:73)*
>
> *The* baraka *for spending in the path of Allah is even more astonishing: The similitude of those who spend their wealth in Allah's path is as the likeness of a grain which grows seven ears, in every ear a hundred grains. (Quran 261:2)*

That is, the return on expenditures whose goal is to help the needy remove the economic barriers in their path to perfection is 700 times the amount of the transfer. Such rewards resulting from rule compliance are not limited to these examples. The responsibility for the supervision and enforcement of the prescribed rules given by the Lawgiver are relegated in the first place to society and then to the legitimate authorities.

Dimensions of Development in Islam

One of the important tests for humans comes about when some individuals and groups experience conditions of plenty while others are faced with scarcity. The rules prescribed by Allah (swt) specify the appropriate response to these tests, which are considered by the Quran to be signs for the true believer. The wealthy are the ones who reject the messages of sharing and giving that have been brought to them by the messengers of Allah (swt). Those who share and spend their wealth in the way prescribed are the adorers of Allah (swt), and He recompenses them for their spending aimed at pleasing Him. These humans recognize that the source of their blessings of bounty is the Creator and not their own doing. There are those, however, who, when faced with an adverse trial, turn to their Creator for help, but once they achieve success, attribute it to themselves.

As mentioned a number of times earlier, in contrast to conventional economics, *scarcity in Islam is not a binding constraint at the level of humanity.* It is only a constraint at a micro-individual level; at this level, it is a test both for the person who is constrained and for the person who is not constrained. For the constrained, it is a test of the strength of belief that has been experientially revealed to the person and is a light shining on the strength and weakness of the self. For those economically better off, it is a test of their recognition of the real source of their wealth and the strength of their rule compliance in helping remove economic constraints, namely, barriers from the path to perfection of those in need of help. There is recognition and an important role for legitimate authorities. The important point is that it is the strength of the rule compliance of rulers, not their cunningness, physical or military prowess, or other worldly advantages, such as riches, that legitimizes their authority to oversee the implementation of the prescribed rules. It is clear that the strength of belief for those who will be vested with legitimate authority must surpass that of a representative believer.

The traditions of the Prophet (sawa) invest the legitimacy of leadership of the community with another dimension, that of *bay'ah*, a contract between the person who is deemed worthy of accession to the office due to demonstrated full compliance with prescribed rules and acceptability by the members of the community. The manner in which the Prophet (sawa) organized the first community as specified in the Quran constitutes legitimate political authority, and He sought acceptability among the multireligious population of Medina. The central term of the contract between the ruler and the ruled is understood clearly: full compliance with the prescribed rules by the legitimate authority. The community and its members commit to following and obeying the legitimate ruler *so long as* he is rule compliant. The legitimate ruler commits not only to complying with all the prescribed rules, among which is the imperative of consultation, but also to ensuring the preservation, cohesion, and well-being of the community in accordance with the duties of the trusteeship-agency office. The strength of the legitimacy of the community is derived from the enforcement of the rules. No authority has any legitimate basis for creating new rules that contradict those specified in the Quran and practiced by the Prophet (sawa). *No political authority selected on the basis of this framework could retain legitimacy in the face of noncompliance with or violation of the rules.* As history shows, governments that violated rules retained power only by force. But such an event is simultaneously and concurrently a failure of rule compliance by the community being ruled by force. Commanding others to rule compliance is part of the cognizance of the love bond between the Creator and the created since rule compliance is the necessary and sufficient condition for staying on the path to perfection. No political authority can violate the prescribed rules and retain legitimacy, and no community can claim that it has remained a believing community while being ruled over by an authority that is noncompliant with and in violation of the prescribed rules. In short, it is the noncompliance with rules that leads to the emergence of unjust, dictatorial, and totalitarian authority.

Commanding what is good and forbidding what is evil is a duty incumbent on individuals as well as on the whole community. It is a promoter of solidarity and achievement and a preserver of social order in the community. *The very existence of oppression, corruption, massive inequality, and poverty in a community is* prima facie *evidence of noncompliance with or outright shirking of this duty on the part of the group's members.* Given the strength of the emphasis on rule compliance by the individual, even the existence of a legitimate political authority does not absolve a human being from the necessity of performing the duty of commanding rule compliance and forbidding rule violation. Coupled with the prescribed rule of consultation, this duty gives every member of society the right, and imposes on him or her the duty, of participating in community affairs. And, since the primary responsibility of the legitimate political authority is to enforce rule compliance, the more active the individuals' roles in assuring that their own behaviors and those of others in the community are rule compliant, the more limited the need for interference of the authority in the socioeconomic life of the community.

The Quran makes it clear that prescribed rules require that economic transactions be based on freedom of choice and freedom of contract, which in turn require property rights over possessions to be exchanged. While the historical evidence strongly suggests that markets already existed in Arabia, it was the Prophet (sawa) who created the first market that was structured with operations in accordance with the prescribed rules of conduct for justice to prevail in exchange and trade. He appointed a market supervisor to promote full compliance with the prescribed rules of market behavior. While the legitimate authority has the obligation of supervising and enforcing rule compliance, market participants are rule compliant as long as they are free from further interference. The history of the market created by the Prophet (sawa) in Medina underlines the importance and centrality of the market and rules.

As stated earlier, the Quran and the traditions of the Prophet (sawa) envision development as composed of three interrelated and interdependent dimensions. The most important of all these is individual human development, without which the other two would not progress as envisioned. The process of human self-development is referred to in the Quran as *rushd*, which is the opposite of *qhay*, meaning deep ignorance. When the process of *rushd* strengthens, the person is said to becoming *rasheed*: that is, someone who is making progress on the path to perfection. This stands in stark contrast to Western economic thought, as it was only in the last three decades of the twentieth century that professionals looked at a broader concept of development beyond the growth of physical capacity to produce goods and services, namely, that economic growth is only an element of the overall progress of human beings and that humans should be the ends, rather than the means, of development. Even in the most sophisticated of concepts—Sen's development as freedom—the imperative of self-development as the prerequisite for a comprehension of the substantive meaning of freedom has received little attention. If development means freedom and functioning, then what guarantee is there that without self-development, doing what one values will not lead to fully self-centered, selfish outcomes? These selfish outcomes include massive poverty and misery for a large segment of humanity side by side with incredible opulence and wealth accumulation for a few. Some minimum level of income is doubtless necessary to avoid destitution and absolute poverty before one is able to reflect upon one's action-decision choices. But beyond that, self-development becomes an imperative for humans to recognize the responsibilities of their *khalifal* state and to develop the earth so as to remove economic barriers and minimize the pain of material paucity for all humans.

Much of the concern with the early formulations of development focused on achieving and maintaining social order. The Islamic concept places great emphasis on the need to focus human energy on the achievement of social solidarity and unity. In turn, that unity is firmly grounded in the purpose of creation, the *walayahh* of the Creator for and over humanity, which invested high dignity in the human state and the responsibilities implied by that state. The *khalifal* functions of each human can be meaningful only in collectivity with other humans. Islam's emphasis on the social dimension is so great that there is not one act of adoration and worship that is devoid of societal implications. The success of each human is dependent on patient and tolerant interaction and cooperation with other humans. The idea is that mutual support and social solidarity bring about a more tolerant and patient response to individual and collective difficulties, heighten cognizance and consciousness of the Creator and of the commonalities of humanity, intensify adoration of Allah (swt) through mutual service to others and the rest of the creation, and ease the path to perfection. Complete success is possible only through appropriate social interaction. The Quran repeatedly urges humans toward social solidarity and a just social order; they must follow the prescribed rules that serve to purify the self and to create social cohesion, namely, the rules that position both individuals and society on a straight path. The fundamental objective is to create a society in which individuals become cognizant of all their capabilities, including the spiritual. When humans realize these capabilities, a life the Quran refers to as *hayat tayyibah*, the good life—a life free of anxiety, fear, and regrets—becomes possible; a life of full awareness of the beauty of the creation and Creator; a life of solidarity with other humans and the rest of creation; and a life lived in the full Grace of Allah (swt).

The central framework and operation of these rules is *justice*. The Prophet (sawa) understood the essential objective of His selection, appointment, and message to be to encourage and insert justice in human societies, as emphasized in the Quran. The Prophet (sawa) taught the responsibility of the individual, the collectivity, and the state. He particularly emphasized the equality of individuals before the law and that all rules that are incumbent on individuals and their collectivity must be more strictly observed by those in positions of authority. Thence the famous saying attributed to him: "Authority may survive disbelief but not injustice." Insistence on justice became the hallmark of the institutional scaffolding of governance, a structure with full transparency and accountability. It was in Medina where the Prophet (sawa) was able to put into operation and implement important rules. The first and the most important of the Prophet's (sawa) efforts was the formation of a society based on Islamic teaching; this He achieved with the assistance of the critical mass of followers who had migrated with Him to Medina. It was first necessary to create peace, social stability, and the means of defending the nascent society from external threats. The social contract with the inhabitants of Medina constituted agreed-on procedures for administering society. Given that Muslims who had migrated with Him were either poor or had lost their wealth fleeing persecution in Mecca, He initiated a contract of mutual support. Next, the Prophet (sawa) clarified rules of property rights over natural resources. Those who had property at the time they entered Islam were given full rights over their property.

Douglass North believes that cognition plays a central role in belief formation, which, in turn, affects preference formation, rational decision making, and institutions. Institutions (rules) have a reciprocal effect on cognition. Beliefs constitute what North refers to as a "mental model."[9] However, whereas North believes that institutions "are clearly an extension to the mental constructs the human mind develops to interpret the environment of the individual," in Islam, rules (institutions) are provided by the Lawgiver. For a believer, the "mental model" is formed by these rules (institutions), which reduce uncertainty for individuals and society, and in turn reduce transaction costs. Above all, the entrepreneurs engaged in production are subject to the rules of economic behavior that stress not cheating, not wasting (*itlaf*) or overusing or overspending (*israf*), and not causing harm to anyone in carrying out production. The Prophet (sawa) said: "There are two characteristics above which there are no other in evil: associating partners with Allah and causing harm to the servants of Allah (other humans)"; "The person who defrauds a Muslim is not of us"; and "Whoever shortchanges the wages of a laborer, his place will be in fire."[10] The exploitation of hired labor, particularly short-changing their wages or refusing to pay labor wages commensurate with their productivity, was the subject of admonishments by the Prophet (sawa): "Whosoever mistreats a laborer in repaying for the work done, Allah will render his own work fruitless and Allah will forbid him the perfume of the Garden."[11]

Distribution Justice, the Market, and the State

Throughout the ages, one of the most important questions confronting humankind has been: What criterion should determine the distribution of economic resources? The answer depends on the underlying concept of justice and fairness, which, in turn, depends on the belief system. Islam considers justice an important attribute of the Creator manifested in His creation. The concept of justice for humans is simple and unambiguous: Justice is obtained when all things are placed where intended by the Creator. How are humans to know where the right (just) place is for everything? The answer is: Follow the rules prescribed by the Creator.[12] By the instrumentality of His *walayahh*, the loving Creator has provided all that is necessary for humans to develop and achieve perfection of the human state. He has also designated the path to perfection and has marked it with rules of behavior in all facets of human life. Rule compliance assures justice. In turn, justice ensures balance for individuals and for their collectivity. Compliance with rules, however, does more

---

[9] North (1995).
[10] Al-Hakimi et al. (1989, p. 367).
[11] Ibid., pp. 366–370.
[12] Ibid., pp. 2–25 and Qutb (1953).

than create balance; it guarantees that humans draw near to their ultimate objective, namely, their Creator. Morality is a result of just behavior. In contrast, nontheocentric thought considers justice "an important subclass of morality in general, a subclass which generally involves appeals to the overlapping notions of right, fairness, equality, and deserts."[13] These systems must find ways in which a consensual agreement is reached on the concept of justice and fairness according to which goods and services produced can be distributed. To do so, they must first devise moral theories that provide reason to justify a particular distributional system. One such theory is utilitarianism, which puts forth a distributional system that avoids justice but is instead based on morality. An action is considered justified if it increases utility, or happiness, of all. Accordingly, there is only one moral issue involved in a course of action or social policy: Does it achieve the greatest aggregate happiness? This is a criterion by which not only individual and social actions are judged, but one according to which various societies are compared. There is much criticism of utilitarianism, but two points stand out. It permits the sacrifice of innocent individuals and their interests if it means increasing the happiness of the whole, thus serving totalitarian objectives; and it assigns equal weights to the happiness of all individuals.

In principle, in economics, it is assumed that a free market that operates on the basis of the self-interest of its participants promotes the general interest of all. Based on a utilitarian concept, welfare economics developed the analytic position that in such a system, in which prices were determined by the free interplay of supply and demand, all factors of production would receive rewards commensurate with their marginal contribution to the production of goods and services. It is important to note that here, too, initial resource endowments as well as the preferences of individuals are taken as a given. Unhappy with utilitarianism, Rawls searched for an alternative principle of distribution by relying on the concept of the social contract.[14] Equating justice with fairness, Rawls attempted to find principles of just distribution with which members of society, with different concepts of good and just, all agree.

To Rawls, distributive justice is a matter of public rather than private choice, although he assumes that citizens are just. Therefore, his principle of justice applies only to social institutions he refers to as the "basic structure." He uses the device of "a veil of ignorance" to ensure fair results. Assuming that people in society are ignorant of all of their particularities, including race, color, creed, or social status, they would come together to choose a rule of

---

[13] Arthur and Shaw (1991, p. 4).
[14] Rawls (1971).

distribution that would then govern all members of society. Rawls concludes that people would choose a rule according to which all "social values—liberty and opportunity, income, wealth, and the basis of self-respect—are to be distributed equally unless an unequal distribution of any, or all, of these values is to everyone's advantage."[15] From this principle, referred to as "the difference principle," two other principles are deduced. First, each individual in society has "equal right to political liberty; freedom of speech and assembly; liberty of conscience and freedom of thought; freedom of the person along with the right to hold (personal) property; and freedom from arbitrary arrest and seizure, as defined by the concept of the rule of law. These liberties are all required to be equal by the first principle, since citizens of a just society are to have the same basic rights." The second principle requires that if there are to be inequalities, they are to everyone's advantage and "attached to positions and offices open to all." These principles are to apply sequentially to the "basic structure" of society. Sequential order is necessary for Rawls to rule out the possibility that a departure from the first principle of equal liberty could or would be compensated by greater economic advantages. Under the veil of ignorance, a fair allocation of primary goods would be the one that members would agree on before they know where they would land in the outcome.

These ideas on distributive justice afford a perspective on Islamic notions of just distribution. An important central difference between Islam's position and those discussed earlier is the role of the market. All these ideas apply to market economies. Markets also play a crucial role in Islam, but with one major difference. Epistemologically, the difference is one of the concept of the market as an ideology and the concept of the market as an instrument. This difference is profound. In societies known widely as market economies, market norms are central to social relations. In turn, market norms are determined by self-interest, which dictate "rational" behavior as maximizing what interests the self, narrowly labeled as satisfaction (utility or profit). Market norms, in turn, determine the pattern of preferences of individuals. As Gomberg argues, market norms and preference patterns are individualist, not communal. They have self-seeking orientations.[16]

In Islam, by contrast, the market is an instrument. It is not an organism that determines the rules and norms of behavior, not even those of its own operation. Rules that shape the pattern of preferences of participants are determined outside the market. Participants internalize them before entering the market. The behavior of consumers, producers, and traders, informed by their preferences, are subject to rules determined outside the market. In a

---

[15] Rawls (1971).
[16] Gomberg (2007).

market where there is full rule compliance, the price that prevails for goods, services, and factors of production is considered just. The resulting incomes are considered justly earned. Therefore, the resulting distribution is just. However, participants will not be allowed to keep their full earnings simply because their income was justly earned. There are rights and entitlements of others in the resulting postmarket distribution of income and wealth that must be redeemed. This is the function of postmarket redistribution, which is governed by its own set of rules. Any remaining wealth that is accumulated is broken up at the end of the person's life and distributed among a large number of beneficiaries spanning at least four generations, according to rules specified in the Quran to avoid the concentration of income and wealth in the hands of a few.

As we have said numerous times, justice is at the heart of an Islamic society. Who is ultimately responsible for establishing a just society? The state's role is one of administrator, supervisor, and protector of society. It is the members of society who ensure that justice prevails. It can be argued that there is no topic more emphasized in Islam than poverty and the responsibility of individuals and society to eradicate it. The Prophet (sawa) said that poverty is near disbelief and that poverty is worse than murder.[17] Thus in any society in which there is poverty, this is sufficient evidence that Islamic rules are not being observed. It means that the rich and wealthy have not redeemed the rights of others in their income and wealth and that the state has failed to take corrective action.

ISLAMIC PERSPECTIVE ON FINANCIAL INCLUSION

There is evidence suggesting that financial development and improved access to finance—also referred to as financial inclusion—in a country is likely not only to accelerate economic growth but also to reduce income inequality and poverty. Despite the essential role of financial inclusion in the progress of efficiency and equality in a society, 2.7 billion people (70% of the adult population) in emerging markets still have no access to basic financial services, and a great part of the them come from countries with predominantly Muslim populations.[18]

Although the linkage of financial development with economic development exists, a high degree of the financial development in a country is not necessarily any indication that poverty has been alleviated in the country. There is a growing realization that in addition to financial development, the

---

[17]Al-Hakimi et al. (1989, pp. 278–468) and Qutb (1953).
[18]Demirguc-Kunt, Beck, and Honohan (2007).

emphasis should be to expand the accessibility to finance and financial services that can play a more positive role in eradicating poverty. Development economists are convinced that the goal should be improving access and making basic financial services available to all members of the society in order to build an inclusive financial system. Enhancing access to and quality of basic financial services, such as availability of credit, mobilization of savings, insurance, and risk management, can facilitate sustainable growth and productivity, especially for small- and medium-scale enterprises.

Understanding the linkage of financial inclusion with economic development is important. There is voluminous literature in economics and finance on the contributions of finance to economic growth and development. The main reason why "finance," "financial inclusion," or "access to finance" matters is that financial development and intermediation have been shown empirically to be key drivers of economic growth and development. Development economists suggest that the lack of access to finance for the poor deters key decisions regarding human and physical capital accumulation. For example, in an imperfect financial market, poor people may find themselves in the poverty trap, as they cannot save at harvest time or borrow to survive a starvation. Similarly, without a predictable future cash flow, the poor in developing countries are also incapable of borrowing against future income to invest in education or healthcare for their children.

Given the significance of financial inclusion, a developed financial sector in a country can play a critical role in promoting growth and in reducing poverty by enabling the poor to borrow to finance income-enhancing assets, including human assets such as health and education, and to become micro-entrepreneurs to generate income and ultimately come out of poverty.[19] In addition, financial sector development could enable the poor to channel the savings to the formal sector (i.e., bank accounts and other saving schemes and insurance), which would allow the poor to establish a buffer against future shocks, thus reducing their vulnerability and exposure, which otherwise could put undue strain on future income prospects.

Modern development theories analyzing the evolution of growth, relative income inequalities, and economic development offer two tracks of thinking. One track attributes imbalances in redistribution of wealth and income in the economy as an impediment to growth while the other track identifies financial market imperfections as the key obstacle.[20] Proponents of the redistribution of wealth claim that redistribution can foster growth and a focus on redistributive public policies, such as land or education reform centering

---

[19] DFID (2004).
[20] Demirguc-Kunt, Beck, and Honohan (2007).

on schooling, saving, or fertility changes, can lead to reductions in income inequalities and poverty.

The other school of thought considers obstacles to growth to be market failure and imperfect information leading to financial market frictions.[21] Financial market frictions can be the critical mechanism for generating persistent income inequality or poverty traps. Such imperfections, including information asymmetries and transaction costs, are likely to be especially binding on the talented poor and the micro- and small enterprises that lack collateral, credit histories, and connections, thus limiting their opportunities and leading to persistent inequality and slower growth.

Risk Sharing and Wealth Redistribution

Islam emphasizes financial inclusion more explicitly, but two distinct features of Islamic finance—the notions of risk sharing and redistribution of wealth—differentiate its path of development significantly from the conventional financial model.

Individuals in a society face two types of risks. The first is the result of the exposure of the economy to uncertainty and risk due to external and internal economic circumstances of the society and its vulnerabilities to shocks. How well the economy will absorb shocks depends on its resilience, which in turn depends on the society's institutional and policy infrastructure. How flexibly these respond to shocks will determine how much these risks impact individual lives when they materialize. The second type of risk individuals face relates to the circumstances of their personal lives. These include risks of injuries, illness, accidents, bankruptcies, or even changes of tastes and preferences. This kind of risk is referred to as idiosyncratic; when such risks materialize, they play havoc with people's livelihoods. This is because often the level of consumption that sustains them is directly dependent on people's income. If their income becomes volatile, so will their livelihood and consumption. Engaging in risk sharing can mitigate idiosyncratic risk and allow consumption smoothing by weakening the correlation between income and consumption such that should these risks materialize, and should the shock reduce income, the individual's consumption and livelihood do not suffer correspondingly.

In a society, risks can be shared among members and/or between members and the state. Both in industrial and developing economies, people find ways and means of sharing risks to their livelihoods. In particular, they use coping mechanisms to increase the variability of their income relative to their consumption. In more developed financial systems, the coping

---

[21] Stiglitz and Weiss (1981).

mechanism is investing in financial assets or acquiring insurance to mitigate personal risks. In developing countries, with weak financial markets, people rely on informal insurance, borrowing, or saving to cope with idiosyncratic risks. In such societies, theory suggests that perfect informal insurance is possible if communities fully pool their incomes to share risks.

According to the Islamic perspective, risks are mitigated in various ways. First, the Islamic economic system is a rule-based system, which has provided rules of behavior and taxonomy of decisions—actions and their commensurate payoffs based on injunctions in the Quran. Complying with these rules reduces uncertainty. Clearly, individuals exercise their freedom in choosing to comply or not with these rules. That rules of behavior and compliance with them reduce uncertainty is an important insight of the new institutional economics. Rules reduce the burden on human cognitive capacity, particularly in the process of decision making under uncertainty. Rules also promote cooperation and coordination.[22] Second, Islam has provided ways and means by which those who are able to mitigate uncertainty by sharing the risks they face by engaging in economic activities with fellow human beings through exchange. Sharing allows risk to be spread and thus lowered for individual participants. However, if a person is unable to use any of the market means of risk sharing because of poverty, Allah (swt) has ordered a solution here as well: The rich are commanded to share the risks that the poor face in their lives by redeeming the rights of the poor derived from the Islamic principles of property rights and sharing their income with them.[23] Islam's laws of inheritance provide further mechanisms for risk sharing.

Islam ordains risk sharing through three main venues:

1. Contracts of exchange and risk-sharing instruments in the financial sector.
2. Redistributive risk-sharing instruments that the economically more able segment of the society utilizes in order to share the risks facing the less able segment of the population.
3. Inheritance rules specified in the Quran through which the wealth of a person at the time of passing is distributed among present and future generations of inheritors.

The second set of instruments meant for redistribution are used to redeem the rights of the less able in the income and wealth of the more able. Contrary to common belief, these are not instruments of charity,

---

[22] Mirakhor (2009).
[23] Iqbal and Mirakhor (2011) and Mirakhor (1989).

altruism, or beneficence; these are instruments of redemption of rights and repayment of obligations.

To avoid opulence alongside poverty, Islam prohibits wealth concentration, imposes limits on consumption through its rules prohibiting overspending, waste, and ostentatious and opulent spending. It then ordains that the net surplus, after moderate spending necessary to maintain a modest living standard, must be returned to the members of the society who, for a variety of reasons, are unable to work; hence, the resources they could have used to produce income and wealth were utilized by the more able.

The Quran considers the more able as trustee-agents in using these resources on behalf of the less able. In this view, property is not a means of exclusion but of inclusion in which the rights of those less able in the income and wealth of the more able are redeemed. The result would be a balanced economy without extremes of wealth and poverty. The operational mechanism for redeeming the rights of the less able in the income and wealth of the more able are the network of mandatory and voluntary payments such as *zakat* (2.5% on wealth), *khums* (20% of income), and payments referred to as *sadaqat* (payments to redeem the rights of others).

The most important economic institution that operationalizes the objective of achieving social justice in Islam is that of the distribution-redistribution rule of the Islamic economic paradigm. Distribution takes place post-production and sale when all factors of production are given what is due to them commensurate with their contribution to production, exchange, and sale of goods and services. Redistribution refers to the postdistribution phase when the charges due to the less able are levied. These expenditures are essentially repatriation and redemption of the rights of others in one's income and wealth. Redeeming these rights is a manifestation of belief in the Oneness of the Creator and its corollary, the unity of the creation in general and of humankind in particular. It is the recognition and affirmation that Allah (swt) has created the resources for all of humankind, who must have unhindered access to them. Even the abilities that make access to resources possible are due to the Creator. This would mean that those who are less able or unable to use these resources are partners of the more able.

Sadaqat are a very important redistributive institution in Islam for two reasons: first, they operationalize the truthfulness of one's belief in Allah (swt) in voluntarily giving of one's income and wealth. Second, the importance of this institution derives from the fact that the receiver is not the person to whom *sadaqat* is given but Allah (swt). Two verses (103 and 104) of the Chapter of Repentance note:

> *of their goods (wealth) take* sadaqah, *so that you might purify and sanctify them; and pray on their behalf. Indeed, your prayers are a*

source of security for them: and Allah *(swt) is One Who Hears and Knows. (103)*

> Do they not know that Allah (swt) accepts repentance from His servants and Receives their Sadaqat, and that Allah (swt) is indeed He, the Oft-Returning, Most Merciful. (104)

Zakat is considered a component of *sadaqat*, but it has been given a special status in the Quran because it is ordained with obligatory prayer in at least 20 verses (see, e.g., 2:110). Moreover, its collection was enforced by the governments in early Muslim history following the passing of the Messenger.

Qardh hassan is a loan mentioned in the Quran as "beautiful" (*hassan*) probably because in all the verses in which this loan is mentioned, it is stipulated that it is made directly to Allah (swt) and not to the recipient (see, e.g., 64:17). It is a voluntary loan without a creditor's expectation of any return on the principal.

Very early in the history of Muslim societies, the institution of *waqf* appeared through which a person could contribute the third of his or her wealth over which he or she is allowed by *Shariah* to exercise control at the time of his/her death. A *waqf* is a trust established when the contributor endows the stream of income accrued to a property for a charitable purpose in perpetuity. This institution has already been partially instrumentalized— although not in the sense used here—since the legality of cash *waqf* (i.e., endowing the future income stream of a cash trust instead of a physical property) has been recognized in most Muslim countries. Here, too, the potential of mobilizing a large amount of financial resources through instrumentalization of this institution by a globally credible Islamic financial institution is substantial.

The third dimension of distributive justice in the institutional scaffolding of an Islamic society is the institution of inheritance, which is crucial in the intergenerational justice framework envisioned by the Lawgiver. Rules governing production, consumption, and distribution ensure conservation of resources for the next generations. Rules of redistribution ensure that those unable to benefit by participating directly in production and consumption in the market, through combination of their labor and their right of access to resources provided by the Supreme Creator for all humans, can redeem their rights through *zakat*, *khums*, *sadaqat*, *waqf*, and other redistributive mechanisms. Once these rights have been redeemed out of the income and wealth of the more economically able, the latter's property rights on the remaining income and wealth is held inviolable. These rights, however, end at the point of passing of a person. At the time of passing, people lose the right to allocate their wealth as they please except for a third of their income, which believers can use to make *waqf*, *sadaqat*, or other transfer contributions as they wish.

Islam provides a set of redistributive instruments that could play a critical role in reducing poverty. Given Islam's emphasis on social and economic justice and the eradication of poverty, we would expect Islamic instruments that address inequity, such as *zakat, khairat, waqf*, and *qardh hassan*, to play an important role in the development of the required institutional structures.[24] Therefore, there is a need to formalize or institutionalize Islamic redistributive mechanisms designed to empower the economically weak segments of society.[25]

By "institutionalization," we mean building nationwide institutions and surrounding legal infrastructure to maximize the effectiveness of these redistributive mechanisms. This institution-building exercise can take place in three steps.

1. Develop the institutions. An institution is nothing more that the legalization of the rules of behavior. Therefore, it would require crafting rules pertaining to these instruments as envisioned by *Shariah.*
2. Establish these institutions and integrate them with the rest of the economic and financial system. In this process, either existing channels of distribution (i.e., banks or post offices) can be utilized to interact with the customers, or new means of leveraging new technologies can be introduced.
3. Ensure enforceability of rules through transparent means.

---

[24]For example, Mohieldin, Iqbal, Rostom, and Fu (2011) estimate the resource shortfall to fill the poverty gap using *zakat* collection and find supporting evidence that 20 out of 39 Organisation of Islamic Cooperation countries actually left the poorest living with incomes under $1.25 per day out of poverty simply with domestic and remittances *zakat* collection. They argue that they do not consider using *zakat* a totally new poverty reduction mechanism, as it is already collected and distributed to the poor in several Islamic countries, but proper collection, streamlining, accountability, prioritization, and allocation to productive activities can have significant impact on enhancing access and opportunity for the poor segment of the society, which will ultimately lead to reduction in poverty.

[25]See Mirakhor (2004) for further details. Given the number of poor in Islamic countries, critics argue that, a priori, Islamic institutions that were meant to redistribute income and wealth from the more well-to-do to the weaker segments of society have not shown the necessary strength in performing their function, and they could be right. Researchers and scholars have devoted little effort in empirically investigating the behavior of Muslims vis-à-vis these institutions (i.e., why the latter have failed to achieve the objectives for which they were designed and how the situation could be remedied). Admitting that these institutions have, by and large, failed to alleviate poverty in Muslim countries does not obviate the need to consider their potential.

The objective of institutionalization of redistributive instruments is to formalize and standardize their operations. For example, for *zakat, khairat,* and *qardh hassan,* a formal network of institutions needs to be developed to collect, distribute, and recycle the funds in the most efficient and the most transparent fashion.[26] In some countries, the point of a financial transaction, such as an automatic teller machine or cash dispensing machine, is used to enable customers to choose to make immediate donations or contributions. The financial institution can collect and aggregate funds and then disburse them to the needy through selected channels.

The use of *qardh hassan* for the microfinance sector should be exploited further. Many characteristics of the *qardh hassan*–based funds could be shared by microfinance institutions. Therefore, the infrastructure of the latter can be utilized to effectively achieve the objectives of the former. While it is difficult to explain why this very important Islamic redistributive institution is so underutilized in the Islamic world—research efforts by sociologists and economists should investigate the behavioral causes—one can speculate that lack of knowledge, in the first instance, and concerns about safety and security of the contributed principal may be important factors. The latter could be provided by a credible Islamic financial institution through issuance of financial instruments that would provide safety and security to the contributors. The Islamic financial institution can also instrumentalize the asset side of its balance sheet. Furthermore, it can provide *qardh hassan* resources to existing microfinance institutions to reduce the burden of their interest rate charges on borrowers. But how would such Islamic financial institutions cover their administrative costs? There are two possible sources: (1) through investing a fraction of the mobilized resources and (2) through profit-sharing via *qardh hassan* resources, through which Islamic financial institutions invest in productive projects of young entrepreneurs who have no access to formal credit markets.

Policy makers need to pay attention to this set of tools to enhance access and should encourage enhancement of such institutions through development of the legal framework to protect the institutions, donors, and stakeholders

---

[26]The institution of *qardh hassan* has been utilized effectively to provide microfinance in the Muslim country of Iran, where these institutions are widespread. They provide small consumer and producer loans and, in some cases, engage in profit-making activities that supplement the principal amounts deposited with the fund. These *qardh hassan* funds are usually associated in each locality with mosques or other religious organizations and, at times, with guilds or professional group associations. The capital is contributed by the more well-to-do who are at liberty to withdraw their funds at any time. These funds operate with very low administrative costs since most are managed through volunteer service contributed by people within the group. See Sadr (2007).

and to ensure transparent governance. With well-developed redistributive institutions supplemented by formal and semiformal sector financial institutions, a more effective approach to poverty reduction is possible.

Given the rules governing property rights, work, production, exchange, markets, distribution, and redistribution, it is reasonable to conclude that in an Islamic society—a rule-complying and Allah (swt)–conscious society—absolute poverty could not exist. It can be argued that there is no topic more emphasized in Islam than poverty and the responsibility of individuals and society to eradicate it. The Prophet (sawa) said that poverty is near disbelief and that poverty is worse than murder. It is almost axiomatic that in any society in which there is poverty, Islamic rules are not being observed. It means that the rich and wealthy have not redeemed the rights of others to their income and wealth and that the state has failed to take corrective action.

SUMMARY

In Islam, economic growth is seen as helpful to the extent that it is focused on spiritual as well material needs, with humans and society as its direct beneficiaries. Economic growth cannot be for growth's sake. The Quran and the life of the Prophet (sawa) provide humans with rules, laws, and institutions to succeed in building a successful society in unity with the Almighty's Creation. In Islam, development has dimensions of self-development, of the physical development of the earth, and of the development of society. The first dimension is the process of the growth of the human toward perfection, the second specifies how natural resources are to be used for developing the earth to provide for the material needs of humanity, and the third dimension encompasses the progress of the human collectivity toward full integration and unity. Together they constitute the rules-based compliance system to ensure progress on the three interrelated dimensions of development.

While Islam attaches great importance to human development and the means for its attainment, the underdevelopment of many Muslim societies has nothing to do with Islam. During the colonial era and even more recently, foreigners plundered many of the Muslim countries in the Middle East, North Africa, and the Far East. After these lands emerged from the yoke of colonialism, autocratic rulers, supported by foreigners, grabbed the reins of power and exploited ethnic and sectarian divisions. In most Muslim societies, efficient institutions, rules, and rule compliance to promote development have not been embraced and practiced.

KEY TERMS

Economic growth

Economic development

Human development

Political freedom

Capabilities and functioning

Cooperation

Coordination

Rules

Trust

Institutions

Qardh hassan (interest-free loan, literally translated as "a beautiful loan")

Sadaqa (payments to redeem the rights of the less fortunate)

Baraka (blessings)

Financial inclusion

QUESTIONS

1. How has the theory of economic development evolved in the West from the writings of Smith to Sen?
2. What are the dimensions of development as derived from the Quran and the practice of the Prophet (sawa) in Islam?
3. What are the dimensions of growth in Islam?
4. Why is freedom so important in human and economic development?
5. Why are institutions important in human and economic development?
6. What constitutes a balanced society in Islam, and why is sharing so important?
7. Identify and describe the areas where you see justice embedded in the Islamic prescription for development and growth.
8. Identify the areas where you see the rights of all generations preserved.

CHAPTER **13**

Economic and Social Welfare

Learning objectives:

1. *The need for a comprehensive social safety net.*
2. *The essential elements of safety nets.*
3. *Ethical principles and institutional measures.*
4. *The distinguishing features of the Islamic perspective on economic and social welfare.*
5. *The role of government in providing safety nets.*

While over the last few decades the international community has adopted the position that broad-based economic growth is necessary for stemming the effects of systemic poverty, a growing consensus has emerged that social safety nets and social protection are also essential elements of any comprehensive framework for poverty alleviation. Not only are provisions that provide basic services, such as healthcare and education, important in their own right, but they are also critical drivers for economic growth and development and an equitable distribution of income and wealth. An adequate social safety net is a central feature of the Islamic economic system and is even more imperative in countries that generate a significant percentage of their current revenues from society's depleting oil and gas reserves. A recent paper confirms that although growth has reduced poverty in Asia, it has been accompanied by increasing inequality (less inclusive than some suggest). The authors go on to suggest a number of policies to support more inclusive growth (reduce poverty more and decrease inequality):

In terms of fiscal policy, these include higher spending on health and education and enhanced social safety nets (e.g., increases in pension coverage and conditional cash transfers). Greater attention must also be paid to labor market reforms that would increase the voice of labor, hence boosting its share in total income (e.g., minimum wages and reducing duality in labor contracts). Finally, building a more inclusive financial system and improved governance should also be part of the policy package.[1]

In the early 1980s, the general prescriptions for growth in developing countries were economic reforms, focusing on developing a prudent combination of policies to enhance stabilization and adjustment while little attention was placed on the potential social costs of reforms. In time, however, more attention was afforded to relieving specific constraints that were binding, including specific provisions for social welfare and protection. Over the years, it has also been recognized that safety nets alone cannot effectively serve as an instrument for alleviating poverty without sound macroeconomic policies that enhance sustainable growth. Economic growth, income redistribution, and social safety nets are all needed in combination to alleviate poverty and afford everyone a fair chance to pursue their dreams. While restructuring efforts may create economic efficiency gains over the long term, they often also lead to social dislocation, particularly over the short term. As Muslim countries adopt much-needed economic reforms to promote fiscal discipline, build effective institutions, and promote economic justice in an effort to stimulate long-term growth, the development of a comprehensive structure to protect the vulnerable from declining deeper into poverty and improving the income distribution becomes even more pressing.

In a recent and much-heralded piece of economic scholarship, Thomas Piketty has argued that income and wealth distribution have deteriorated globally because of a fundamental shift in economic and financial fundamentals.[2] The rate of return to capital has exceeded economic growth. This shift has favored the owners of capital relative to labor, in turn widening the wealth and income distribution globally. He has called for heavy and progressive taxation of wealth to address this growing inequality because economic growth will not by itself address this growing chasm.

For social protection policies to be effective in Muslim countries, they should be complementary to the principles of economic justice as enunciated

---

[1]Balakrishan, Steinberg, and Syed (2013, p. 29).
[2]Piketty (2014).

in Islam. In this chapter, we explore the critical aspects of Islamic safety net arrangements, strategies for poverty alleviation, and equitable income distribution. In this context, we also explore the current role of social safety net policies in some Muslim countries. We conclude by discussing how countries can allocate their resources more efficiently to minimize social dislocation and ensure equity in accordance with Islamic principles. In order to understand the core principles underlying economic welfare and poverty alleviation, it is necessary to have a thorough understanding of available tools for income distribution and redistribution in Islam. (See discussion in Chapter 12.)

SOCIAL SAFETY NET PROVISIONS

Many observers contend that Islam played such a critical role in the development of the Arab societies that it allowed them to flourish and to have a transformative effect throughout the world.[3] Although conventional economics addresses the issue of the allocation and distribution of resources, it lacks the spiritual or moral foundation to achieve social goals. The Quran assumes conventional economic principles, such as the laws of supply and demand, based on individual enterprise and reward but set within a moral framework to ensure equal opportunities and support for all.[4]

We begin by providing a brief description of the foundation of an Islamic social safety net system. To fully implement Islamic economics requires more than a simple paradigm shift away from classical economics. Rather, Islam conceptualizes human behavior with regard to the distribution of resources and the requisites for human welfare somewhat differently from what is done in Western economic theory. For example, classical economics assumes that (1) individuals are rational actors in the economy, (2) resources are scarce, and (3) personal demands or wants are unlimited. However, the underlying factors determining the extent of poverty are unlimited wants, resource scarcity, and, to some degree, the distribution of output.

Similar to classical economic theory, Islam recognizes that individuals are rational actors; however, in Islam, the underlying cause of poverty is seen differently. Scarcity is not afforded an overriding importance in explaining poverty in Islam. Islam asserts unambiguously that poverty is neither caused by scarcity and paucity of natural resources, nor is it due to the lack of proper synchronization between the mode of production and the relation of distribution, but as a result of waste, opulence, extravagance, and nonpayment of what rightfully belongs to the less able segments of the society. This position is

---

[3]Chapra (1991).
[4]Iqbal (1987, p. 79).

illustrated by the prophetic saying "Nothing makes a poor man starve except that with which a rich person avails in luxury." That is to say, the right to advance one's own personal utility cannot impinge on the rights of others. Corruption (the stealing of what belongs to society, such as oil), mal-distribution of wealth and income, and the accompanying waste are seen as the root causes of poverty, deprivation, and need. Put somewhat differently, the principle is to protect against the eventual degeneration and disintegration of the community that result from placing narrow self-interests above ethical values. The Quran (28:58–59; 9:24) cautions individuals against allowing ephemeral worldly desires to subsume Allah's desires for humankind.[5]

Thus in sharp contrast to classical economics, resource constraints are in fact not seen as the binding constraints to prosperity and economic welfare in Islam. Rather, Allah (swt) granted humankind enough to meet everyone's basic needs (the Almighty did not create the world haphazardly); however, as a result of an unjust social and economic order, there is an inequitable distribution of these resources between the artificial boundaries of the state and people within countries, with waste and poverty seen as the twin results. God's entrustment of these resources to humankind as a whole can be duly discharged only when everyone has enough to satisfy at least their basic needs.[6] This point is particularly relevant to the major oil exporters, as the states' survival and ability to provide their people with basic services has been up to now dependent on revenues from oil—a depleting natural resource entrusted to all (current and future generations). Accordingly, poverty in rich oil-exporting countries is a result of corruption, misallocation of resources, and resultant waste (Quran 4:130–131; 15:19–20; 27:16; 16:71; 34:39).

Islamic teachings limit humankind's material wants if they adversely affect society's well-being: No one should be denied their basic needs or sustenance and live in poverty and deprivation. While vulnerability (disability, sickness, etc.) is a product of the human condition and prevalent in all societies, its attendant impact, resulting in poverty, is fundamentally a consequence of people's deference to Allah's (swt) guidance.[7] In this regard, Islam calls on its believers to be content with their material lot in life while also giving to charity if the capacity exists and not engaging in wasteful consumption. Although Islam envisages an established safety net system, it is not meant to replace the essential element of hard work. The Prophet (sawa) repeatedly stressed Allah's (swt) disapproval toward those who depended on

---

[5] Quranic quotes are taken directly from Asad (2005).
[6] Ahmad (1991).
[7] Ul-Haq (1996).

charity although they could earn enough to fulfill their livelihood through their own labor.[8]

The Islamic method to alleviate poverty and to realize an equitable distribution of income is fundamental to achieving the Islamic vision of a just social and economic order.[9] Injustice is believed to ultimately impede the realization of human welfare, exacerbate social unrest and malaise, and retard development.[10] Justice demands that all, regardless of race, color, sex, nationality, and even religion, share the benefits of development equitably; and distributive justice is recognized as central to the Islamic vision of an economic system (Quran 4:135; 5:8; 16:90).[11]

The principle of justice also demands an economic system that ensures equal access to basic needs that promote human well-being (including shelter, food, healthcare, and education) for all, thus creating a level playing field. For instance, equal access to education is essential to promoting equality of opportunity, as it minimizes social stratification and employment segmentation. Where provisions have been developed to ensure the individual's access to basic needs and equal opportunity, it is also under the state's authority to redistribute wealth. While Islam recognizes that some have been endowed with more worldly goods than others, it also creates mechanisms for redistribution, such as *zakat* (compulsory alms tax), calling on believers to engage in economic justice.

CONCEPT OF SAFETY NET AND WELFARE

According to the Quran, poverty and denial of assistance to the needy is forbidden. The Quran goes on to explain that material inequalities are not a manifestation of spiritual inequalities. Rather, such inequalities should be overcome through human effort and are thus meant to foster brotherhood, again stressing the importance of *zakat* (Quran 43:32). Islam also stresses the principle of economic prudence. With respect to the use of public funds and personal wealth, waste is forbidden. Islam views extravagant expenditures and conspicuous consumption with acute opprobrium (Quran 17: 26–27).

Islam enjoins the ethical principles with institutional measures to create a framework for poverty alleviation to ensure that basic needs can be met. The

---

[8] Ahmad (1995).
[9] Ibid.
[10] Chapra (2003).
[11] Ibid.

measures to alleviate poverty and achieve an equitable distribution of wealth and resource are threefold and include:

1. The development of ethical and moral values, such as justice, equality, honesty, and the like.
2. Economic tools and instruments, such as *zakat, sadaqa,* and inheritance and property laws.
3. The development of the institutional capacity and political will to ensure that these principles and norms are adequately upheld.[12]

Similar to many publicly organized social safety net systems, the purpose of *zakat* is to guarantee a minimum standard of living by helping the poor meet the costs of basic needs, protecting the vulnerable against shock, and fostering an equitable income distribution. Its primary objective is to serve the cause of social justice and a moral purpose; it is not a mechanism for charity. According to Islam, the role of the state includes the administration of a social security system in which the religiously decreed *zakat* assumes a central position. The Islamic system levies a *zakat* on all Muslims who meet a minimum level of wealth to help finance eight categories of welfare that are mentioned in the Quran (9:60), including poverty alleviation, the emancipation of slaves, pilgrimage, and assistance to those serving Islam.

In much of the literature on safety nets in the Muslim world, Islamic institutions such as *zakat* are considered to be part of the informal safety net or on the fringes of a welfare system. While the *zakat* system is a fundamental element and the cornerstone of social safety nets, its effective implementation has been less than optimal. Recent evidence indicates that donors prefer to give *sadaqa* directly to private individuals or charities.[13] An Islamic safety net system constitutes a number of other institutional arrangements that facilitate voluntary spending for the needy. *Waqf* is another mechanism whereby an individual donates a certain asset, such as land and buildings, for a designated specific purpose under a legal deed. It has been useful in transferring wealth from private ownership to collective ownership to be used for social advancement. Loss of confidence between *zakat* payers and *zakat* institutions should lead Muslim countries to seek alternatives that are permissible in Islam, such as state taxation of income.

---

[12] Iqbal (1987, p. 79).
[13] Salih (1999).

EMPIRICAL EVIDENCE ON SOCIAL WELFARE FROM SELECT MUSLIM COUNTRIES

Some historical background will provide a context for the establishment of current social welfare policies in Muslim countries in the Middle East and North African countries. The years 1950s to 1970s marked a formative period for many of these countries. Not only had most gained independence from colonial rule (with the prominent exception of Iran), but for the major oil exporters in particular, this period also marked a dramatic increase in oil export proceeds. These two events gave rise to the development of an implicit social contract in which citizens exchanged political liberties for economic and social stability. Elements of the social contract essentially endorsed state paternalism and included a preference for equity and redistribution in social and economic policy and a preference for protectionism and state control of markets. The social contract was later consolidated through adoption of an elaborate social welfare framework, financed by oil revenues for oil-rich countries or by assuming large external debt for those that did not have oil. The Islamic ethos of equity, equality, and justice had long disappeared from the landscape, and ruling class hierarchies, gender inequality, and other modalities of social stratification prevailed while rulers used economic benefits in the form of subsidies to buy domestic support and hold on to power.

The entrenchment of these open-handed welfare policies has posed challenges to development and economic reform in the region. Despite the bloated and in some cases unsustainable safety net system, meaningful reforms would inevitably be met with fierce political opposition as citizens see safety net provisions as part of the social contract. The wealthier countries (whose wealth is generated from depleting oil and gas exports) are often criticized for offering generous universal cash transfers and subsidies, particularly in times of budgetary surpluses resulting from higher oil prices. Safety net mechanisms should be developed for the purposes of ensuring a reasonable level of equity and for alleviating poverty and not for buying political support to hold on to power.

Research on the topic is difficult at best due to lack of data, collected or made public, on poverty and income distribution for many countries in the Middle East and North Africa (MENA) region. However, where data does exist, we can get a sense of the progress made in poverty alleviation. Despite the abundance of natural resources, nearly all countries in the MENA region are faced with the challenges of addressing significant levels of poverty. The exceptions are perhaps the wealthier, less populated oil-exporting countries in the Persian Gulf (Kuwait, Qatar, and the United Arab Emirates [UAE]).

TABLE 13.1   Regional Poverty Comparisons

	Poverty Head Count Ratio at $1 a Day (PPP) (% of population)				Poverty Head Count Ratio at $2 a Day (PPP) (% of population)			
	1981	1990	2002	2008	1981	1990	2002	2008
East Asia and Pacific	57.7	29.6	11.6	12.46	84.8	69.9	40.7	33.24
Europe and Central Asia	0.7	0.5	2.1	0.66	4.7	4.9	16.1	2.2
Latin America and Caribbean	9.7	11.3	8.9	5.53	26.9	28.4	23.4	12.38
Middle East and North Africa	5.1	2.3	1.6	N/A	28.9	21.4	19.8	N/A
Sub-Saharan Africa	41.6	44.6	44	N/A	73.3	75	74.9	N/A

Source: World Bank, World Development Indicators (2011).

For the region as a whole, about 2% of MENA's population lived on the less than US$1-per-day poverty line and nearly 25% live below the US$2 poverty line. Given the region's overall level of development, income poverty in MENA is actually low compared to the rest of the developing world. (See Table 13.1 for regional comparisons.) Poverty levels do vary significantly between the oil-rich countries and the resource-poor countries, signaling large regional disparities. For instance, while 2% of Iranians live on less than US$1 per day, in Yemen nearly 16% fall under that absolute poverty threshold.[14] Iraq is a special case with extensive poverty that is likely to be higher than the MENA average.

Focusing on Iran, statistics indicate that within the last decade, about 7% of Iranians fell below the US$2-per-day poverty line. However, national poverty rates often obscure pervasive distortions in relative depravation and inequalities in human development. For instance, the statistics on national poverty measures (calculated based on food intake of less than 2,200 calories per day) reveals a more alarming picture of deprivation than the US$1-per-day indicator: Nearly 15% in urban areas and 17% of Iran's rural population. Moreover, while 10.4% of Iran's urban population lives below the *absolute poverty line* (minimum requirement for food, clothing, healthcare, and shelter), 22.6% of rural inhabitants live in absolute poverty.[15] Although Iran has made remarkable improvements in poverty alleviation and in key human development indicators, these gains have been achieved primarily through charitable handouts and subsidies rather than through empowerment and

[14]World Bank (2011).
[15]United Nations (2003).

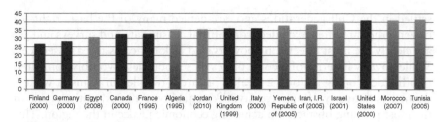

FIGURE 13.1 Gini Index for Select OECD (Organisation for Co-operation and Development) and MENA (Middle East and North Africa) Countries

employment. Moreover, such gains could not have been achieved without a large dependence on oil revenues.

An indicator of income distribution is the Gini index or coefficient (with 0 indicating perfect equality and 100 indicating perfect inequality, or one person enjoying all the income). Iran's Gini index provides a striking view of its skewed income distribution, with an index higher than even other countries in the MENA region (except Morocco and Tunisia, which have less access to a steady revenue base from oil; see Figure 13.1). Moreover, Iran's income distribution figures further indicate widespread disparities with a 10.5 to 1 ratio between the income/consumption of the richest and the poorest 20% of the population. The fact that the wealthiest 20% of the population in the richest provinces consume nearly 32 times what the poorest 20% consume in the poorest provinces shows the regional challenges Iran faces in addressing income inequalities.[16] This disparity goes beyond income and consumption standards and, as expected, permeates into access to basic services. For instance, in Sistan and Baluchistan Province (perhaps the poorest province in Iran), only 55% of the population has access to safe water; the national average is 83%. The gaps between national and provincial literacy, nutrition, and birth registration indicators are similarly wide. Yemen is a particularly interesting case in the region. In contrast to Iran, it is one of the poorest countries and has limited natural resources (on a per capita basis); however, its Gini index reveals a significant level of income equality.

While the labor-importing countries (Bahrain, Kuwait, Oman, Qatar, Saudi, UAE) do not have indices on poverty and income distribution, such statistics may, in any case, be obscured by the enormous presences of an expatriate labor force. For instance, the composition of nonnationals ranges from a high of 81% in the UAE to a low of 20% of the total population in Oman.[17] Immigrants, many of whom are from neighboring countries and

---

[16]United Nations (2003).
[17]Kapiszewski (2006).

settled in the Gulf generations ago, are denied many of the basic rights of citizens; they are often excluded from official census data and surveys and yet are clearly the most affected by poverty and lack of access to basic services. While poverty in terms of income places these countries favorably compared to other developing regions, a bleaker picture is revealed in terms of what is defined as "poverty of opportunity."[18] Inequality of opportunities is one of the most pressing obstacles to achieving economic justice in the region. This point becomes particularly stark as we explore labor market and education outcomes.

Provisions that provide for basic needs, such as quality healthcare, education, employment, and consumer goods, play a vital role in reducing generational poverty and enhancing equal opportunities, particularly over the long term. Outcome indicators and government expenditures in the various areas of the social sector afford a sense of government priorities and the efficiency, sustainability, and equitability with which public funds are being spent. We examine these indicators for MENA countries relative to other comparator groups ("comparators" are based on World Bank–designated low-income, middle-income, and high-income groupings) in the areas of health and education, and other components of the social safety net.

Formal social safety net programs, including employment guarantees, consumer subsidies, cash transfers, and universal health and education services, play a prominent role throughout the Middle East and North Africa region. However, safety net arrangements in many countries tend to be heavily concentrated in providing universal subsidies on consumption goods, which are characterized as being regressive (i.e., the rich receive a larger share of the benefits than the poor), inefficient, and poorly targeted. MENA countries spend on average 5% of gross domestic product (GDP) for social safety net–type programs (including social insurance and social assistance), which is slightly higher than in other developing regions but significantly below levels seen among countries in the European Union.[19] While the level of government spending on social assistance in the MENA region is comparable to that of other middle-income countries, a large share does not reach the poor. For example, Jordan's national assistance fund covers only 22,000 households, compared to Egypt's social assistance program that affects an estimated 2.7 million beneficiaries. While health and education outcomes have made notable improvements in the last few decades, the current level of spending is unsustainable in some cases and coverage is limited. In the

---

[18]UNESCO defines poverty of opportunity "as a multidimensional concept. It embraces not only critical elements of lack of education, proper health and economic assets, but also social exclusion and political marginalization." UNDP (2002).
[19]Hoftijzer (2006).

absence of sound safety net provisions, many of the poor in the region tend to rely on informal mechanisms, which may be adequate to smooth out idiosyncratic shocks but are limited in their ability to address an economic crisis.

Healthcare

A sound healthcare system not only maximizes health outcomes, but it also protects the population against the potentially devastating financial costs of healthcare, provides equitable and high-quality access to services, and is financially sustainable given anticipated economic growth and demographic factors. National health account estimates and indicators on health outcomes for the MENA countries and the comparator groups reveal a telling trend with regard to equitable, efficient, and sustain resource allocation.

In Table 13.2, we provide a snapshot of national health accounts estimates for a select set of MENA countries. Total healthcare expenditures as a percentage of GDP for the MENA region are on par with international trends. However, for a number of countries in the region, health outlays as a percentage of GDP have decreased. This relative reduction is most likely a result of GDP growth (particularly for the oil-exporting countries in the first part of this decade) outpacing growth in healthcare outlays, rather than a reduction in real terms. On average, total per capita healthcare expenditures for most MENA countries (with the most notable exceptions of Iraq and Yemen) are higher than those of the low- and middle-income group of countries. However, the regional disparities in this indicator are striking: In Qatar, total per capita expenditures is $1,489; in Yemen, it is $72 per person. Between the MENA countries, there is also a broad range in government outlays on healthcare as a percentage of total government expenditures: Algeria, Iran, Iraq, and Tunisia allocate about 10% of government expenditures toward healthcare (Jordan nearly 20%), while Yemen spends less than half of that figure (4.3%). Overall, private sector healthcare expenditures as a percentage of total healthcare expenditures have increased for most of MENA; however, there are variations in the ratio of private expenditures to public expenditures in the region. High private expenditures in some countries may signal inadequacies in publicly provided healthcare.

Despite vast disparities in expenditures on healthcare, basic health standards in areas such as infant mortality, immunization, and life expectancy rates have improved significantly for all countries in the MENA region (see Table 13.3). In MENA (with the exception of Iraq), during the period 1990 to 2002, infant mortality decreased, with an overall regional average lower than the low-income group of countries. However, infant mortality in the region was still about 10% higher than that of the middle-income group.

TABLE 13.2 National Health Accounts Estimates for Select MENA Countries

	Total Expenditure on Health (THE) % GDP			General Government Expenditure on Health (GGHE) % THE			Private Expenditure on Health (PvtHE) % THE			GGHE % General Government Expenditure			THE per Capita at Exchange Rate (US$)			GGHE per Capita at Exchange Rate (US$)		
	1998	2001	2010	1998	2001	2010	1998	2001	2010	1998	2001	2010	1998	2001	2010	1998	2001	2010
Algeria	4.1	3.8	4.34	73.7	77.4	79.87	26.3	22.6	20.13	9.7	9.5	8.97	66.6	67.7	198.1	49.1	52.4	158.3
Egypt	4.8	5.4	4.74	33.8	39.9	39.21	66.2	61.1	60.79	6.5	7.1	6.12	62.3	76.5	127.8	21.1	30.5	50.1
Iran	5.9	6.3	5.29	44.6	44.5	40.21	55.4	55.5	59.79	10.9	11.5	10.06	95.9	109.7	...	42.8	48.8	...
Iraq	2.3	1.6	8.52	51	27.1	81.18	49	72.9	18.82	1.9	1.2	10.20	10.5	12.1	215.8	5.4	3.3	175.2
Jordan	8.9	9.4	8.32	54.9	45.7	67.60	45.1	54.3	32.40	13.1	9.8	19.25	153.2	171.7	363.7	84.1	78.5	245.9
Kuwait	4.3	3.6	2.63	78.8	77.7	80.37	21.2	22.3	19.63	6.6	6.2	6.86	632.6	625.0	1194.4	498.5	485.7	959.9
Qatar	4.2	2.9	2.06	73	74.1	77.46	27	25.9	22.54	6.8	6.8	5.19	784.8	836.5	1488.6	572.9	619.8	1153.1
Saudi Arabia	5	4.7	4.01	79.1	78.6	65.98	20.9	21.4	34.02	11.4	9.9	6.84	378.5	415.9	659.0	299.4	326.9	434.8
Tunisia	5.5	5.7	5.72	49.7	49.6	54.25	50.3	50.4	45.75	7.1	7.6	10.85	128.5	130.0	240.5	63.9	64.5	130.5
UAE	4.1	3.7	3.70	78.4	78.3	73.00	21.6	21.7	27.00	7.9	7.7	8.79	1126.0	1213.7	1467.5	882.8	950.3	1071.2
Yemen	5	5	5.59	40.4	42.8	21.03	59.6	57.2	78.97	5.5	6.5	4.33	18.9	27.0	72.1	7.6	11.5	15.2
MENA	5	5	4.64										129.4	146.0	305.1			
Low-income	5	5	5.74										13.6	12.7	30.3			
Middle-income	6	6	5.77										74.9	77.4	228.9			
High-income	10	11	12.40										2819.6	3328.7	4114.2			

Source: World Bank, World Development Indicators 2011.

TABLE 13.3 Key Health Indicators for Select MENA Countries

	Life Expectancy at Birth, Total (years)			Mortality Rate, Infant (per 1,000 live births)			Immunization, DPT (% of children ages 12–23 months)			Immunization, Measles (% of children ages 12–23 months)		
	1990	2002	2011	1990	2002	2011	1990	2002	2011	1990	2002	2011
Algeria	67	71	73	54	35*	26	89	86	95	83	81	95
Egypt	63	70	73	76	26*	18	87	97	96	86	97	96
Iran	65	69	73	54	34	21	91	99	99	85	99	99
Iraq	61	63	69	40	102	31	83	81	77	80	90	76
Jordan	68	71	73	33	23*	18	92	95	98	87	95	98
Kuwait	75	77	75	14	9	9	71	98	99	66	99	99
Qatar	72	75	78	19	11	6	82	96	93	79	99	99
Saudi Arabia	69	73	74	34	23	8	92	95	98	88	97	98
Tunisia	70	73	75	41	21*	14	93	96	98	93	94	96
UAE	74	75	77	12	8	6	85	94	94	80	94	94
Yemen	55	60	65	98	82	57	84	69	81	69	65	71
MENA	64	69	73	57	44	24	88	92	91	84	92	90
Low-income	57	59	59	93	79	63	64	65	79	57	65	77
Middle-income	68	70	69	40	30	35	88	85	82	89	80	85
High-income	76	78	80	8	5	5	86	95	96	76	90	93

Source: World Bank, World Development Indicators 2011.

Moreover, infant mortality figures varied significantly between countries in the region, from a low of 6 per 1,000 live births in Qatar and the UAE to a high of 57 in Yemen. During that same period, overall life expectancy also increased—with an average higher than that of the low-income group and only slightly lower than that of the middle-income countries. Indicators also revealed significant improvement in child immunization, with the 2002 estimate higher than even the high-income comparator group of countries.

A balanced healthcare system is financed through an equitable contribution from the various partners, including insurance providers, households, and governments. Provisions for universal healthcare coverage have ensured more than 90% of the population in the region is given access to at least basic health services.[20] However, full healthcare coverage is also incomplete. For instance, in Saudi Arabia, free healthcare is considered a right for all expatriates employed by the public sector and all Saudi citizens. Health coverage for non-nationals employed in the private sector (a sizable portion of Saudi Arabia's population) is the responsibility of their employers and/or sponsors. Similarly, Iran faces difficulties in meeting its commitment to universal healthcare—nearly all Iranians have access to public healthcare services and limited curative care, and yet a significant portion of the population lacks services to the full range of care through Iran's various health networks. Like most safety net arrangements in MENA, public expenditures for healthcare and health coverage are regressive. In some cases, government-financed outlays often accrue to high-tech hospitals that provide expertise and services for diseases that typically afflict the affluent. Government facilities are usually the social safety nets for the poor and other vulnerable groups. However, such facilities often provide incomplete and insufficient care, particularly in the rural areas, where facilities face severe budgetary limitations. For most of these countries, contributions from private insurance provide only modest financing, and private insurance is out of reach for the impoverished in need of quality care. Similar to many countries in MENA, while Iran does provide universal healthcare coverage, those who can afford it seek services from private sources because of the quality difference between private and public sector healthcare services. Iran's overall high expenditure on private healthcare (as a percentage of total healthcare expenditures) is almost definitely a result of the rich seeking higher-quality services. High overall out-of-pocket expenditures in the region signals that many households absorb a significant proportion of healthcare costs and that there may be little to no financial protection in the event of illness or injury. Poorer families tend to allocate a higher share of their income to healthcare services. For instance, in Algeria, household health

---

[20]World Bank (2002).

expenditure for the poorest 10% of the urban population is three times higher than for the wealthiest 10% of urbanites; for the rural population, it is two times as large.[21]

The issue of sustainability of the healthcare sector is a critical dimension. Improved healthcare standards are associated with significant population growth, which in turn have placed greater pressure on public healthcare systems in the region. Without adequate healthcare system controls that improve efficiency and coverage, population growth can threaten the sustainability of the entire healthcare system. For instance, at the current average annual rate of growth in population, Saudi Arabia's population is expected to grow by 75% by the year 2020. Population aging alone will require total per capita spending to increase by 12%.[22] Given the public sectors' dominance in the healthcare field, it is unlikely MENA countries will be able to continue to provide free cradle-to-grave healthcare indefinitely.

Education

In today's information age, it is clear that the knowledge gap, rather than the income gap, determines a country's competitiveness in the global economy. Education is essential to expanding human capacities and opportunities as well as being a tool for reducing poverty.[23] Moreover, there can be no mistake about the prominence and importance Islam places on the acquisition of knowledge. The Quran calls on humankind to use intellect, to reflect and to think, because the objective of life is to seek and discover truths.[24] Throughout the Middle East, most countries have adopted a policy of universal education. However, for a number of countries, this has not necessarily resulted in increased school performance and access.

Overall, the average education expenditures in MENA (see Table 13.4) are higher than the low- and middle-income comparator groups. However, there are significant disparities in the amount each country in the region spends. For instance, in some countries (Iran, Saudi Arabia, Tunisia, Morocco, and Kuwait), expenditures on education (as a percentage of GDP) are higher than the average for the MENA region as a whole and even for the high-income group of countries. By contrast, expenditures as a percentage of GDP for the UAE and Qatar are lower than those of the middle-income countries. Indicators measuring the quality of education, such as

---

[21] Tzannatos (2000).
[22] Statistics have been gathered from various World Health Organization reports.
[23] UNDP (2003).
[24] Knowledge (*ilm*) and its derivatives are mentioned 811 times in the Quran, the same number of times as faith (*iman*) and its derivatives.

TABLE 13.4 Education Financing and Outcome Indicators for Select MENA Countries

| | Education Financing | | | | | | | Education Outcomes | | | | | |
| | Public Spending on Education (% of Total Gov't Expend.) | | Public Spending on Education (% of GDP) | | Expenditure per Student, Primary (% of GDP per capita) | Expenditure per Student, Secondary (% of GDP per capita) | Expenditure per Student, Tertiary (% of GDP per capita) | Primary Enrollment Rate (Net) | | Secondary Enrollment Rate (Net) | | Tertiary Enrollment Rate (Gross) | |
	1991	2008	1991	2008	2008	2008	2008	1991	2008	1991	2008	1991	2008
Algeria	22	20.3	5.1	4.3	11.32475 (c)	17.16166 (c)		88.8	97.0	63.8	66.66182 (b)	11.3	19.35763 (b)
Egypt	3.9	11.9		3.8				84.1	96.70379 (g)		68.20011 (d)	15.8	30.4
Iran	22.4	20.0	4.1	4.8	16.6	20.4	20.8	92.4	99.58808 (g)			10.2	36.3
Iraq								94	89.22668 (e)				16.35853 (h)
Jordan	19.1		8		12.3	14.8		94.1	89.7	79.2	84.5	22.9	41.1
Kuwait	3.4	12.92772 (a)	4.8	3.76001 (a)	10.0	13.7		49	92.1		89.0		21.86206 (b)
Morocco	26.3	25.7	8	5.6	16.2	34.0	71.6	55.9	87.51 (d)		35.07 (c)	10.6	12.6
Qatar		7.1	3.5	2.5	9.9509 (d)	10.57179 (d)		89.4	91.96845 (g)	69.6	83.41422 (g)	23.2	11.5
Saudi	17.8	19.3	5.8	5.6	19.32681 (e)	19.26211 (e)		59.3	96.57535 (g)	30.9		10.3	30.3
Syria	14.2	18.8	3.9	4.6	16.78 (d)	14.25 (d)		90.9	91.6	42.7	66.5	17.7	
Tunisia	14.3	22.7	6	6.3	17.3	24.3	46.1	94.1	97.7				33.6
UAE	15	25.04606 (b)	1.9	1.10189 (b)	4.23993 (b)	5.52489 (b)		99	88.37658 (a)	59.6	81.04002 (a)	7.6	28.1
MENA	4.5	17.4	19.1	4.7	14.201665 (f)	18.496945 (f)		83.5	91.6		67.4	12.6	6.6
Low-Income	3.2	17.4		3.7					79.7		32.7	5.2	
Middle-Income	16.2	17.0	3.9	4.6				92.4	89.6		61.9	11.3	23.9
High-Income	14.3	12.4	5	5.1	19.7	25.0	27.3	95.4	96.8	84.8	90.9	46.3	68.2

Source: World Bank, World Development Indicators 2011.

Notes: a: 2006, b: 2004, c: 2003, d: 2009, e: 2007, f: 2002, g: 2010, h: 2005

outlays for education at each level (primary, secondary, tertiary), reveal a similar trend: Saudi Arabia spends far more per student at the primary level (percentage of per capita GDP) than the MENA regional average and the average of the middle-income group of countries. Nearly one-third of public spending on education is devoted to university-level education in Egypt, Jordan, and Kuwait. In Morocco, expenditures per student on tertiary education are particularly high as a percentage of GDP per capita. Per capita expenditures in the UAE are far lower in part because GDP per capita is high and many nationals go abroad for university education.

While there is limited data on equity within the education systems in the region, we can make some broad conclusions based on available data. Generally, high expenditures on education have done little to enhance and ensure potential spillover and safety net effects. Admittedly, adult and youth literacy rates have improved markedly for all countries in the region. However, greater expenditures on education have not been met by demand-side policies that raise the overall enrollment rates and supply-side policies that raise the quality of education. While the average primary school enrollment rate for MENA is higher than that of the low-income group, for a number of countries, enrollment has decreased (see Table 13.4).

Inefficiencies constrain the ability of systems to provide quality and well-targeted education in nearly all spheres of education management, including finance and delivery mechanisms. The inability of public school systems to provide students with critical high-order cognitive and analytical skills jeopardize the MENA region's international competitiveness as the countries attempt improve their economic growth record and attract investment. Government spending on public education is often highly concentrated on tertiary education and vocational training. Yet despite high expenditures, the quality of education in its current form cannot generate the caliber of employees required by the private sector. As we will see, high investments in tertiary education have not been met with positive labor market outcomes, signaling a low or even negative return to education expenditures. For instance, while enrollment rates in tertiary education has outpaced enrollment in primary and secondary schools, Iran continues to have a high level of unemployment. Moreover, the rate and the number of women enrolling in higher education institutions is higher than that of men (in 2000–2001, 88,000 men versus 90,000 women), yet women face an inordinately difficult time finding employment.[25]

While initially proportionally higher investment on tertiary education may be associated with lower unemployment rates and employment in skill-intensive jobs, such untargeted policies are in reality regressive, diverting

---

[25]United Nations (2003).

public resources from broad-based educational opportunities. Subsidies on higher education tend to produce inequitable outcomes because students who pursue university education tend to be from higher income levels. The case of Egypt provides a poignant example: It is estimated that 54% of Egypt's university-level spending accrues to the wealthiest one-third of households while only 10% goes to the poorest one-third.[26]

Employment and Labor

Initiatives that help to generate employment tend to have an equalizing effect across society—one of the core goals of the safety net. Equality of opportunity in wage-earning is one of the most important strategies for poverty reduction.[27] For many of the MENA countries, labor market distortions are one of the most formidable challenges to achieving sustainable levels of equity and poverty alleviation. According to some estimates, nearly 100 million new jobs will have to be created between the years 2000 and 2020 to keep pace with current demographic trends.[28] According to some estimates, Iran alone will have to create at least half a million new jobs per year over the next decade. The challenges presented by this growth include developing a labor market with the needed absorptive capacity and fostering human resource development that will be competitive in international and domestic markets. Successfully facing such challenges requires reforms in education and labor market policies as well as policies that generate private sector growth.

Among countries in the MENA region, the employment generation and social safety net program of choice has historically been guaranteed public sector employment. Public sector employment has created deficit-financed jobs to absorb the excess supply of labor, thereby acting as a welfare program for those who could not successfully integrate into the private sector. Even as structural reforms were implemented and economic outcomes seemed to have improved, employment and job creation in the private sector remain low, in part because the public sector continues to be the employer of last resort, resulting in significant labor market distortions.

The average unemployment rate for the MENA region as a whole is more than twice as high as the high-income country average. The high ranges from nearly 24% and 18% in Algeria and Morocco to a low of about 2% to 3% in the UAE and Kuwait. In Iran, the official unemployment rate has grown from 9% in 1996 to 12.2% in 2005 and over 15% in 2011. The rate continues to grow as a result of a population bulge between the ages of 10 to 20 and

---

[26]Doraid (2000).
[27]Roemer (1999).
[28]Hoftijzer (2006).

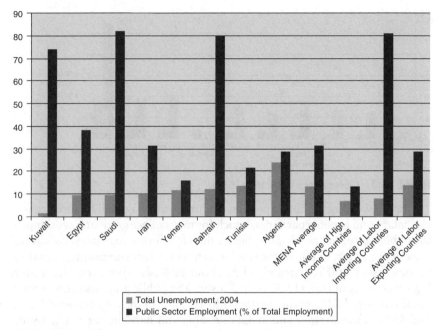

FIGURE 13.2 Employment Outcomes

women entering the workforce. This same trend can be found in many countries throughout the MENA region.

While overall total unemployment is low among the labor-importing countries of Kuwait, Qatar, Saudi Arabia, and the UAE, unemployment rates among nationals are much higher (see Figure 13.2). This may be a sign of the limited absorptive capacity of the public sector and the skill mismatch among nationals. For instance, according to 2004 estimates, the total unemployment rate in Kuwait was 1.7%; however, the unemployment among the citizen population was 4.9%. In the UAE, total unemployment was 3%, but unemployment among Emeriti citizens accounted for 11.4% of the total national labor force. Moreover, public sector employment is much higher in the rich countries of the Persian Gulf because governments are employers of last resort and use this approach for affording the general population a wasteful subsidy from depleting oil revenues.

As indicated in Figure 13.3, the wage bill consumes a high of 40% of total current expenditures in Saudi Arabia and a low of 15% in the UAE. Even for the less affluent countries in the region, a sizable portion of the government budget is committed to public sector salaries. For instance, 54% of Morocco's current expenditures are allocated toward the wage bill; in Yemen, this number is nearly 25%.

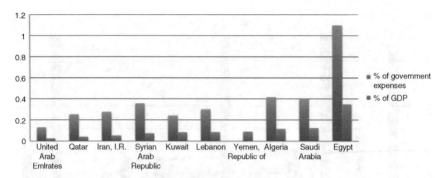

FIGURE 13.3 Government Wage Bill (2011)

In the wealthier labor-importing countries, the wage bill finances generous salary and benefits packages, which for new college graduates working in the public sector are nearly 50% higher than for those expatriates working in the private sector. Public sector employment in the labor-importing countries in the Persian Gulf is extremely high: about 80%, far above the average for high-income countries (13.5%). In Kuwait, the public administration sector alone employed 52% of the total workforce, 79% of the national workforce, and 46% of expatriates; and in Saudi Arabia and Bahrain, the public sector employs over 80% of the total labor force (see Figure 13.2).[29] Despite a high government wage bill in many countries, the trends for the labor-exporting countries are slightly different. This group of countries tends to have lower employment levels in the public sectors—on average 28.7% of total employment.

Not only do employment guarantees strive to promote the redistribution of wealth, they also attempt to protect a sizable portion of the workforce from the consequences of economic volatility. However, these policies fall short in a number of crucial ways. First, they are offered at the expense of the development of a vibrant private sector that can absorb the expanding labor capacity through legitimate market mechanisms. Second, as is the problem with other safety net policies in the region, government sector employment is extended to the more educated and wealthier groups.[30] These policies are regressive and suffer from poor targeting. Job promotions are often based on tribal affiliation. While some of the smaller and wealthier countries, such as the UAE, Qatar, and Kuwait, may have sufficient resources to pay reasonable salaries to new entrants in the government sector, this strategy results in gross inefficiencies and acts as a disincentive for citizens to seek gainful employment

---

[29]Hoftijzer (2006).
[30]Yousef (2004).

in more productive sectors of the economy and to gain skills that are actually relevant to the needs of the private sector. Statistics indicate, for instance, that only 33% of Emiratis and 66% of non-nationals who graduated from college pursued degrees in fields that were most relevant to the private sector, such as engineering, medicine, and other sciences.[31] Similarly, the Gaza Strip and Saudi Arabia had the lowest percentages of science graduates in higher education (16% and 17%, respectively) in the MENA region, while Algeria and Iran had the highest (58% and 61%, respectively).[32] Finally, wasteful subsidies financed by depletable oil and gas reserves (consumption of oil revenues as opposed to their transformation into other forms of capital) deprive the future generations from their birthright.

In more recent years, most countries in the MENA region have begun to institute a number of strategies to increase private sector employment, such as passive and active labor market policies. Some examples of reform initiatives include Saudi Arabia's Human Resource Development Fund (HRDF). The objective of HRDF is to increase private sector employment among nationals by providing temporary wage subsidies and financial assistance for training. One of the major obstacles to this approach may be that many young Saudis resist taking blue-collar jobs as a matter of social status; such attitudes first need to change.[33] In Tunisia, public works programs are also an important source of employment targeted specifically to the poor. During the years from 1987 to 1991, such programs in Tunisia employed nearly 75,000 workers per year.[34] However, evidence seems to suggest that active labor market programs have a limited effect on long-term job creation and wage growth. Moreover, jobs created by these programs are short term in nature and do little to reduce the longer-term challenges of competing in the job market. Reforms continue to need to be made in public sector employment in the areas of recruitment, linking wages and productivity, and rationalizing public sector wages and benefits.

Subsidies

Nearly all of the MENA countries provide generous universal subsidies on essential goods such as water, electricity, fuel, and food. The most common policy provision is to create a price ceiling, making goods and services more affordable to all households. There are generally no provisions for setting limits on the quantity a single consumer can purchase at the subsidized price,

---

[31] Figures are based on various International Monetary Fund reports and country data.
[32] Fergany (2000).
[33] Mellehi (2000).
[34] World Bank (2002).

nor is eligibility limited based on income. For resource-rich countries in particular, consumer subsidies and transfers are one of the most formidable mechanisms through which these countries attempt to transfer oil wealth that accrues initially to the government. But, like most safety net policies in the region, subsidies are untargeted, highly regressive, and drain public resources from those most in need. Moreover, as a result of shifts in demographic trends (population growth) and depleting oil reserves, estimates indicate that it will become increasingly difficult for these countries to support the demands for high living standards for future generations. As a result of the dramatic fall in oil prices during the 1990s, many countries in the region were forced to take on increasingly high levels of debt in an effort to maintain subsidies. The lack of fiscal sustainability plus inefficiency and regressiveness highlight the need for MENA countries to reevaluate and reform their subsidy policies.

It is crucial to understand the composition of these subsidies to evaluate their impact on poverty alleviation and income distribution. Most countries in the region spend less than 1% of GDP on cash transfers, which, if administered properly, have been found to be a far more efficient and effective safety net mechanism than subsidies, such as providing government employment or cheap electricity and water. In 2010, nearly 25% of Kuwait's budget is allocated toward public subsidies and transfers, the lion's share of these subsidy expenditures went toward water and electricity.[35] Iran's implicit fuel subsidy accounts for nearly 15.5% of GDP[36]—that is more than government expenditures on health and education combined. In contrast, very little is spent on subsidies that typically target the most vulnerable and poor or that have higher social returns (see Figure 13.4). In 2004, Iran spent only 2% of

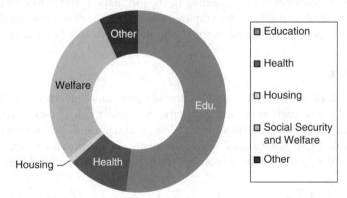

FIGURE 13.4 Total Current Expenditures on Social Services for Iran 2002–2003

---

[35] Statistics based on various IMF reports and country data.
[36] Ibid.

GDP on subsidies for welfare and social security, and both Qatar and Saudi Arabia spent less than 1% of total expenditures on social services (subsidies). Similarly, while it is estimated that Syria's fuel subsidies could grow to be 14.5% of GDP, it allocated only 1.1% of GDP to social assistance programs (including its pension system). Yemen currently spends nearly 5% of GDP on subsidies—equivalent to its expenditures on health. With that said, Yemen has also made substantial progress in reducing its overall subsidy bill, which in 1996 reached a high of 18% of total expenditures and over 7% of GDP.

In the case of subsidies, the price of domestically produced commercial goods (e.g., energy) is set considerably below market levels. Since consumption is generally higher among wealthier segments of the population, a higher portion of the subsidy accrues to them. The leakage rate for Iran's fuel subsidy—that is, the proportion of the subsidy transferred to the economically more advantaged—is 94% in that nation's urban areas and 89% in its rural areas.[37] Moreover, of the poorest 10% of households, less than half receive general welfare benefits in cash or in kind and only one-quarter of assistance accrues to the second poorest segment of the population. Similarly, Syria's policies on fuel subsidies have also created inequitable outcomes. According to some estimates, the richest population deciles benefit 25 times more that the poorest deciles, while the poorest half of the population captures less than 20% of total benefits.[38] In addition to being regressive, subsidies have resulted in illegal smuggling to neighboring countries. At the height of Yemen's subsidy program, only one-third of the subsidy actually reached consumers; the rest was captured by importers, distributors, and smugglers in neighboring countries.

More recently, authorities in Iran instituted reforms to the fuel subsidies in an attempt to reduce the fiscal burden and the environmental degradation caused by overconsumption.[39] The program offers a "smart card" to all car owners, fixing the subsidized fuel allowance and forcing consumers to pay market prices when consumption exceeds the amount rationed.[40] The scheme has shortcomings. The very poor have no cars, while others exchange their smart cards for cash or other goods at a disadvantageous exchange ratio. Moreover, economic inefficiencies associated with high administrative costs and leakages to the economically more advantaged could be mitigated if the

---

[37]Iqbal (2006).

[38]Various IMF reports and country data.

[39]Universal fuel and energy subsidies have resulted in some of the worst environmental degradation and pollution in the world. According to the World Resources Institute, Tehran is one of the most polluted cities in the world as a result of excessive fuel consumption.

[40]World Bank (2006).

public was simply provided with cash transfers and gasoline prices were raised to prevailing world market prices.

Reforms

How can the countries in the MENA region better address the needs of the disadvantaged in an Islamic context? An effective, efficient, and equitable social safety net should include three main elements: (1) a well-targeted provision for health and education; (2) a self-funded social security system providing coverage for all workers; and (3) government-funded programs that protect the vulnerable and poor from facing excessive risk. Individual reforms that develop better targeting mechanisms, reduce wasteful government expenditures on subsidies and employment guarantees, and improve education and human resources capacity are an indispensable basis for creating an Islamic safety net system. However, such reforms will have to be slow and progressive, given considerable political constraints. Moreover, reform must be compatible with preexisting economic conditions, social institutions, and cultural realities.

There seems to be a general assumption that all countries in the MENA region have access to vast amounts of oil revenues to fund safety net programs. However, this is far from the case. As indicated in Table 13.5, the smaller, less densely populated countries in the Persian Gulf have greater access to energy reserves. Yemen, Egypt, and Tunisia may be rich in oil (natural gas), but on a per capita basis reserves are quite small. In Jordan and Lebanon, there are no oil reserves. And yet one cannot ignore the reality that natural resource endowments present a unique opportunity for some countries to strengthen the welfare of their citizens. For the major oil-exporting countries, the capacity to address issues of economic vulnerability should be made more tenable by the sheer access to oil and gas revenues. For this group of countries, oil, a depletable resource, must benefit all generations, and governments must proceed with this fact in mind.

For the broad citizenry to take seriously any proposition regarding the management of exhaustible resources, it must be compatible with basic Islamic teachings on ownership rights of depletable resources and the role of the state. Islam is very clear in its treatment of land and in the depletion of minerals. In the specific case of resources below the ground, Islam is unambiguous. Anything underground belongs to society at large; that is, all citizens should have an equal share in the fruit of what is under the land. This incorporates both current and all future generations. A relevant and touchy issue is to what extent these resources should be shared with other countries.

The major oil exporters in the region have an additional means to address the needs of all members of society, especially the disadvantaged. They can

TABLE 13.5 Oil Exports and Per Capita Proven Reserves

	Oil Products Exports: 1,000 Metric Tons Oil Equivalent, 2003	Proven Oil and Gas Reserves: Sustaining Gains in Poverty Reduction Barrel Oil Equivalent per Capita, 2004
Qatar	32,418	788,564
UAE	112,304	187,754
Kuwait	97,869	115,384
Saudi Arabia	40,0189	18,442
Libya	59,366	6,862
Iraq	43,256	5,616
Oman	41,702	5,074
Iran	133,395	4,753
Bahrain	12,378	1,290
Algeria	73,233	389
Syrian	17,217	173
Yemen	17,805	144
Tunisia	3,207	69
Egypt	9,524	54
Jordan	0	0
Lebanon	0	0
Morocco	849	N/A

Source: Statistics on oil products exports: World Resources Institute. Figures for proven oil reserves: barrels oil equivalent/per capita are based on author's calculations, using data from *British Petroleum Statistical Year Book* and World Development Indicators.

Notes: Excludes Israel and Malta; data for Djibouti is unavailable. Per capita figures for the Gulf Cooperation Council countries based on national population. All statistics based on oil equivalents.

use current oil and gas revenues directly, but this solution may not benefit future generations. Alternatively, they can use oil revenues to establish an oil fund and use the earnings from the fund to meet social needs and possibly to supplement the income of even the nondisadvantaged while treating all generations equitably.[41] While this may be a solution for the richer countries in the Persian Gulf, it would have to be combined with more active safety net provisions in the case of the more populated countries (Algeria, Egypt, Iran, and Saudi Arabia), and it is of course irrelevant to the resource-poor countries

---

[41] See Hossein and Arfaa (2007). Also see Askari, Abbas, Jabbour, and Kwon (2006) for the mathematical derivation of the required annual transfers from oil and gas revenues and the estimated size of payments in these six countries.

in the region. For these latter more populous countries, an effective progressive income tax is an absolute necessity to address equity issues and to support government programs.

While many countries in the region do not have vast oil reserves, cash transfers are still a viable policy option to help alleviate poverty and to keep the poor from falling deeper into poverty. Of course, the devil is in the details, and how these mechanisms actually are designed and administered is crucial, as such programs have failed to increase welfare in many instances. However, there are also positive examples within and outside the region. For instance, in Jordan, after the economic crisis of 1989, the government decided to replace widely used subsidies with a means-tested cash payment program administered by the National Aid Fund (NAF). The number of NAF beneficiaries grew from 8,000 households in 1987 to 66,000 in 2002. Furthermore, nearly 7.4% of the population was able to access this assistance program in 2002, as opposed to 2.6% earlier. While poverty rates did grow following the crisis, empirical evidence seems to suggest that Jordan's cash transfer program had a crucial role in relieving poverty during the latter half of the 1990s.[42] As described in Box 13.1, a number of Latin American countries have found success with conditional cash transfers.

BOX 13.1 LATIN AMERICA: CONDITIONAL CASH TRANSFERS

The objective of the conditional cash transfer (CCT) in Brazil is to reduce poverty by transferring cash to poor families while also mitigating the generational effects of poverty. Beneficiaries of the Bolsa Familia program are required to have their children vaccinated, their health monitored, and to be enrolled in school. Part of Bolsa Famlia's success can be attributed to the government's efforts to streamline various safety net provisions previously administered by various federal agencies into a more consolidated system. Moreover, the task of monitoring the program's implementation has been relegated to the local community, thus increasing efficiency. Evidence of progress can be seen by the increase in the number of children attending school. Under the old initiative, only 19% of schools reported that children of beneficiaries were regularly attending classes; however, under the new program the number of children has increased to 79%.

---

[42] Various IMF country reports.

Mexico launched a similar CCT program in 1997 called Oportunidades, which provides cash transfers to nearly 5 million households (consisting of about one-fourth of Mexico's population). Payments made to female heads of households are conditional upon child school attendance and grades as well as the family's regular visit to health clinics. The rapid expansion of Oportunidades helped Mexico reduce poverty levels even during the country's economic downturn from 2000 to 2002. Indicators suggest that during that period, extreme poverty was reduced from 15.2% to 12.6%. These results challenge standard notions that there must be social costs in the wake of economic crises in the developing world.

Source: "Anti-Poverty Schemes in Latin America," *Economist*, September 16, 2005.

In addition to the establishment of cash transfer programs and individual reforms, a broader and more progressive tax base that raises government revenues efficiently and fairly would help to increase the overall sustainability of the current safety net while improving intergenerational equity. Islam envisages and endorses a system of taxation where revenues are used to fulfill basic social needs. Yet most of the countries in the MENA region lack an effective income tax system. While reforms to the existing safety net policies and institutions, including the introduction of cash transfers, are essential, these reforms cannot replace the critical element of developing the human resource capacity of the region.

SUMMARY

Policies in the Middle East and North African have not broadly reflected the social welfare principles enunciated in Islam. The Quran and the *Sunnah* provide both normative and ethical guidance on how to develop a fair economic order—with justice at the center of the paradigm. Islam clearly demands that basic needs be met, that equality of opportunity be achieved, and that depletable resources be used to benefit all members of current and future generations equitably.

While governments in the region, particularly those in the oil-exporting countries, may have designed safety net mechanisms that meet the basic needs of some of their population, such policies cannot be said to be fully Islamic for a number of reasons. Perhaps most crucially, state paternalism comes at enormous social and political costs. The combination of universalized, untargeted, and regressive subsidies and high expenditures and poor quality services results in a safety net system that is inefficient and wasteful. Finally, those institutional features of an Islamic economic system, such as *zakat*, that do exist are poorly administered. Many throughout the Muslim world have lost confidence in the ability of these institutions to alleviate poverty and distribute income equitably in order to establish societies that are just, as required by Islam.

KEY TERMS

Safety net	*Khums*
Ethics	Employment
Poverty	Healthcare
Wealth distribution	Education
Income distribution	Unemployment benefits
Sadaqa	Subsidies
Qardh hassan	Reforms
Zakat	Microfinance

QUESTIONS

1. What is the purpose of a safety net?
2. What are the elements of a comprehensive safety net?
3. Do you think that a safety net should be an integral element of a caring and ethical society?
4. How should governments finance safety nets?
5. Detail the safety net measures prescribed in Islam.
6. Given the importance of work in Islam, how important is the achievement of full employment and a just wage?
7. Do safety nets reduce work incentives?
8. Do you agree with minimum wage legislation? Why or why not? Does minimum wage legislation violate Islamic principles?
9. What kinds of subsidies are most efficient?

CHAPTER 14

Economic State of Affairs in OIC Countries

Learning objectives:

1. *The common elements of development in the conventional and the Islamic system.*
2. *The role of the concept of* ummah *in Islam.*
3. *How to measure key objectives of Islamic law* (maqasid-al-Shariah).
4. *The actual performance of Islamic countries in comparison to Islam's ideal concept of economic and social justice.*

In the Islamic economic system, the government is empowered to undertake all programs that are helpful to the development and the well-being of the community (*ummah*), where collective action, as opposed to individual action, is called for and when individuals fail in their duty to follow the rules laid down by the Almighty and to confront and stand up to transgressors and oppressors. Thus the central purpose of public policy is to promote the goals of a healthy society where individuals can flourish and develop as envisaged in the Quran and implemented by the Prophet (sawa) in Medina.

In the realm of human economic pursuits, Islam encourages economic prosperity and development. Islam embraces capitalism, but capitalism with a strong dose of morality and justice—the type of capitalism advocated by Adam Smith in his less quoted book, *The Theory of Moral Sentiments*. But Islam goes much further in stressing the foundation of justice and the practice of equity in everything on this plane of existence. In fact, to our mind, the absence of morality, fairness, and justice is the Achilles' heel of today's capitalist system, as being played out in the global crisis that has enveloped the world since 2007. It is a crisis that will continue for many years to come, not only because of economic and financial mismanagement but because of injustice, human selfishness, and inept public policies.

In Islam, public policy embraces these areas:

- Public sector governance (accountability, efficiency, stability, regulatory and supervisory quality, enforcement, and absence of corruption and violence)
- Integrity of the legal system (judicial independence and impartial courts)
- Preservation of human freedom
- Absence of all discrimination (gender, religious, ethnic, sectarian, and tribal)
- Preservation of the environment (water, air, biodiversity and habitat, and treatment of depletable resources as capital)
- Promotion of all policies that promote economic and social prosperity in line with the Islamic vision

In this chapter, we focus on the public policies and priorities that deal most directly with economic prosperity and how successfully they have been implemented in Muslim countries.

PUBLIC POLICY IN THE ISLAMIC ECONOMIC SYSTEM

All public policies shape economic developments in a community. The direct policies needed to support development in the Islamic economic system are those that are targeted to achieving the Islamic vision, which consists of these areas:

- Freedom for all members of society to pursue their economic interests
- Economic justice for humans of all generations while preserving the interests of all living creatures
- Equal opportunity (education, healthcare, and equality before the law) to succeed
- Provision of good jobs for all who can and want to work
- Personal property rights and sanctity of contracts
- Equitable distribution of income and wealth
- Poverty eradication
- Basic need fulfillment of food, shelter, and clothing when private alms giving is insufficient

- Management of natural and depletable resources to benefit all members of current and future generations
- Abolition of corrupt practices
- Supportive financial system that excludes debt and interest
- Minimum level of public debt (of course, not tied to interest)

Given the Islamic preoccupation with individual *rights* as well as *obligations*, the role of the state (Chapter 9) should be minimal in an Allah (swt)-conscious and law-abiding community. Humans aware of the rules set out in Islam would abide by them and do all that they can to ensure that all members of society are rule compliant because they realize that life on this plane of existence is merely a test for the Judgment Day that all must face. If a community follows the set rules, it will thrive. State policies and intervention are thus only needed as collective action because individual action is not possible—in areas such as construction of infrastructure, safeguarding the interests of future generations, establishing and implementing a just legal system, and providing for national defense—or when individual humans have not complied with the set rules and society needs state intervention to get back on the right path.

It is almost impossible to measure and assess the adherence of Muslim countries to all these Islamic teachings on economic governance and management. However, we can get an indirect insight into some of these areas, including those listed next:

- Quality of institutions
- Quality of governance
- Market freedom (for goods, labor, and financial markets)
- Economic freedom
- Corruption elimination
- Progress in poverty eradication
- Overall income distribution
- Prevalence of wealth hoarding
- Quality and availability of education
- Employment opportunities
- Equity of benefits derived from natural resource depletion
- Independence, effectiveness, and fairness of the legal system
- Level of private and public debt

The brief discussion that follows assesses the broad performance of members of the Organisation of Islamic Cooperation (OIC) countries in some of these objectives that are important elements stressed in the Islamic system—education, gender, health, income (wealth), inequality, poverty, and environment/sustainability—relative to other country groupings.

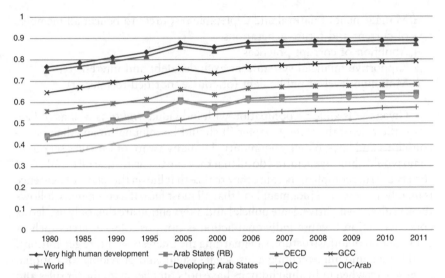

FIGURE 14.1 UN Human Development Index Trends for Groups of Muslim Countries and Non-Muslim Comparator Groups
Source: United Nations Development Programme, Human Development Reports, "Human Development Index," http://hdr.undp.org/en/statistics/hdi.
Note: The UN Human Development Index measures development by combining the three dimensions of health, education, and living standards into a composite index, which is expressed as a number between 0 and 1.

DIMENSIONS OF ECONOMIC AND SOCIAL ACHIEVEMENTS IN MUSLIM COUNTRIES

In Figure 14.1, we show a 30-year trend of overall human development for the OIC countries in comparison to other regional and country groupings.[1] We use the United Nation's Human Development Index (HDI), which is a composite of three indexes: the Education Index, the Health (Life Expectancy)

---

[1] The figures are based on three papers: Scheherazade Rehman and Hossein Askari, "How Islamic Are Islamic Countries?" *Global Economy Journal* 10 (May 2010): 1–37. Scheherazade Rehman and Hossein Askari, "An Economic Islamicity Index," *Global Economy Journal* 10 (September 2010): 1–37. Hossein Askari and Scheherazade Rehman, "The Economic Development of OIC Countries: A Survey," in *Islamic Finance and Economic Development*, edited by Zamir Iqbal and Abbas Mirakhor (Washington, DC: World Bank, 2013), pp. 299–324.

Index, and the Income (Wealth) Index.[2] It is clear that over a long period of time, the OIC countries have consistently underperformed relative to the world average in broad-based economic and social development. What stands out in the figure is that the OIC countries as a group have consistently underperformed many other country groupings. However, a subset of the OIC, the six countries of the Gulf Cooperation Council (GCC)—Bahrain, Kuwait, Oman, Qatar, Saudi Arabia, and the United Arab Emirates—have performed above the world average (although still below the countries from the Organisation for Economic Co-operation and Development [OECD]) over this same 30-year period.

In Figure 14.2, we display the 30-year educational progress of the OIC countries as measured by the UN Education Index.[3] Education is generally accepted as a major input into economic growth and development. Moreover, "education" (including its attributes, such as "knowledge") is the second most often repeated word in the Quran and was also repeatedly stressed by the Prophet (sawa) during His lifetime. Over the last 30 years, it would appear that OIC performance has been consistently well below the world average. It should again be noted that a subset—the GCC countries—has performed above the world average but has still remained well below the OECD average.

The empowerment of women and gender equality are key to achieving a healthy and sustainable economic and social development. They not only promote economic efficiency but, as the World Bank notes, aid in enhancing other types of development by "removing barriers that prevent women from having the same access as men to human resource endowments, rights, and

---

[2] As explained on the United Nations Development Programme Human Development Reports (HDR)Web site, "The scores for [these] three HDI dimension indices are then aggregated into a composite index using geometric mean" (http://hdr.undp.org/en/statistics/hdi).

[3] According to the HDR Web site, the Education Index of the human development index (HDI) is "measured by mean of years of schooling for adults aged 25 years and expected years of schooling for children of school entering age. Mean years of schooling is estimated based on educational attainment data from censuses and surveys available in the UNESCO Institute for Statistics database and Barro and Lee (2010) methodology. Expected years of schooling estimates are based on enrolment by age at all levels of education and population of official school age for each level of education. Expected years of schooling are capped at 18 years. The indicators are normalized using a minimum value of zero, and maximum values are set to the actual observed maximum value of mean years of schooling from the countries in the time series, 1980 to 2010. Expected years of schooling are capped at 18 years. The Education Index is the geometric mean of two indices" (http://hdr.undp.org/en/statistics/hdi).

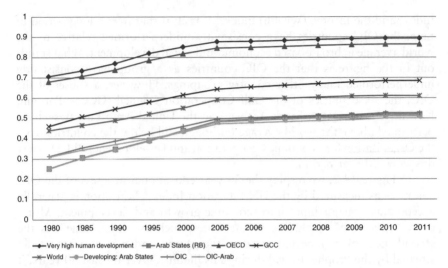

FIGURE 14.2 UN Index of Education Achievement for Groups of Muslim Countries and Non-Muslim Comparator Groups
Source: United Nations Development Programme, Human Development Reports, "Human Development Index," (http://hdr.undp.org/en/statistics/hdi).
Note: The UN Human Education Index measures the adult literacy rate (with a two-thirds weight) and the combined primary, secondary, and tertiary gross enrollment ratio (with a one-third weight). The adult literacy rate gives an indication of the ability to read and write, while the tertiary gross enrollment ratio gives an indication of the level of education from nursery school and kindergarten to postgraduate education. The Education Index is expressed as a number between 0 and 1.

economic opportunities. Giving women access to equal opportunities allows them to emerge as social and economic actors, influencing and shaping more inclusive policies. Improving women's status also leads to more investment in their children's education, health, and overall wellbeing."[4] In Figure 14.3, we measure how active women are in the labor force.[5] When it comes to women's participation in the workforce and in the economy, the OIC countries have fared much better than the Arab region of the OIC—particularly the GCC countries. The gender performance of OIC countries, excluding the Arab countries, has been almost consistently above the world average and that of

---

[4]The World Bank, Data, Gender, Gender Equality Data & Statistics (http://data.worldbank.org/topic/gender).
[5]Gender equality measures how active women are in the labor force by calculating the average of the labor force rate, female rate (percentage of female population ages 15 plus), and labor participation rate (percentage of total labor force).

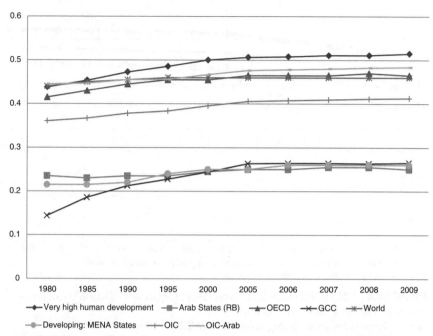

FIGURE 14.3 Gender Inequality (Labor Force Participation) for Groups of Muslim Countries and Non-Muslim Comparator Groups
Source: The World Bank, Data, Gender, Gender Equality Data & Statistics (http:// data.worldbank.org/topic/gender).
Notes: The data represent the average participation of females (ages 15 plus) in the total labor force.
MENA = Middle East and North Africa

the OECD countries, but the performance of the Arab countries in fostering gender equality is disturbing, namely, it lags well behind the world average and all regions.

To assess progress in addressing health issues over time, we use the UN Health Index, measuring life expectancy at birth. Human health conditions in the OIC countries are far below world standards (see Figure 14.4).[6] In this indicator, the Arab countries have consistently performed better than the non-Arab OIC countries.

---

[6]The life expectancy at birth component of the HDI is calculated using a minimum value of 20 years and maximum value of 83.4 years. This is the observed maximum value of the indicators from the countries in the time series, 1980 to 2010. Thus, the longevity component for a country where life expectancy birth is 55 years would be 0.552 (http://hdrstats.undp.org/en/indicators/72206.html).

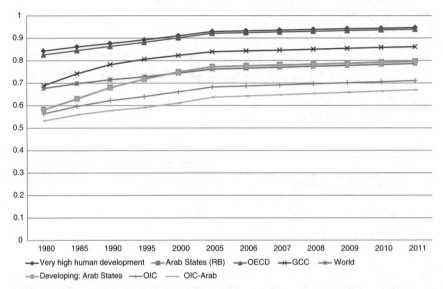

FIGURE 14.4 UN Health Index (Life Expectancy) for Groups of Muslim Countries and Non-Muslim Comparator Groups
Source: http://hdrstats.undp.org/en/indicators/72206.html.
Notes: The UN Health Index measures life expectancy at birth. The Health Index is expressed as a number between 0 and 1.

To assess the income or wealth of a region, we use the Income (or Wealth) Index of the United Nations.[7] The Income Index measures the living standards of countries in terms of gross national income (GNI) per capita in terms of purchasing power parity in U.S. dollars (PPP$). The results can be seen in Figure 14.5. Overall OIC living standards are well below those of the developing Arab countries, as the per capita income of the GCC countries is on par with the highly developed countries of the world and the OECD. To get a more comprehensive picture of the wealth of various regional and country groupings, we also examine income and wealth distribution. Again, as we have said many times before, economic and social justice is at the heart of the Islamic system—equity and the eradication of poverty are absolutely central.

---

[7] "For the wealth component, the goalpost for minimum income is US$100 (PPP) and the maximum is US$107,721 (PPP), both estimated during the same period, 1980–2011. The decent standard of living component is measured by GNI per capita (PPP$) instead of GDP per capita (PPP$). The HDI uses the logarithm of income to reflect the diminishing importance of income with increasing GNI," United Nations Development Programme, Human Development Reports (http://hdr.undp.org/en/statistics/hdi).

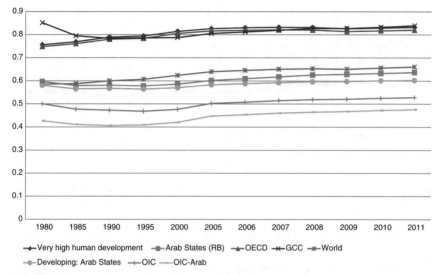

FIGURE 14.5 UN Income (Wealth) Index for Groups of Muslim Countries and Non-Muslim Comparator Groups

Source: http://hdr.undp.org/en/data-explorer.

Notes: The UN Income (Wealth) Index measures GNI per capita (PPP$). The Income Index is expressed as a value between 0 and 1.

In Figure 14.6, we present the Gini coefficient of the regional and country groupings. The information concerning the Gini coefficient is mixed because of missing data and, as a result, may be somewhat misleading. Although this should not negate the fact that income disparity in the OECD countries has risen and is now on par with that of the developing and emerging world, it should be underscored that income disparity in the OIC group, and in the Arab region, has remained constant over the last 30 years. To gain further insight into the overall income-wealth picture of various regional and country groupings, it may be helpful to look into prevailing poverty levels.[8] In Figure 14.7, we display the poverty levels, as measured

---

[8] Poverty is measured by the Poverty Headcount Ratio at US$1.25 a day (PPP) (percentage of population). These countries had no data available for any category in the Poverty Index: Brunei Darussalem, Kuwait, Lebanon, Libya, Oman, Saudi Arabia, Somalia, United Arab Emirates, and the West Bank and Gaza. Data from United Nationals Development Programme, Human Development Reports (http://hdr.undp .org) and World DataBank (http://databank.worldbank.org).

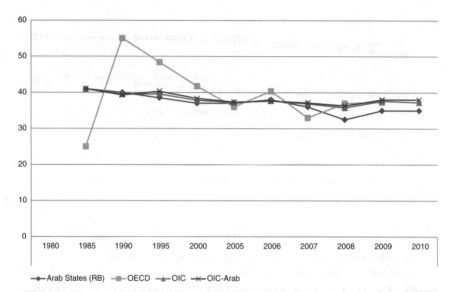

FIGURE 14.6 Gini Coefficient (Income Distribution) for Groups of Muslim Countries and Non-Muslim Comparator Groups
Source: The World Bank, Poverty & Equity Data (http://povertydata.worldbank.org/poverty/home).
Notes: The data represent the Gini coefficient. These countries had no available data: Brunei Darussalem, Kuwait, Lebanon, Libya, Oman, Saudi Arabia, Somalia, United Arab Emirates, and the West Bank and Gaza. Data for Iceland were also not available and thus not calculated with the OECD country grouping. Because data were missing for 1995 for the OECD countries, the data were derived by averaging the 1990 and 2000 data points.

by the percentage of the population that lives on US$1.25 (PPP) or less per day, in various regions and county groupings.

Because of data limitations, we were not able to assess environmental management over time. We can only examine the latest available data for the Environmental Performance Index (EPI) for 2010 (see Figure 14.8). The "overall EPI rankings provide an indicative sense of which countries are doing best against the array of environmental pressures that every nation faces."[9] It represents both the environmental health and the ecosystem vitality

---

[9]The 2010 Environmental Performance Index was developed by the Yale Center for Environmental Law and Policy and the Center for International Earth Science Information Network at Columbia University in collaboration with the World Economic Forum and the Joint Research Center of the European Commission (http://www.carboun.com/wp-content/uploads/2010/04/EPI-2010-Full-report.pdf).

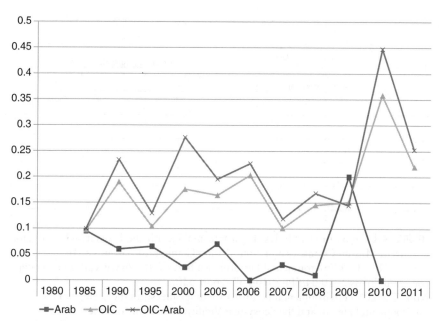

FIGURE 14.7 Poverty (Living on US$1.25 per Day as a Percentage of Total Population) for Groups of Muslim Countries and Non-Muslim Comparator Groups
Sources: United Nations Development Programme, Human Development Reports (http://hdr.undp.org) and World DataBank (http://databank.worldbank.org).
Note: The Poverty Headcount Ratio measures poverty at US$1.25 a day (PPP) (as a percentage of the population).

of countries. The OIC countries trail the world when it comes to environmental responsibilities.

As we have emphasized a number of times, there is little evidence to attribute the subpar economic performance of Muslim countries to Islamic teachings. Just because countries that profess Islam have had subpar economic performance does not mean that Islamic teachings are the basis for their failure. To the contrary, as discussed, Islamic teachings are fully supportive of sustained growth and prosperity and hold as central tenets efficient and sound institutions, free markets, market supervision, sound governance, equal opportunity, sanctity of honestly earned income and wealth, rule enforcement, transparency in all business dealings, the importance of education and good health, poverty eradication, financial stability (by embracing equity as opposed to debt financing), admonitions against corruption and hoarding, and so on.[10] In

---

[10] For detailed discussion of this point, see Mirakhor and Askari (2010).

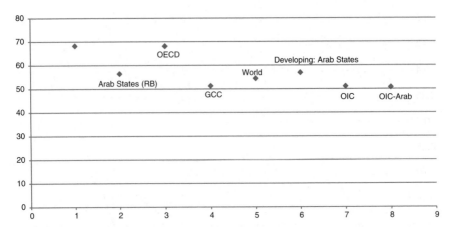

FIGURE 14.8 Environment Index (Environmental Health and Ecosystem Vitality) for
Groups of Muslim Countries and Non-Muslim Comparator Groups 2010
Source: The 2010 Environmental Performance Index (http://www.carboun.com/wp-
content/uploads/2010/04/EPI-2010-Full-report.pdf).
Note: The 2010 Environmental Performance Index measures the average of the
Environmental Health and the Ecosystem Vitality Indexes of countries.

fact, it can be argued that Islamic teachings on economic development and
growth are similar to the foundational elements of capitalism, as espoused by
Adam Smith, which are the evolving recommendations of modern economic
development theories—but with a strong dose of justice.

SUMMARY

The Islamic goal for society is to develop and grow on the basis of Allah's (swt)
Divine rules and the guidance provided by the Prophet (sawa). If humans follow
His rules, development and growth would be balanced—political freedom,
freedom of choice, trustworthy society, equal opportunities for all with the
preservation of all rights of the disabled, equality of religion, race and gender,
no extremes of wealth or poverty, good jobs for all those who can work,
provision of a dignified life for the disadvantaged and the disabled, and
preservation of the rights of all humans of every generation in the environment
and the natural resources bestowed by Allah (swt). If humans follow His rules,
they would develop and grow beyond their wildest dreams, be spiritually
fulfilled, be materially satisfied, share with other humans and remove stumbling
blocks to their development and fulfillment, be exhilarated by life in a just
society, and experience the embrace of Allah's (swt) unity of creation. Allah's

(swt) prescription from about 1,400 years ago of rules, rule compliance, and effective institutions is valid for all time. Conventional economic thinking, since the writings of Adam Smith, has arrived at a similar point but unfortunately without the scaffolding of sharing, ethical behavior, and justice.

In the West, the issue of justice has taken on increasing importance in the last 40 or so years as a result of John Rawls's seminal contributions (*A Theory of Justice*, 1971) to advancing the conception of justice and to a vast body of empirical economic analysis showing the shameful and growing disparity of wealth and income between the haves and the have-nots. While Rawls's theory has not been operationalized into rules that could be implemented, let alone practiced anywhere, the rules laid down in Islam about 1,400 years ago were designed to develop a system that had justice at its foundation. If these rules are followed, justice would be established with "everything in its right place" and everyone "receiving their just due."

KEY TERMS

Human development	Poverty
Economic development	Wealth
Equality	Environment
Gender equality	Justice
Growth	Rules
Education	Institutions

QUESTIONS

1. How would you describe the current state of human and economic development in Muslim countries?
2. To what do you attribute the achievements or underachievements in Muslim countries?
3. Do you think that conditions would be very different if Muslims and Muslim rulers had followed the rules prescribed in Islam?
4. What reforms do you suggest?
5. How can Muslim countries begin to develop effective institutions?
6. Where should Muslim countries begin to reform their economies?
7. Have colonial powers played a destructive role in the socioeconomic development of Muslim countries? Why or why not? Explain your answer

Glossary of Arabic Terms

A'mal salih Righteous work. Rule-compliant work.

Ábd Servant-adorer.

Ádl 'dalah Justice, balance.

Ahadeeth Reported sayings or actions of the Messenger (singular *hadeeth*).

Akhlaq Moral ethical disposition.

Al-amal Work in Islam.

Al-Ameen The one who is trustworthy.

Al Amr A command or a decree.

Al-amr bil-ma'ruf wa Al-nahy 'an il munkar Commanding the good and forbidding the evil. Encouraging rule compliance and discouraging rule violation.

Al-Faridhatu Al-Ádilah The just duties.

Al-Insan-ul-Kamil Perfected human being.

Al-Rahman The Universally Merciful Allah.

Al-riba Interest rate.

Al-Sunnatu Al-Qa'imah The established tradition.

Amanah Trust.

Áqd Agreement, contract.

Áql Contemplative intelligence. The root verb also means "to restrain" or "to withhold." To indicate restraint on impulsive action or response.

Aslamtu I have delivered myself into safety/security (comes from *Salám*) of Allah (swt).

Ayah Sign; something that stands in relation to something else such that cognizance of the sign leads to the cognizance of the thing represented by the sign.

Ayatu Al-Muhkamah Firm signs.

Baraka Blessings (plural *barakat*).

Bay' Exchange.

Bay'ah A contract between the person who is deemed worthy of accession (who has demonstrated full compliance with prescribed rules) to the office according to the first dimension of legitimacy and the members of the community.

Bay' al-muajjil Sales contract with deferred payment.

Bay' salám Sales contract with deferred delivery.

Dayn Debt.

Deen A way of living; obedience to a set of rules of behavior; a way of conduct in service of something or someone. It covers customs, habits, religion, ideology, cosmology, praxis, conduct, and rules of behavior (institutions).

Du'a Prayer.

Fadl Grace or blessing from Allah (swt).

GLOSSARY OF ARABIC TERMS

Falah   Success and salvation.

Fiqh   Knowledge of issues regarding jurisprudence.

Fitrah   The primordial nature of humans.

Fuqaha   Jurists (singular *faqih*).

Gharar   Excessive information; asymmetry in a contract or exposure to excessive risk.

Hajr   Sequestration of property due to violation of rule compliance (e.g., wasting of resources at one's disposal).

Halal   Permissible.

Haram   Unlawful.

Hawa   Whim and caprice.

Hayat Tayyibah   Purified, blissful life that results from complete rule compliance.

Hijra   The migration of the Prophet (sawa) and his followers from Mecca to Medina until AH 450 (AD 1058).

Hisab   Account.

Ibadah   Worship; acts of communion; connotes both adoration and service (singular *ibadat*).

Ihsan   Acts of beneficence; *mohsin*: a person whose actions become acts of beneficence.

Ihtikar   Hoarding of commodities and productive resources from the market for the purpose of pushing up the prices.

Ijarah   Leasing contract.

Ijma'   Consensus of jurists.

Ijtihad   From the root *jahd*, meaning "struggle."

Ikrah hukmi   Aversive ruling.

Ílm   Knowledge (plural *ulum*).

Imamah   The principle of governance in which the Imam as the leader of the society is fully rule compliant.

Imamate   Temporal and spiritual leadership of the society.

Iman   A word derived from the verb *amina*, meaning safety and security

Iman   The position associated with entrance into the sanctuary of safety and security of Allah (swt).

Infaq   Expenditures.

Insan   Human.

Iqta'iddar   Devoting land for building houses.

Israf   Extravagance.

Istihsan   Judicial preference.

Isti'mar   Physical development of the earth.

Istisna   Consignment or contract to manufacture or develop an asset.

Itlaf   Wasting, destruction.

Itraf   Opulence.

Jannah   Paradise.

Jihad   Struggle.

Jo'ala   Offering a service for a predetermined fee or commission.

Karamah   Human dignity.

Khairat   Benevolent contribution.

Kharaj   Taxes and rents on public lands used by private producers.

Khilafa Agency trustee.

Khilafah Agent/trustee.

Khisarah Probability of loss.

Khums Means one-fifth of income (Chapter 8 of the Quran) given to the Messenger or his legitimate successor for the expenditure and transfer payments.

Khyar Haywan When the subjects of the negotiations were pack animals, the buyer had the right to return the animal up to three days after the deal was consumed.

Khyar Majlis When sellers and buyers could terminate negotiation before leaving the location in which the negotiation is taking place.

Khyar Moddah When a delivery period was specified but the product was not delivered on time.

Khyar Qashsh When the buyer discovers that the quality of the product is not what was expected.

Khyar Rou'yah When a buyer has not seen the commodity subject of the negotiation but after seeing it finds it unacceptable.

Khyar Shart When the side conditions that were specified during the negotiations were left unfulfilled.

Kifala Suretyship or guarantee contract.

Kufr Rejection of faith. Covering of truth.

La dharar wa la dhirar No harm no injury.

Ma'rifa Intimate knowledge gained through struggle (*jihad*) to become fully rule compliant.

Maád The return of creation to its origin and accountability of humanity (individually and collectively) for acts of commission and omission, success, and failure in achieving, establishing, upholding justice toward their selves, others of their kind, and the rest of creation.

Madhahib Schools of thought.

Mafsada Disutility.

Maqasid Objectives.

Maqasid-al-Shariah The key objectives of *Shariah*.

Maslaha Utility.

Maslahah Society's interests; public interest.

Maysir Speculative risk.

Meethaq Covenant; the Primordial Covenant that all humans were called before their Supreme Creator and asked to testify that they recognize in Him as the One and Only Creator and Sustainer of the entire Creation and all other implications flowing from this testimony.

Millah Belief.

Mu'min Someone who has entered the sanctuary.

Muamalat Transactions.

Mubadilah al-maal bi al-maal Exchange of property with property.

Mubayaá Political allegiance; a contract between the ruler and the community that the leader will be rule-compliant in the discharge of the duties of the office (from the word *bay'ah*).

Mudarib Asset/investment manager.

Mudharabah A contract between a capital provider (*rab-al-mal*) and an asset manager (*mudarib*) with the profits and losses shared according to the contractual agreement.

Muhkam Unambiguous.

Muhtasib Person in charge of holding market participants to accountability.

Musharakah An equity partnership where partners participate in risk-sharing contract.

Nafaqa A man's financial support for his wife.

Nisab A minimum amount of wealth to qualify for *zakat*.

Niyyah Intent combined with commitment to a rule-complying action.

Nubbowah Prophecy; the continuous chain of humans appointed by the Creator to remind, warn, cleanse, teach, and induce humans to bring about and uphold justice within the created order through their position of agency-trustee assigned and empowered by the Supreme Creator.

Qaba'il Tribes.

Qaflah Negligence, inattention, and carelessness.

Qardh Hassan A beautiful loan (interest free).

Qaum People.

Qhay Deep ignorance.

Qist Mutual and interrelational justice among humans and between them and the rest of creation.

Qiyas Analogy.

Rabb or Allah The Cherisher Lord.

Rasheed Someone who is making progress on the path to perfection.

Rububiyyah The manifestation of the actions of the *Rabb* expressing the twin ideas of "cherishing" and "Lordship."

Ruh Spirit.

Rushd Enlightened (opposite of *qhay*).

Sadaqa From the root word meaning "truthfulness" and "sincerity" (plural *sadaqat*). Transfer payments for the purpose of relieving monetary constraints on those in need.

Sadaqat Payments to redeem others' rights and a demonstration of the veracity of one's claim to Islamicity.

Sakiynah Tranquility.

Sakk Certificate of ownership.

Salaam Sales contract.

Salah Ritual individual and congregational prayers.

Salámah or Salám Connoting the verbal idea of "entering safety and security" or "becoming safe and secure."

Shahadah Witnessing; the witnessing of Allah as the One and Only Creator, Sustainer, and Cherisher of the creation, and the witnessing of the Messengership of Muhammad (sawa).

Shariah Islamic law.

Shirakah Contract of partnership.

Shirk Associating partners with Allah. It also expresses the idea that undermining the human dignity of the individual through discrimination on whatever basis connotes that their Creator is different from one's own.

Shu'ub Branches of humanity (singular *Sha'b*).

Sukuk Commonly known as Islamic bonds (plural *sakk*).

Ta'seer Price controls.

Tafakkur Reflective meditation—reasoning, i.e., observing, considering, and reflecting on the significance of things and phenomena.

Takaful Contract of mutual care; same as Islamic insurance based on the concept of solidarity and mutual help.

Talaqqa ArRukban The prohibition of interference with supply before entrance into the market.

Taqwa An intense awareness of the presence of the Cherisher Lord; Allah-consciousness.

Tatfeef Short-changing a buyer—not giving full weight and measure.

Tawbah Repentance.

Tawheed Connotes the idea of the belief in the One-and-Onlyness of the Creator.

Tazakkiy The cleansing-purification process that makes becoming fully rule compliant possible.

Tijarah Trade.

Úbudiyyah Expresses the twin ideas of "adoration" and "service" in responding to the *walayahh* of Allah given through *Rububiyyah*.

Ukhuwwah Brotherhood (comes from *a'kh* meaning "brother").

Ulil-albab Those who attain an ever-active full consciousness of the Presence of Allah (swt).

Ummah Community of believers.

Urf Customs.

Waad Promise.

Wakil Representative in principal/agent contract.

Walayahh Mandate; the unconditional, dynamic, active, ever-present love of the Supreme Creator for His Creation manifested through the act of creation and provisioning of its sustenance; being, or working, in the closest possible proximity to someone.

Wali Protector/guardian.

Waliyy The one who is doing *walayahh* (plural *aulia'*).

Waliyy-u-Allah Devotee of Allah.

Waqf Designated assets whose underlying income flows are used to support building and maintaining public infrastructures.

Wikala Representation contact or principal/agent contract.

Yaqeen The state of full certainty.

Zakat The rights of others to one's income and wealth designated by the Messenger (sawa) as being about 2.5 percent of annual net wealth.

Bibliography

Ahmad, Abdul Rahman Yousri. (2011). "The Scientific Approach to Islamic Economics: Philosophy, Theoretical Construction and Applicability," in Habib Ahmed and Muhammad Sirajul Hoque, eds., *Handbook of Islamic Economics*, vol. 1 (Jeddah, Saudi Arabia: Islamic Research and Training Institute), pp. 6–7.

Ahmad, I. (1944). *The Social Contract and the Islamic State* (Allahabad: Urdu Publishing House).

Ahmad, Ziauddin. (1991). *Islam, Poverty, and Income Distribution* (Leicester, UK: Islamic Foundation).

Akerlof, George A. (1970). "The Market for 'Lemons': Quality Uncertainty and the Market Mechanism," *Quarterly Journal of Economics* 84, no. 3, pp. 488–500.

Akerlof, George A., and Robert J. Shiller. (2009). *Animal Spirits: How Human Psychology Drives the Economy, and Why It Matters for Global Capitalism* (Princeton, NJ: Princeton University Press).

Al-Hakimi, M. R., M. Al-Hakimi, and Ali Al-Hakimi. (1989). *Al-Hayat*, vol. 6 (Tehran: Maktab Nashr Al-Thaqrafa Al-Islamiyyah), pp. 324–451.

Al-Hasani, Baqir, and Abbas Mirakhor, eds. (2003). *Essays on Iqtisad: The Islamic Approach to Economic Problems* (New York: Global Scholarly Publications).

Alpay, Savas, Murat Atlamaz, and Esat Bkimli. (2011). "Trade among OIC Countries: Limits of Islamic Solidarity," *Insight Turkey* 13, no. 2, pp. 145–170.

Al-Sadr, M. B. (1968). *Iqtisaduna*, 2nd ed. (Beirut: Dar al Fikr).

———. (1980). *Falsafatuna*. (Beirut: Dar Al-Ta'arof Lil-Matbu'at).

Al-Sadr, Shaheed Seyyed M. B. (1979). *Iqtisaduna*. (Beirut: Dar Al-Ta'arof Lil-Matbu'at).

Andersen, Torben M. (2008). "The Scandianavian Welfare Model—Prospects and Challenges," *International Tax and Public Policy* special issue 15, pp. 45–66.

———. (2010). "Income Taxation: Incentive vs. Insurance," working paper (Denmark: Aarhus University, School of Economics and Management).

———. (2011). "Collective Risk Sharing: The Social Safety Net and Employment," working paper (Denmark: Aarhus University, School of Economics and Management). oekonomi@econ.au.dk.

Anderson, William G. "Who Rules America?" http://www2.ucsc.edu/whorulesamerica/power/wealth.html (accessed June 15, 2013). All data reported here are taken from Anderson. For Organisation for Economic Co-operation and Development (OECD) data, see "Growing Unequal? Income Distribution and Poverty in OECD Countries," http://www2.ucsc.edu/whorulesamerica/power/wealth.html.

Aoki, Masahiko. (2001). *Toward a Comparative Institutional Analysis* (Cambridge, MA: MIT Press).

"Approach to Islamic Economics: Philosophy, Theoretical Construction and Applicability." (2009). In Ahmed Habib and Mirakhor Abbas, "Islamic Economics and Finance: An Institutional Perspective," *IIUM Journal of Economics and Management* 17, no. 1.

Arrow, K. J., and G. Debreu. (1954). "Existence of Equilibrium for a Competitive Economy," *Econometrica* 22, pp. 262–290.

Arthur, J., and W. H. Shaw. (1991). *Justice and Economic Distribution* (Upper Saddle River, NJ: Prentice Hall), p. 4.

Asad, Muhammad. (2005). *Message of the Quran* (Louisville: Fons Vitae of Kentucky).

Askari, H., V. Nowshirvani, and M. Jaber. (1997). *Economic Development in the Countries of the GCC: The Curse and Blessing of Oil* (Stamford, CT: JAI Press).

Askari, H., Z. Iqbal, N. Krichene, and A. Mirakhor. (2010). *The Stability of Islamic Finance: Creating a Resilient Financial Environment for a Secure Future* (Singapore: John Wiley & Sons).

Askari, Hossein. (2006). *The Middle East Oil Exporters: What Happened to Economic Development?* (Cheltenham, UK: Edward Elgar).

Askari, Hossein, and Abbas Mirakhor. (2010). *Islam and the Path to Human and Economic Development* (New York: Palgrave Macmillan).

Askari, Hossein, with B. Dastmialtsch. (1990). *Saudi Arabia: Oil and the Search for Economic Development* (Stamford, CT: JAI Press).

Askari, Hossein, F. Abbas, G. Jabbour, and D. Kwon. (2006). "An Economic Manifesto for the Oil-Exporting Countries of the Persian Gulf: Oil Depletion, Economic Efficiency and Intergenerational Equity," *Banca Nazionale Del Lavoro Quarterly Review* 59, no. 239, pp. 363–388.

Askari, Hossein, John Cummings, and Michael Glover. (1982). *Taxation and Tax Policies in the Middle East* (London: Butterworth).

Askari, Hossein, and Noora Arfaa. (2007). "Social Safety Net in Islam: The Case of Persian Gulf Oil Exporters," *British Journal of Middle Eastern Studies* 34, no. 2, pp. 177–202.

Askari, Hossein, Vahid Nowshirvani, and Mohammed Jaber. (1997). *Economic Development in the Countries of the GCC: The Curse and Blessing of Oil* (Stamford, CT: JAI Press).

Askari, Hossein, Zamir Iqbal, and Abbas Mirakhor. (2009). *Globalization and Islamic Finance: Convergence, Prospects, and Challenges* (Singapore: John Wiley & Sons).

Ayyagari, M., T. Beck, and A. Demirgüç-Kunt. (2007). "Small and Medium Enterprises across the Globe," *Small Business Economics* 29, pp. 415–434.

Azid, T., M. Asutay, and U. Burki. (2007). "Theory of the Firm, Management and Stakeholders: An Islamic Perspective," *Islamic Economic Studies* 15, no. 1 pp. 1–2.

Balakrishan, Ravi, Chad Steinberg, and Mrtaza Syed. (2013). "The Elusive Quest for Inclusive Growth: Growth, Poverty, and Inequality in Asia," International Monetary Fund Working Paper no. WP/13/152, June.

Ball, R. et al. (2003). "Risk Transfer and Value for Money in PFI Projects," *Public Management Review* 5, no. 2.

Bendjilali, and Farid B. Taher. (1990). "A Zero Efficiency Loss Monopolist: An Islamic Perspective," *American Journal of Islamic Social Sciences* 7, no. 1, pp. 219–232.

Bracy, N., and S. Moldovan. (2006). "Public-Private-Partnerships: Risks to the Public and Private Sector," paper presented at the 6th Global Conference on Business and Economics, Boston, October, 15–17.

Brav, Alon, George M. Constantinides, and Christopher C. Geczy. (2002). "Asset Pricing with Heterogeneous Consumers and Limited Participation: Empirical Evidence," *Journal of Political Economy* 110, no. 4, pp. 793–824.

Buchanan, James M. (1984). "The Ethical Limits of Taxation," *Scandinavian Journal of Economics* 86, no. 2, pp. 102–114.

Canadian Council for Public Private Partnerships. (1996). Best Practice Guidelines.

Chapra, M. U. (1992). *Islam and the Economic Challenge* (Leicester, UK: Islamic Foundation).

———. (2000). *The Future of Economics* (Leicester, UK: Islamic Foundation).

———. (2007). *What Is Islamic Economics?* (Saudi Arabia: Islamic Research and Training Institute, Islamic Development Bank).

———. (2010). *Muslim Civilization: The Causes of Decline and the Need for Reform* (Leicester, UK: Islamic Foundation).

———. (2011). "What Is Islamic Economics?" in Ahmed Habib and Muhammad Sirajul Hoque, eds., *Handbook of Islamic Economics*, vol. 1 (Jeddah, Saudi Arabia: Islamic Research and Training Institute).

Chapra, M. Umer. (1991). "The Need for a New Economic System," *Review of Islamic Economics* 1, no. 1, pp. 9–47.

———. (2001). "Islamic Economic Thought and the New Global Economy," *Islamic Economic Studies* 9, no. 1, p. 5.

———. (2003). "Development Economics: Lessons that Remain to Be Learned," *Islamic Studies* 42, no. 4, pp. 1–12.

Choudhry, Nurun N., and Abbas Mirakhor. (1997). "Indirect Instruments of Monetary Control in an Islamic Financial System," *Islamic Economic Studies* 4, no. 2, pp. 27–65.

Crane, Brinton. (1967). "Enlightenment," in *The Encyclopedia of Philosophy*, vol. 2 (New York: Macmillan and the Free Press), pp. 520.

Demirgüç-Kunt, Asli, Thorsten Beck, and Patrick Honohan. (2007). *Finance for All? Policies and Pitfalls in Expanding Access*. World Bank Policy Research Report (Washington, DC: World Bank).

Department for International Development (London). (2004). "The Importance of Financial Sector Development for Growth and Poverty Reduction," policy division working paper.

Doraid, Moez. (2000)."Human Development and Poverty in the Arab States," United Nations Development Program, New York. www.arab-hdr.org/publications/other/undp/hdr/2000/arab/poverty2000.pdf.

Dornbusch, R. (1971). "Note on Growth and the Balance of Payments," *Canadian Journal of Economics* 4, no. 3, pp. 389–395.

———. (1976). "Capital Mobility: Flexible Exchange Rates and Macroeconomic Equilibrium," in E. Claassen and P. Salin, eds., *Recent Issues in International Monetary Economics* (Amsterdam: North Holland).

Easterlin, Richard, Laura Angelescu McVey, Malgorzata Switek, Onnicha Sawangfa, and Jacqueline Smith Zweig. (2011). "The Hapiness-Income Paradox Revisited," discussion paper, no. 5799 (Bonn, Germany: Institute for the Study of Labor).

Economist. (2013). "Levying the Land," *Economist* 70, http://www.economist.com/news/finance-and-economics/21580130-governments-should-make-more-use-property-taxes-levying-land.

Edgeworth, Francis. (1881 [1961]). *Mathematical Psychics: An Essay on the Application of Mathematics to the Moral Sciences* (New York: Augustus M. Kelly), p. 101.

Epstein, L., and J. Allen Hynes. (1983). "The Rate of Time Preference and Dynamic Economic Analysis," *Journal of Political Economy* 91, pp. 611–635.

Ernst & Young. (2009). "Islamic Funds Growth Stalls but Investable Assets Grow Says Ernst & Young," http://www.bi-me.com/main.php?id=36874&t=1 (accessed July 18, 2014).

Fergany, Nader. (2000). *Arab Higher Education and Development: An Overview* (Cairo: Almishkat Center for Research).

Frenkel, J. A. (1971). "A Theory of Money and Trade and the Balance of Payments in a Model of Accumulation," *Journal of International Economy* 1, no. 2, pp. 159–187.

———. (1976). "A Dynamic Analysis of Balance of Payments in a Model of Accumulation," in Jacob A. Frenkel and Harry Johnson, eds., *The Monetary Approach to the Balance of Payments* (London: George Allen and Unwin).

Frenkel, J. A., and C. Rodriguez. (1975). "Portfolio Equilibrium and the Balance of Payments: A Monetary Approach," *American Economic Review* 65, pp. 674–688.

Frenkel, J. A., and S. Fischer. (1972). "International Capital Movements along Balanced Growth Paths: Comments and Extensions," *Economic Record* 48, pp. 266–267.

Gomberg, Paul. (2007). *How to Make Opportunity Equal* (Malden, MA: Blackwell).

Greve, C. (2003). "When Public-Private Partnerships Fail. The Extreme Case of NPM—Inspired Local Government of Forum in Denmark," paper presented at the EGPA Conference, Oerias, Portugal, September 3–6.

Groenwegen, John, Christos Pitelis, and Sven-Erik Sjöstrand, eds. (1995). *On Economic Institutions: Theory and Applications* (Cheltenham, UK: Edward Elgar).

Habachy, S. (1962). "Property, Right, and Contract in Muslim Law," *Columbia Law Review* 62, no. 3, pp. 450–473.

Hall, Robert E., and Alvin Rabushka. (1995). *The Flat Tax*, 2nd ed. (Stanford, California: Hoover Institution Press).

Hassan, Zubair. (1987). "Distributional Equity in Islam," in Munawar Iqbal, ed., *Distributive Justice and Need Fulfillment in an Islamic Economy* (International Institute of Islamic Economics: Islamabad), pp. 25–54

———. (1992). "Profit Maximization: Secular versus Islamic," in Sayyid Tahir, Aidit Ghazali, and Syed Omar Syed Agil, eds., *Readings in Microeconomics: An Islamic Perspective* (Petaling Jaya: Longmann Malaysia).

———. (2002). "Maximization Postulates and Their Efficacy for Islamic Economics," Munich Personal RePEC Archive.

———. (2011). "Scarcity, Self-Interest, and Maximization from an Islamic Angle." MPRA Paper 31631, University Library of Munich, Germany.

Hefner, Robert W. (2006). "Islamic Economics and Global Capitalism," *Society* 44, no. 1, p. 16.

Heiner, Ronald A. (1983). "The Origin of Predictable Behavior," *American Economic Review* 73, pp. 560–595.

Hodge, G. A. (2002). "Who Steers the State When Governments Sign Public-Private Partnerships?" *Journal of Contemporary Issues in Business and Government* 8, no. 1, pp. 5–18.

———. (2004). "Risks in Public-Private Partnerships: Shifting, Sharing or Shirking," *Asia Pacific Journal of Public Administration* 26, no. 2, pp. 155–179.

Hoftijzer, Margo. (2006). *Opportunity, Security, and Equity in the Middle East and North Africa* (World Bank, Washington, DC).

Hoynes, H. W., and E. F. P. Luttmer. (2010). "The Insurance Value of State Tax-and-Transfer Programs," working paper no. 16280, National Bureau of Economic Research, Boston.

Hoynes, Hilary, and E.F.P. Luttmer. (2010). "The Insurance Value of State Tax-and-Transfer Programs," NBER Working Papers 16280, National Bureau of Economic Research, Boston, MA.

Human Development Report. (2008). United Nations Development Programme, New York.

Iqbal, Farrukh. (2006). *Sustaining Gains in Poverty Reduction and Human Development in the Middle East and North Africa* (Washington, DC: World Bank).

Iqbal, M. (1992). "Organization of Production and Theory of Firm Behaviour from an Islamic Perspective," in A. Ahmad and Kazim Awan, eds., *Lectures on Islamic Economics* (Jeddah, Saudi Arabia: IRTI), pp. 205–215.

Iqbal, Munawar, ed. (1987). *Distributive Justice and Need Fulfillment in an Islamic Economy* (Islamabad, Pakistan: International Institute of Islamic Economics).

Iqbal, Munawar. (1992). "Organization of Production and Theory of Firm Behaviour from an Islamic Perspective," in Ausaf Ahmad and Kazim Raza Awan, eds. *Lectures on Islamic Economics* (Jeddah, Saudi Arabia: Islamic Research and Training Institute).

Iqbal, Zamir, and Abbas Mirakhor. (2007). *An Introduction to Islamic Finance: Theory and Practice* (Singapore: John Wiley and Sons).

———. (2011). *An Introduction to Islamic Finance: Theory and Practice*, 2nd ed. (Singapore: John Wiley and Sons).

Irfan, Ul Haq. (1996). *Islamization of Economic Doctrines of Islam: A Study in the Doctrines of Islam and Their Implications for Poverty, Employment, and Economic* (Herndon, VA: International Institute of Islamic Thought, 1996).

Ishigami, K. (1995). "New Approaches to Public-Private Projects in Japan," www.nri .co.jp/nri/publications/nriqF/95winter/gaiyo.html#contents.

Islahi, A. A. (1982). *Economic Concepts of Ibn Taimiyah* (London: Islamic Foundation).

———. (1986). "Ibn Taimiyah's Concept of Market Mechanism," *Journal of Research in Islamic Economics* 2, no. 2, pp. 55–66.

Islamic Research and Training Institution. (2000). *Resolutions and Recommendations of the Council of the Islamic Fiqh Academy, 1980–2000* (Jeddah, Saudi Arabia: Islamic Research and Training Institution).

Jacobson, L. (1998). "Partnership Problems," *Government Executive* 30, no. 5.

Jobst, A., (2009). "Islamic Securitization after the Subprime Crisis," *Journal of Structured Finance* 14, no. 4, pp. 41–57.

Judd, K. L. (2000). "Is Education as Good as Gold: A Portfolio Analysis of Human Capital Investment," National Bureau of Economic Research, Public Economics, Cambridge, MA. http://dev3.cepr.org/meets/wkcn/3/3507/papers/judd.pdf.

Junaid, S. A. H. (1992). "Factors of Production and Factor Pricing from an Islamic Perspective," in A. Ahmad and Kazim Awan, eds., *Lectures on Islamic Economics* (Jeddah, Saudi Arabia: IRTI), pp. 185–204.

Kahf, Monzer. (2006). "Definition and Methodology of Islamic Economics Based on the Views of Imam al Sadr," paper presented at the International Conference on Imam Sadr's Economic Thoughts. Qum, Islamic Republic of Iran, May.

Kapiszewski, Andrzej. (2006). "Arab versus Asian Migrant Workers in the GCC Countries," United Nations Expert Group Meeting on International Migration and Development in the Arab Region (Beirut: United Nations, May 15–17).

Keynes, John Maynard. (1930). *A Treaties on Money* (London: Macmillan).

———. (1936, rev ed. 1970). *The General Theory of Employment, Interest, and Money* (London: Macmillan).

Khan, Fahim. (2011). "Fiqh Foundations of the Theory of Islamic Economics: A Survey of Selected Contemporary Writings on Economics Relevant Subjects of Fiqh," in Habib Ahmed and Muhammad Sirajul Hoque, eds., *Handbook of Islamic Economics*, vol. 1 (Jeddah, Saudi Arabia: Islamic Research and Training Institute), p. 192.

Khan, M. Fahmin. (1984). "Macro Consumption Function in an Islamic Framework," *Journal of Research in Islamic Economics* 1, no. 2, p. 6.

Khan, Mohsin, and Abbas Mirakhor. (1987). *Theoretical Studies in Islamic Banking and Finance*, (Houston: IRIS Books).

Khurshid, Ahmad. (2011) *First Principles of Islamic Economics* (Leicestershire, UK: Islamic Foundation).

Kindleberger, C., and R. Aliber. (2005). *Manias, Panics and Crashes* (New York: Basic Books).

Knight, Risk. (1971). *Uncertainty and Profit* (Chicago: University of Chicago Press).

Kotlikoff, Laurence J. (2010). *Stewart Is Dead: Ending the World's Financial Plague with Limited Purpose Banking* (Hoboken, NJ: John Wiley & Sons).

Kristol, Irving. (1981). "Rationalism in Economics," in Daniel Bell and Irving Kristol, eds., *The Crisis in Economic Theory* (New York: Basic Books), p. 215.

Krugman, Paul. (2013). "The Decline of E-Empires," *New York Times*, August 25.

Lane, E. W. (2003). *An Arabic-English Lexicon* (Lahore: Suhail Academy).

Lawson, M. M. (1997). "Economic Development Corporation of Utah: Lessons Learned from the First 10 Years," *Economic Development Review* 15, no. 3.

Levitsky, J. (1986). *World Bank Lending to Small Enterprises: A Review* (Washington, DC: World Bank).

Long, D. Stephen. (2000). *Divine Economy, Theology and the Market* (London: Routledge).

McMillan, J. (2002). *Reinventing the Bazaar: A Natural History of Markets* (London: W.W. Norton).

Mehanna, Rock-Antoine. (2005). "International Trade, Religion, and Political Freedom; an Empirical Investigation," *Global Business & Economics Review* 5, no. 2, pp. 284–296.

Mellehi, Kamel. (2000). Human Resource Development through Vocational Education in Gulf Cooperation Countries: The Case of Saudi Arabia," *Journal of Vocational Education and Training* 52, no. 2, pp. 329–344.

Metwally, M. M. (1981). "A Behavioural Model of an Islamic Firm," Research Series in English, no. 5 (Jeddah, Saudi Arabia: King Abdulaziz University, International Centre for Research in Islamic Economics).

Metzler, L. (1951). "Wealth, Savings and the Rate of Interest," *Journal of Political Economy* 59, pp. 93–116.

Metzler, Lloyd A. (1952). "Reply," *Journal of Political Economy* 60, p. 249.

Michihiro, Kandori. (1992). "Social Norms and Community Enforcement," *Review of Economic Studies* 59, p. 63.

Mirakhor, Abbas. (1983). "Muslim Contribution to Economics," first presented at the Midwest Economic Association Meeting, April 7–9, and reprinted in Baqir Al-Hassani and Abbas Mirakhor, *Essays on Iqtisad* (New York: Global Scholarly Publication).

———. (1985). "Theory of an Islamic Financial System," in Baqir Al-Hassani and Abbas Mirakhor. *Essays on Iqtisad* (New York: Global Scholarly Publication).

———. (1992). "Equity, Efficiency and Firm Behavior in an Islamic Economy," in A. Ahmad and K. R. Awan, eds., *Lectures on Islamic Economics* (Jeddah, Saudi Arabia: Islamic Development Bank and Islamic Research and Training Institute).

———. (1993). "Equilibrium in a Non-Interest Open Economy," *Journal of King Abdulaziz University* 5, pp. 3–23.

———. (2004). "Islamic Finance and Instrumentalization of Islamic Redistributive Institutions," paper presented at Ibn Rushd Memorial Lecture, London, April.

———. (2007). "A Note on Islamic Economics," Islamic Research and Training Institute, Jeddah, Saudi Arabia.

———. (2007). "Islamic Finance and Globalization: A Convergence?" *Journal of Islamic Economics, Banking and Finance* 3, no. 2, pp. 11–72.

———. (2009) "Islamic Economics and Finance: An Institutional Perspective," *IIUM Journal of Economics and Management* 17, no. 1, pp. 31–72.

———. (2011). "Epistemology of Finance: Misreading Smith," *Islamic Finance Review* 1, pp. 9–15.

————. "Equity, Efficiency and Firm Behavior in an Islamic Economy," Working paper (INCEIF, Kuala Lumpur, Malaysia).

Mirakhor, Abbas, and Hossein Askari. (2010). *Islam and the Path to Human and Economic Development* (New York: Palgrave Macmillan, 2010).

Mirakhor, Abbas, and N. Krichene. (2009). "The Recent Crisis: Lessons for Islamic Finance." Second public lecture on financial policy and stability. Islamic Financial Services Board, Kuala Lumpur, Malaysia.

Mirakhor, Abbas, and Zaidi Iqbal. (1988). "Stabilization and Growth in an Open Islamic Economy," Working paper no. 88/22 (International Monetary Fund, Washington, DC).

Modigliani, Franco, and Lucas Papademos. (1975). "Targets for Monetary Policy in the Coming Year," Brookings Papers on Economic Activity, Economic Studies Program, Brookings Institution, 6, no. 1, pp. 141–166.

Mohieldin, Mahmoud, Zamir Iqbal, Ahmed Rostom, and Xiaochen Fu. (2011). "The Role of Islamic Finance in Enhancing Financial Inclusion in Organization of Islamic Cooperation (OIC) Countries," Policy Research Working Paper WPS5920, World Bank, Washington, DC.

Montiel, P. (1986). "An Optimizing Model of Household Behavior Under Credit Rationing," *IME Staff Papers* 33, no. 3, pp. 583–615.

Mundell, R. (1960). "The Public Debt, Corporate Income Taxes and the Rate of Interest," *Journal of Political Economy* 68, pp. 622–626.

Naqvi, Haider, and Syed Nawab. (2002). "Economics, Ethics and Religion: Jewish, Christian and Muslim Economic Thought," *Islamic Studies* 41, no. 3, pp. 516–520.

North, Douglass C. (1995). "Five Propositions about Institutional Change," in J. Knight and I. Sened, eds. *Explaining Social Institutions* (Ann Arbor: University of Michigan Press), pp. 15–26.

————. (2003). *Understanding the Process of Economic Change* (Princeton, NJ: Princeton University Press).

Nozick, R. (1974). *Anarchy, State, and Utopia* (New York: Basic Books).

Olson, M., and M. J. Bailey. (1981). "Positive Time Preference," *Journal of Political Economy* 89, pp. 1–25.

Osborne, S., ed. (2001). *Public-Private Partnerships: Theory and Practice in International Perspective* (New York: Rutledge).

Patinkin, D. (1965). *Money, Interest, and Prices*, 2nd ed. (New York: Harper & Row, 1965).

Payandeh, A. (1984). *Nahjulfasahah: Collected Short Sayings of the Messenger* (Tehran: Golestanian).

Perrot, J. Y., and G. Chatelus. (2000). *Financing of Major Infrastructure and Public Service Projects: Public Private Partnerships, Lessons from French Experience Throughout the World* (Paris: Presses de l'Ecole Nationale des Ponts et Chaussées).

Piketty, Thomas. (2014). *Capital in the Twenty-First Century* (Cambridge, MA: Belknap Press of Harvard University Press).

Pope John Paul II. (2005). *The Encyclicals*, ed. Joseph G. Donders (Maryknoll, NY: Orbis Books).

Putterman, Louis. (1993). "Ownership and the Nature of the Firm," *Journal of Comparative Economics* 17, no. 2, pp. 243–263.

Qutb, Shaheed Seayyied. (1953). *Social Justice in Islam*, rev. ed. J. B. Hardie., trans. (N.p.: Reprinted by American Council of Learned Societies).

Rāghib al-Aṣfahānī, al-Ḥusayn ibn Muḥammad. (2009). Mufradāt alfāz_al-Qur'ān al-Ṭab'ah 4, 4th ed. (Beirut, Lebanon: al-Dār al-Shāmīyah).

Rawls, John. (1971). *A Theory of Justice* (Cambridge, MA: Belknap Press of Harvard University Press).

Roemer, John. (1999). *Equality of Opportunity* (Cambridge, MA: Harvard University Press).

Sadr, Kazem. (2007). "Gharzul-Hasaneh Financing and Institutions," presented at the First International Conference on Inclusive Islamic Financial Sector Development, jointly organized by Islamic Research and Training Institute of the Islamic Development Bank and the Centre for Islamic Banking Finance and Management, Universiti Brunei Darussalam.

Salih, Siddig Abdelmageed. (1999). *Challenges to Poverty Alleviation in IDB Member Countries* (Jeddah, Saudi Arabia: Islamic Development Bank).

Savoie, D. (1999). "Public-Private Partnerships: A Word of Caution," *Insight* 4, no. 1.

Schotter, Andrew. (1981). *The Economic Theory of Social Institutions*. (Cambridge, UK: Cambridge University Press)

Schumpeter, Joseph A. (1954). *History of Economic Analysis* (New York: Oxford University Press).

Sen, Amartya. (1994). *Development as Freedom* (New York: Anchor Books).

———. (2010). *The Idea of Justice*. (London: Penguin).

Sheng, Andrew. (2009). *From Asian to Global Financial Crisis* (Cambridge, UK: Cambridge University Press).

Shiller, R. J. (2003). *The New Financial Order: Risk in the 21st Century* (Princeton, NJ: Princeton University Press).

Siddiqui, Mohammad Nejatullah. (1995). "An Overview of Public Borrowing in Early Islamic History," *Islamic Economic Studies* 2, no. 2, p. 10.

———. (2010). "History of Islamic Economic Thought," in Habib Ahmed and Muhammad Sirajul Hoque, eds., *Handbook of Islamic Economics*, vol. 1 (Jeddah, Saudi Arabia: Islamic Research and Training Institute), pp. 95–110.

Sinn, Hans-Werner. (1995). "A Theory of the Welfare State," *Scandinavian Journal of Economics* 97, pp. 495–526.

———. (1996). "Social Insurance, Incentives and Risk Taking," *International Tax and Public Finance*, 3, no. 3, pp 259–280.

Sirajul Hoque, Muhammad, ed. (2011). *Handbook of Islamic Economics*, vol. 1 (Jeddah, Saudi Arabia: Islamic Research and Training Institute).

Smith, Adam. (1976 [original 1776]). *An Inquiry into the Nature and Causes of the Wealth of Nations*, 2 vols. W. B. Todd, ed. See vol. 2 of the *Glasgow Edition of the Works and Correspondence of Adam Smith* (Oxford: Clarendon Press).

————. (2006 [original 1790]). *The Theory of Moral Sentiments* (New York: Dover Publications).

Solow, Robert M. (1974). "Intergenerational Equity and Exhaustible Resources," *The Review of Economic Studies* 41; Symposium on the Economics of Exhaustible Resources, p. 41.

Stiglitz, Joseph. (1993). "Perspectives on the Role of Government Risk-Bearing within the Financial Sector," in *Government Risk-Bearing* (Cleveland: Federal Reserve Bank of Cleveland), pp. 109–130.

Stiglitz, Joseph, and Andrew Weiss. (1981). *"Credit Rationing in Markets with Imperfect Information,"* *American Economic Review* 71, no. 3, pp. 393–410.

Sugema, Iman, Toni Bakhtiar, and Jaenal Effendi. (2010). "Interest versus Profit-Loss Sharing Credit Contracts: Efficiency and Welfare Implications," *International Research Journal of Finance and Economics* 45, pp. 58–67.

Tamari, Meir. (1987). *"With All Your Possessions": Jewish Ethnic and Economic Life* (New York: Free Press).

Thornton, H. (1939 [original 1802]). *An Inquiry into the Nature and Effects of the Paper Credit of Great Britain*. F. Hayek, ed. (New York: Rinehart, 1939).

Tzannatos, Zafiris. (2000). *Social Protection in the Middle East and North Africa: A Review* (Washington, DC: World Bank).

Udovitch, A. L. (1970). *Partnership and Profit in Medieval Islam* (Princeton, NJ: Princeton University Press).

Ul-Haq, Mahbub. (1995). *Reflections on Human Development* (New York: Oxford University Press).

Ul Haque, N., and A. Mirakhor. (1999). "The Design of Instruments for Government Finance in an Islamic Economy," *Islamic Economic Studies* 6, no. 2, pp. 27–42.

United Nations. (2003). *United Nations Common Country Assessment for the Islamic Republic of Iran*.

United Nations Development Program. (2002). *Human Development Report 2002: Deepening Democracy in a Fragmented World* (New York: Oxford University Press).

————. (2003). *Arab Human Development Report 2003: Building a Knowledge Society* (New York: Oxford University Press).

Uzawa, Hirofumi. (1969). "Time Preference and the Penrose Effect in a Two-Class Model of Economic Growth," *Journal of Political Economy* 77, pp. 628–652.

Waud, R. N. (1970). "Inflation, Unemployment, and Economic Welfare," *American Economic Review* 60, no. 4, pp. 631–641.

Weitzman, Martin. (1984). *The Share Economy* (Cambridge, MA: Harvard University Press).

————. (1986). *The Case for Profit Sharing* (London: Employment Institute).

Weitzman, Martin, and Douglas Kruse. (1990). "Profit Sharing and Productivity," in A. Blinder, ed., *Paying for Productivity: A Look at the Evidence* (Washington, DC: Brookings), pp. 288–298.

World Bank. (2002). *Reducing Vulnerability and Increasing Opportunity: Social Protection in the Middle East and North Africa* (Washington, DC: World Bank).

————. (2011). *World Development Indicators* (Washington, DC: World Bank).

World Bank, Middle East and North Africa Region, Office of the Chief Economist. (2006). *Middle East and North Africa Economic Developments and Prospects 2006: Financial Markets in a New Age of Oil* (Washington, DC: World Bank).

World Development Indicators. (2004). Washington, DC: World Bank.

Wright, Brian D. (1993). "Public Insurance of Private Risks: Theory and Evidence from Agriculture," in Mark S. Sniderman, ed., *Government Risk-Bearing* (Boston: Kluwer Academic Publishers), pp. 45–65.

Yousef, Tarik M. (2004). "Employment, Development and the Social Contract in the Middle East and North Africa," World Bank, http://siteresources.worldbank.org/INTLM/Resources/390041-1103750362599/MENA_paper.pdf.

Zöngür, Yasemin. (2010). "Comparison between Islamic and Conventional Securitization: A Survey," *Review of Islamic Economics* 13, no. 2, pp. 81–118.

Index

Page numbers followed by *f* and *t* indicate figures and tables.

Takaful (insurance) (*Continued*)
 distinctive features of, 210–211
 operating models, 212–214, 213*t*
Tawheed (oneness), 30, 33
Taxation:
 flat tax, 258, 259
 as policy instrument, 228–229, 255–256,
  257–259
 progressive, and income and wealth
  disparities, 11
 wealth tax, 258–259
Theory of Moral Sentiments, The (Smith),
  3–7, 307–308, 311, 361
Theory of the firm, 105–112, 106–109
Tijarah (commerce), 65, 86, 282
Time horizon, output determination and,
  143
Time value of money, 82
Total cost (TC), 107
Total revenue, 106
Trade. *See* International trade
Transaction velocity of money, 149
Transfers:
 distributive justice and, 80–81
 income from, 137
 property rights and, 55
Transitory income, 141
Transparency, as function of financial system,
  190
Treasury securities, in Islamic monetary
  policy, 300–302
Trust, Islamic rules of conduct, 60–62
Tunisia, 341, 343, 347, 353, 356
Two-tier *Mudarabah* model, of Islamic
  banking, 194, 195
Two-windows model, of Islamic banking, 89,
  194, 195–196

Udovitch, A. L., 22
Ul-Haq, Mahbub, 14–15, 20
Unemployment, 144, 152–154
 in classical versus Keynesian economics,
  144–148, 147*f*
 trade-off between inflation and, 274–276,
  275*f*
United Arab Emirates (UAE), 341, 346, 347,
  350, 351, 352, 365
United Kingdom, 8
United States, 10, 12*f*, 13*t*
Unity, in Islamic economic system, 30–31, 44,
  45

Utilitarianism, 320
Utility, consumer behavior and, 102–105

Value judgments, excluded from conventional
  economics, 96–97, 104–105, 107,
  122–123

Wadia (deposits) contract, 193, 197
Wage rigidity of, 152–153
Waliullah, Shah, 24
Walayahh (Creator's love), 29, 33, 34, 47,
  319
Wants, needs versus, 100–102
Waqf (endowment):
 redistribution and, 327
 role in fiscal policy, 255–256
 social welfare and, 338, 340*t*, 341*f*
Waste, prohibition of, 34–36, 38, 57, 59, 67,
  68, 101
Wealth, 68–69
 disparities in, 10–12, 13, 42
 government debt repayment and, 249–250
 noncirculation of, 84–85
 of OIC region, 368–370, 369*f*, 370*f*, 371*f*
 rules for accumulation and utilization of,
  66–68
 rules for distribution/redistribution of,
  68–69
 See also Zakat
Wealth of Nations, The (Smith), 2, 3, 7,
  311
Well-being. *See* Human welfare
What/how/whom, as fundamental economic
  questions, 98
Wikala (principal/agent representation)
  contract, 193, 194, 196
 Takaful and, 212–213
Work (*al-amal*):
 distributive justice and, 80–81
 incentive-compatible labor contracts,
  110–111
 Islamic rules of conduct, 69–70
 national income and, 133–135
 property rights and, 55–57
 role of state in labor markets, 222

Yediyildiz, Bahaeddin, 256
Yemen, 340, 343, 346, 355, 356

Zakat (2% tax on wealth), 69, 104, 137, 230,
  257, 259, 326, 327–329, 338